Janet Swan Hill, BA, MA
Editor

Education for Cataloging
and the Organization
of Information:
Pitfalls and the Pendulum

Education for Cataloging and the Organization of Information: Pitfalls and the Pendulum has been co-published simultaneously as *Cataloging & Classification Quarterly*, Volume 34, Numbers 1/2 and 3 2002.

More pre-publication
REVIEWS, COMMENTARIES, EVALUATIONS . . .

"USEFUL, THOUGHT-PROVOK-
ING. . . . Lively reading–full of
wisdom, provocative, challenging,
and firmly supportive of cataloging as
a core competency of librarianship in
a time when the 'simplicity' of
metadata is so seductive. I hope this
book will reach beyond its obvious
audience–catalogers and cataloging
educators–who will like it very much.
Library administrators and public service librarians will benefit from the
clear focus on the value of cataloging
to the library and its clientele."

Margaret Rohdy
Head of Research, Training,
and Quality Management
University of Pennsylvania
Libraries

"Timely. . . . A useful compendium written by highly regarded cataloging educators, administrators, and practitioners . . . also
provides interesting insights from
several recent library and information science graduates. . . .
DISCUSSES INNOVATIVE METH-
ODS OF EDUCATING CATALOG-
ERS. I highly recommend this book
to cataloging practitioners and educators, library administrators, and
all students currently enrolled in library and information science programs."

Andrea L. Stamm, MLS, MA
Head
Catalog Department
Northwestern University Library

The Haworth Information Press
An Imprint of The Haworth Press, Inc.

Education for Cataloging and the Organization of Information: Pitfalls and the Pendulum

Education for Cataloging and the Organization of Information: Pitfalls and the Pendulum has been co-published simultaneously as *Cataloging & Classification Quarterly*, Volume 34, Numbers 1/2 and 3 2002.

Cataloging & Classification Quarterly™ Monographic "Separates"

Below is a list of "separates," which in serials librarianship means a special issue simultaneously published as a special journal issue or double-issue *and* as a "separate" hardbound monograph. (This is a format which we also call a "DocuSerial.")

"Separates" are published because specialized libraries or professionals may wish to purchase a specific thematic issue by itself in a format which can be separately cataloged and shelved, as opposed to purchasing the journal on an on-going basis. Faculty members may also more easily consider a "separate" for classroom adoption.

"Separates" are carefully classified separately with the major book jobbers so that the journal tie-in can be noted on new book order slips to avoid duplicate purchasing.

You may wish to visit Haworth's Website at . . .

http://www.HaworthPress.com

. . . to search our online catalog for complete tables of contents of these separates and related publications.

You may also call 1-800-HAWORTH (outside US/Canada: 607-722-5857), or Fax 1-800-895-0582 (outside US/Canada: 607-771-0012), or e-mail at:

getinfo@haworthpressinc.com

Education for Cataloging and the Organization of Information: Pitfalls and the Pendulum, edited by Janet Swan Hill, BA, MA (Vol. 34, No. 1/2/3, 2002). *Examines the history, context, present, and future of education for cataloging and bibliographic control.*

Works as Entities for Information Retrieval, edited by Richard P. Smiraglia, PhD (Vol. 33, No. 3/4, 2002). *Examines domain-specific research about works and the problems inherent in their representation for information storage and retrieval.*

The Audiovisual Cataloging Current, edited by Sandra K. Roe, MS (Vol. 31, No. 2/3/4, 2001). *"All the great writers, teachers, and lecturers are here: Olson, Fox, Intner, Weihs, Weitz, and Yee. This eclectic collection is sure to find a permanent place on many catalogers' bookshelves. . . . Something for everyone. . . . Explicit cataloging guidelines and AACR2R interpretations galore."* (Verna Urbanski, MA, MLS, Chief Media Cataloger, University of North Florida, Jacksonville)

Managing Cataloging and the Organization of Information: Philosophies, Practices and Challenges at the Onset of the 21st Century, edited by Ruth C. Carter, PhD, MS, MA (Vol. 30, No. 1/2/3, 2000). *"A fascinating series of practical, forthright accounts of national, academic, and special library cataloging operations in action. . . . Yields an abundance of practical solutions for shared problems, now and for the future. Highly recommended."* (Laura Jizba, Head Cataloger, Portland State University Library, Oregon)

The LCSH Century: One Hundred Years with the Library of Congress Subject Headings System, edited by Alva T. Stone, MLS (Vol. 29, No. 1/2, 2000). *Traces the 100-year history of the Library of Congress Subject Headings, from its beginning with the implementation of a dictionary catalog in 1898 to the present day, exploring the most significant changes in LCSH policies and practices, including a summary of other contributions celebrating the centennial of the world's most popular library subject heading language.*

Maps and Related Cartographic Materials: Cataloging, Classification, and Bibliographic Control, edited by Paige G. Andrew, MLS, and Mary Lynette Larsgaard, BA, MA (Vol. 27, No. 1/2/3/4, 1999). *Discover how to catalog the major formats of cartographic materials, including sheet maps, early and contemporary atlases, remote-sensed images (i.e., aerial photographs and satellite images), globes, geologic sections, digital material, and items on CD-ROM.*

Portraits in Cataloging and Classification: Theorists, Educators, and Practitioners of the Late Twentieth Century, edited by Carolynne Myall, MS, CAS, and Ruth C. Carter, PhD (Vol. 25, No. 2/3/4, 1998). *"This delightful tome introduces us to a side of our profession that we rarely see: the human beings behind the philosophy, rules, and interpretations that have guided our professional lives over the past half century. No collection on cataloging would be complete without a copy of this work."* (Walter M. High, PhD, Automation Librarian, North Carolina Supreme Court Library; Assistant Law Librarian for Technical Services, North Carolina University, Chapel Hill)

Cataloging and Classification: Trends, Transformations, Teaching, and Training, edited by James R. Shearer, MA, ALA, and Alan R. Thomas, MA, FLA (Vol. 24, No. 1/2, 1997). *"Offers a comprehensive retrospective and innovative projection for the future." (The Catholic Library Association)*

Electronic Resources: Selection and Bibliographic Control, edited by Ling-yuh W. (Miko) Pattie, MSLS, and Bonnie Jean Cox, MSLS (Vol. 22, No. 3/4, 1996). *"Recommended for any reader who is searching for a thorough, well-rounded, inclusive compendium on the subject." (The Journal of Academic Librarianship)*

Cataloging and Classification Standards and Rules, edited by John J. Reimer, MLS (Vol. 21, No. 3/4, 1996). *"Includes chapters by a number of experts on many of our best loved library standards. . . . Recommended to those who want to understand the history and development of our library standards and to understand the issues at play in the development of new standards." (LASIE)*

Classification: Options and Opportunities, edited by Alan R. Thomas, MA, FLA (Vol. 19, No. 3/4, 1995). *"There is much new and valuable insight to be found in all the chapters. . . . Timely in refreshing our confidence in the value of well-designed and applied classification in providing the best of service to the end-users." (Catalogue and Index)*

Cataloging Government Publications Online, edited by Carolyn C. Sherayko, MLS (Vol. 18, No. 3/4, 1994). *"Presents a wealth of detailed information in a clear and digestible form, and reveals many of the practicalities involved in getting government publications collections onto online cataloging systems." (The Law Librarian)*

Cooperative Cataloging: Past, Present and Future, edited by Barry B. Baker, MLS (Vol. 17, No. 3/4, 1994). *"The value of this collection lies in its historical perspective and analysis of past and present approaches to shared cataloging. . . . Recommended to library schools and large general collections needing materials on the history of library and information science." (Library Journal)*

Languages of the World: Cataloging Issues and Problems, edited by Martin D. Joachim (Vol. 17, No. 1/2, 1994). *"An excellent introduction to the problems libraries must face when cataloging materials not written in English. . . . should be read by every cataloger having to work with international materials, and it is recommended for all library schools. Nicely indexed." (Academic Library Book Review)*

Retrospective Conversion Now in Paperback: History, Approaches, Considerations, edited by Brian Schottlaender, MLS (Vol. 14, No. 3/4, 1992). *"Fascinating insight into the ways and means of converting and updating manual catalogs to machine-readable format." (Library Association Record)*

Enhancing Access to Information: Designing Catalogs for the 21st Century, edited by David A. Tyckoson (Vol. 13, No. 3/4, 1992). *"Its down-to-earth, nontechnical orientation should appeal to practitioners including administrators and public service librarians." (Library Resources & Technical Services)*

Describing Archival Materials: The Use of the MARC AMC Format, edited by Richard P. Smiraglia, MLS (Vol. 11, No. 3/4, 1991). *"A valuable introduction to the use of the MARC AMC format and the principles of archival cataloging itself." (Library Resources & Technical Services)*

Subject Control in Online Catalogs, edited by Robert P. Holley, PhD, MLS (Vol. 10, No. 1/2, 1990). *"The authors demonstrate the reasons underlying some of the problems and how solutions may be sought. . . . Also included are some fine research studies where the researchers have sought to test the interaction of users with the catalogue, as well as looking at use by library practitioners." (Library Association Record)*

Library of Congress Subject Headings: Philosophy, Practice, and Prospects, by William E. Studwell, MSLS (Supp. #2, 1990). *"Plays an important role in any debate on subject cataloging and succeeds in focusing the reader on the possibilities and problems of using Library of Congress Subject Headings and of subject cataloging in the future." (Australian Academic & Research Libraries)*

Authority Control in the Online Environment: Considerations and Practices, edited by Barbara B. Tillett, PhD (Vol. 9, No. 3, 1989). *"Marks an excellent addition to the field. . . . [It] is intended, as stated in the introduction, to 'offer background and inspiration for future thinking.' In achieving this goal, it has certainly succeeded." (Information Technology & Libraries)*

National and International Bibliographic Databases: Trends and Prospects, edited by Michael Carpenter, PhD, MBA, MLS (Vol. 8, No. 3/4, 1988). *"A fascinating work, containing much of concern both to the general cataloger and to the language or area specialist as well. It is also highly recommended reading for all those interested in bibliographic databases, their development, or their history." (Library Resources & Technical Services)*

Cataloging Sound Recordings: A Manual with Examples, by Deanne Holzberlein, PhD, MLS (Supp. #1, 1988). *"A valuable, easy to read working tool which should be part of the standard equipment of all catalogers who handle sound recordings." (ALR)*

Education and Training for Catalogers and Classifiers, edited by Ruth C. Carter, PhD (Vol. 7, No. 4, 1987). *"Recommended for all students and members of the profession who possess an interest in cataloging." (RQ-Reference and Adult Services Division)*

The United States Newspaper Program: Cataloging Aspects, edited by Ruth C. Carter, PhD (Vol. 6, No. 4, 1986). *"Required reading for all who use newspapers for research (historians and librarians in particular), newspaper cataloguers, administrators of newspaper collections, and–most important–those who control the preservation pursestrings." (Australian Academic & Research Libraries)*

Computer Software Cataloging: Techniques and Examples, edited by Deanne Holzberlein, PhD, MLS (Vol. 6, No. 2, 1986). *"Detailed explanations of each of the essential fields in a cataloging record. Will help any librarian who is grappling with the complicated responsibility of cataloging computer software." (Public Libraries)*

AACR2 and Serials: The American View, edited by Neal L. Edgar (Vol. 3, No. 2/3, 1983). *"This book will help any librarian or serials user concerned with the pitfalls and accomplishments of modern serials cataloging." (American Reference Books Annual)*

The Future of the Union Catalogue: Proceedings of the International Symposium on the Future of the Union Catalogue, edited by C. Donald Cook (Vol. 2, No. 1/2, 1982). *Experts explore the current concepts and future prospects of the union catalogue.*

Education
for Cataloging
and the Organization
of Information:
Pitfalls
and the Pendulum

Janet Swan Hill, BA, MA
Editor

Education for Cataloging and the Organization of Information: Pitfalls and the Pendulum has been co-published simultaneously as *Cataloging & Classification Quarterly*, Volume 34, Numbers 1/2 and 3 2002.

The Haworth Information Press
An Imprint of
The Haworth Press, Inc.
New York • London • Oxford

Published by

The Haworth Information Press®, 10 Alice Street, Binghamton, NY 13904-1580 USA

The Haworth Information Press® is an imprint of The Haworth Press, Inc., 10 Alice Street, Binghamton, NY 13904-1580 USA.

Education for Cataloging and the Organization of Information: Pitfalls and the Pendulum has been co-published simultaneously as *Cataloging & Classification Quarterly*, Volume 34, Numbers 1/2 and 3 2002.

Cover design by Marylouise E. Doyle.

Library of Congress Cataloging-in-Publication Data

Education for cataloging and the organization of information : pitfalls and the pendulum / Janet Swan Hill, editor.
    p. cm.
    Co-published simultaneously as Cataloging & classification quarterly, v. 34, nos. 1-3, 2002.
    Includes bibliographical references and index.
    ISBN 0-7890-2028-9 (alk. paper) – ISBN 0-7890-2029-7 (pbk : alk. paper)
    1. Catalogers–Training of. 2. Catalogers–In-service training. 3. Cataloging–Computer-assisted instruction. 4. Library education. 5. Library education (Continuing education) 6. Library education–United States. 7. Library education (Continuing education)–United States. I. Hill, Janet Swan. II. Cataloging & classification quarterly.
    Z682.4.C38 E385 2002
    023'.8–dc21

                                 2002015053

Indexing, Abstracting & Website/Internet Coverage

This section provides you with a list of major indexing & abstracting services. That is to say, each service began covering this periodical during the year noted in the right column. Most Websites which are listed below have indicated that they will either post, disseminate, compile, archive, cite or alert their own Website users with research-based content from this work. (This list is as current as the copyright date of this publication.)

(continued)

Special Bibliographic Notes related to special journal issues (separates) and indexing/abstracting:

- indexing/abstracting services in this list will also cover material in any "separate" that is co-published simultaneously with Haworth's special thematic journal issue or DocuSerial. Indexing/abstracting usually covers material at the article/chapter level.
- monographic co-editions are intended for either non-subscribers or libraries which intend to purchase a second copy for their circulating collections.
- monographic co-editions are reported to all jobbers/wholesalers/approval plans. The source journal is listed as the "series" to assist the prevention of duplicate purchasing in the same manner utilized for books-in-series.
- to facilitate user/access services all indexing/abstracting services are encouraged to utilize the co-indexing entry note indicated at the bottom of the first page of each article/chapter/contribution.
- this is intended to assist a library user of any reference tool (whether print, electronic, online, or CD-ROM) to locate the monographic version if the library has purchased this version but not a subscription to the source journal.
- individual articles/chapters in any Haworth publication are also available through the Haworth Document Delivery Service (HDDS).

Education for Cataloging and the Organization of Information: Pitfalls and the Pendulum

CONTENTS

ALTERNATIVES FOR INSTRUCTIONAL DELIVERY

ABOUT THE EDITOR

Janet Swan Hill, MA (Library Science), is Professor and Associate Director for Technical Services at the University of Colorado Libraries in Boulder. She began her professional career at the Library of Congress in 1970 as an intern, map cataloger, and then as Head of the Map Cataloging Unit in the Geography and Map Division. Between 1978 and 1989, she was Head of Cataloging at the Northwestern University Library. Ms. Hill received the Margaret Mann Citation from ALA/ALCTS in 1993, and the Library of Congress Meritorious Service Award for her work on the revision of the Library of Congress Classification Schedule, Class G, in 1975.

Ms. Hill founded ALA's Cataloging and Classification Section's Task Force (later Committee) on Education, Training, and Recruitment for Cataloging. Highlights of her ALA service include being President of ALCTS and serving for eleven years on ALA's Committee on Cataloging: Description and Access, including six years as the ALA representative on the Joint Steering Committee for the Revision of AACR2. She is currently in her third term on the ALA Council and has served on three Presidential Task Forces (Outsourcing, Core Values for the Profession, and Membership Meeting Quorum).

Ms. Hill is also a figure skating judge, judging singles, pairs, and ice dancing for the United States Figure Skating Association. She competes in synchronized skating and has skated in seven National Synchronized Skating Championships.

Pitfalls and the Pendulum:
Reconsidering Education for Cataloging and the Organization of Information:
Preface

In the past century and a half, education for cataloging might be regarded as a pendulum, swinging slowly from near one extreme to another. Prior to Melvil Dewey's founding of the first library school in 1887, most of those who would become librarians learned their craft on the job, either through a kind of apprenticeship under the tutelage of an experienced staff member, or by figuring things out for themselves as best they could.

With the formalization of education for librarianship begun by Dewey, the pendulum swung away from individual "apprenticeships," as much that librarians might need to know became a part of a curriculum–one in which instruction in cataloging was one of the main required components. The existence of a course of instruction in a library school never entirely eliminated the need for on the job training for catalogers, but for nearly three-quarters of a century, what librarians learned in library school was sufficient for them to begin work as catalogers, and it was also generally sufficient to last them for most of their careers. The days of the cataloger-as-apprentice, and employer-as-educator were no more (for a while).

[Haworth co-indexing entry note]: "Pitfalls and the Pendulum: Reconsidering Education for Cataloging and the Organization of Information: Preface." Hill, Janet Swan. Co-published simultaneously in *Cataloging & Classification Quarterly* (The Haworth Information Press, an imprint of The Haworth Press, Inc.) Vol. 34, No. 1/2, 2002, pp. xix-xxiii; and: *Education for Cataloging and the Organization of Information: Pitfalls and the Pendulum* (ed: Janet Swan Hill) The Haworth Information Press, an imprint of The Haworth Press, Inc., 2002, pp. xv-xix. Single or multiple copies of this article are available for a fee from The Haworth Document Delivery Service [1-800-HAWORTH, 9:00 a.m. - 5:00 p.m. (EST). E-mail address: getinfo@haworth pressinc.com].

xv

The application of computers to cataloging, and the adoption of shared cataloging through bibliographic networks began another swing of the pendulum. Increased cataloging productivity, increased availability of pre-existing cataloging copy that could be adapted for local use by non-professionally trained catalogers, and the seemingly limitless capability of computers for search and retrieval contributed to a perception that education for cataloging was no longer particularly important. The cataloging portion of library school curricula shrank. Many introductory courses in cataloging were replaced by general introductions to bibliographic control. Sometimes, even an introduction to bibliographic control was no longer considered an essential part of every librarian's education, and both it and an introduction to cataloging were dropped out of the core of required courses.

Library automation and bibliographic networks did indeed radically change life for catalogers, and at first, most of those changes were of the sort that had been predicted. More copy and automation did lead to greater productivity and less need for professionally trained catalogers. But this trend never reached the expected (by some) conclusion. "The computer" turned out not to be so wonderfully, magically capable as had been anticipated. Computers actually accentuated the importance of some aspects of cataloging (e.g., authority work) that had nearly withered away in the last days before online catalogs. Increased availability of cataloging for mainstream titles in mainstream formats highlighted the need to provide catalog access for other materials–rare, or local items, and materials in formats other than books–or to provide better cataloging for material previously given short shrift (e.g., by analyzing contents and series). Technology brought a proliferation of almost metastatic proportions of types of information resources acquired by libraries. Even the basic view of the role of the catalog changed.

While library schools had decreased their commitment to bibliographic control and to the education of those who would provide it, the need for both increased, and librarians and their employers had to pick up the slack. The pendulum swung toward a situation where the needs of libraries and their users could only be satisfied by a return of a system of cataloger-as-apprentice and employer-as-educator. And while what catalogers learned either as apprentices, or in library school used to serve them for most of their careers, this became no longer the case. The materials, the technologies, and the expectations are all undergoing rapid change, and all require response. That response includes a commitment to continual (rather than continuing) education, exploration of alternatives for instructional delivery, and a reassessment of priorities and expectations leading to a reconsideration of education for bibliographic control. The papers in this collection were solicited with that in mind.

The four authors contributing papers to the section "A Matter of Opinion" were asked to consider some of the issues that have traditionally plagued cataloging instruction, and to express opinions about them as provocatively as they wished. Michael Gorman addresses the most basic issue of all: whether cataloging should be taught. Sheila S. Intner tackles the theory vs. practice issue, discusses how education for handling different materials formats should be handled, and also considers the appropriate setting for cataloging education. Heidi Lee Hoerman asks why so many people hate cataloging, and suggests both reasons and solutions. Robert P. Holley proposes ways in which cataloging education can be made both more effective and more interesting.

In the next section, "The Context," papers set the context in which education for cataloging and bibliographic control must operate today. Those who employ catalogers have been aware for some time that the supply of qualified catalogers is insufficient to meet their needs. Stanley J. Wilder's exploration of the demographics of librarians, especially catalogers, confirms that perception, and suggests that the worst is yet to come. Beginning in the 1980s there have been numerous surveys of curricular offerings in cataloging and classification. Daniel N. Joudrey's detailed survey, from which he provides extensive data and draws interconnections, provides concrete information about the status of cataloging instruction today. In the course of his survey, he also gathered information about which textbooks are being used in conjunction with graduate courses in cataloging related subjects. This information, originally written as an appendix to the larger paper, is presented here as a "stand-alone" companion piece. Jerry D. Saye examines cataloging instruction in accredited library programs from an entirely different perspective–that of the structure and atmosphere of library school programs, the outlook, background, and influence of the faculty, and the impact of operating within the larger academic arena. The section concludes with reports of two opinion surveys. In the first, Beatrice Kovacs and Nancy Dayton surveyed graduates of the University of North Carolina at Greensboro program on their opinions about the usefulness of their cataloging instruction. In the second, Michelle R. Turvey and Karen M. Letarte surveyed library educators, both those who taught cataloging and those who did not, on their perceptions of the importance of cataloging competencies to graduates.

Rapid changes in the environment in which bibliographic control is provided, as well as changes in rules and technologies, have increased the importance of, altered the need for, or changed the methods that need to be used, in particular aspects of cataloging education. In "Education for Specific Purposes," a few of these are covered. Clément Arsenault and John E. Leide consider the possible impact of the proliferation of formats in which information resources are being produced, and of format integration on the organization of the cataloging curriculum. Ingrid Hsieh-Yee examines issues surrounding digital resources, and proposes a model curriculum covering the provision of metadata and cataloging for these materials. Another area where philosophy and practicality sometimes lead to different approaches in education is that of subject cataloging. Arlene G. Taylor and Daniel N. Joudrey cover many of these arguments, including whether subject analysis should be taught in a separate course, what should be covered, and in what manner. Authority control is an area of cataloging rarely taught separately, and often hardly addressed in library schools. Rebecca L. Mugridge and Kevin A. Furniss ask and answer a pertinent question: "Whose Responsibility Is It?" The final paper of this section is supplied by the Editor, Janet Swan Hill, who lists many of the skills needed by catalogers and those who manage cataloging, including those that cannot be acquired in library school, and discusses ways to acquire them.

The final section, "Alternatives for Instructional Delivery," reflects major changes in education for cataloging, in terms of who should be responsible for instruction, when and where instruction should or could be delivered, and how technology can be used to conduct or enhance education and training. Gertrude S. Koh conducts a historical survey of innovation in classroom instruction for cataloging from a content point of view, and follows that with a description of how today's students, their experiences, and the technologies with which they must work influence the design of a cataloging curriculum and choice of pedagogical methods. She then describes the use of expert practitioners as online mentors for students in a course on Internet resources. Two brief papers accompany this piece: One was written by the students registered in Koh's course in the fall of 2001, and the other is by two of the online mentors, Kate Harcourt and Susan M. Neumeister. The vexing issue of the suitability of distance education for cataloging is the subject of Elaine Yontz's "When Donkeys Fly," in which Yontz covers its advantages and disadvantages, and describes her own conversion. A special instance of distance online continuing education is OCLC's Web-based class in cataloging Internet resources. Robert Ellett reports on a study of the effectiveness of the course. Anna M. Ferris, a participant in both the course and the study, describes the learning experience from her perspective. Certain kinds of education can probably never be handled by library schools, nor perhaps, should they. Cooperative programs are critical to the cataloging endeavor, but presuppose institutional cooperation and the participation of individuals who have a significant amount and quality of on the job experience. Carol G. Hixson and William A. Garrison describe the development and components of the training programs of the Program for Cooperative Cataloging. Another example of a training program devised for participants in a cooperative program is covered by Sue Kriegsman, who discusses the content and the challenges of training people who may not be catalogers, and who may not even be librarians, in providing intellectual control through creating cataloging and metadata records for the Colorado Digitization Project. Although Judith Hopkins' paper is the final paper in this section, its position is determined only by logic, not importance. In a time when it has become clear that library schools cannot handle all the education that catalogers will need, and that continual education is essential, the "Community of Catalogers" is a critical piece of the educational puzzle.

Janet Swan Hill

A MATTER OF OPINION

Why Teach Cataloguing and Classification?

Michael Gorman

SUMMARY. Enemies of cataloging today include ill-informed administrators, information scientists in library schools, and those who think that alternatives to vocabulary control and bibliographic architecture–such as Google–are better and cheaper than cataloging. Bibliographic control and cataloging should be at the heart of library education. An ideal library school is described. *[Article copies available for a fee from The Haworth Document Delivery Service: 1-800-HAWORTH. E-mail address: <getinfo@haworthpressinc.com> Website: <http://www.HaworthPress.com> © 2002 by The Haworth Press, Inc. All rights reserved.]*

KEYWORDS. Cataloging education, library education, library school curricula

Michael Gorman is Dean of Library Services, California State University, Fresno.

[Haworth co-indexing entry note]: "Why Teach Cataloguing and Classification?" Gorman, Michael. Co-published simultaneously in *Cataloging & Classification Quarterly* (The Haworth Information Press, an imprint of The Haworth Press, Inc.) Vol. 34, No. 1/2, 2002, pp. 1-13; and: *Education for Cataloging and the Organization of Information: Pitfalls and the Pendulum* (ed: Janet Swan Hill) The Haworth Information Press, an imprint of The Haworth Press, Inc., 2002, pp. 1-13. Single or multiple copies of this article are available for a fee from The Haworth Document Delivery Service [1-800-HAWORTH, 9:00 a.m. - 5:00 p.m. (EST). E-mail address: getinfo@haworthpressinc.com].

1

INTRODUCTION

Those of us who have spent the past few decades thinking about librarianship and its concerns are afflicted with a species of existential dread when confronted with such a question. Before the great gas bubble of digitization came along, the answer would have been so obvious that only a ninny would have even posed the question. That obvious answer is: "We should teach cataloguing and classification[1] because it is essential that those who wish to be librarians (not just those who wish to be cataloguers) understand the way in which recorded knowledge and information is organized for retrieval." (As the post-trendy would say "*Duh!*".) That answer sufficed from the great days of Anthony Panizzi and the debates over the catalogues of the British Museum, to the golden age of which Cutter wrote, to the Paris Principles and the steely intellect of Seymour Lubetzky, even unto MARC and the online catalogues of the 1970s and 1980s. The world of the Web and of metadata–a world in which would-be librarians are taught ephemera such as Java script and how to construct Web pages (something that is self-evidently within the powers of any fool)–has lost that certainty and a central part of librarianship is in danger of neglect. How can such a thing have come to be?

ENEMIES OF CATALOGUING

I believe that there are three major enemies of cataloguing–one relatively long-standing, the others relatively new. The first group consists, broadly speaking, of ill-informed library administrators, almost invariably lacking a technical processing background, who have come of age as administrators since OCLC came to be a dominant force. They do not understand the essential truth that OCLC's success was built on its nature as one of the most successful socialist endeavors in American history–*from each library according to its means, to each according to its needs*. The contribution of the smallest library is as important as the contribution of the Library of Congress in such an enterprise. Even the largest library benefits from the contributions of the smallest and the flow of cataloguing copy is dependent on all contributors living up to the implicit agreements that are the basis of all library cooperation. Lacking knowledge of the fundamentals of OCLC, those administrators believe that OCLC records grow on trees and their libraries can safely dispense with original cataloguers to rely on ill-paid staff to pick the fruit of the OCLC trees and construct incoherent catalogues of increasingly less use to their users. All this without such a library contributing anything to the OCLC enterprise. Since these administrators do not value cataloguing enough to maintain effective cataloguing departments, it is scarcely likely that they will value it enough to demand a sound cataloguing education of new employees in other parts of the library.

One reasonable way to look at library education is that the variations on library schools produce a product (graduates) of value to consumers (library administrators). If the latter do not require recent graduates to have a sound knowledge of cataloguing, there is no pressure on the producers to build such knowledge into the curriculum. In addition to those who are indifferent to cataloguing, there are many administrators who would like newly hired librarians to know about bibliographic control but feel powerless to affect "library schools" or their curricula. In this sense, practicing librarians today are very like automobile purchasers of the 1970s. Those purchasers wanted higher mileage and more safety but were at the mercy of an industry abusing its perceived monopoly and ignoring the consumers' desires. The sad thing for libraries is that there is no Japanese library education industry capable of coming to the rescue.

Powerless or indifferent library administrators combine, unwittingly or wittingly, with the second group of enemies of cataloguing. That group consists of the "information scientists" increasingly infesting many of the successors to library schools. Knowing nothing of libraries, library history, or bibliographic control, they press for cataloguing to be succeeded by courses that suit their non-library objectives and research interests and, thus, deprive their hapless students of skills that could make them employable in libraries. This sinister trend is reinforced as the demographic shifts that are taking place throughout academia affect LIS schools. There are numerous instances in which older LIS teachers of cataloguing have retired and been replaced by adepts of other, marginal or non-library, disciplines. Proclaiming that they produced "information professionals" capable of working within or without libraries was popular in LIS education a scant few years ago. Some even dedicated themselves to producing mostly non-librarians or bragged of the high percentage of their graduates who found jobs outside libraries. The collapse of many sectors of the "new economy" has taken some of the glitter off that boast, but the fundamental split personality remains. If LIS schools are to produce both librarians and non-librarians (in any combination), what is the suitable curriculum for each? Assuming most LIS schools do not follow the example of that at Berkeley and light out for the territories, some percentage of their intake will consist of people who wish to pursue careers in librarianship. Would it not make sense for those people to be offered a curriculum that would equip them for such work? It is hard to understand the more virulent IS types, but perhaps they believe that they should not produce people capable of working in libraries as they are (not that most have any experience with such) but for hypothetical libraries in a totally digitized world.

If there were to be such a future for libraries, the third group of enemies of cataloguing would come into their own. These are those who think that there are alternatives to vocabulary control and bibliographic architecture that are as effective and far cheaper than real cataloguing. The more moderate such push metadata and the extremists search engines, but both are seeking results without effort and spun gold out for garbage in. We should note that neither class contains many, if any, librarians.

Metadata–literally "data about data" (a definition that would include real cataloguing if taken literally)–arose from the desire of non-librarians to improve the retrievability of Web pages and other Internet documents. After many papers and numerous conferences (a process in which renegade librarians joined), a quasi-standard called The Dublin Core emerged as the shining example of metadata and what it could achieve. The Dublin Core (DC) consists of 15 denotations, each of which has a more or less exact equivalent in the MARC record. As any cataloguer knows, MARC contains far more than 15 fields and sub-fields, in addition to the information contained in coded fixed fields. In addition, there are MARC formats for a variety of different kinds of publication, from books to electronic resources, which adds to the variety of denotations. Those who advocate metadata and, implicitly or explicitly, believe that the whole range of bibliographic data for documents in all formats can be contained in 15 categories, ignore a simple fact. The MARC formats are not the result of whimsy and the baroque impulses of cataloguers but have evolved to meet the real characteristics of complex documents of all kinds. What we have is a simplistic (in many ways naïve) short list of categories that is expected to substitute for cataloguing when put in the hands of non-cataloguers.

The literature of metadata is littered with references to "MARC cataloguing," an ignorant phrase that betrays the hollowness of the metadata concept.[2] MARC, as any cataloguer knows, is a framework standard for holding bibliographic data. It does not dictate the content of its fields–leaving that to content standards such as *AACR2*, LCSH, etc. People who talk of "MARC cataloguing" clearly think of cataloguing as being a matter of identifying the elements of cataloguing record without specifying the content of those elements. It is, therefore, clear that those people do not understand what cataloguing is all about. The most important thing about bibliographic control is the *content* and the controlled nature of that content, not the denotations of that content. So, when all the tumult is over and the metadata captains and kings have spoken, we are left with the absurd proposition that a 15 field subset of the MARC record, with no specification of how those fields are to be filled by non-cataloguers, is some kind of substitute for real cataloguing. The fact that metadata and the Dublin Core have been discussed *ad nauseam* for about five years with very few people pointing out this obvious flaw in the argument is reminiscent of the story of the little boy and the naked Emperor. In this case, however, the Emperor keeps swaggering around *sans* clothes (controlled content), at least so far.

OF ARMS AND THE GOOGLE

Metadata is, when compared with search engines, a triumph of bibliographic philosophy. Search engines use keyword searching in a vain attempt to retrieve relevant electronic documents, as anyone who has used them can attest. This record of futility does not prevent eminent non-librarians from being their champions. Take, for example, the case of William Y. Arms, professor of computing at Cornell University and self-appointed expert on digital libraries. In a remarkable paper published in 2000, Arms displays the combination of arrogance and ignorance that is characteristic of his type.[3] I would cite:

> *Progress is being made in reducing material[s] costs. Open access materials on the Internet are making many primary materials available at no cost.*[4]

Oh, really? What is the percentage of scholarly materials that is available on the Internet at no cost? How many of them are derived from the print industry? Just hand-waving and vagueness from Professor Arms, because his real target, having disposed, to his satisfaction, of the inconvenient facts of the cost of scholarly books, journals, etc., is the role of the librarian and how to get rid of the latter because:

> *If professional and research information is to be available more widely, either users will have to bypass libraries, or libraries will have to employ fewer people.*[5]

Having delivered himself of this magisterial *non sequitur*, Arms goes on to talk about the tasks of librarians (always to him "professional librarians," presumably to distinguish them from amateur librarians) and how computers could perform them. He starts with cataloguing and an attempt at equivalence between library cataloguing and search engines. He grants that "almost everything that is best about a library catalog service is done badly by a Web search service," but hastens to add that Web indexing services are cheap and cover more documents than library catalogues. This argument beggars belief. It would be far cheaper to have surgery performed by your brother-in-law Arnold armed with a saw and instructions from the Internet than it would be to go to the Mayo Clinic (another institution with high labor costs). Also, once he got into the swing of it, Arnold could probably perform many more operations than a team of surgeons at the Mayo Clinic.

Arms then compares Google to Inspec (the indexing/abstracting service for computer science), with a tip of his hat to the former. The history of indexing is littered with scientists and technologists making generalizations based on their own discipline, conveniently ignoring the problems of vocabulary in the social sciences and arts/humanities. He compounds this elementary error:

> But its [Google's] greatest strength is that everything in its indexes is available online with open access . . . Inspec references [sic] a formally published version, which is usually printed or online with restricted access.[6]

So, there we are. Google is "better" than Inspec because everything to which it gives access is online and costs nothing. Perhaps you can find everything that you need in computer science online and free. However, in the vast majority of disciplines, serious research and scholarship are not possible without access to "formally published versions" in print and/or online by subscription.

Arms goes on to question the future of reference librarians and, grudgingly, comes to the conclusion that " . . . nothing on the horizon approaches human judgement in understanding such subtleties."[7] He remains confident that this is a transient phase and that, though there are "tough technical and organizational problems," there is "nothing that cannot be solved in twenty years of natural evolution."[8] He concludes that not only will automated digital libraries replace real libraries, but also that librarians have no skills that can be used to achieve this happy state of affairs.

Arms' paper is dotted with laudatory references to Google and the power and authority of its algorithms. I decided to test the system he likes so much by using it to attempt to retrieve electronic documents by or about Dr. Arms. It is pertinent to note that a Google search using "William Arms" yields "about 1,350" results in no useful order and, though the good professor's home page is the first thing retrieved, the *first 10* results (deemed by Google's "powerful algorithms" to be the most relevant) include the coat of arms of a member of the British Royal Family; symbols of the city of Thunder Bay, Canada; and miscellaneous songs by one William Arms Fisher. Bizarrely, refining the search to "William Y. Arms" yields 1,460 results (110 more than the coarser search). Since they too are in no useful order, I could not be bothered to check them all and can only assume they all relate to our Arms and, therefore must include relevant items not retrieved by Google's "powerful algorithms" on the first search. "William Yeo Arms" yields "about 34" results. Librarians and cataloguers may be about to pass from the stage of history, but we do know a little bit about vocabulary control, relevance and recall in indexing, and arranging search results in a useful order. Please note that these searches are in the relatively orderly world of personal names and do not involve the complexities of free-text searching vs. controlled subject searching in non-technical fields or the even more freakish results of the former.

The reader may be asking why I have devoted a number of paragraphs to one article by one person. The answer is that he is one of many, unfortunately influential, people who speak and write against the interests of real libraries. No straw man he–this consultant to the Library of Congress, influential member of the National Research Council and other gatherings of the great, and author of *Digital Libraries*.[9] No doubt it is only a matter of time before he is invited to an ALA Conference to tell us how outmoded we are. Certainly, it will be far longer before a "professional librarian" is invited to a computer science conference to tell them how passé they are and how misguided their endeavors.

A CATALOGUING CURRICULUM

Let us assume that the combined efforts of library administrators, information scientists, metadatologists, and Dr. Arms come to naught and cataloguing continues as a basic discipline within librarianship. Let us also assume that LIS schools are ready to restore cataloguing to its previous unavoidable status as a central part of and education to be a librarian. (Or even an "information professional," come to that, as cataloguing is the one unique thing that a graduate of an LIS school has to offer to employers in non-library fields.)[10] If these happy and supremely rational states of affairs were to come about, what should the cataloguing curriculum look like?

ALA has embarked on a quest for a list of agreed "core competences." A "penultimate" report by a task force is under consideration by the ALA Executive Board at the time of this writing. The task force has come up with a list of the core competences that begins:

Organization of Knowledge Resource

The ability to organize collections of informational materials in order that desired items can be retrieved quickly and easily is a librarian's unique competency *[sic]*. Well-organized collections are the foundation for all library service. Competence in organizing collections involves thorough knowledge of bibliographic and intellectual control principles and standards, understanding of how to apply these principles and standards in practical, cost-effective operations; and, the ability to collaborate with those who provide systems for managing organizational functions such as library vendors and institutional computer center staff members."[11]

There are many striking, and most welcome, things about this statement, despite the barbarity of its expression (what, for example, is an "Organization of knowledge resource?"). The placement of the organization of knowledge at the head of a sometimes bromidic (e.g., "connecting people to ideas") list and its identification as the unique competence of a librarian are, in themselves, a forceful argument for restoring cataloguing to the center of library education. The insistence that all librarians should have a "thorough knowledge of bibliographic and intellectual control principles and standards" and should understand how to apply them reinforces the argument. Finally, the role that bibliographic control plays in constructing and understanding automated systems, in acquisitions, and in collection development is recognized. It is worth remembering that the task force was set up by the ALA-sponsored Congress on Professional Education as a response to the perceived need for a basic education that all librarians should receive. The response of LIS schools to this unequivocal statement will be a test of the professional resolve of ALA and its ability to influence education for the profession it represents. If they embrace it and restore cataloguing to a central place in the curriculum, the seemingly unbridgeable and seemingly ever-widening gulf between librarians and educators will be bridged. If they reject it, ALA will have to bid the LIS schools farewell and create another approach entirely to library education. In either event, the content and place of the cataloguing curriculum must be decided. Library education in the U.S. and Canada has been largely a matter of local control–which is why we have got to the point at which graduates of some LIS schools have no, or only the most cursory, acquaintance with cataloguing. One thing that should result from the core competences debate is an insistence by ALA that curricula in LIS schools *must* include cataloguing to a certain standard (a "thorough knowledge" would be a good start) as well as other core areas if the program is to be accredited.

WHAT LIBRARIANS DO

The ALA task force, after its clear statement on the "organization of knowledge," states that the core competences are (in paraphrase): Connecting users with information; Connecting people to ideas; Facilitating learning; Management; Technology; and, Research.[12] This is a somewhat soggy list combining the obvious with aims rather than competences. One suspects that their hearts are in the right place but they suffer from neophilia made manifest in the reluctance to use words and phrases like "cataloguing," "reference," "instruction," "collection development," "children's libraries," and the rest of the Oldspeak used in actual libraries. "Connecting people to ideas" and "connecting users to information" are both vague to the point of incoherence. Let us begin the analysis with some basics. Libraries deal with information and, more importantly, with recorded knowledge. In order to make these goods of the mind (to use Mortimer Adler's phrase), librarians engage in the following activities.

- *Collection development and acquisitions:* They select, acquire, and give access to carriers of recorded knowledge and information in all formats.
- *Cataloguing:* They organize those carriers and arrange access to them by creating catalogues, indexes, and other controlled guides to those carriers and their contents. (Note that the term "organization of knowledge" is profoundly flawed–we do not organize knowledge as such, only recorded knowledge. Equally, we do not

provide connections to "ideas"–only to those ideas embodied in recorded knowledge and information.)

- *Reference and library instruction:* They provide assistance and instruction on how to find, select, and evaluate recorded knowledge and information.
- *Circulation, maintenance, preservation, etc.:* They arrange access to physical carriers, maintain the collections of such carriers, and preserve recorded knowledge and information in all formats.
- *Systems:* They install, modify, maintain, and, in increasingly rare instances, create computer systems to assist in and improve all the foregoing activities.
- *Management:* They manage and administer the libraries in which these activities take place. This includes all library services, staff, and the environment in which the library exists.
- *Types of library:* All these activities take place in one form or another in every library, but the relative importance and nature of each vary greatly depending on the type of library. Librarians need an education in those differences.

There is a changing penumbra around these activities (these days, various aspects of computer science, personnel, information theory, budgeting/accounting, etc.) but the basic list is surprisingly unchanging over the years. Unless you believe that digitization, the "information revolution," etc., are going to bring an end to libraries as we know them, it seems reasonable to ask for a nationally agreed curriculum that ensures that every graduate of a LIS school has a good grounding in all the subjects named above, as well as in the penumbral areas of the moment.

THE HEART OF LIBRARY EDUCATION

Cataloguing is not just for cataloguers. It is possible that the decay of cataloguing education is, in part, due to a failure to grasp this fact. It is essential that libraries have a supply of educated and dedicated cataloguers in order to provide coherent local catalogues and to contribute to the great national and international networks of which OCLC is the shining exemplar. It is equally essential that *all* librarians have a thorough knowledge of cataloguing standards and principles for what should be an obvious reason and for another, more subtle, reason. The obvious reason is that knowledge of bibliographic control is essential to all aspects of the work of librarians. How can one be an effective reference librarian, collection developer, library instructor, or, come to that, children's librarian without knowledge of bibliographic control? How can a reference librarian assists a library user if she knows nothing of the architecture of catalogues and the ways in which subjects are expressed and collated? How can an instruction librarian teach the use of the library and information literacy without knowing the central issues of bibliographic control? These rhetorical questions apply with equal force to collection development, acquisitions, and even management. In the latter case, it may not be the only way to judge a library administrator, but ignorance of bibliographic control is an almost infallible indicator of flawed and ineffective library management. Last but by no means least, systems work is rooted in a thorough knowledge of bibliographic control. Anyone who has had to suffer in a library with a systems person who is technologically knowledgeable but has not the foggiest about the content of MARC records (and only a little learning about MARC itself) will be keenly aware of what I speak. Similarly, the implementation of even the simpler forms of library systems is virtually impossible without the contribution of cataloguers. Such an attempt in libraries without cataloguers is almost too horrible to contemplate.

I referred earlier to a more subtle reason for the teaching of cataloguing to all would-be librarians. It is this: cataloguing is the intellectual foundation of librarianship–it is the way in which good librarians, in all fields, think. A good reference librarian will not only map a question to the way in which recorded knowledge and information is organized, but will also follow elementary precepts of cataloguing and classification such as proceeding from the general to the special and following the syndetic structures of bibliographic control. Collection development and preservation librarians think of their responsibilities in terms of the subject groupings of classifications and subject headings lists. When asked for a recommendation for a good book to read, a children's librarian thinks, consciously or subconsciously, in terms of subject and genre groupings derived from cataloguing practice as well as the age-suitability–another organized grouping of like materials. If you cannot think like a cataloguer, you cannot think like a librarian and, therefore, cannot deliver effective library service.

THE CURRICULUM

I have a concept of an ideal library school, and there may yet be some such. I use the term "library school" intentionally here. I believe there is a need, now more than ever, for such institutions, whether stand-alone (my preference) or as part of some structure that teaches "information science" and "information studies," to those who feel a need for them. The library school component in such structures would have its own core faculty and would draw on other faculty for the penumbral courses. In that ideal library school, all students would take the same courses in the first year. The second year would consist of elective courses, using which students would build on their foundation year and explore related areas of interest in greater depth. The first year–a form of General Education curriculum for librarians–would include not only the core competences (cataloguing, reference work, collection development, etc.) but also such basic courses as the history of libraries, the role of libraries in society, and the ethics and values of librarianship. If a student completed the first year satisfactorily, the second year would build on the basic learning experience and would be informed by it. Students would not be encouraged to declare an interest in a particular branch of librarianship or type of library in the first year in the hope that the "GE" educational experience might well change a premature initial decision. For example, someone with no knowledge of, or interest in, cataloguing on entering the library school might be transformed into someone with a keen interest in the topic by the first year experience. The reverse might be the case and, in either instance, the unified first year concept would have proved itself.

The first year cataloguing curriculum would cover all aspects of bibliographic principles and standards and their application in libraries and library services. The topics would include descriptive cataloguing (both access points and bibliographic description), subject headings, classification, filing rules, authority control, indexing and abstracting principles and practice, the organization and management of the cataloguing process, and cooperative cataloguing structures. Given that thorough knowledge, the students would then be equipped to take on the elective courses of the second year. The "cataloguing thread" would include classification theory, history of cataloguing, advanced descriptive and subject cataloguing (separate courses), indexing theory, design of online catalogues, bibliographic control of electronic resources, and archival cataloguing. Though one might expect those who wish to be cataloguers to be the bulk of students in these courses, the fact is that many of them would benefit librarians who wish to toil in other vineyards.

ENVOI

If one believed only the evidence of library literature, conferences, etc., one would readily conclude that this is a profession in crisis, fragmented, drifting, and in a state of existential panic. Who are we? What are we doing here? The portrait is of a profession as Admiral Stock-dale–grinning amiably while shambling toward oblivion. The facts on the ground contribute to a quite different picture. Libraries are flourishing, even when, as is too often the case, they are underfunded. Far from the virtual fantasies of information scientists, real libraries are getting on with the job–cataloguing, giving service and instruction to millions of library users, developing collections in all formats, encouraging wonder in children and wisdom in the old, and making the difference one life at a time. I believe that cataloguing is a central part of that mission in ways both obvious and subtle, and that we must devise ways in which education for our profession understands and communicates that centrality.

ENDNOTES

1. I will use "cataloguing," "cataloguing and classification," and "bibliographic control" interchangeably in this paper–each refers to the organization of recorded knowledge and information in all its aspects.

2. See, for example among many such: Weibel, Stuart. CORC and the Dublin Core. *OCLC newsletter*, no.239 (May/June 1999).

3. William Y. Arms, "Automated digital libraries: how effectively can computers be used for the skilled tasks of professional librarianship?" *D-Lib magazine*, v.6, no. 7/8 (July 2000), [9 p.].

4. William Y. Arms, "Automated digital libraries," p. 1.

5. William Y. Arms, "Automated digital libraries," p. 2.

6. William Y. Arms, "Automated digital libraries," p. 3.

7. William Y. Arms, "Automated digital libraries," p. 8.

8. William Y. Arms, "Automated digital libraries," p. 8.

9. William Y. Arms, *Digital Libraries*. (Boston: MIT Press, 2001).

10. Michael Gorman, "library schools.com." *California Libraries* (July 2000) p. 3.

11. ALA Task Force on Core Competencies *[sic]*. Draft report, 2002. http://www.ala.org/congress/draft.html.

12. *Ibid.*

Persistent Issues in Cataloging Education:
Considering the Past
and Looking Toward the Future

Sheila S. Intner

SUMMARY. Describes and analyzes the following three issues which elicit strong but divergent views among cataloging faculty, students, and practitioners, and seem to have done so for as long as people have been writing about cataloging education: (1) practice versus theory in cataloging education; (2) dividing book and nonbook cataloging into separate classes versus teaching the cataloging of all materials in a single class; and (3) what setting is best for teaching cataloging–formal graduate school courses, on the job training, or continuing education offerings. Speculates on how these issues may play out in the future as cataloging education continues to evolve in the 21st century. *[Article copies available for a fee from The Haworth Document Delivery Service: 1-800-HAWORTH. E-mail address: <getinfo@haworthpressinc.com> Website: <http://www.HaworthPress.com> © 2002 by The Haworth Press, Inc. All rights reserved.]*

KEYWORDS. Cataloging education, continuing education, theory vs. practice

Sheila S. Intner is Professor, Graduate School of Library & Information Science, Simmons College, and Director of GSLIS in Western Massachusetts, Mt. Holyoke College, South Hadley, MA 01075 (E-mail: sheila.intner@simmons.edu or shemat@aol.com).

[Haworth co-indexing entry note]: "Persistent Issues in Cataloging Education: Considering the Past and Looking Toward the Future." Intner, Sheila S. Co-published simultaneously in *Cataloging & Classification Quarterly* (The Haworth Information Press, an imprint of The Haworth Press, Inc.) Vol. 34, No. 1/2, 2002, pp. 15-29; and: *Education for Cataloging and the Organization of Information: Pitfalls and the Pendulum* (ed: Janet Swan Hill) The Haworth Information Press, an imprint of The Haworth Press, Inc., 2002, pp. 15-29. Single or multiple copies of this article are available for a fee from The Haworth Document Delivery Service [1-800-HAWORTH, 9:00 a.m. - 5:00 p.m. (EST). E-mail address: getinfo@haworthpressinc.com].

INTRODUCTION

Twenty-plus years of personal experience teaching cataloging, discussing cataloging education with colleagues, reading relevant literature, and examining student evaluations of basic cataloging courses have led me to believe that certain issues are eternally debatable and quite unresolvable in ways that satisfy everyone. No sooner does one choose a particular resolution to one of these issues than criticism will erupt claiming that a different option would do a better job of addressing this or that matter, or answering this or that need. Among these thorny issues are: (1) the proper balance between teaching theory and practice; (2) the proper division into discrete courses of a curriculum covering the cataloging and classification of books and other types of materials (called variously nonbook, nonprint, and/or audiovisual materials, including electronic resources); and, (3) the relative merits of teaching cataloging in formal graduate school courses or nonacademic venues such as on-the-job training, workshops, and other continuing education offerings.

At the outset, I freely admit that I have strong feelings on each of these three issues, arguing always for the greatest possible emphasis on theory, an integrated approach to materials, and more of all types of cataloging education in all possible venues; but I have spent a good part of my teaching career doing other than following my own preferences. In the article that follows, I tackle the issues one by one, giving the background and laying out arguments for and against various kinds of resolution, trying all the while to put personal preferences aside and to weigh the alternatives objectively. At the end of the exercise, I shall suggest the resolutions that make the most sense educationally and practically, given the current and likely future environment in which cataloging is taught–if, in fact, it continues to be taught. For the purposes of this article, I use the term "cataloging" to refer to both cataloging and classification, unless otherwise noted.

CURRICULAR FRAMEWORKS

Before discussing the three issues to which this article is devoted, two practical matters about curriculum bear examination. The first is the different status of required versus elective courses and the other is the nature of beginning versus advanced level courses. Designating a course "required" means that every student in the academic program must take that course in order to be eligible to receive a degree. Occasionally, students with long experience in a particular required subject may petition successfully to waive a required course, but this is not typical. When it occurs, it indicates that the student does have knowledge in the required area. One can assume, therefore, that having earned the professional degree, graduate librarians have covered the subject areas of the required curriculum.

More than one author has demonstrated that over the last several decades cataloging courses–even the most basic courses–have been shifting from required to elective status.[1] By definition, "elective" means that students can opt *not* to take such courses. Students holding the professional master's degree may or may not have taken any particular set of elective courses, as White pointed out.[2] If all cataloging courses are assigned elective status, it cannot be taken for granted that graduates of accredited professional school programs will have learned anything about the subject. More likely, only a small proportion of the total academic population will take cataloging, and fewer still will take more than one cataloging course.

This brings us to the second matter–beginning versus advanced level courses. If several cataloging courses are included in the curriculum of a particular academic program, it is likely that one will be designated a beginning level course (often called "Introduction to Cataloging" or "Basic Cataloging" to identify its nature) while the others are designated advanced level courses. Beginning level courses are usually prerequisites for all the others and are most likely to be part of the required curriculum, while the advanced-level courses are all elective. When a program offers a single cataloging course, it is most likely to be a beginning level course, since students could not be expected to be ready for courses at more advanced levels without first having had the introductory material. This may seem to be self-evident academic gobbledygook, but its significance for our discussions will soon become clear.

THEORY *versus* PRACTICE

The battle between theory and practice is not confined to cataloging–it appears in comments made by students on course evaluation forms for subjects as diverse as archives management and intellectual freedom, reference and collection development. Hardly any subject is completely free of it. Recently, one student said succinctly, "learning about cataloging isn't nearly as interesting as doing it," and joined numerous peers in recommending that to improve the specific class being evaluated, a great deal more class time and homework assignments should be spent on actual cataloging and discussion of practical matters, and a whole lot less on "theory," by which the student appeared to mean anything that was not part of a catalog record.

Observation of student performance in formal library school cataloging classes for 40 semesters leads me to conclude that a direct relationship exists between the amount of hands-on cataloging done in the course through homework assignments and in-class exercises, and the ability of students to assimilate the factual material associated with cataloging practice and make it part of their personal knowledge. On the other hand, just memorizing the facts will not help these students function over the long run of their careers as rules, tools, methods, and technologies change. Only a thorough understanding of the principles that underlie cataloging rules can guide good decision-making in response to or in anticipation of changes occurring in the field. Yet, learning basic cataloging facts can be so time-consuming that no time is left for learning the underlying theory; and, similarly, learning the facts is so large a task for true neophytes–those who start out without any preexisting knowledge–that both learning them and putting them all into a coherent framework can appear impossible, indeed.

One element of learning cataloging that poses special problems is its arcane vocabulary. If ever any group of librarians can be said to speak Biblish[3] [footnote Walt Crawford's article in the *LITA Newsletter*], it is catalogers. Who ever heard of titles proper? Or emanations of corporate bodies? Or, for that matter, of corporate bodies? They sound like murdered dot-coms. And those are but a few examples from descriptive cataloging. On the subject side, we talk about coextensivity, specificity, syndetics, and cuttering, to say nothing of coordination, synthesis, and faceting. What student new to cataloging could possibly be expected to know the meaning of these terms? Add to this our penchant for turning every name and phrase into an abbreviation or acronym and what we present to newcomers is a bewildering tongue, made all the more difficult to understand if they only hear it spoken, rather than seeing it written. Thus, for example, RLIN becomes ARLIN, RLAN, RLIND, or RLINT (variations of the acronym for the Research Libraries Information Network seen on student papers), and PRECIS, the computer-assisted subject heading system once used by the British Library, becomes PRAY-C.

Expressions of cataloging theory are few and succinct, but carrying them out often presents sophisticated, complex problems. Cutter's ob-

jects offer a good example. Cutter said the catalog should show what the
library has by an author, of a title, or in a subject, and enable the
searcher to select what is wanted from among the gathered works of an
author, editions of a title, or books on a subject or in a genre of literature.[4] That sounds simple, but putting it into practice is anything but. To
show what the library has, catalogers expect to use the exact wordings
for names, titles, and subjects as they appear on the items they catalog.
If they do so, however, they may necessarily use different words for the
same thing–different names for the same person, different titles for the
same work, and different terms for the same subject. Therefore, to draw
together related items despite the variations in words and word-forms
they might bear, catalogers select authoritative forms of names, titles,
and subject terms, and use these in place of the variants that appear on
the items themselves. As a result, being faithful in "showing what the library has" sometimes obfuscates "drawing together the related items"
and vice versa.

Subject theory is full of tricky ideas. For instance, take specific and
direct entry, one of the principles David Judson Haykin discussed in his
seminal book on Library of Congress subject headings.[5] Haykin meant
that the term assigned to an item being cataloged should reflect its subject exactly and not be broader or narrower than it should be, nor should
it be preceded by a broader term, which would create an indirect entry
of the desired term. For example, if one is cataloging a book about
worms of many kinds, then the subject should be WORMS, not
ANIMALS, which is broader; and not EARTHWORMS, which is narrower; nor should the term be constructed in a heading-subdivision format such as ANIMALS–WORMS or INVERTEBRATES–WORMS,
which are indirect ways of saying "WORMS." Another way of putting
the concept is that the subject heading used for an item being cataloged
should be coextensive with the subject matter of the item. Coextensivity
relates to how specific a subject heading is with regard to the topic the
cataloger wants to represent, while direct entry dictates that one should
go straight to the term without any intervening hierarchy of subject matter being offered first. There, everybody got it now? Unfortunately,
about 10%-15% of the students in every cataloging class this author has
taught, and occasionally more, garble the notes they take on this notion
to such an extent that they cannot answer examination questions correctly that deal with the meanings and implications of specificity, direct
entry, and coextensivity. Indeed, one must consider that perhaps there
are in each class a few more students who have no more idea what specificity, direct entry, and coextensivity are than their colleagues who got

these questions wrong, but who have just managed to guess the answers correctly.

These few examples are meant to illustrate the fact that, while doing cataloging is difficult, understanding the underlying principles on which the rules for doing it depend is even more difficult and is couched in its own strange language. Some instructors take the easy way out, teaching practice alone and answering questions about why something is done one way and not another with the stock phrase, "that's how it's done." The problem with this strategy is that there are always a few people in every class who refuse to be satisfied with such an answer and plague the instructor to supply reasons that make sense. This can turn out to be both time consuming and embarrassing for an instructor who is not comfortable discussing theoretical matters. At the same time, instructors who teach theory are not totally better off, because in my experience, there are always a few students in every class who manage to jot down notes reading exactly the opposite of what the instructor has said and then study them diligently, thus insuring that the errors become permanently fixed in their vision of cataloging. Fortunately, in the long run, logic suggests that their classmates who write accurate notes will be prepared to do better cataloging. Most students exposed to cataloging theory will "get it" (or some of "it," at any rate) and will be able to make decisions for new items based on the principles; whereas students who are not exposed at all to theoretical principles have nothing to help them make decisions as they catalog items that differ in any significant way from the ones they have learned to catalog by rote.

The key question instructors need to ask at every point when they teach how to do cataloging is "Why do we do this?" If students cannot answer that question, the future of library organization is at risk. Students need to know why we transcribe titles properly with scrupulous accuracy, even going so far as copying errors and misprints, but at the same time take a number of allowable liberties in constructing uniform titles. They should know what happens when coextensive subject headings are assigned and what changes occur in retrieval if the headings aren't coextensive; and they should be able to visualize and explain differences in access when those headings are expressed directly and indirectly. People who don't understand the difference between retrieval using subject headings and retrieval using keywords are likely to be persuaded that subject headings are passé, when nothing could be further from the truth. People who don't understand the value of name authorities or transcribed descriptive information will not make good decisions about managing their libraries' catalog systems, or lobbying the vendors of their online public access catalogs for new features that can benefit the users of their catalogs. Furthermore, if the people who don't know about cataloging principles happen to be reference librarians, they won't shine at performing at information retrieval on behalf of their clients, either.

LEARNING ABOUT BOOKS AND NONBOOKS

Before the 1950s and 1960s, most libraries collected and cataloged books, and cataloging departments had few concerns about creating catalog records for items in the media we now generically call nonbook materials–nonbooks, for short. Periodicals and other serials were also part of library collections, but these materials tended to be handled differently by specially-designated serials/periodicals staff, even when catalog records for the titles were filed in the same catalog with records for books. Often, however, serials weren't cataloged fully. Instead, title lists were maintained, sometimes with holdings added, sometimes not. In those days, the need to teach students how to catalog serials did not have the same priority as the need to teach them how to catalog books. One could reasonably claim that educators' current actions–which have squeezed cataloging curriculum down from multiple courses at beginning and advanced levels to just one or two (if that)–are evidence of a belief that materials other than books should still have low priority. Since the 1960s, however, learning how to catalog nonbooks has become more and more important as library acquisitions of nonbooks increased and fewer sources of cataloging data were available to copy, dictating that buyers had to catalog a large proportion of their purchases from scratch, by themselves. Today, being able to catalog nonbooks is an essential skill at the majority of libraries. The question for library schools thus became: How should this knowledge be covered?

The options for nonbook cataloging curriculum were mainly limited to the following: (1) combining the rudiments of cataloging for all material types into a beginning level course and following it up with advanced level courses that also cover all material types; and, (2) excluding nonbooks from the beginning-level cataloging course and teaching about them solely in one or more advanced-level courses. [Note: In my school, two advanced level courses cover nonbooks–one for printed nonbook forms such as maps and music, the other for nonprint forms such as video recordings, sound recordings, visual materials and electronic resources.] A third option–ignoring nonbooks altogether–was also available, leaving the subject area for post-graduate continuing education, and some schools with limited resources made that choice.

The first two options have both advantages and disadvantages. Regarding the first, while it sounds relatively easy to combine the rudiments of cataloging all materials into one course, and logical to put these same discussions for different material types into the same course, in practice, it takes a great deal longer to teach such a combined course. Real neophytes, who lack previous exposure of any kind to library cataloging and are easily confused by the jargon and large number of esoteric procedures, can find the variations among different media incomprehensible. Explanations about how to handle each step of the process for each type of material must be given and absorbed, and variations for monographic and serially published items must be covered in some detail. Doing a thorough job for both descriptive and subject cataloging can easily take more than a semester, yet one semester is the usual time period into which a beginning level required cataloging course must be fitted.

Regarding the second option, leaving all discussion of nonbooks for standalone, advanced level, elective classes–which solves the time crunch–clearly means that many students are never going to be exposed to it. Given the situation in the field today in the 21st century, this outcome is counterproductive to good practice. The pool of titles requiring original cataloging in cataloging departments in all types of libraries are not run-of-the-mill, easy-to-catalog, hardcover trade books–those can be expected to have Cataloging-In-Publication records appearing in the books themselves or, lacking that, a catalog record in a cooperative database originating from some major cataloging source.[6] The things local libraries are left to handle themselves are the uncommon titles, including video recordings, visual materials, and electronic resources. Electronic resources–the newest and most sophisticated type of material to be cataloged for library collections–have, at this writing, something more than 500,000 titles cataloged in library network databases, despite the fact that large databases like OCLC's WorldCat contain more than 48,000,000 discrete records. Putting two and two together, one is prompted to ask: If most librarians graduate from master's degree programs with no education in cataloging nonbook titles,[7] how well are they prepared to handle the materials that will most likely need cataloging "from scratch?" The answer, I fear, is "Not well at all!"

One simple-sounding strategy for responding to the shift in the kinds of media being acquired by libraries requiring original cataloging in library cataloging departments is to alter the basic cataloging course from book cataloging to electronic resources cataloging. Since electronic resources are the most difficult materials to catalog, it is reasonable to believe that anyone who can catalog electronic resources can also catalog books or other kinds of material that require full original cataloging in a library. Part of implementing such a strategy would be the immediate need for all cataloging educators to become fully conversant with electronic resources cataloging–a situation that would not only augment the ranks of those who can understand and debate its highest-level issues and problems, but could also have spinoff benefits such as sparking interest in scholarly studies of electronic resources cataloging and improving the tools available for it. Both the spinoff benefits named would by themselves make such a curricular shift worthwhile. Nonprint catalogers learn quickly that few comprehensive tools like *Books in Print* exist for any of the nonprint formats, let alone for all of them.

ACADEMIC versus NONACADEMIC CATALOGING EDUCATION

A question the foregoing discussion seems to beg is, "If all cataloging knowledge is not taught and learned in formal academic programs, where else might it be taught and learned?" Furthermore, once venues other than the graduate school curriculum are identified, one can fairly ask, "Which, of all the available possibilities, is best?"

The most obvious place to turn for needed professional knowledge once someone has earned his or her master's degree is to his or her job. On-the-job training is accepted as part of the work-life of most librarians, especially in large institutions with numerous staff members at varying levels of expertise. For example, a few years ago, a large university seeking a new staff member whose first round of searching failed to produce a successful outcome revised their posting to emphasize the many kinds of training the person serving in the position would receive. The new advertisement produced a much better pool of candidates and resulted in hiring the kind of person they wanted.[8] Ongoing change in computer systems for all types of library work has prompted so much training and retraining that it has become part of the landscape of functioning as a librarian, rather than an unusual event that might happen once or twice in an entire career or in the case of significant change to the job held.

Copy catalogers often are taught to do the kind of cataloging they do by means of on-the-job training.[9] Similarly, reference librarians, bibliographers, and other specialized public services staff members who perform or supervise the cataloging of selected types of material (Internet resources or special collections materials, for example) might be expected to receive on-the-job training in relevant areas.

A second time-honored method of acquiring needed knowledge after leaving academia is the continuing education workshop, institute, seminar, or conference program. Professional organizations at all levels–national, regional, and local–and of all persuasions–type-of-library-related, type-of-job-related, type-of-computer-system-related, and type-of-material-related–take quite seriously the responsibility of providing educational offerings of interest and use to their members. Schools offering the master's degree feel a similar obligation and have programs of continuing education for all members of the profession. (Some schools give tempting discounts to their alumni, but the cost of their programs tend to be affordable even for nonalumni.) The number of events held in a year to which librarians might go to learn about cataloging might not be exceptionally large, but nearly every state library association, vendor user group, and local bibliographic network provides some, and usually in locations close enough to home that most people can attend. The American Library Association, American Society for Information Science, Special Libraries Association, and similar national groups offer a dazzling array of educational events every year, many at their annual meetings and conferences, although not all of their events are both conveniently situated and affordable. Still, when a librarian is motivated and/or a library makes professional development a priority benefit for its employees, people get there, no matter what.

The Internet has rapidly become a fruitful learning environment, both for graduate and post-graduate programs of all kinds. Internet access has made it possible for students and practitioners alike to take regular credit-bearing classes and all sorts of continuing education offerings as well as to learn from less formal interactions with people who have similar interests via discussion lists and informative Websites. "Virtual" conferences have had varying success in attracting audiences for many reasons, but as interactive technologies improve, their successes might be expected to increase, adding to the list of remote learning opportunities. Certainly, for the telecommuter, virtual learning is already *de rigueur*.

Peer teaching and learning circles are other ways that working professionals acquire new knowledge. Both could be employed by libraries to update the knowledge and skills of people whose professional education occurred before current media were available or before current cataloging procedures were instituted. Neither require making any large up-front investments. What they do require is a knowledgeable person willing to teach his or her colleagues, time allowed for both teaching and learning (that is, practicing what has been taught), and a quiet place in which to do it. Lacking a knowledgeable person on staff, a library can bring someone in from outside the staff to do the teaching. Sometimes, such a person commands greater attention and respect simply because of being an outsider.

Which of these alternatives is best? The answer is each is "best" for some purposes, but not for all. Fundamental to the matter, cataloging education has to be an ongoing process over a professional's entire career, not a one-time exposure followed by practice alone. One must learn about and absorb the implications of the application of new and changed cataloging rules, new materials, and new policies formulated to account for new types of searching tools, technologies, and services.

Theory, background, and history of the various operations we call cataloging are best taught in academic classrooms by instructors whose business it is to know them thoroughly and keep up with research in all their many aspects. It is difficult to stop the work of a real cataloging department to explain such things, which take the time of a master cataloger but produce no catalog records or other immediate tangible benefits to the library. Hands-on cataloging of items, also, is best begun in a laboratory setting where mistakes can be made and corrected without costing anyone money or wreaking havoc in a library's catalog; but, once a person moves on to advanced levels, few laboratory experiences can furnish the needed practice afforded by a constant flow of new and varied materials such as are found in a real cataloging department. Thus, on-the-job training should properly follow an academic program providing thorough grounding in theory and laboratory practice.

In 1989, Barbra Higginbotham, who once served as head of original cataloging at a large university research library, suggested that large university research libraries should contribute to the post-graduate education of college and public library catalogers by providing them with internships in university cataloging departments.[10] Smaller institutions lacking the research imperative, whether college or public libraries, most likely to be willing to hire newly-graduated catalogers lacking professional experience, simply do not have an adequate flow of materials appropriate for advanced learning. Higginbotham's motives were not entirely self-sacrificing. Experiences in hiring and training catalogers for the university taught her that a few years of college or public library experience made potential new hires only slightly more effective in a large university research library setting than candidates right out of graduate school. Learning at advanced levels not only takes time, it requires exposure to sophisticated materials in all forms accompanied by the guidance of knowledgeable supervisors and/or peers.

When a cataloger succeeds in becoming an effective professional, he or she is entitled to congratulate himself or herself, but only for a moment. As time passes, he or she can only remain effective and current by continuing to learn. This is the point at which continuing education naturally comes into play, exposing participants to new materials, tools, technologies, and ideas. Continuing education should, as its name implies, continue from that time forward to the end of the cataloger's career.

One problem our profession faces in promoting continuing education opportunities is that people are not universally motivated to participate. With few exceptions, employing libraries do not require ongoing learning through continuing education, unlike teaching, for example, which both requires and rewards it with pay raises. Some libraries fail to reward ongoing learning either through monetary support, moral support, or potential for job advancement. Some librarians are hindered by barriers that discourage them–some imposed by their employers, such as rigid scheduling that prohibits attending continuing education offerings–even if they want to participate and are willing to pay for it out of their own pockets. Library and information science might take a lesson from medicine, which not only imposes demanding requirements for passing extensive qualifying examinations before allowing new physicians to practice their specialties, but makes them retake the examinations periodically to insure they keep abreast of new developments and continue learning.

A well-prepared cataloging librarian needs a tripartite education. First, he or she should have both beginning and advanced level coursework, including laboratories, taken in an academic program. Second, once graduated, academic coursework should be followed by on-the-job training–training that is extensive if her or his employer has complex cataloging operations and systems, or less so if in-house cataloging is limited and uncomplicated. Third, on-the-job training should be augmented on a regular basis by continuing education offerings that suit the libraries' and the catalogers' needs and interests, and keep their knowledge up-to-date.

Responsibility for the three types of education and training is necessarily shared among professional school faculties, employers, and cataloging librarians. Obtaining a good educational preparation is largely the responsibility of professional school faculty, who determine the curriculum, as well as the students who must apply themselves assiduously and work hard to learn all they can. Employers are responsible for on-the-job training, not only for new hires but for all employees as they need it. Budget must be set aside to pay for it; time must be allocated to enable it to be done; and good trainers need to be provided to give it. Until and unless it becomes a requirement of practice, continuing education is primarily an optional endeavor and is, therefore, the responsibility of the cataloging librarian herself or himself. Employers may encourage continuing education by allowing personnel to take time off, covering costs of travel and registration fees, and providing rewards of one kind or another to those who participate. Another way to promote continuing education is to encourage librarians to serve on professional association committees and boards. A spinoff benefit is that they become aware of and part of the organization's activities, some of which, inevitably, are educational. Those who are naturally curious are likely to be drawn to education events; those who are not might participate in them simply because they are already on-site for other meetings or because a colleague invites them to attend.

CONCLUSIONS

In writing about the three persistent issues in cataloging education selected for this article (theory/practice, book/nonbook, and school/job/ other), I am struck by how much more important than anything else it is that cataloging education be recognized as a process–more specifically, as a process that does not end until a cataloger's career ends, though it could certainly continue into retirement. How much attention is given to theory and how much to practice is certainly important, also; but as long as instructors attempt to explain why things are done, students will be made to realize that cataloging is not a rote, mechanical business without any challenging decision making. Similarly, while it is important in today's environment that librarians understand the processes of cataloging nonbooks as well as books, it is unrealistic to expect they will unless, by some stroke of good fortune, professional schools alter their curricula to integrate the cataloging of all media into a required course. If such a course at the beginning level were followed by a required advanced level course, it would be ideal; however, students intending to follow career paths other than cataloging might mutiny at being made to commit so many hours to cataloging.

What needs to be borne in mind as practitioners, educators, administrators, and others consider the cataloging curriculum is this: So long as library directors and committees comprised of noncataloging department staff make the managerial decisions about catalogs and cataloging systems, they, too–not just the catalogers–need to understand the implications of their decisions concerning the catalog. They need to be sufficiently sensitive to the issues to know that the catalog is the primary reference tool used by both librarians and the public, and, therefore, that spending money and time on cataloging education and ongoing cataloging operations is, in effect, an investment in quality public service.

ENDNOTES

1. See, for example, Roxanne Sellberg, "The Teaching of Cataloging in U.S. Library Schools," *Library Resources & Technical Services* 32, no. 1 (Jan. 1988): 30-42, and Mary Ellen Soper, "Descriptive Cataloging Education in Library Schools, Using the University of Washington as a Specivic Example," *Cataloging & Classification Quarterly* 7, no. 4 (Summer 1987): 47-55.

2. See, for example, Herb White, "The Education and Selection of Librarians: A Sequence of Happenstance," *Library Journal* 115, 20 (Oct. 15, 1990): 61-62; and Herbert S. White and Sarah L. Mort, "The Accredited Library Education Program as Preparation for Professional Library Work," *Library Quarterly* 60, 3 (July 1990): 187-215.

3. Walt Crawford, "Speaking the Language," [Letter to the Editor] *LITA Newsletter* 30 (fall 1987): 19.

4. Charles A. Cutter, *Rules for a Dictionary Catalog*, 4th ed. (Washington, DC: Government Printing Office, 1904), 12.

5. David Judson Haykin, *Subject Headings: A Practical Guide* (Washington, DC: U.S. Government Printing Office, 1951), p. 7-9.

6. In addition to the large amount of cataloging done by national agencies such as the Library of Congress, National Library of Canada, and British Library, a relatively small number of large university research libraries and city public libraries tend to do a great deal of first-time original cataloging for trade books that small libraries can subsequently copy from network databases. Small non-research libraries may come close to finding 95% or more of the books they buy already cataloged.

7. This author teaches the nonprint cataloging course at Simmons College, one of the largest graduate programs in North America. In 17 years, she averaged about 15 students in a class, totalling 255 graduates with knowledge of the nonprint formats. (In reality the total is fewer, since nonprint cataloging was not taught when the author was on sabbatical.) Assuming the advanced cataloging course had similar average enrollment during those years, only about 510 students will have been educated in cataloging anything other than books. The school graduated approximately 2,550 students in 17 years, which means 80% had no exposure to nonbook or nonprint cataloging.

8. D. Whitney Coe, "Recruitment, a Positive Process," in *Recruiting, Educating, and Training Catalog Librarians*, Sheila S. Intner and Janet Swan Hill, eds. (Westport, CT: Greenwood Press, 1989): 53-65.

9. Copy catalogers do not catalog "from scratch," but find an existing record in a source database and edit it as required by local library policies. Editing may take the form of correcting obvious errors, adding or deleting information that appears in the item being cataloged or in the source record, respectively, and–sometimes–changing elements such as call numbers that individual libraries choose to do differently than their peers. Whoever trains the copy cataloging crew usually is expected to supervise the work they produce and correct their understanding of procedures as necessary to insure that quality standards are maintained.

10. Barbra B. Higginbotham, "Standards, Volume, and Turst in the Shared Cataloging Environment: Training Approaches for the Smaller Library," in *Recuiting, Educating, and Training Cataloging Librarians*, Sheila S. Intner and Janet Swan Hill, eds. (Westport, CT: Greenwood Press, 1989): 355-366.

Why Does Everybody Hate Cataloging?

Heidi Lee Hoerman

SUMMARY. An opinionated and *very* informal exploration of the reasons that cataloging is often disparaged or undervalued, with suggestions for initiatives that might improve perceptions and enable advancement of cataloging agenda. *[Article copies available for a fee from The Haworth Document Delivery Service: 1-800-HAWORTH. E-mail address: <getinfo@haworth pressinc.com> Website: <http://www.HaworthPress.com> © 2002 by The Haworth Press, Inc. All rights reserved.]*

KEYWORDS. Cataloging education, cataloging

INTRODUCTION

Okay, so maybe *everybody* doesn't hate cataloging. I don't hate cataloging. I am what I like to refer to as a "dyed-in-the-wool cataloger." I even went to library school knowing that I wanted to be a cataloger and that I never wanted to spend *my* precious time answering inane questions at some reference desk. Besides, as I knew from my pre-professional work in the Yale University Cataloguing (with a "u") Department of the early '70s, this was where the *real* work of libraries happened. We attended meetings where we heard about international conferences on cataloging code revision. We were computerizing. I was

---

Heidi Lee Hoerman, BA, MLIS, CPh, is Instructor, College of Library and Information Science, University of South Carolina, Columbia, SC 29208.

[Haworth co-indexing entry note]: "Why Does Everybody Hate Cataloging?" Hoerman, Heidi Lee. Co-published simultaneously in *Cataloging & Classification Quarterly* (The Haworth Information Press, an imprint of The Haworth Press, Inc.) Vol. 34, No. 1/2, 2002, pp. 31-41; and: *Education for Cataloging and the Organization of Information: Pitfalls and the Pendulum* (ed: Janet Swan Hill) The Haworth Information Press, an imprint of The Haworth Press, Inc., 2002, pp. 31-41. Single or multiple copies of this article are available for a fee from The Haworth Document Delivery Service [1-800-HAWORTH, 9:00 a.m. - 5:00 p.m. (EST). E-mail address: getinfo@haworthpressinc.com].

inputting OCLC records before some of my MLIS students were born! So, it came as a bit of a shock to me that cataloging was widely viewed with about as much enthusiasm as week-old fish.

In the ensuing years, I've witnessed a great deal of disparagement of cataloging, some serious, some humorous. The distaste for cataloging is found among library school students, experienced librarians, and administrators. Even catalogers themselves sometimes loathe the work they've chosen. And in those several years as a doctoral student that I read, read, read, read, READ about cataloging, I found that this was nothing new. Cataloging is much whined about and always has been.

What should be done about this? We could choose to ignore it, but some of the people who dislike cataloging control our budgets. We, ourselves, could choose to disparage those who so undervalue that which is clearly central to librarianship, but those who are disparaged have a tendency to get insulted and cut off what little empathy they have for us to begin with. We *could* examine the various flavors in which this belittlement occurs and try to determine its causes. By knowing these, perhaps we can work together to change people's minds and gain their support.

THEY START YOUNG

It may start in library school; it often starts before that. With a few exceptions (among them those of us who were privileged to work in cataloging departments and those who have catalogers in their families), most students come to MLIS programs with the reference librarian as their model. These are the librarians they've seen. They come to library school because they want to do what they've seen done; they want to help people find information.

We tend to dislike on principle that which we do not know or understand. Cataloging is done behind the scenes. In many public library branches, it is done by someone else somewhere else. In school libraries and other one-librarian libraries, it may be done grudgingly and badly by someone who never had time to learn about how to do it. A colleague, who was director of a small public library before joining an LIS faculty, said she lived in dire terror that a cataloging professor would come to her town, look in her catalog, and be appalled at what was found there. Fear of the "Cataloging Police" is widespread. Students who haven't worked in cataloging departments are unlikely to have known librarians who gushed, "Go to library school so you can learn the joys of cataloging!"

The catalog isn't much used by MLIS students before they come to library school. Think back. How much did you use the catalog in the library when you were growing up? For term papers, we used the *Reader's Guide to Periodical Literature*.[1] To find books, we browsed the shelves. We may, on occasion, have looked things up in the catalog, but only to get our bearings. Upon finding a call number for something, *any*thing, we headed to the stacks to wander. Many times, our use of the catalog frustrated us. It led us astray. We had much better luck asking the kindly reference librarian to help us–unless it was that same reference librarian who had crankily sent us to the catalog in the first place. "Look it up in the card catalog and see if you can find it before you bother me," she seemed to say. A career in making that catalog? Oh, please!

Then we get them in library school and the disillusionment continues. We tell them that they must learn about cataloging, no choice. Then we start throwing the scary terminology at them: universal bibliographic *control*, name authority *control*, cataloging *rules*, a government agency that issues *rule interpretations*. (Do you hear the black helicopters just over the hill? We really must change our terminology to something more positive.) Then we teach them the rules for things we can't truly justify (main entry, the *rule* of three). We try to explain LCSH to them and direct-and-specific entry and MARC tags and Dewey number building and some of them get sucked in and decide to take more cataloging electives, while the rest run screaming from the room.

We acknowledge that the catalog doesn't work very well. They learn how to use other bibliographic retrieval tools that have far more bells and whistles. I receive periodic emails from a former student who then and now keeps wailing, "Why can't the OPAC be more like Amazon. com?" Is it laziness, he wonders? Lack of vision? Stubborn resistance to change? I give him the simple answer we always fall back on: too much to do, too little money. It rings pretty hollow to him, more and more so to me.

WHY DON'T THE KINDLY REFERENCE LIBRARIANS DEFEND US?

To reference librarians we are more often seen as an impediment than an aid. We have a tendency to turn down their requests. We refuse to change subject headings or call numbers for them. As a former cataloging administrator, I could defend this at length. If we change this call number what about the next one that comes in and the next and the next? We follow national standards without concern about their efficacy for local retrieval. We share cataloging so we must follow the LCRIs. We say, "Sorry, we can't *afford* to customize cataloging for local needs." We are usually telling the truth but it is a bitter pill to swallow. Given the state of our acceptance of cataloging of iffy quality into our catalogs through copy cataloging, our insistence on this seems disingenuous to our reference colleagues.

We work days. Oh, yes, on occasion some of us spend some evening or weekend time on the reference desk, but for the most part, we work days. We answer reference department requests 9-to-5, Monday-to-Friday. You need something we have in process on Saturday afternoon? Sorry, the cataloging department is locked. Come back Monday. I can also argue all the reasons why reference librarians, with their strange schedules, have more flexibility in their work than catalogers strapped to a desk chair, but that is for another discussion. For now, we are looking through reference department eyes. We work days and have regular coffee breaks. In some libraries, the cataloging department is open less than half the hours that the reference desk is staffed. It is hard to argue the essential nature of our services when a lot of the time the library operates just fine without us.

To reference librarians, we have a disproportionate view of the catalog. The library catalog is just one of many bibliographic retrieval tools. It is fairly limited in what it can do. It's full of inconsistencies, the subject headings are gibberish and too few in number. The online catalog interfaces are primitive in comparison to some of the CD-ROM or Web-based bibliographic tools. Our bibliographic records lack abstracts. What is listed in the catalog is a very limited subset of what is available in the library. Few catalog entries are hyper-linked to full text. You and I could explain why all of this is true–but we cannot seem to "fix it." For many librarians, particularly in smaller libraries where shelf browsing prevails, the catalog is just not something they use very often.

Catalogers have a different view, a rather peculiar view. We are blindly planting and pampering individual trees little aware of the forest we have created. We make individual bibliographic records with loving care. We typically don't use the catalog much either. Often catalogers are more aware of the strictures of LCRIs than of the effect these might have on record retrieval. We can find the basis for many LCRIs in LC budget cuts–they were, on the whole, devised to improve workflow, not access. Some catalogers rarely, if ever, use the public interface to their catalog. Few catalogers are familiar with the leaps and bounds of functionality made by other bibliographic tools.

We really are quite provincial. We are quite proud of our extensive knowledge of the minutiae of cataloging. We can divine the difference between a true new edition and a new printing of a Latin American paperback. We know what a colophon is. We can read and actually understand *AACR2*. We know when to use a name-title added entry. We understand how the MARC tags work in authority records. Reference librarians don't know any of this stuff and we think them rather ignorant because of this. They can't catalog. We can. But we can't answer reference questions. Not really. In the time we spent learning our cataloging craft, reference librarians learned the world of information retrieval. If we disparage their skills, why are we surprised that they discount our knowledge?

IT COSTS TOO DARN MUCH

Administrators have been whining about the cost and labor-intensiveness of cataloging for as long as there have been catalogers. Why does it take so many people? Why does it take so long for the books to hit the shelves? Why does it cost so much? Isn't there some way to make cataloging cheaper? Panizzi, Cutter, Jewett, all faced these questions. None of them could create the catalog they wanted to create for lack of money and time. It's a problem that won't go away.

We've come up with a variety of ways to trim cataloging costs. First, there is shared cataloging–a great idea with a several hundred-year history that became ubiquitous, or so it seems, in the twentieth century. If one person catalogs an item following an agreed-upon set of standards, the rest of us can use that cataloging at less expense. In fact, we can use cheaper, less well-trained and less well-compensated, personnel to handle items with cataloging we can "share." (This is a special library definition of sharing, "*I* share *your* cataloging.")

For most libraries, the vast majority of bibliographic records that enter the local catalog were created elsewhere and are added to the catalog with little local quality control. Even if the cataloging we "share" meets the agreed upon standards, these are *de facto* standards designed for very large research libraries (in fact, for the most part, for one *very* large research library) using a strict set of ever-changing rules. Don't get me wrong; I am an LC fan. But let's face it, our standard is to catalog like LC because that is the cheap way to go.

Another way we've tried to limit the costs of cataloging is by redefining what we mean by cataloging to a very low common denominator. We create very short bibliographic records compared to the records of many abstracting and indexing services. Then we go a step further by developing minimal record standards that eliminate retrieval-friendly things like subject headings and classifications. Oh, yes, we can't afford to do full cataloging so we do what are basically inventory records and wonder why the catalog is little respected.

Often, we don't take care of the catalog that results from our efforts. Rare is the catalog that is fully maintained. Few have even those minimal cross-references that up-to-date authority records could provide. Collocation is a dream more often than a reality. This is not new with online catalogs. Few cataloging departments were able to keep up with authority work in their card catalogs either. And who is to blame us? Those of us who remember changing thousands of cards to implement *AACR2* headings changes know the labor that was involved. Some catalog maintenance is less labor intensive in an online environment but authority control remains problematic and many libraries devote scant labor to clean up, hoping that someday *someone* will develop a solution and fix their catalog. Meanwhile, in countless catalogs, users do not find cross-references between Samuel Clemens and Mark Twain. They often find items listed both places–sometimes we mean for that to happen, sometimes we don't. Explain that to users and reference librarians.

THE CATALOGER SHORTAGE

For at least the last twenty years, there has been a shortage of catalogers. Please, remember that I mean no insult to my many fine colleagues, but let us face it. We have filled cataloging positions with whomever we could find. Cataloging departments are, on occasion, the dumping ground for the gift that keeps on giving: the bad employee who is too awful to let loose on the public anymore but not quite bad enough to fire. We catalogers joke about it. We are the ones who wear the rubber soled shoes so we can sneak up behind the copy catalogers and sneer at their work. Cataloging departments are a haven for the weird and the near-weird. We are not the happy, free-wheeling group like those out at the reference desk.

But, more seriously, the shortage of available catalogers has meant, in many cases, that cataloging positions have been unfilled or replaced by lower-ranked, less expert staff. We start to think cataloging is something that can be done by anyone. Maybe it can. To be honest, at this stage, it is in many cases being done by *anyone*, and that anyone has very little training. We then take the cataloging done by this untrained person and "share" it, unexamined, into our catalogs.

BESIDES, YOU CAN OUTSOURCE MOST OF IT, CAN'T YOU?

Outsourcing is just sharing taken to its logical conclusion. And, yes, we can outsource most cataloging. We do. As soon as we download, with little local quality control, a bibliographic record that was created elsewhere, we have outsourced the responsibility for that cataloging. Outsourcing the whole cataloging operation is just the next step. Many libraries survive without onsite catalogers. Academic, municipal and county branch libraries come to mind. The only difference between doing central processing and outsourcing to a commercial cataloging firm may be some loss of local influence on individual cataloging decisions.

Wait, I'm starting to scare myself. I do know the reasons why it is better to have in-house expertise in cataloging. Local expertise could develop a local catalog that meets local needs. That is what the catalogers at the Hennepin County Public Library were trying to do under the direction of Sandy Berman. To do what they were trying to do is very expensive. They were scoffed at by many–including me. The economics of "lowest-common denominator" shared cataloging won again over attempts to use local cataloging expertise to improve access. We do not have research to prove that Berman's subject headings improved relevant retrieval by users but at least he and his staff were trying something!

LIBRARY SCHOOLS DON'T TEACH CATALOGING ANYMORE

Over dinner with a fellow cataloging teacher, far more august than I, we tried to count the number of people we would think of as active "cataloging professors." Admittedly, our definition was fairly strict. We counted not all those who teach cataloging but those who really, we felt, identify themselves as cataloging teachers. We also only counted those who were full time faculty in ALA-accredited programs. We estimated that there are approximately fifteen people who fit this category and that quite a few of these are approaching retirement. There are over fifty ALA-accredited programs. These are desperate times for the teaching of cataloging.

When cataloging professors retire or leave or simply change their teaching and research emphasis to another subject area, replacements are needed. There are not many replacements in the doctoral student pipeline. With retirements and changes in emphasis, there are fewer places each year to pursue an LIS doctorate with a concentration in cataloging. LIS education is very short on new blood in all subject areas but cataloging vies with children's services and school libraries for the worst shortages. Thus, a strategy used by many LIS schools is to augment the full-time faculty with the use of adjunct instructors drawn from the "real world" of libraries. Adjunct instructors often have the specialized expertise not held by the faculty and are commonly used to teach in specialized subject areas as preservation, law and medical librarianship, and, increasingly, cataloging.

One of the problems with relying on adjunct faculty to teach specialized courses is that the knowledge in those courses becomes marginalized. The isolation of adjunct faculty from the full time faculty means that their concerns are not voiced in faculty meetings. They tend not to be part of the planning process. It is not as easy for them to have informal conversations with the regular faculty about the place of their subject in the overall curriculum and in the courses of those other faculty. They tend to have fewer resources devoted to the teaching of their courses and their courses tend to be offered less often. Adjunct cataloging faculty may have little experience outside their present environment and may teach a single model for cataloging services based on one type of library, often the academic research library, to students who will work in many types of libraries.

Some adjunct faculty are excellent instructors, but these are often the exception rather than the rule. I place the blame here not with the adjunct faculty but with the LIS programs. Adjuncts tend to be paid very little, teach the course in addition to their full time library position, and rarely have the luxury of graduate assistants. If they are asked to teach cataloging because the expertise to teach it no longer exists among the faculty, they also have no local mentor as a cataloging instructor. Teaching cataloging is a daunting task, one that becomes easier with time and practice. It is not simply a more extensive version of the training one does in libraries. For many adjuncts, the meager rewards do not sufficiently balance the difficulties and they teach only once or a very few times.

Daniel N. Joudrey, in a recent survey found that the teaching of cataloging *per se* is diminishing in the LIS programs, often being replaced by courses more generally addressing the organization of information, indexing and abstracting, and metadata.[2] Some of this is due, as he points out, to the mistaken belief that cataloging is passé, but this is not the only reason. As an MLIS instructor who clings fast to teaching library cataloging in its traditional form, I, too, find I must move some things aside to cover other topics. My core technical services students won't hear my lecture on CONSER this term because I decided it more important for them to learn about aggregator databases. My syllabi are full. I cannot simply add content; I must drop existing important topics to add new ones.

CHANGING PERCEPTIONS

What is to be done about this sorry state of affairs? Well, one of the advantages of teaching is that one gets to suggest solutions without worrying about such practical matters as staffing and budgeting. So, for those of you who have made it this far in reading this long and perhaps infuriating rant, I shall now prescribe solutions without worries of practicality.

First, we need to stop whining about the state of cataloging and do something about it. We need to come out from behind our desks and figure out ways to enjoy what we do. Catalogers have spent too long coloring inside the lines. Maybe it is time to throw out the baby with the bath water and stop rearranging deck chairs on the Titanic. I'm sorry: too many metaphors. Right now our catalogs are messy and ineffective. So farm out as much vanilla-flavored cataloging as possible, not to eliminate cataloging positions, but to free personnel to (1) work on catalog maintenance which has as its sole aim the improvement of the user-services aspect of the catalog, and (2) think and experiment with new ways to provide access to the library's priceless store of information.

To my mind, no professional cataloger should be spending most of his or her time making our dreadfully short standard bibliographic records. Train and oversee paraprofessionals to do it. Outsource it. Stop ill-using your professionally educated brain to make individual bibliographic records and start making catalogs. If you are a cataloging administrator, set your professional catalogers free to exercise their minds. There are too few of us thinking about what catalogs should look like and how they should work. Cutter said, "The golden age of cataloging is over," when card catalogs reduced our work from making a new book catalog to making a single card. Most of us have never made a catalog; we make bibliographic records. Our present catalogs are based on a 100-year-old model and we rarely take the time to think clearly about that.

Second, stop trying to do cataloging "on the cheap." Yes, there is never enough money to do everything you want to do but we must change or be left behind. Cheap cataloging is still too expensive in the minds of many administrators. Try to look at it from their point of view. Take what is spent on cataloging, look at the use of the catalog and the *usefulness* of the catalog and compare it to other information access tools the library has. Can you justify the expense of the cataloging operation by the quality of the catalog as compared to other tools? Justify the costs of cataloging. Show the rest of the library what makes the catalog worth the money that is spent on it. To do this, you may have to improve the catalog. Do not just assume your catalog is fine; every cataloger should go out and use the catalog like a user with the public interface.

Third, change our terminology and the way we speak of standards. "Authority control" has got to go. In fact, all use of "control" should be eschewed. In industry, there has been a change from "quality control" to "quality assurance." Authority control doesn't begin to tell the story. What about "Heading Access Assurance?" That is what we mean. All discussion of cataloging should be made with improving access as paramount.

If you hear yourself say in answer to a public services request, "No, we can't change that because the Library of Congress does it that way," go directly to the rest room and wash your mouth out with soap. You *choose* to do things the way the Library of Congress does them because that is the cheap way to go. You can change anything you wish in your local catalog–as long as you are fully aware of all the implications of making that change. Be honest. Tell the reference librarians that you *will* not change the subject heading because to do so would cost too much money. Then explain to them exactly what the expenses are. After awhile you may find in listening to yourself that there are changes you can make that are both affordable and encouraging of access.

Third, get involved with the LIS schools. Help grow faculty. Help the programs that are drifting away from librarianship to see the exciting things that are happening in libraries. Work with those of us who are schools of Library and Information Science to stay vital. Donate money to the schools and make sure their university administrations hear from outside about the importance of programs to create faculty in library science; university presidents pay more attention to donating alumni. Consider doing the doctorate yourself and joining an LIS faculty. If there are no faculty to hire who are librarians-to-the-bone, it is little wonder that the schools sometimes seem to turn their backs on the profession.

Fourth and finally, help recruit the brightest and best to cataloging. Go out and talk to undergraduates and high school students about careers in library technical services. Volunteer to organize a booth at local career fairs. Do a public lecture on the broad range of what librarians do. Find the brightest and best and send them to me. Okay, I'll share with the other cataloging faculty. But do look to see who is teaching cataloging and how often it is offered before you recommend your alma mater. You don't want to do the hard work of encouraging fresh recruits only to have them arrive to find the cataloging professor has retired and an adjunct is nowhere to be found.

ENDNOTES

1. More recently, younger MLIS students have never heard of the *Reader's Guide to Periodical Literature* as other computerized competitors abound.

2. Daniel N. Joudrey, "A New Look at US Graduate Courses in Bibliographic Control," *Cataloging & Classification Quarterly*, 34, 1/2 (2002): 59-101.

Cataloging:
An Exciting Subject for Exciting Times

Robert P. Holley

SUMMARY. Cataloging remains a fundamental component of library and information science and has many lessons to teach the architects of the Internet age. All students can benefit from taking a cataloging course, especially if it stresses cataloging as one specific answer to the problems of managing information and places cataloging within a larger context that also includes indexing and Internet search engines. Students deserve cataloging courses that combine theory and practice, avoid memorization, and require them to show a mastery of core principles rather than picky details. This paper includes specific suggestions on how to make cataloging exciting. *[Article copies available for a fee from The Haworth Document Delivery Service: 1-800-HAWORTH. E-mail address: <getinfo@haworthpressinc.com> Website: <http://www.HaworthPress.com> © 2002 by The Haworth Press, Inc. All rights reserved.]*

KEYWORDS. Cataloging education, cataloging curriculum

MY BACKGROUND

I set myself the goal of becoming the best cataloging professor in North America when I had the opportunity in 1993 to become a library

Robert P. Holley is Professor, Library & Information Science Program, 106 Kresge Library, Wayne State University, Detroit, MI 48202 (E-mail: aa3805@wayne.edu).

[Haworth co-indexing entry note]: "Cataloging: An Exciting Subject for Exciting Times." Holley, Robert P. Co-published simultaneously in *Cataloging & Classification Quarterly* (The Haworth Information Press, an imprint of The Haworth Press, Inc.) Vol. 34, No. 1/2, 2002, pp. 43-52; and: *Education for Cataloging and the Organization of Information: Pitfalls and the Pendulum* (ed: Janet Swan Hill) The Haworth Information Press, an imprint of The Haworth Press, Inc., 2002, pp. 43-52. Single or multiple copies of this article are available for a fee from The Haworth Document Delivery Service [1-800-HAWORTH, 9:00 a.m. - 5:00 p.m. (EST). E-mail address: getinfo@haworthpressinc.com].

educator after over 20 years as a practitioner. I remember the first semester when I taught two sections of "Introduction to Technical Services" to 50 students. I did some things right and many other things wrong, but I had a firm sense of what I wanted to accomplish. Fate, however, intervened before my second semester because the Dean asked me to take over as Director of the Wayne State University Library and Information Science Program. While Director, I taught Advanced Classification and Cataloging; but, in the meantime, the Program hired another professor to be the cataloging specialist. Thus, I taught other non-cataloging courses and expect to do the same now that I am returning to full-time teaching once again.

Nonetheless, I have thought very much about the debates that have raged in the professional literature and within ALA Council about the importance of professional education in cataloging, not only for catalogers but also for all information professionals. While I am aware of the pronounced tendency of graduates to flatter their former professors, I have been pleased at the number of students who have taken the time to tell me that they still remembered a good bit of what I taught them in that one semester of cataloging. Many hasten to add that they didn't think at the time that the course would ever be useful in their future careers and that they considered me the "professor-from-hell" for requiring them to understand cataloging principles.

I have a long background in cataloging and technical services. In the early 1970s, I started my career in the Cataloging Department, Sterling Memorial Library, Yale University, as a subject cataloger. Soon after, I was promoted to Assistant to the Head of the Cataloging Department where I had a major role in introducing OCLC. I became Assistant Director for Technical Services at the Marriott Library, University of Utah, in 1980 with responsibility for acquisitions, serials, and cataloging. I've been at Wayne State University since 1988 as Interim Dean, Associate Dean, Director of the Library and Information Science Program, and Professor.

My chief love has always been cataloging. I remained intellectually involved even after I moved away from daily involvement in bibliographic control. I have been most professionally active in ALCTS where I was President in 1994-1995 and have served on at least one ALCTS committee each year since the mid-1970s. From 1981-1995, I held various offices in the IFLA Division of Bibliographic Control where I acquired a broader international perspective. Finally, I have been an active scholar with the majority of my work on cataloging topics including frequent contributions to *Cataloging & Classification Quarterly.*

WHY TEACHING CATALOGING IS IMPORTANT

I hope to avoid the traditional clichés in this section. For example, as a classics major, I always bristle when someone proposes learning Latin as a way to improve English vocabulary comprehension. After all, this is a very small advantage compared with acquiring a perspective on the world view and literature of an important culture.

Information Control Is the Foundation of Librarianship

I am using the more general term information control rather than bibliographic control because I will suggest later in this article that cataloging should be presented as a specific case of the more general goal of controlling information. At the most fundamental level, the main task of librarianship and much of information science is to organize information, often in large quantities, in a way that is useful for information seekers. Cataloging and indexing are two principal means to achieve this goal. While full-text indexing and search engines have a role in information control, knowledge of cataloging and indexing helps understand their strengths and limitations.

Librarians Will Be More Effective If They Understand the Construction of Their Information Seeking Tools

Librarians will be more effective in finding information both for themselves and for their patrons if they understand the structure of records in the online catalog, the principles of authority control including cross references, and the MARC format insofar as it affects indexing. Often a successful search strategy requires understanding the type of entry to which the search term belongs according to cataloging rules. Librarians should also understand that the same records can be indexed, retrieved, and displayed differently according to specific rules of various online catalogs. This is especially true since the Web allows searching multiple catalogs with multiple online systems that do not behave in the same way. Even with a Z39.50 connection, librarians should know that certain searches that work in their online catalog may not be successful in another vendor's online catalog because that vendor does not support the same indexing structures.

Librarians provide better reference services if, for example, they know:

- the strengths and weakness of subject headings and classification as subject retrieval tools;
- the impossibility of directly answering a patron query if the indexing language does not provide the level of specificity required;
- tricks for finding needed information through multiple searches that build upon the structure of cataloging records; and
- the required access points for special format material.

More Patrons Use the Online Catalog Than Ask a Reference Question

I have often wondered why so little attention has been paid to the fact that relatively few users, at least in public and academic libraries, ever ask a question at the reference desk in comparison with those that use the records in the online catalog or bibliographic databases. For this reason, I would think that libraries would pay special attention to providing accurate cataloging records, to selecting well-indexed databases, and to choosing the best retrieval tools available since these are excellent ways to assist users who are reluctant to ask for help at the reference desk, and also to make it less necessary that they do so. The digital library further reinforces the wisdom of this strategy by distancing users from reference support and making them more dependent upon their own knowledge.

Cataloging Has Valuable Lessons for the Internet Age

Traditional cataloging has much to teach the architects of the Internet age. Experts who have the goal of taming the Internet and providing effective access to its resources can learn much from the history and current practice of cataloging because catalogers have attempted to solve similar problems for over a century. The goal of combining like items and distinguishing unlike items is just as needed on the Internet as in any library catalog though it will be much harder to achieve. Catalogers have already faced the issues of multiple languages, non-Roman scripts, and varying cultural traditions of information creation and dissemination. They therefore have important lessons to share as information on the Internet becomes increasingly available in languages other than English. E-merchants are facing the issue of subject access and classification as customers with varying mental topologies access their sites and will make a purchase only if they find what they are looking for.

SUGGESTIONS FOR CATALOGING PROFESSORS

Based upon my experiences as a cataloger, reference librarian, and educator, I make the following suggestions to improve the teaching of cataloging in North American library and information programs. Many overlap and are not mutually exclusive.

Teach As If Your Students Are Not Going to Be Catalogers When They Graduate

I believe strongly that a professor should not teach cataloging with the assumption that students will become catalogers when they graduate. To do so requires paying too much attention to the immediate cataloging environment. In any case, a professor who attempts to create a trained cataloger in one course is doomed to failure because there is too much to learn and because local practice, which cannot and should not be taught in library school, is such an important part of any cataloger's training for a specific position. By assuming that students will not be catalogers, the professor will be able to concentrate on the parts of cataloging that are necessary for success in any library and information science position.

Students who intend to become catalogers should take an advanced cataloging course if one is available, sign up for a practicum in a cataloging department, or seek a part-time position at any level that includes cataloging responsibilities. Even if none of these suggestions are possible for an individual student, I hope that cataloging administrators will hire bright students who have a grasp of principles and show interest in learning the practicalities.

Don't Allow Students with a Practitioner Background to Skip the Course

On a related issue, I would recommend not allowing students with cataloging experience to test out of a beginning cataloging course if it is required within the curriculum. The course should present a theoretical perspective that they may lack, should show where cataloging fits within the profession, and should help them distinguish between cataloging as a professional responsibility and local practice within their institution. In addition, their presence in the classroom can be used to enrich the experience for others.

Teach Cataloging Within the Context of Indexing and Information Science

I believe that the current trend to have a course with a title such as "Organization of Knowledge" is a step in the right direction towards enabling student learning. In my own institution, I supported a curriculum revision that created a course that would prepare students to specialize further in either cataloging or indexing. To use an analogy, cataloging is Newtonian physics within the larger context of the Einstein universe that is the organization of knowledge. Cataloging and indexing standards are specific examples of answers to more general problems of information control. Even if the course is called cataloging, placing cataloging within this broader context will help students better understand the fundamental issues and get a better perspective on what are core issues in comparison with peripheral concerns.

Create and Grade Practical Exercises Within a Broader Context

Students should learn the truth that what looks simple in theory may become complex in practice. The emphasis, however, should be on problem solving and on understanding the larger issues rather than on mastering small, picky points. I am not suggesting that students should not be required to complete practical exercises. Cataloging without practice would be like taking a computer-programming course without writing code. The professor should avoid teaching mechanical solutions that may work in the short run but that do nothing to increase the students' understanding of the principles involved. For example, choosing the correct access points is much more important than knowing how many spaces to put between data elements, especially now that the computer can handle these chores automatically. At all costs, the professor should avoid the horrible grading practice of requiring that everything be perfect before giving any points for an answer that is fundamentally correct but inaccurate in some small detail.

Stress the Goals of Cataloging Rather Than the Rules

I firmly believe that the goal of cataloging is to help users find what they need rather than to follow the rules blindly. One of the main reasons for having rules is that skilled users can predictably find what they need by following the patterns that they have learned from prior experience. Students should come to understand the importance of rules that favor access such as providing a supplementary added entry to take care of an ampersand (&) in a title so that the user who has heard about the item does not need to know the specific typography of the title page. But students should also realize that rules are made to be bent. If researchers refer to an item as the *Trainer Report*, the cataloger should include this commonly used title as an added entry with the appropriate note as justification.

Mimic the Real World Wherever Possible

I strongly favor replicating the real world experience of practitioners wherever possible. Rather than using structured exercises where the students progress from one cataloging principle to the next, I had my class catalog ten items that I chose from the materials put aside for the library book sale. I took care to choose different types, to avoid too many "easy" items, and to make sure that current AACR2 cataloging was not available on OCLC. Both the students and I learned a great deal about these ten books as we progressed through the syllabus–description, name access, subject access, and classification. Somewhat to my surprise, a sound recording presented an ambiguous chief source of information where it was impossible to tell whether *The Who Live at Leeds* was a title or statement of responsibility plus title. Since this recording was much harder to catalog than anticipated, we spent class time discussing the two ways to provide access so that users would find the catalog record no matter how they or the cataloger interpreted the chief source of information. I also noticed that easy items in one cataloging category were very difficult in others. A book with simple description and name access presented a thorny problem when assigning the Dewey Decimal Classification number.

I realize that this approach will not systematically cover all the rules on a given topic, but it avoids the artificiality of a structured exercise where students quickly figure out which resource to use and move quickly from one section to the next without much thought. Using a set of real items mimics the actual cataloging experience where librarians sometimes encounter surprising difficulties in cataloging items that look superficially simple.

De-Emphasize Memorization

I believe that one of the main reasons that many students dislike cataloging classes is the emphasis upon memorization. As someone with an excellent conceptual memory but a poor literal memory (numbers, tags, etc.), I strongly recommend that cataloging professors mimic the real world by allowing students to use their notes and cataloging tools during examinations. Catalogers and reference librarians are usually hired and evaluated not on how much they have memorized but rather on how well they can find the appropriate answers. In my opinion, a good examination should stress understanding concepts. In any case, students who have not mastered the material will spend so much time looking for the answers that they will not successfully finish a well-crafted examination. But students who know what they are doing but have forgotten a small fact should be able to look it up.

Give Technology an Appropriate Emphasis

In my experience, some students mistake technological competence for cataloging mastery. They believe that the ability to input a record into a bibliographic utility is the most important part of cataloging. In some ways, this attitude is understandable because it is satisfying to see the completed bibliographic record as an end product. Furthermore, students may get immediate valuable feedback if they make fatal errors in the MARC format in a system that is programmed to reject incorrect values. The professor should, however, emphasize that technology is only a tool. The important part is the validity and usefulness of the cataloging record for information retrieval.

Encourage Students to Trust Their Own Judgment

Professors should encourage students to trust their own judgments and to work through their cataloging assignments on their own. Compulsive students, and I confess to having been one, do not often resist the temptation to check their assigned items on OCLC, RLIN, or some other source of cataloging data. In general, doing so ends up confusing students as they encounter records created under earlier editions of the cataloging code, the classification scheme, or the subject heading list that may or may not be correct under current practice. As I stated earlier in the section on practical exercises, grading should reinforce this trust by assigning major credit for important decisions and overlooking minor mistakes, especially those that the student could not be expected to avoid. I also let my students know that I had looked at the available cataloging records and would be much less sympathetic in the case of errors made from copying them.

Require a Thought Paper and Include Essay Questions in Examinations

To underline the intellectual component of cataloging, a cataloging class should include a brief thought paper; and essay questions are quite appropriate for in-class or take-home examinations. The suggested topics should allow students to prove that they understand the concepts of cataloging. With the professor's approval, some students may even wish to investigate a topic of special personal interest. Added benefits will be increased familiarity with the professional literature, exposure to points of view beyond what the professor has taught in class, and first hand experience with the intellectual foundations of cataloging.

For example, I might suggest the following questions for a thought paper or an essay question:

- Is main entry still needed in the age of online and Internet access?
- What are the relative advantages of subject access versus classification at the reference desk?
- Is authority control worth the cost?
- If you were able to design the ideal online catalog, what retrieval functions would you consider to be most important? Please base your answer on the material covered in this class.

Obviously, grading should take into account the knowledge levels of students; but I think that professors would be surprised at the sophistication of many students' thinking.

Avoid Apologies for Teaching Cataloging

If professors don't value what they are teaching, neither will students. I cringe each time I hear a speaker on a cataloging topic tell the audience that they can take a nap during the speech because it will deal with dull issues that focus on boring details. These "dull issues" and "boring details" often make the difference in providing effective library service to users. After all these years and at some distance from day-to-day issues, I remain excited about cataloging and would hope to convey this excitement to my students.

CONCLUSIONS

Much of what I have said above could be placed within the context of the perpetual debate between "theory" and "practice" in library education. What I am suggesting is the potential for a synthesis of these two dichotomies. The successful cataloging class should provide practical experience that will be useful to the new graduate in almost any library or information science position, but this practice should be informed with theory. The professor should lead students to understand the theory behind the specific examples and tasks encountered in class. The professor should focus on "why" rather than "how." On the other side, practice is also important for its role in undermining theory that sometimes overemphasizes certainty and order. The real world of cataloging is often messy. Even experts can disagree over rule interpretations in specific cases. Catalogers must often make compromises to meet user needs or to deal with financial realities.

Most of all, learning cataloging does not have to be a dull exercise in memorizing rules. Bibliographic control is a key foundation of librarianship and information science. The issues are complex and have occupied some of the best minds in librarianship. The experiences learned in controlling a bibliographic universe of 48 million catalog records is a good first step towards taming the Internet. Why not allow our newest colleagues to share the excitement that has kept us in the field?

THE CONTEXT

Demographic Trends Affecting Professional Technical Services Staffing in ARL Libraries

Stanley J. Wilder

SUMMARY. This paper presents demographic data from the Association of Research Libraries to argue that professional staffing in technical services/cataloging positions is declining. Two factors are identified as possible causes: first, a consistent and long-term drop-off in hiring, and second, unusually high retirement rates resulting from the advanced age of these staff. *[Article copies available for a fee from The Haworth Document Delivery Service: 1-800-HAWORTH. E-mail address: <getinfo@haworthpressinc.com> Website: <http://www.HaworthPress.com> © 2002 by The Haworth Press, Inc. All rights reserved.]*

Stanley J. Wilder is Assistant Dean, Information Management Services, River Campus Libraries, University of Rochester.

[Haworth co-indexing entry note]: "Demographic Trends Affecting Professional Technical Services Staffing in ARL Libraries." Wilder, Stanley J. Co-published simultaneously in *Cataloging & Classification Quarterly* (The Haworth Information Press, an imprint of The Haworth Press, Inc.) Vol. 34, No. 1/2, 2002, pp. 53-57; and: *Education for Cataloging and the Organization of Information: Pitfalls and the Pendulum* (ed: Janet Swan Hill) The Haworth Information Press, an imprint of The Haworth Press, Inc., 2002, pp. 53-57. Single or multiple copies of this article are available for a fee from The Haworth Document Delivery Service [1-800-HAWORTH, 9:00 a.m. - 5:00 p.m. (EST). E-mail address: getinfo@haworthpressinc.com].

KEYWORDS. Demographics, aging, librarianship, cataloging, retirements, hiring, library staffing

The supply of professional expertise in Association of Research Libraries (ARL) technical services operations has tumbled in recent years, due to two separate-but-related phenomena: a drastic reduction in hiring, and high levels of retirements. Viewed at the level of an individual library, reducing the resources devoted to professional technical services staffing may be a natural response to increased productivity. Viewed collectively, however, the speed and extent of these changes are more troubling, calling into question whether the future supply of technical services expertise can satisfy even a reduced level of need.

The data supporting these assertions come from the unpublished data sets of the *ARL Annual Salary Survey* from 1980 to 2000.[1] Most of the variables in these sets appear annually, but age data exist only for the years 1986, 1990, 1994, 1998, and 2000. It is also important to note that while catalogers were considered as part of the undifferentiated technical services job category prior to 1983, they were thereafter counted separately. Similarly, reference librarians were counted among public services positions until they too got their own category in 1983. For the purposes of this paper, the cataloger and technical services categories are considered together unless otherwise noted.

ENTRIES

The first problem facing professional technical services staffing lies in reduced hiring. The number of individuals hired for technical services/cataloging jobs dropped 46% between 1985 and 2000. This drop was not part of a general trend in ARL, because the overall number of new hires increased by 27% in the same period. Put another way, technical services/cataloging jobs accounted for 23% of all hiring in ARL libraries in 1985, but fell to just 10% of all hiring by 2000.

A similar phenomenon is taking place among new professionals, which can be defined as new hires in their first professional position. In 1980, 36% of new professionals filled technical services/cataloging positions, compared to just 12% in 2000. Over the same period, about 40% of new professionals consistently filled public services/reference positions.

New professionals are critically important for the entire population, as the primary source of young people, and an indicator of hiring trends. But new professionals are especially important to technical services/cataloging positions because these have historically been, along with public services/reference positions, the most important point of entry for new professionals in ARL libraries. In 1980, for example, 69% of all new professionals were hired for these two categories alone.[2]

The *Salary Survey* data cannot answer all the questions these numbers raise. For example, it is conceivable that there has been an analogous reduction in the number of library school students inclined to take up technical services/cataloging careers, or that some portion of the explanation lies in unsuccessful recruitment efforts. But the extent of the drop, its consistency over an extended period of time, and across a large number of large academic libraries, makes unavoidable the conclusion that a fundamental shift has occurred in the staffing priorities of academic libraries away from professional technical services/cataloging positions.

Whatever its source, the effect of the drop in hiring of new and experienced professionals to technical services/cataloging positions has had the inevitable effect of reducing the overall number of staff in these areas, down 35% between 1985 and 2000. This change is more remarkable given that the 2000 data contain six additional libraries.

RETIREMENTS

The drop in hiring, and especially the drop in hiring of new professionals, is certainly an important part of a related phenomenon, the advancing age of cataloging staff. As a group, librarians are older than comparable professionals,[3] but catalogers are old relative to other librarians. For example, 16% of ARL catalogers were aged 60 and over in 2000, compared with 10% of the overall ARL population. Most if not all of that 16% can be expected to retire by 2005. Viewed from another perspective, 32% of catalogers are aged 55 and over, almost twice as many as in the comparable reference population. It is thus possible that fully one-third of the 2000 ARL cataloging population will retire by 2010.

Catalogers were old in the 2000 data, but it is the aging of that population that poses the most substantial problem. As Figure 1 illustrates, just over 40% of catalogers were under age 40 in 1986, which made them somewhat younger than the larger ARL population of the time. This is as one would expect, considering the prominent role cataloging served as a point of entry for young librarians noted above. In only 14 years, cataloging has gone from being one of ARL's youngest subgroups to one of its oldest.

FIGURE 1

%	<24	25-29	30-34	35-39	40-44	45-49	50-54	55-59	60-64	65+
1986	0.2	6.5	15.1	18.2	15.2	11.9	12.5	9.9	7.2	3.5
2000	0.2	3.6	5.5	8.7	13.9	15.8	19.9	16.3	8.6	7.5
N										
1986	2	74	173	209	174	136	143	113	82	40
2000	2	29	44	70	112	127	160	131	69	60

Taken as a whole, the situation is something of a vicious circle: it starts with a sharp drop in hiring of technical services/cataloging staff, especially new professionals. With the supply of recruits reduced, the number of catalogers drops, and the group that remains begins to age quickly, approaching retirement at a higher rate. It could be that reduced hiring for technical services/cataloging staff serves as a disincentive to library schools' students who might otherwise choose careers in these areas. This might account for some of the difficulty libraries have had in recruiting staff for these positions.

CONCLUSION

Professional technical services/cataloging jobs are by their nature apprenticeships, requiring long years of experience to obtain full proficiency. As these data show, however, ARL libraries are voting with their feet: they clearly do not need as many of these staff as they once did. Nonetheless, it doesn't seem likely that the need for advanced bibliographic expertise will go away altogether. In a period when large numbers of the most experienced technical services/cataloging staff reach retirement age, it remains to be seen whether libraries will be able to secure enough of this expertise to satisfy their lower level of need.

ENDNOTES

1. ARL Annual Salary Survey, Martha Kyrillidow (Washington, DC: Association of Research Libraries).
2. For a more detailed analysis of new hires in ARL libraries, see: Wilder, Stanley. The Changing Profile of Research Library Professional Staff. *ARL: A Bimonthly Report on Research Library Issues and Actions from ARL, CNI, and SPARC.* 1-5 <*http://www.arl.org/newsltr/208_209/chgprofile.html*>, and "Generational Change in

Librarianship." Video produced for the Librarians' Association of the University of California, the Association of Research Libraries, and the Arizona Library Association, November 17th, 2000. <*http://128.151.244.9:8080/ramgen/Wilder/swilder.rm*>.

3. Wilder, Stanley. The Changing Profile of Research Library Professional Staff. *ARL: A Bimonthly Report on Research Library Issues and Actions from ARL, CNI, and SPARC*. 1. <*http://www.arl.org/newsltr/208_209/chgprofile.html*>.

A New Look at US Graduate Courses in Bibliographic Control

Daniel N. Joudrey

SUMMARY. The current state of graduate bibliographic control education in the United States is examined through reviewing the literature, analyzing Web sites for 48 LIS programs, and corresponding with and interviewing bibliographic control educators. In reviewing the recent bibliographic control education literature, six primary themes were identified: background/contextual information, theory versus practice, responsibilities and skills needed by catalogers, relations between educators and practitioners, the universality of cataloging, and curricular issues. Each of these areas is examined in depth. The study conducted examined the number and types of bibliographic control education available in LIS programs in the US. It also collected information on which textbooks were being used in each course. It appears from the study that some courses are increasing in number. The primary areas of bibliographic control education examined include organizing information, technical services, classification theory, indexing, thesaurus construction, cataloging technology, and basic, advanced, descriptive, subject, non-book, Internet resources, and music cataloging courses. *[Article copies available for a fee from The Haworth Document Delivery Service: 1-800-HAWORTH. E-mail address: <getinfo@haworthpressinc.com> Website: <http://www.HaworthPress.com> © 2002 by The Haworth Press, Inc. All rights reserved.]*

Daniel N. Joudrey, MLIS, has begun a doctoral program at the University of Pittsburgh. This paper was written to fulfill a requirement for a doctoral seminar in the organization of information held by Dr. Arlene G. Taylor (E-mail: djoudrey@mail.sis.pitt.edu).

The author wishes to thank Dr. Arlene G. Taylor, Harry M. Field, Bryan Carson, Judith Silva, Jen-Chien Yu, and Jesús Alonso Regalado for their support.

[Haworth co-indexing entry note]: "A New Look at US Graduate Courses in Bibliographic Control." Joudrey, Daniel N. Co-published simultaneously in *Cataloging & Classification Quarterly* (The Haworth Information Press, an imprint of The Haworth Press, Inc.) Vol. 34, No. 1/2, 2002, pp. 59-101; and: *Education for Cataloging and the Organization of Information: Pitfalls and the Pendulum* (ed: Janet Swan Hill) The Haworth Information Press, an imprint of The Haworth Press, Inc., 2002, pp. 59-101. Single or multiple copies of this article are available for a fee from The Haworth Document Delivery Service [1-800-HAWORTH, 9:00 a.m. - 5:00 p.m. (EST). E-mail address: getinfo@haworthpressinc.com].

59

KEYWORDS. Cataloging education, classification education, library education, library schools, bibliographic control courses

INTRODUCTION

Library and Information Science (LIS) graduate education in bibliographic control is changing, and how could it not? Over the past ten years the profession has seen the development of the MARC21 format, the continuing expansion of bibliographic utilities, and the births of the Web, XML, and the Dublin Core. "Metadata" has become the word of the decade and in many schools, courses on organizing information have displaced traditional cataloging and classification courses. In LIS education, the definition and scope of bibliographic control are continually expanding, yet classroom contact hours are not increasing. Contributing to the squeeze on time in the classroom is the fact that traditional theory and practice cannot (and should not) be eliminated. As of December 2000, only seven US LIS graduate schools offer specialization tracks in bibliographic control, with three of these schools offering fewer than four courses.

With rapidly occurring changes, persistent rumors from the uninformed that there are no jobs for catalogers, and a certain lack of enthusiasm on the part of many LIS educators and librarians for cataloging, what *is* the current state of bibliographic control education? What courses are being taught? Are there fewer courses being offered? What textbooks are being used? This paper begins looking for answers to these questions by examining the journal literature from the past decade. It then describes a small study conducted in the autumn of the year 2000 to determine what courses are being taught, which of those courses are required of all LIS students, and what trends are apparent.

METHODOLOGY

This paper examines the graduate-level, bibliographic control courses offered in 48 ALA-accredited LIS schools in the United States.[1] These graduate-level courses fall into a dozen areas, as indicated in Figure 1.

This examination of bibliographic control education was conducted by analyzing the Web sites of the 48 ALA-accredited LIS schools in the United States, excluding only the program at the University of Puerto Rico (which had no Web site and did not respond to e-mail inquiries).

FIGURE 1. Areas of Bibliographic Control

Organizing Information	Basic Cataloging
Descriptive Cataloging	Subject Analysis
Classification Theory	Advanced Cataloging
Non-Print Materials Cataloging	Internet Resources Cataloging
Indexing and Abstracting	Cataloging Technology
Music Cataloging	Thesaurus Construction

Course rosters were consulted to find the bibliographic control courses offered by each institution. Then, the course description and the syllabus for each course were examined to determine the nature of the course and the textbooks used.[2] If a current syllabus was not available on the Web site, the school's cataloging faculty was contacted by e-mail. In a few cases, telephone interviews were conducted to obtain the needed information. Data collection occurred between September 14, 2000 and February 12, 2001.

TERMINOLOGY

Throughout this paper, the term *bibliographic control* includes the concepts of organizing information, indexing and abstracting, thesaurus construction, and all forms of cataloging and classification. The term *cataloging* refers to the areas of descriptive cataloging, subject analysis, and classification, unless otherwise specified. The individual components are referred to separately as needed. Courses that attempt to cover a non-venue specific, broader view are referred to here as *organizing* courses.

REVIEWING THE LITERATURE

This paper explores what is being taught in the area of bibliographic control. It looks at the following questions: Are similar courses being offered to all library school students in the United States? Are library school students even exposed to the theory and practice of bibliographic control? Are there fewer courses today than three, four, or fourteen years ago?

During a literature search for journal articles on the primary text-books of bibliographic control, it was quickly discovered that very little has been published on the topic. Only a single 1987 article by Lois Mai Chan addressed the use of textbooks, and it was within the broader context of instructional materials used in cataloging courses.[3]

Journal literature regarding trends, theories, needs, and the curricula of bibliographic control education is more readily available, with the most recent article being Michael Gorman's *California Libraries* article.[4] For the sake of currency, the articles reviewed for this paper were primarily published between 1990 and 2001. A small number of pre-1990 articles are included because the information they contain is particularly relevant. The articles focus primarily on cataloging education in the United States. In the process of analyzing the articles, it became clear that there are six recurring themes/areas prevalent in the discussions of bibliographic control education. This literature review examines each of those areas: background information/contextual information, theory versus practical application, responsibilities and skills needed by catalogers, the relationship between educators and practitioners, the universality of cataloging, and curricular issues. The history of bibliographic control education is not addressed in this paper, as others have written on this topic.[5,6]

Contextual Information: Many of the articles attempt to provide some context or background for the discussion of bibliographic control education. This is most often discussed in terms of changes in technical services and in the poor image of catalogers and cataloging among libraries and librarians.

Taylor points out that major changes in cataloging have occurred over the past thirty-six years. "There have been major technological changes: 'white out' has come and gone and catalog records are now in the form of computer printouts."[7] Callahan and MacLeod state that "cataloging departments have been reorganizing since the 1970s when they prepared for the installation of bibliographic utilities" and "must always be viewed within the context of change."[8] In recent years, this has been exacerbated by the ownership versus access debate, the increasing responsibilities in database management, and reductions in technical services staff. El-Sherbini and Klim state, "The role of the cataloging librarian is changing. Catalogers are becoming managers, teachers, and trainers of non-professionals. They manage outsourcing projects, provide quality control and database management."[9] The changes in function are also reflected in the changing names of cataloging departments.[10]

Clack states that cataloging is a big-ticket item (with high costs). As budgets shrink, cataloging departments are forced to reorganize, take short cuts, and use more paraprofessionals. She also states that changes are often unplanned and unsystematic, with departments being reactive to new developments in the field, not proactive.[11] Hill too concludes that cataloging is a greatly changing specialization where technology and economics have tremendous impact on operations, and therefore, on the skills needed by cataloging professionals.[12]

The other most common contextual issue addressed in the literature is that of the poor image of catalogers and cataloging, especially in respect to the classroom. Clack discusses the "serious image problem of the specialty." Lack of time to cover everything creates the impression that bibliographic control education is not keeping pace with current trends. "Cataloging has not as yet been embraced by a large number of students as a favorite course of study"[13]–dullness, drudgery, and difficulty being cited as primary culprits. Dr. Clack also refers to the image of pseudo-scholars and recluses as typical and that there are impressions that cataloging positions are dead-ends with no rewards, recognition, or opportunities for advancement.[14] Riemer mentions the dullness factor–that people do not view cataloging as interesting.[15] Taylor alludes to colleagues who went "away with the idea that cataloging had to be endured and that it had no future application for them. Librarians who had that experience, unfortunately, sometimes tell the clerks and students who work for them that if they go to library school they will hate cataloging."[16] Saye too states that "the subject of cataloging and classification is perceived by all too many students as a rite of passage that must be endured."[17] This image problem has resulted in a shortage of qualified catalogers and Saye recognizes that some of the responsibility for this situation lies with LIS educators.[18] This can occur through poor delivery of courses, through having non-cataloging educators teach core courses in bibliographic control, or through dismissive attitudes toward the specialization in general (by both cataloging and non-cataloging educators). The last is a situation this author has experienced all too frequently while attending library school.

These issues present serious challenges to bibliographic control education. While the environment of constant change may not be within the control of the specialization, the image of cataloging is; changing it is the responsibility of all catalog librarians, both educators and practitioners. Cataloging could and should be a source of pride, yet it has become a pariah. That "cataloging is librarianship's unique contribution"[19] to academia and the world does not seem to matter. Bibliographic control needs to be embraced again by this profession.

Theory versus Practical Application: The single most frequently discussed issue in the recent literature on bibliographic control education was that of theory versus practical application in LIS schools. Many of the articles described this issue as one of balancing both of these very necessary components. While all of the authors expressed an appreciation for theory and endorsed its place in the curriculum, many also stated a need for more practical education. This is supported by a number of surveys (of practitioners and recent graduates) that indicate that entry-level catalogers are unprepared to perform their practical cataloging responsibilities. Callahan and MacLeod found that 63% of entry-level catalogers felt unprepared for their first professional cataloging position and that 67% of employers found entry-level catalogers to be without the necessary skills to perform their duties.[20,21] These figures are startling and demand attention from LIS educators. To remedy this, Garrett believes it is more natural to begin with the specific task, work through understandings of the general model, and then learn the theory behind it all. In other words, student catalogers would learn more effectively if the order in which theory and practice are taught were inverted. Findings of a study at the University of Hawaii seem to support this assertion.[22]

Connaway believes that theory should be combined with the practical side of cataloging in order for entry-level catalogers to perform their positions adequately.[23,24] MacLeod and Callahan acknowledge that LIS educators have struggled to find the proper balance and focus for their students in order to give them a solid foundation in the principles of cataloging and to make them professionally competent. They come to the same conclusion as Connaway, pointing out the impression of employers that entry-level catalogers are completing library schools without developing the practical skills required to perform the job.[25] Evans, a practitioner and an educator, wonders, "where are the new librarians going to get the remaining skills" that she expects as a supervisor, when she herself (as a cataloging educator) cannot cover all of the material needed for successful job performance.[26] Olson phrases it somewhat differently, stating that professionals need to understand their catalogs in a holistic manner, knowing each element in both theory and practice.[27] Romero[28] and Zyroff[29] discuss how the pendulum of theory versus practice has swung back and forth over the years. Both mention the lack of practical experience in the education of today's entry-level catalogers. They appear to suggest preparation that is more practical, as does Evans.[30] Practitioners and employers seem to adopt a more pragmatic view, expecting recent graduates to have practical skills in cataloging. This is not to say, however, that employers find LIS education without its benefits, as Xu discovered.[31] She found that recent graduates are generally more competent with the latest technologies and thus require far less training in that area.

While practical preparation is important, educators are sometimes concerned that students may encounter the challenges of being in administrative or supervisory positions that require a solid grounding in cataloging theory. Lubetzky once wrote, "the subject of cataloging should not be treated as a how-to-do-it, routine outline in so many rules."[32] Taking it to an extreme though, Fallis and Fricke have stated that practical skills are not appropriate for graduate education, which is for intellectual pursuits, academic study, learning theory, and conducting research.[33] If there is a need for practical skills, internships may be a solution. Their beliefs are not popular in the field, however, if the response letters to their article are any indication.[34]

While this author disagrees with much of what they have said, Fallis and Fricke are right about the benefits of a practicum, internship, or field placement. Sluk states many students are often quoted as saying that their practicum was their best experience in library school. He goes on to state, "cataloging is learned by doing *and* by studying with one who knows the field well."[35] For this author, the practicum was greatly beneficial, making the theory more concrete and solidifying the practical skills obtained in courses. The benefits of the practicum or field placement should not be underestimated.

In the theory versus practice debate, the strength of the practitioner/employer's perspective is that there are generally more jobs for cataloging practitioners than for directors or coordinators of cataloging or technical service departments.[36] While the job market demands the pragmatic rather than the theoretical, it is also clear that both are necessary for catalogers to perform their tasks with understanding and competency. Riemer, a practitioner, states that a mix is needed and that practice without theory risks being blind.[37] One is of little value without the other. As Hill states, no one knows the best mix,[38] and as Intner points out, no one can absolutely define what is practice and what is theory,[39] but it is imperative that educators aim for balance between the two.

Responsibilities and Skills of Catalogers: Closely related to the issue addressed above is the discussion of the changing responsibilities of catalogers and the skills that entry-level catalogers need. "It is rare to find a catalog librarian whose job assignment is limited to the tasks of cataloging."[40] Figures 2 and 3 are a compilation of the skills, responsibilities, and qualities that practitioners are looking for in new hires as stated in four journal articles addressing this topic. Numbers in parentheses indicate the number of articles in which the topic was mentioned. Nothing is terribly surprising in the accumulated list save that many of the desired qualities cannot be or are not taught in library school.[41,42,43,44]

In a not-so-scientific analysis of the skills, responsibilities, and qualities below, it can be seen that of the thirteen items mentioned more than

FIGURE 2. Catalogers' Responsibilities

Developing cataloging policies and procedures (2)*	Editing and revising the work of paraprofessionals*	Interpreting and applying rules and standards*
Managing time	Following rules and standards*	Prioritizing
Management	Problem solving	Hiring
Workflow management	Training	Supervising paraprofessionals
Researching and making decisions	Selecting and maintaining automated systems*	Using judgment

*Cataloging-related

FIGURE 3. Skills, Qualities and Knowledge Needed by Catalogers

Knowledge of automated library systems*	Knowledge of cataloging tools and resources*	Knowledge of the cataloging vocabulary*
Knowledge of LCSH (2)*	Foreign language skills (2)	Knowledge of MARC (3)*
Computer skills/Internet skills (3)	Knowledge of LCRIs*	People skills/supervisory skills (2)
Research skills	Knowledge of AACR2 (2)*	Knowledge of/skills with OCLC (3)*
Knowledge of various formats (2)*	Understand library economy	Knowledge of DDC/LCC*
Knowledge of the essentials of retrieval	Service oriented vision/Users' needs (3)	Ability to get the job done
Knowledge of authority work*	Adaptability to new ideas	Theory and foundation of cataloging (2)*
Flexibility (2)	Communication skills (2)	

*Cataloging-related

once, over half (those marked by an asterisk) are specifically cataloging-related. It too can be seen that of the entire thirty-eight items listed above, nearly half of them are specifically cataloging-related. An area of further investigation might be to compare these or other lists of skills, responsibilities, and qualities desired in a cataloger to course outlines and objectives in bibliographic control education.

The Relationship Between Educators and Practitioners: Another issue raised in the literature was the perception of a communication gap between educators and practitioners. Connaway states that library directors rated fewer than half of the entry-level librarians they hired as satisfactorily trained for their positions. She stresses the importance of practitioner input in the development of LIS education.[45,46] O'Neill feels the job of educating new librarians should not be the sole responsibility of LIS faculty. Practitioners must be involved.[47]

With a different point of view, Jeng,[48] citing Kathryn Henderson, suggests that practitioners are less important in cataloging education because they are biased toward particular systems. This seems a misapplication of Henderson's original statement that "an educator not aligned to any library *can* have a broader, more unbiased view of the total task at hand in teaching cataloging."[49]

MacLeod and Callahan report that 98% of the educators they surveyed stated they considered the needs of practitioners in designing courses. Fifty-three percent of practitioners did not see this reflected in the curricula of library schools. The concept of the lack of communication between educators and practitioners pervades this 1995 MacLeod and Callahan article, which focuses on the differing perspectives of educators and practitioners regarding the preparation of students for professional cataloging. They conclude that the differences are attributable to "the nature of their respective responsibilities." Their study indicates that the two groups are "not as distant as their history of discord indicates" and they found "a number of encouraging conclusions and constructive recommendations" that apply to all the participants in their study.[50]

Concurring, Romero repeatedly refers to practitioners and educators as agreeing, as having the same concerns, and as benefiting mutually or gaining insight from the results of her study.[51] While MacLeod and Callahan and Romero recognize the mutual interests of both groups, they do not indicate that communications between the two groups have improved or that the groups are in any way working together to improve the quality of bibliographic control education. LIS educators must take the lead in improving these relationships. Only when practitioners' opinions, through guest lecturing, adjunct faculty positions, or inclusion in curriculum development activities, are welcomed into the realm of academia, will this "rift" end.

Cataloging: A Universal Skill: The fifth issue that this author found raised in the journal literature is the need to acknowledge cataloging as a skill that is important in all aspects of librarianship. Gorman calls bibliographic control the heart of librarianship and feels that it should be taught as such.[52] Romero considers cataloging a universal skill for librarians. She cites Hopkins,[53] agreeing that "a cataloging course is important for all librarians, not only those intending to become catalogers." She also implies that this view is commonly held throughout the profession.[54] In fact, there was overall agreement among the recent bibliographic control education articles on the topic of the universality of cataloging skills. Zyroff stresses this point; indeed, it is the primary focus of her article. She considers cataloging so basic to librarianship that it must be included in the core curriculum, and worries about the "professional perception that cataloging has become an optional skill for librarians."[55] Gorman, in a piece written for *California Libraries*, discusses the dangers of this attitude:

> Why are the managers of dot.coms keen to employ information managers (knowing full well that they are librarians under another name)? The ultimate irony is that the skills that make those information managers marketable are the very skills that the former library schools are abandoning . . . what makes them want to hire librarians is the knowledge, conscious or subconscious, that librarians have unique skills in organizing documents (including electronic documents) for speedy retrieval and that those skills are as useful when it comes to the organization and retrieval of data and pieces of information. (We call those skills cataloguing, classification, and bibliographic organization in oldspeak.) Ah, but there's the rub. New graduates from LIS schools could be assumed to have a grasp of the basics of librarianship as recently as ten years ago. Now there is no guarantee that new graduates from many such schools have taken cataloguing courses . . . so, here we are. The dot.commanders are smart enough to know what they lack. They are, apparently, turning to new graduates of LIS schools in the hope that they can supply that lack. This is all happening at a time when those schools are abandoning the teaching of the skills that the dot.coms want in favor of skills that are found plentifully and more abundantly in the graduates of other, non-LIS, programs. Since so much of the new econ-

omy is made up of smoke and mirrors, perhaps this tragi-comic misunderstanding will be just another illusion in the dot.com funhouse. Bit of a shame, though, that just when librarians are in demand, library education is walking away from everything that makes librarians distinct and valuable.[56]

Zyroff points out that familiarity with cataloging skills provides an "in-depth perspective on the structure of information."[57] It is her contention that the critical thinking skills of catalogers are crucial to successfully accessing information and that even systems librarians need to comprehend cataloging theory and practice in order to design better OPACs. Zyroff notes that learning to use controlled vocabulary also assists in searching and retrieval, necessary skills for all librarians. The cataloging skills that "assure consistency, predictability and repeatability of access" are just as useful as ever, she notes,[58] though it may not be so easy to convince students of this. Frost states she has had to work hard to convince LIS students that a public services librarian needs to know cataloging principles.[59]

O'Neill believes educators should emphasize the importance of technical services work to all aspects of library service:

> Educators must convey their belief in, and enthusiasm for, the importance of all technical services functions to their students. All introductory and advanced courses should emphasize that technical services functions are necessary in all information environments and for all modes of information delivery. Whether information is transmitted by cuneiform clay tablets, printed books and serials, electronic resources or whatever lies beyond, someone must be responsible for identifying, acquiring, organizing and preserving the information stored in these various formats.[60]

She goes on to stress the importance of technical services, discussing how the work done will have an impact upon the ability of the library to provide access to information. This point is especially important for students who do not plan to become catalogers. They too must understand how technical services affect their jobs, as this will make them better librarians. She does remind us, however, that for most students the processes involved in technical services will be only a part of their jobs, not their main focus.[61]

Williamson writes in her 1997 article that understanding the process of subject analysis is important for all librarians since subject analysis is

all about retrieval. "Locating information by subject is one of the fundamental approaches to all information-seeking. It is essential that *all* information professionals have a basic knowledge of the principles of
subject analysis and an understanding of their application in indexing
and retrieval in online systems of various kinds."[62] Finally, Xu describes a picture of holistic librarians, those librarians who function
equally well throughout the various departments of the library. The "holistic librarian" notion is one view of the future of librarianship and one
that might affect library education. Unfortunately, however, Xu reveals
that according to her analysis of job advertisements from 1971 to 1990,
there is no evidence to show the emergence of the holistic librarian in
the profession.[63]

The themes expressed in these articles, as well as old-fashioned common sense, indicate that cataloging is the backbone of librarianship.
Without the organization of information, retrieval of information (an essential or perhaps *the* essential function of libraries) would be impossible.
It is therefore only reasonable to state that all librarians must have a basic
understanding of and possess basic skills in bibliographic control.

Curricular Issues: The final area to be discussed in this literature review involves curricular issues. The curriculum is one way a library
school is evaluated for currency and relevancy. It is the manifestation of a
school's beliefs on education and indicates a program's understanding of
the profession and its needs. The LIS school curriculum should reflect the
needs of students about to enter the workplaces of today and tomorrow as
well as reflecting the needs of and skills required by employers. Is bibliographic control education meeting the needs of students and their future
employers? In order to start looking for answers to this question, this paper will look at the ALCTS Education Policy Statement, the results of
two studies, and the opinions of several LIS educators.

In 1995, the Association for Library Collections and Technical Services (ALCTS) Board of Directors approved the ALCTS Educational
Policy Statement that embodied a vision of necessary outcomes for the
education of catalogers. It had several lists of core competencies attached as an appendix.[64,65] These core competencies reflect both the
practitioner's and the educator's points of view. It provides a comprehensive and realistic approach to the theoretical foundations of practice.
This list is a good baseline when discussing bibliographic control curricular issues. With these competencies in mind, educators must look at
what actually comprises the current cataloging curricula and decide
whether they are adequate to meet the needs of students and employers.
Figure 4 provides an interpretive list of these core competencies.

In 1987, *Cataloging & Classification Quarterly* (*CCQ*) conducted a study to look at what courses were being offered in 55 ALA-accredited library schools in the U.S. and Canada.[66] The survey provided a list of the library schools that responded and the courses those schools reported that they offered. The survey found 209 courses being offered, which leads to an average of 3.8 courses being offered per school. The *CCQ* staff did not attempt to categorize the different types of courses being offered. Instead, the article provided the raw data that was collected. This allows researchers to use this information as a baseline for comparison. The *CCQ* study is used for that purpose in this current study. The survey shows that each of the 55 schools offered between one and ten courses. It did not indicate, however, which courses were required and which were electives. Based on categorizations made by this author fourteen years later, it appears that 49 basic cataloging courses were offered in 1987, as were 14 organizing courses. Fifty-one of 55 schools (or 92.7%) offered some introductory cataloging or introductory organizing course.

Based on Sherry Vellucci's 1997 article,[67,68] in which all cataloging courses are roughly categorized into introductory and advanced

FIGURE 4. Core Competencies/Core Knowledge in Bibliographic Control

Information-seeking behavior	User needs
Theory of organization of information	Theory of access
National and international standards	Subject analysis
Thesaurus construction	Indexing
Classification	Description
Access	Syndetic structure
Bibliographic relationships	Controlled vocabulary
Information retrieval theory	Searching techniques
Data and record structures	Precision and recall
Cataloging tools	Bibliographic utilities
Library administration and management	Evaluating information retrieval systems
Database design	Data management concepts
Planning and designing user-driven systems	State-of-the-art research and practice

courses, 92% of fifty-two ALA-accredited library school programs provided an introductory course in cataloging with 63% of the programs making it a required course. Introductory organizing courses were offered at 20 (38%) of the schools (all of which were required). All of the schools in her survey offered some introductory course, either cataloging or organizing. In 90% of the schools, the introductory course was required.

In 1998, Spillane[69] found that the numbers of some bibliographic control courses might be lower than those reported by Vellucci. Spillane reported in her study that only 55.4% of schools required a basic cataloging course and that the number of programs with integrated (organizing) courses was 15. She did find, however, that the average number of courses being offered per school had risen from 3.8 in 1986 to 4.[70] The discrepancies between this and the Vellucci study may result from differences in the institutions that were surveyed. They may also arise from differences in the definitions of cataloging and integrated (organizing) courses. These issues may also affect comparisons that may be made between these two earlier studies and the current study being reported.[71]

According to Vellucci, the majority (73%) of the fifty-two ALA-accredited library schools in her study provided at least one type of advanced cataloging course. She also found that 73% of the programs offered only three or fewer cataloging courses.[72,73] Can one to three cataloging courses meet the ideals in the ALCTS core competencies?[74] Can four or five courses? When reminded of the Callahan and MacLeod study (in which 63% of entry-level catalogers felt they were not prepared for their first cataloging job),[75,76] it appears that one to four courses may indeed be too low and that the current cataloging curricula meet the needs of neither the students nor the employers. So, whose needs *are* being met by bibliographic control education?

Another issue that arises when discussing the curriculum is how new technologies have increased the amount of material that needs to be taught in cataloging courses. This new material, of course, is reducing the time that is available to cover existing issues of importance, both theoretical and practical. Taylor has said:

> [There have] been major additions to the material covered and virtually no subtractions. Since 1966, we have had the development of LC's Cataloging-in-Publication (CIP) program, the International Standard Bibliographic Descriptions (ISBD), and the Machine-Readable Cataloging (MARC) formats. Bibliographic networks have de-

veloped and have drastically changed the way in which local cataloging is done. Cooperative cataloging has taken on greatly increased importance. The online catalog has become the format of choice. Computer files, audiocassettes, videocassettes, compact discs, and three-dimensional materials have been added to the list of non-book materials that students should learn to catalog.[77]

Saye believes that LIS programs cannot "be expected to have the time to teach everything the entry-level individual needs to know"[78] and this is coming from someone teaching in a two-year program. Both the MacLeod and Callahan[79] and the Zyroff[80] articles cite the trend among library schools to yield to students' interests to the detriment of core cataloging competencies. MacLeod and Callahan[81] and Evans[82] echo concerns about a minimalist approach to cataloging, stating that since students are perceived as being less interested in the cataloging field, courses have gotten broader and have begun neglecting traditional cataloging skills.

Some curricular issues are mentioned in only one article, but bear repeating. MacLeod and Callahan[83] call for more management coursework due to changes in the field. Clack raises the issue that many LIS educators just do not like cataloging, which is related to the image issues addressed earlier. She states that fewer required courses exist and students are not being encouraged to take cataloging as an elective, despite the fact that cataloging is more complex and more sophisticated than ever before.[84] Frost believes "cataloging and classification have evolved into courses that cover organization of information of all kinds with an emphasis on digital data . . . [and this change] presents opportunities to teach and learn cataloging in new and exciting ways."[85]

Riemer believes that descriptive cataloging, in particular, is being ignored despite engaging and controversial issues related to:

- Multiple Versions
- Latest versus Successive Entry
- Brief Displays
- Corporate Entry
- Need for MARC
- Main Entry
- *AACR2*
- Corporate Authorship[86]

Romero and others express their views of what belongs in cataloging curricula. Romero's article discusses specific areas that she feels are lacking, namely instruction in MARC coding, better explanation of the areas of description, and the importance of consulting sources when making cataloging decisions.[87] Connaway believes catalogers should be taught personnel management and supervision; have a familiarity with OCLC, MARC, cataloging resources, and cataloging tools; understand bibliographic control of all formats; and possess computer skills. She advocates a practical approach with an end result of students creating a cataloging portfolio that can be presented to potential employers.[88,89] Clack feels that catalogers need exposure to:

- Standards
- Searching
- *AACR2*
- LCRIs
- ISBD
- MARC
- Online Systems

- Access Points
- Theory and Practice
- Subject Analysis
- Classification
- Authority Work
- Management
- Bibliographic Networks[90]

When Evans teaches, she addresses the following in her syllabus:

- Reading Title Pages
- Vocabulary
- *AACR2*
- LCSH
- Catalog Management

- MARC
- OCLC
- DDC
- Searching
- Management Issues[91]

She fears the minimalist approach (one to three cataloging courses) is just not enough.

Saye teaches both basic and advanced cataloging courses. He feels the basic course should provide minimal level cataloging skills and should acquaint the student with the basic tools and resources available. The basic course needs to be everything to everyone (including non-cataloging students). Saye's advanced course includes some of the same concepts as the basic level course (description, access, DDC, LCSH, etc.), but these are treated, presumably, in more depth. Topics such as *LCRI*s, antiquarian materials cataloging, serials, and additional classification work are included in the advanced course. In addition, Saye states, in an early article from 1987, that the basic course, plus one or two electives is enough to train the entry-level cataloger; any more than that is just exotica, ephemera, useless information.[92] Saye's article, however, was written before the studies indicating a certain level of incompetence in entry-level catalogers[93,94] were published. Finally, Williamson states,

There are those that feel that with advances in computer technology, the predominant use of copy cataloging, and the growing trend towards outsourcing, formal instruction in these subjects [cataloging and classification] should no longer be required. Indeed many programs have eliminated such courses from their core curricula. Others have called for the reinstatement of courses related to an area that they believe to be a fundamental preserve of the information professions.[95]

She sensibly and non-dramatically states,

> given the length of most programs, it is not possible to cover all bases, let alone create experts. A short basic course is not sufficient for intelligent use of the present retrieval systems let alone coping with the future. A knowledge of principles backed up with application is essential and advanced courses covering such areas as classification theory and its systems, thesaurus design and construction, various kinds of indexing . . . are needed.[96]

Given that LIS educators cannot do everything needed, the length of most programs is too short, and the attitudes of many library directors towards bibliographic control are less than positive, what *is* being done in bibliographic control education? What is being offered today?

STUDY OF BIBLIOGRAPHIC CONTROL COURSES

Introduction

With Nancy J. Williamson's sensible words in mind, this study began in September 2000 for an organizing information doctoral seminar at the University of Pittsburgh. Data collection was conducted between September 14, 2000 and February 12, 2001. Forty-eight Web sites were analyzed, 315 e-mail messages were exchanged, and five telephone interviews were conducted to obtain the necessary information. All of the information sought about the 48 schools included in the study was obtained. For each area of bibliographic control education, the collected data are addressed separately, after discussions of the general results and of the information collected on required courses in LIS education.

In each section that follows, the results from the current study are compared with three previous studies: Vellucci's in 1997,[97] Spillane's from 1998,[98] and the 1987 *Cataloging & Classification Quarterly* (*CCQ*) survey.[99] The numbers used for comparisons are based on the raw data provided by the *CCQ* study, on Figure 3 in Spillane's article, and on Vellucci's Table 3. As mentioned above, the *CCQ* data had not been categorized, therefore all labels applied to the courses and all totals of these courses reflect this author's definitions of categories and this author's tallying of the courses.

In her research, Spillane surveyed 56 schools and 221 courses. The *CCQ* study looked at 55 schools with 209 courses. The current study surveyed 48 schools and 199 courses, while Vellucci surveyed 52 schools with 156 courses. These three other surveys, unlike the current one that focuses on US schools, included the Canadian LIS schools.

As noted above, true comparisons of the three studies may be nearly impossible due to variations in terminology and/or the differing sizes and compositions of the samples. Despite these differences, some data comparisons are presented, though determining whether or how much some of the numbers have actually changed may be difficult. The most reliable comparisons may be between the current study and the 1987 *CCQ* survey for the reasons explained above. In many cases, the numbers in the 1998 Spillane survey are more extreme than in the other three surveys. The *CCQ*, Vellucci, and Joudrey studies together generally tend to show smooth progressions. With the Spillane numbers included, there is often a sharp increase or decline in the numbers. Further investigation is needed to determine the cause of these fluctuations.

General Results

It was found in this current survey of 48 LIS schools[100] that a total of 207 courses are listed in the course rosters for the areas of bibliographic control. This results in an average of 4.31 courses per school. No school had fewer than two offerings, nor did any school offer more than seven courses in bibliographic control. When inquiring about various courses, it was found that (at least) eight courses that are not taught remain on the rosters. This leaves 199 courses in bibliographic control. This results in an average of 4.15 courses per school, a number slightly higher than the 4 courses per school found by Spillane.[101] The 199 bibliographic control courses divide into 49 required courses and 150 electives. There is an average of 1.02 required courses and 3.13 electives at each school (see Table 1). See "Textbooks Used in Bibliographic Control Education Courses" by Daniel N Joudrey in this volume, for information regarding textbook usage.

Table 2 provides a general overview of the number of courses offered in each area of bibliographic control and the number of schools offering those courses (see Table 2). From this chart, it can be seen that the area offered by the greatest number of schools is Indexing. The area with the greatest number of courses in it, though, is Basic Cataloging. It can also be seen that in the first five areas (organizing, cataloging, technical services, advanced cataloging, and descriptive cataloging), schools may offer more than one course, but in the last eight, only one course per school is offered.

Table 3 compares the numbers of introductory cataloging and organizing information courses from the four surveys. This table shows, despite conventional wisdom, that the number of introductory organizing and cataloging courses seems to be increasing, not decreasing. The current study, which has the smallest sample of schools, shows more introductory courses in these areas than the studies conducted three, four, and fourteen years ago. Without having access to the raw data of the other studies though (with the information of how each course in each school was categorized), it is impossible to state definitively that introductory courses are increasing.

From this comparison, it appears that the average number of introductory organizing and cataloging courses per school has risen from 1.14 in 1986 to 1.5 in 2000.

TABLE 1. Overview of Courses

Number	199 courses	49 required	150 electives
School average	4.15 per school	1.02 per school	3.13 per school

TABLE 2. Overview of Courses in the Areas of Bibliographic Control

	Organizing	Basic Cataloging	Technical Services	Adv. Cat.	Descriptive Cat.	Subject Cat.	Classification
Schools (n = 48)	26 54.2%	40 83.3%	11 22.9%	27 56.3%	4 8.3%	10 20.8%	7 14.6%
Courses (n = 199)	29 14.6%	43 21.6%	12 6%	29 14.6%	5 2.5%	10 5%	7 3.5%
	Non-book	Internet		Indexing	Thesaurus	Music	Cat. Technology
Schools (n = 48)	7 14.6%	5 10.4%		39 81.3%	8 16.7%	1 2.1%	4 8.3%
Courses (n = 199)	7 3.5%	5 2.5%		39 19.6%	8 4%	1 .5%	4 2%

Table 4 shows a comparison of the other types of bibliographic control courses in the four surveys. Many of the categories show great variations in the number of schools offering that course type. Differences in sample sizes and variations in terminology, as well as the natural evolution of the LIS programs, most likely cause these variations.

Graph 1 shows the number of bibliographic control courses offered per institution. It compares the results of the four studies. It appears that since the *CCQ* study in 1986, the average number of bibliographic control courses offered per institution is increasing rather than decreasing. The 2000 study shows an average of 4.15 courses per school, a number

TABLE 3. Comparison of Introductory Courses

Study	No. of Schools	Organizing*	Basic Cat.	Total	Average
CCQ	55	14	49	63	1.14 per school
Vellucci	52	20	48	68	1.3
Spillane	56	15	56	71	1.3
Joudrey	48	29	43	72	1.5

*Spillane refers to these courses as "integrated courses."

TABLE 4. Comparison of Other Types of Courses

Course Type	Joudrey 2000	Spillane 1998	Vellucci 1997	*CCQ* 1986
Technical Services	12	≈19 (7)[a]	Unknown	17 (5)
Adv. Cat./Special Topics	29	≈52 (23)	38 (9)	42 (13)
Subject Cataloging	10	10	13 (3)	18 (8)
Descriptive Cataloging	5	≈5	5	13 (8)
Classification Theory	7	10 (3)	13 (6)[b]	9 (2)
Special Formats[c]	12	≈7 (−5)	5 (−7)	10 (−2)
Indexing	39	≈42 (3)	Unknown	15 (−24)
Cataloging Technology	4	≈4	4[d]	9 (5)
Other[e]	9	1	10	13 (4)

≈ Approximation
a. Numbers in the parentheses indicate the difference between that study and the current one.
b. Includes classification theory and advanced classification.
c. Includes non-print and Internet resources cataloging.
d. Included in the other cataloging electives.
e. Includes internships, music cataloging, thesaurus construction, serials, bibliography, and miscellaneous courses.

GRAPH 1. Number of Bibliographic Control Courses Offered by Schools According to Four Studies

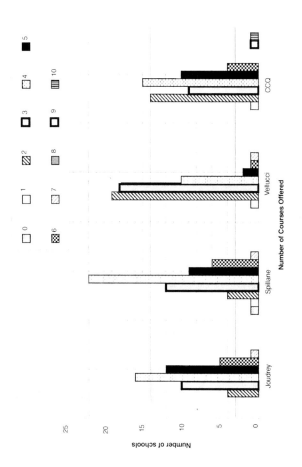

slightly higher than the 4 courses per school found by Spillane[102] and the 3.8 figure found by the *CCQ* survey.[103] This information seems to contradict popular thought. This increase may be the result of increasing numbers of organizing information courses and special format cataloging courses (see discussion below).

Required Courses[104]

In the current survey, there are 49 course requirements in bibliographic control among the 48 LIS schools. Fifty-two courses can be used to fulfill these 49 requirements. These courses are not spread evenly throughout the schools. Only 44 of the 48 schools (91.7%) have a required course in bibliographic control. Four schools have no requirements in this area, but offer instead three to five elective courses. Thirty-nine schools have one required course; five schools have two.

As seen in Figure 5, of these 44 schools, four schools have one technical services course requirement. Sixteen have one cataloging requirement. Seventeen have one organizing requirement. One school has two organizing course requirements. Three have one organizing course requirement and one cataloging requirement. Three other schools allow various options for fulfilling their bibliographic control course requirements.

Twenty-three out of 48 schools (47.9%) now require an organizing course (or allow an organizing course to fulfill a bibliographic control requirement), 21 schools (43.8%) require (or may require) a cataloging course, and five schools (10.4%) require (or may require) a technical services course. One school allows indexing to fulfill their bibliographic control requirement and another allows a subject course to fill this requirement (2.1% each). Three of the schools have options for fulfilling bibliographic control requirements, which can lead to a variety of configurations.

A breakdown of the 52 courses that can be used to fulfill the 49 bibliographic control requirements is seen in Figure 6.

Compared with Vellucci's study, the percentage of programs that require organizing information courses has increased from 38% to just under 50% and the percentage of programs that require a basic cataloging course has declined from 63% to 43.8%. Those that have both an organizing and a cataloging requirement have decreased from 12% to 6.3%. Schools with a requirement in bibliographic control (no matter the type) have increased slightly, from 90% to nearly 92%.[105]

FIGURE 5. Bibliographic Control Requirements

Type of requirements	# of Schools
One Organizing requirement	17
One Cataloging requirement	16
One Technical Services requirement	4
Two Organizing requirements	1
One Organizing **and** one Cataloging requirement	3
One Organizing **or** one Subject requirement	1
One Cataloging **or** one Technical Services requirement	1
One Organizing **and** either one Cataloging **or** one Indexing requirement	1

FIGURE 6. Breakdown of Required Courses

Type of course	# of Courses	% of total courses	% of Required Courses
Organizing	24	12.1%	46.2%
Cataloging	21	10.6%	40.4%
Technical Services	5	2.5%	9.6%
Subject	1	0.5%	1.9%
Indexing	1	0.5%	1.9%

Since Spillane did not specify the number of required organizing courses being offered, only required cataloging courses can be compared with the current study. Spillane found that there were 31 required cataloging courses in 1998.[106] The current study finds 21 required cataloging courses, a larger discrepancy than one would expect, though it may be explained by differences in terminology as well as an evolutionary shift away from cataloging courses toward more general organizing courses.

Organizing Courses: As mentioned earlier in this paper, organizing courses are those required and elective courses that take a broader view of organizing information in various settings. They may not be as detailed as traditional cataloging courses. From this survey, it appears that the number of organizing courses is increasing, when compared with the studies by Spillane,[107] *CCQ*,[108] and Vellucci[109] (see Table 5).

Twenty-six schools (54.2%) offer courses in organizing information; twenty-two schools (45.8%) do not (see Table 6). As indicated in the previous section, 22 of 48 (45.3%) schools require an organizing course. Of the schools that offer organizing courses, 84.6% require it for all library graduate students. One school surveyed allows students to take an organizing course or another course to fulfill their bibliographic control requirement. Three schools offer organizing as an elective only. Of the 22 schools without organizing courses, fourteen have cataloging requirements, four require a technical services course, three have no requirements in this specialization at all, and one allows students to choose between a cataloging and a technical services requirement.

Nineteen, or 39.6% of all schools have one required organizing course. One school requires two organizing courses (2.1%). Two schools have an organizing elective and an organizing requirement (4.2%); one school has one organizing course that may fulfill a requirement or may be taken as an elective; three schools (6.3%) have only elective courses in organizing.

These 26 schools offer 29 different courses in organizing information. These courses comprise 14.6% of the total courses offered in bibliographic control. Of these 29 courses, 23 or 79.3% are required. One course may be required or may be taken as an elective (3.5%). Five of the courses (17.2%) are electives only. As seen in Table 3, the number of organizing courses seems to be rising when compared to the studies of Spillane (15 courses)[110] and Vellucci (20 courses)[111] and *CCQ* (14 courses).[112]

Basic Cataloging Courses: Basic cataloging courses are those introductory courses (required or elective) that introduce students to the concepts of traditional library cataloging. Forty (83.3%) of the 48 ALA-accredited LIS schools in the US offer at least one course in basic

TABLE 5. Schools Offering Organizing Courses

	#	%	Required	%	May Require	%	Elective	%
Schools w/ Org. (n = 26)	26	100%	22	84.6%	1	3.9%	3	11.5%
All Schools (n = 48)	26	54.2%	22	45.8%	1	2.1%	3	6.3%

TABLE 6. Organizing Courses

	#	%	Required	%	May Require	%	Elective	%
Org. Courses (n = 29)	29	100%	23	79.3%	1	3.5%	5	17.2%
All Courses (n = 199)	29	14.6%	23	11.6%	1	0.5%	5	2.5%

cataloging (see Table 7). Nineteen (39.6%) schools require it for all library school students. Of the 40 schools with basic-level cataloging courses, 47.5% require it. Two schools give students the option of taking an introductory cataloging course to fulfill a core requirement. Nineteen schools offer basic cataloging only as an elective. Of the 21 schools that require or may require basic cataloging, 15 of the schools (71.4%) offer no organizing courses, two schools (9.5%) have an organizing elective, and four schools (19.1%) require an organizing course as well. Of the eight schools without basic cataloging courses, six have organizing requirements and two require a technical services course. Of those eight schools, four schools offer a combination of subject analysis and descriptive cataloging courses in place of cataloging.

At these 40 schools, 43 basic cataloging courses are offered (see Table 8). These 43 courses are 21.6% of the total bibliographic control courses. Of these 43 courses, 22 are electives, 19 are required, and two courses may fulfill a core requirement or be taken as an elective.

As mentioned earlier, Spillane found 56 introductory cataloging courses, with 31 of them (55.4%) being required.[113] This number is considerably higher than the 43 basic cataloging courses in the current study, 19 of which (44%) are required. Vellucci found 48 basic cataloging courses, 33 (68.8%) of which were required courses.[114] The *CCQ* study found 49 basic cataloging courses; the number of which that were required being unknown.[115] These numbers and those in the previous section suggest a trend in LIS education of moving away from basic cat-

TABLE 7. Schools with Basic Cataloging

	#	%	Required	%	May Require	%	Elective	%
Schools w/ Basic Cat. (n = 40)	40	100%	19	47.5%	2	5%	19	47.5%
All Schools (n = 48)	40	83.3%	19	39.6%	2	4.2%	19	39.6%

TABLE 8. Basic Cataloging Courses

	#	%	Required	%	May Require	%	Elective	%
Basic Cat. Courses (n = 43)	43	100%	19	44.2%	2	4.65%	22	51.2%
All Courses (n = 199)	43	21.6%	19	9.6%	2	1%	22	11.1%

aloging courses toward more general organizing information courses to fulfill bibliographic control requirements. The numbers also show, however, that basic cataloging still has a strong foothold, being taught in over 83% of the LIS schools in the United States.

Technical Services: Similar to organizing information courses, technical services courses are generally broader than cataloging courses. They are designed to introduce students to the various activities that take place within a technical services department of a library. Technical services courses are less common in LIS education than are organizing or cataloging courses. There are eleven schools that offer these courses, of which four require the course, one school offers students an option of taking a technical services course to fill a core requirement, and six schools offer only electives in this area (see Table 9).

At these eleven schools, twelve courses are offered. One school has both a required course and an elective (see Table 10). The twelve courses break down into four required courses, one course that may or may not be used to fulfill a core requirement, and seven electives. Vellucci did not specifically mention technical services courses, so there can be no comparison with that survey. Spillane, however, did find that nineteen courses of this type existed.[116] This number is a great deal higher than in the current study. More investigation is necessary to determine the source of this discrepancy. At the time of the *CCQ* study, seventeen technical services courses were being offered.[117] If not for the Spillane study, one would think this type of course was showing signs of vanishing, but with her figure of nineteen courses in 1998, one must question the figures.

TABLE 9. Schools with Technical Services Courses

	#	%	Req.	%	May Require	%	Elective	%
Schools w/ T. S. (n = 11)	11	100%	4	36.4%	1	9.1%	6	54.5%
All Schools (n = 48)	11	22.9%	4	8.3%	1	2.1%	6	12.5%

TABLE 10. Technical Services Courses

	#	%	Required	%	May Require	%	Elective	%
T. S. Courses (n = 12)	12	100%	4	33.3%	1	8.3%	7	58.3%
All Courses (n = 199)	12	6%	4	2%	1	0.5%	7	3.5%

Elective Courses

The courses that are represented in this section are those that generally do not fulfill requirements for a graduate program in library and information science. This does not mean there are not a few exceptions. Due to this change, the tables in the following section focus primarily on comparing the current data with the three previous studies.

Advanced Cataloging: Advanced cataloging courses in this study consist of Cataloging and Classification II, Advanced Cataloging, seminars, or courses in advanced topics or issues. Twenty-seven schools, or 56.3%, have advanced cataloging offerings in the form of 29 courses (see Table 11). Twenty-four schools offer both basic cataloging and advanced cataloging; one school offers a combination of descriptive cataloging and subject analysis before offering advanced cataloging; and two schools offer only an organizing course before advanced cataloging.

These 29 courses constitute 14.6% of the total course offerings in bibliographic control education. None of these courses are required of all students. The 29 courses can be broken down into six Advanced Issues courses/Seminars (20.7%), 16 Advanced Cataloging and Classification courses (55.2%), and 7 Cataloging and Classification II courses (24.1%). Table 11 below shows a comparison of the results of the three studies. These figures seem to indicate a drop in the number of advanced cataloging courses from the previous two studies. Except for the spiked number in the Spillane study,[118] it appears that a gradual decrease of advanced cataloging courses is occurring over time.

Subject Courses: Subject courses are those courses that focus solely on the subject analysis process, including analyzing information packages, applying controlled vocabulary, and assigning classificatory symbols. Subject courses are offered in ten schools with one course each (see Table 12). At nine of these schools, the courses are electives. At one school, a subject course may be used to fulfill a bibliographic control requirement.

Similarly, nine of the ten courses are elective courses, while one course may be used to fulfill a bibliographic control requirement. The numbers

TABLE 11. Advanced Cataloging

	Joudrey	Spillane	Vellucci	*CCQ*
Schools with Adv. Cataloging	27 (56%)	Unknown	38 (73%)	37 (67%)
Number of Courses	29 (14.6%)	≈52 (24%)	38 (24%)	42 (20.1%)

from the current study are close to those of the two most recent, previous studies; however, there is a 33% decrease in the number of schools offering subject courses from the 1987 *CCQ* study to the current one (see Table 13).[119]

Descriptive Cataloging: While creating separate courses for the subject approach to information seems relatively common (20.8% of the schools surveyed), the same cannot be said about descriptive cataloging. Only four schools offer courses that focus solely on description and access. The five courses in descriptive cataloging are all electives. While the three most recent studies show similar numbers, there has been a sharp decline in the number of descriptive cataloging courses over the past fourteen years. Table 14 illustrates this dramatic decrease. Does this reflect a change in pedagogical thought indicating that educators find that description and subject cataloging should be taught as a whole and not separately or is this change a reaction to a perceived lack of interest in the topic?

TABLE 12. Schools with Subject Courses

	Joudrey	Elective	May req.	Spillane	Vellucci	*CCQ*
Schools w/Subject	10	9 (90%)	1 (10%)	≈10	13	15
% of all Schools	20.83%	18.75%	2.08%	≈18%	25%	27%

TABLE 13. Subject Courses

	Joudrey	Elective	May req.	Spillane	Vellucci	*CCQ*
Subject courses	10	9 (90%)	1 (10%)	10	13	18
% of all courses	5.03%	4.52%	.50%	4.5%	8.33%	8.6%

TABLE 14. Descriptive Cataloging: Schools and Courses

	Joudrey	Spillane	Vellucci	*CCQ*
Schools w/ Desc. Cat.	4	≈5	5	11
% of All Schools	8.33%	≈8.93%	10%	20%
Desc. Cat. Courses	5	≈5	5	13
% of All Courses	2.51%	≈2.26%	3.21%	6.22%

Classification Theory: Seven classification theory courses are offered in seven different schools (see Table 15). All courses are offered as electives only. The comparisons with Vellucci,[120] CCQ,[121] and Spillane[122] seem to indicate an initial increase and then a reduction in courses of this type. This also may have been affected by the differences in the samples used.

Non-Traditional Formats/Non-Book Cataloging: Courses in non-book cataloging may include the cataloging of multimedia, realia, and audiovisual resources. There are seven cataloging courses for non-book materials at seven schools, none of which are required courses.

The figures in Tables 16 and 17 need some explanation. Neither Vellucci nor Spillane separated Internet resources from other non-traditional formats. (Internet resources cataloging would have been unheard of in 1987.) This author feels this is an area to be watched. Accordingly, Internet resources have been broken out in this study so that future comparisons can be made. The charts, however, include both the combined figures and the separate figures so that comparisons can be made. It appears from the three studies that this will be an area of growth in bibliographic control education. From these charts, it becomes clear that one-quarter of the schools in this survey are now offering some sort of non-traditional format cataloging courses. This shows a significant increase since the previous two studies were conducted.

Internet Cataloging/Metadata: Five courses in Internet resource cataloging/metadata for electronic resources may be found in five schools. None are required courses. This is a growing area in bibliographic control education and therefore the numbers have been separated from other non-book cataloging courses. In addition, courses focusing on the Dublin Core and other forms of metadata are likely to increase as electronic resources continue to challenge the profession. As stated above, neither Vellucci's nor Spillane's studies separated Internet resource cataloging from other non-traditional formats, so the charts include both

TABLE 15. Classification Theory: Schools and Courses

	Joudrey	Spillane	Vellucci	CCQ
Schools w/Class Theory	7	≈10	13	8
% of All Schools	14.58%	17.86%	≈25%	14.54%
Classification Courses	7	10	13	9
% of All Courses	3.52%	4.55%	8.33%	4.3%

the combined figures and the separate figures so that comparisons can be made.

Indexing and Abstracting: Of all the areas in bibliographic control education, indexing is offered at more schools than any other area (see Tables 18 and 19). Forty-two schools have indexing listed in their course rosters, however it was found that three schools are not currently teaching the course. So, thirty-nine schools offer thirty-nine courses in indexing and abstracting. This represents over 81% of the schools in this survey. No school offers more than one indexing course. Of the 39 schools offering it, only one school allows students to take an indexing course to fulfill a core bibliographic control requirement. All the other schools offer it as an elective only.

Vellucci did not include indexing courses in her study, so no direct comparisons are possible. Spillane found that in 1998, approximately 42 courses were offered (presumably, in 42 schools). This means that approximately 75% of the schools Spillane surveyed offered indexing and that indexing courses constituted approximately 19% of the courses offered in the schools in her study.[123] These percentages are only slightly lower than those found in the current study. The raw number in Spillane's study is equal to the number of courses in the current study,

TABLE 16. Non-Book Cataloging

	Joudrey Non-Book Only	Joudrey Non-Book + Internet	Spillane Non-Book + Internet	Vellucci Non-Book + Internet	CCQ Non-Book
Schools w/Non-Book	7	12	≈7	5	10
% of All Schools	14.6%	25%	≈12.5%	10%	18.2%
Non-Book Courses	7	12	≈7	5	10
% of All Courses	3.5%	6 %	≈3.2%	3.2%	4.8%

TABLE 17. Internet Cataloging

	Joudrey Internet	Joudrey Non-Book + Internet	Spillane Non-Book + Internet	Vellucci Non-Book + Internet
Schools w/Non-Book	5	12	≈7	5
% of All Schools	10.4%	25%	≈12.5%	10%
Non-Book Courses	5	12	≈7	5
% of All Courses	2.5%	6 %	≈3.2%	3.2%

TABLE 18. Schools with Indexing

	#	%	Elect.	%	May req.	%
Schools w/Indexing (n = 39)	39	100%	38	97.4%	1	2.6%
All Schools (n = 48)	39	81.3%	38	79.2%	1	2.1%

TABLE 19. Indexing Courses

	#	%	Elect only	%	May req.	%
Indexing Courses (n = 39)	39	100%	38	97.4%	1	2.6%
All Courses (n = 199)	39	19.6%	38	19.1%	1	0.5%

before three were removed for not being taught. In the *CCQ* study, however, only 15 courses were offered at 13 schools.[124] This indicates that over the fourteen-year period between the current study and the 1987 study there has been a dramatic increase in indexing and abstracting courses. Further research is needed to explain the rising popularity of indexing and abstracting courses.

Thesaurus Construction/Controlled Vocabulary: Closely related to indexing and abstracting (in fact, its materials are often incorporated into those courses) are the thesaurus construction and controlled vocabulary courses. Eight schools (16.7%) offer a total of eight electives in this area. Thesaurus construction courses represent 4% of bibliographic control courses offered in the United States. The only truly unexpected finding in this area is that one school offers thesaurus construction, but no indexing course. Neither Vellucci nor Spillane reported results for this area of bibliographic control, so no comparisons can be made with those studies. The *CCQ* survey found only two courses of this kind in two schools.[125]

Other Bibliographic Control Courses: The final two areas of bibliographic control to be discussed are music cataloging and cataloging technology. Only one school offers a course in music cataloging. This music cataloging course represents one-half of one percent of the total bibliographic control courses offered. It is offered at two percent of the LIS schools in the survey. Vellucci, *CCQ*, and Spillane do not mention music cataloging courses.

The category of cataloging technology is a hodgepodge of technology-related courses with titles such as "OCLC Systems and Services," and "On-line Technical Services." These courses are offered at four (8.3%) of the 48 schools in this survey. Spillane's[126] and Vellucci's[127] studies both listed approximately four courses of this type, similar to the current study. The *CCQ* study, however, showed nine cataloging technology courses at nine schools indicating a decline in the number of these types of courses over the past fourteen years.[128]

CONCLUSIONS AND RECOMMENDATIONS

Despite the beliefs of many library administrators and LIS educators, the reports of the death of cataloging are greatly exaggerated. In reviewing the current literature on bibliographic control education, it becomes apparent that there are problems. Students, practitioners, and employers are all dissatisfied with bibliographic control education. There is continuing debate about the balance of theoretical and practical approaches. There is a lack of confidence that educators understand the needs and concerns of practitioners. There are concerns that the depth of bibliographic control education is becoming more shallow, as library educators are forced to add more to already crowded syllabi.

At the same time that many doubt the abilities and education of entry-level catalogers, there are still fairly large numbers of job postings in the cataloging and technical services areas of the profession.[129] Cataloging positions exist in libraries, at bibliographic utilities, at dot.coms, and for organizations providing cataloging-for-pay services as well as generic institutions needing information management. Someone must be trained to fill these positions.

Despite the dreams of information technology professionals and library directors everywhere, cataloging and classification are still human-based, expensive activities and will remain so until technology advances tremendously. The profession has been too quick to jettison cataloging staff and move away from technical services in general to embrace the promises of technological innovation. Those promises have not yet been fulfilled and there is now a lack of qualified, interested professionals to perform these activities that are the backbone of librarianship.

In the course of this paper, a number of questions have been raised. This paper has attempted to answer them by looking at the courses offered and the recent journal literature. Some of the questions are shown in Table 20.

TABLE 20. Questions Raised in This Paper

What *is* the current state of cataloging education? What courses are being taught?

The current state of cataloging education is perhaps not as bad as one might think. There are 199 courses offered throughout the US. Forty-four of the 48 schools require at least one bibliographic control course, so a great majority of librarians in the country are exposed to some form of bibliographic control. The average number of bibliographic control courses per institution is increasing. The number of required courses in bibliographic control is increasing. The number of introductory courses is increasing. The number of specialized courses (e.g., Internet resources cataloging) is increasing. As seen throughout this paper, numerous courses are being offered in a variety of areas of bibliographic control, everything from music cataloging to thesaurus construction.

Are some types of course becoming less available?

Apparently so. Traditional cataloging courses seem to be declining in number, though the number of cataloging courses is still fairly high, with over 83% of schools offering at least one basic course. It also appears that over the past fourteen years (comparing the *CCQ* numbers with those of the current study) the greatest decreases in the number of courses taught have been seen in: Descriptive cataloging (a 62% decrease), Cataloging technology (55%), Subject analysis (44%), and Advanced cataloging (30%).

What do new librarians learn about bibliographic control? Are most library students even exposed to the theory and practice of bibliographic control?

It would seem that new librarians/library students are still being exposed to bibliographic control. The change may be in the depth of knowledge. A trend of moving toward organizing information courses and away from traditional cataloging seems to be underway. Instead of learning to catalog and focusing on the rules and procedures, it seems that a general, broad approach is the goal. New librarians may know nothing about *LCRI*s or number building in Dewey, but they will have a familiarity with metadata, ISBD, EAD, and general classification concepts.

If approximately half of the skills, desired qualifications, etc., are cataloging-related, why do library schools offer so few courses in bibliographic control?

That may be changing. As stated above, the number of courses offered by each institution may be rising. However, as most programs are still twelve courses/36 credits/one-year programs, that may have little impact. Are employers' expectations too high for graduates of a one-year program? Are educators' goals too low? Is one year too little time to study bibliographic control? The answers to these three questions appear to be "yes."

Do 1 to 4 cataloging courses meet the ideals proclaimed in ALCTS' Educational Policy Statement?

With the various studies about cataloger competency, the lack of time to adequately cover the material needed for competency, the increasing amount of information/developments/changes, and with the fourteen competencies that ALCTS has listed for catalogers, the answer would have to be no.

Whose needs are met by bibliographic control education?

From the various studies and the literature, it appears that both students and employers find the LIS programs inadequate for preparing new catalogers to enter the job market. Are the only persons satisfied with bibliographic control education the educators? Are they satisfied? If the answers to these two questions are yes, then the profession really is in trouble.

As stated earlier in this paper, it is difficult to draw any conclusive comparisons with the Spillane and Vellucci studies due to differences in terminology. Without knowing how the other researchers classified any given course, following trends over time is difficult or impossible. Assuming a certain integrity to the definitions though, the following trends can be seen:

- The number of introductory organizing and cataloging courses is increasing.
- The average number of courses offered per institution is increasing.
- Nearly 92% of LIS schools in the United States require some course in bibliographic control.
- Nearly 96% of LIS schools in the United States offer courses beyond the introductory level.
- Nearly fifty percent of schools now require organizing courses.
- The number of schools with cataloging requirements has shrunk to 44%, but more than 83% of schools offer at least one traditional cataloging course.
- The number of indexing courses has increased dramatically over the past fourteen years and has become the most frequently offered elective in bibliographic control.
- Internet, metadata, and non-book formats cataloging courses are increasing in numbers and are likely to continue to increase, as more resources are available in electronic formats.
- Descriptive cataloging courses are decreasing as are cataloging technology, subject analysis, and advanced cataloging courses.
- There seems to be a growing tendency for courses to be broader than traditional library cataloging and classification.
- More bibliographic control requirements are being fulfilled by organizing information courses rather than cataloging courses.

Nancy J. Williamson was right when she said, "given the length of most programs, it is not possible to cover all bases, let alone create experts. A short basic course is not sufficient for intelligent use of the present retrieval systems let alone coping with the future."[130] While LIS educators may not be able to create experts, there are some things that can be done to improve the situation. After undertaking this study and reviewing the bibliographic control education literature, this paper makes the following recommendations to LIS educators:

- Embrace the field of cataloging again. Cataloging is the heart of librarianship. Without the organization of information, retrieval (an essential, if not *the* function of libraries) is impossible. The less well organized information is, the more difficult it is to retrieve.
- Ensure that all librarians have basic skills and a solid understanding of bibliographic control.
- Aim for balance between theory and practice, neglecting neither.
- Create enthusiasm for this core competency.
- Be positive about cataloging or be quiet. Do not disparage what you do not understand. Organizing information should and could be a source of pride; it is "librarianship's unique contribution"[131] to academia and the world.
- Expand graduate programs to 1.5 or 2 years[132,133,134,135,136] with a required practicum for cataloging students.
- Half of the skills needed by catalogers are specifically cataloging-related. Allow students the time to develop these cataloging skills by studying in 1.5 to 2 year specialization tracks that cover a greater percentage of the needed skills.[137,138]
- Revise current courses and add new courses to the curriculum to enhance the students' development of practical skills, while maintaining a strong theoretical foundation.
- Include current practitioners in curriculum development and hire them as adjunct faculty to ensure that the working professional's perspective is present in the students' learning experience. It is only when practitioners' opinions, through guest lecturing, adjunct faculty positions, or inclusion in curriculum development activities, are welcomed into the realm of academia that we can ensure that *all* aspects of bibliographic control education are being addressed.
- Bibliographic control instructors–Keep current!

ENDNOTES

1. See Appendix 1 for the schools included in this study.

2. See the author's "Textbooks Used in Bibliographic Control Education Courses," *Cataloging & Classification Quarterly* 34. no. 2/3 (2002) 103-120, for a brief look at the textbooks used in the various areas of bibliographic control education.

3. Lois Mai Chan, "Instructional Materials Used in Teaching Cataloging and Classification," *Cataloging & Classification Quarterly*, 7, no. 4 (1987): 131-144.

4. Michael Gorman, "library schools.com," *California Libraries* 10, no. 7 (2000): 3.

5. Jodi Lynn Spillane, "Comparison of Required Introductory Cataloging Courses, 1986 to 1998," *Library Resources & Technical Services* 43, no. 4 (1999): 227-228.

6. Roxanne Selberg, "The Teaching of Cataloging in US library schools," *Library Resources & Technical Services* 32, no. 1 (1988): 30-42.

7. Arlene G. Taylor, "A Quarter Century of Cataloging Education," in *Technical Services Management, 1965-1990 A Quarter Century of Change and a Look to the Future. Festschrift for Kathryn Luther Henderson,* eds. Linda C. Smith and Ruth C. Carter, (New York: The Haworth Press, Inc., 1996): 300.

8. Daren Callahan and Judy MacLeod, "Management Issues and the Challenge for Cataloging Education," *Technical Services Quarterly* 13, no. 2 (1996): 15.

9. Magda El-Sherbini and George Klim, "Changes in Technical Services and Their Effect on the Role of Catalogers and Staff Education: An Overview," in *Cataloging and Classification: Trends, Transformations, Teaching, and Training,* eds, James R. Shearer and Alan R. Thomas (New York: Hawthorn Press, 1997).

10. Callahan and MacLeod, "Management Issues," 16-17.

11. Doris H. Clack, "Education for Cataloging: A Symposium Paper," *Cataloging & Classification Quarterly* 16, no. 3 (1993): 30-32.

12. Debra W. Hill, "Requisite Skills of the Entry-Level Cataloger: A Supervisor's Perspective," *Cataloging & Classification Quarterly* 23, no. 3 (1997): 75.

13. Clack, "Education for Cataloging," p. 30-31.

14. Ibid.

15. John J. Riemer, "A Practitioner's View of the Education of Catalogers," *Cataloging & Classification Quarterly* 16, no. 3 (1993): 43.

16. Taylor, "A Quarter Century," p. 303.

17. Jerry D. Saye, "The Cataloging Experience in Library and Information Science Education: An Educator's Perspective," *Cataloging & Classification Quarterly* 7, no. 4 (1987): 27-28.

18. Ibid.

19. Jane B. Robbins, "Educating Cataloging Librarians: Its Art and Craft," in *Recruiting, Educating and Training Cataloging Librarians,* eds. Sheila Intner and Janet Swan Hill, (New York: Greenwood Press, 1989).

20. Callahan and MacLeod, "Management Issues," p. 19.

21. Daren Callahan and Judy MacLeod, "Recruiting and Retention Revisited: A Study of Entry-level Catalogers," *Technical Services Quarterly* 11, no. 4 (1994): 34.

22. LeAnn Garrett, "Dewey, Dale, and Bruner: Educational Philosophy, Experiential Learning, and Library School Cataloging Instruction," *Journal of Education for Library and Information Science* 38, no. 2 (1997): 129-136.

23. Lynn S. Connaway, "Educating Catalogers to Meet the Needs of Diverse Users in a New Technological Environment," *Colorado Libraries* 25, no. 3 (1999): 49.

24. Lynn S. Connaway, "A Model Curriculum for Cataloging Education," *Technical Services Quarterly* 15, no. 1/2 (1997): 37.

25. Judy MacLeod and Daren Callahan, "Educators and Practitioners Reply: As Assessment of Cataloging Education," *Library Resources & Technical Service* 39, no. 2 (1995): 154.

26. Anaclare F. Evans, "The Education of Catalogers: The View of the Practitioner/Educator," *Cataloging & Classification Quarterly* 16, no. 3 (1993): 50-51.

27. Hope A. Olson, "Thinking Professionals: Teaching Critical Cataloging," *Technical Services Quarterly* 15, no. 1/2 (1997): 52.

28. Lisa Romero, "An Analysis of Entry-level Cataloging Errors," *Journal of Education for Library and Information Science* 35, no. 3 (1994): 210.

29. Ellen Zyroff, "Cataloging is a Prime Number," *American Libraries* 27 (1996): 47-48.

30. Evans, "The Education of Catalogers," p. 50-51.

31. Hong Xu, "The Impact of Automation on Job Requirements and Qualifications for Catalogers and Reference Librarians in Academic Libraries," *Library Resources & Technical Services* 40, no. 1 (1996): 25.

32. Seymour Lubetzky, "On Teaching of Cataloging," *Journal of Education for Librarianship* 5, no. 1 (1964): 255-258.

33. Don Fallis and Martin Fricke, "Not by Library School Alone," *Library Journal* 124, no. 17 (1999): 44.

34. "Not by Theory Alone," *Library Journal* 125, no. 3 (2000): 134.

35. John M. Sluk, "James Harold Moon: Cataloger, Teacher, Friend," *Cataloging & Classification Quarterly* 25, no. 2/3 (1998): 209-215.

36. In a quick examination (Feb 2001) of Autocat postings for a two-month period in 2000, there were 64 bibliographic control positions. Of these, 23% were manager/supervisory/department head positions and 77% were not.

37. Riemer, "A Practitioner's View," p. 40.

38. Hill, "Requisite Skills," p. 76.

39. Sheila S. Intner, "Cataloging Practice and Theory: What to Teach and Why," *Journal for Library and Information Science* 30, no. 4 (1990): 333-336.

40. Callahan and MacLeod, "Management Issues," p. 17.

41. Ibid.

42. Connaway, "Educating Catalogers," p. 43-44.

43. Evans, "The Education of Catalogers," p. 50.

44. Hill, "Requisite Skills," p. 72-82.

45. Connaway, "Model Curriculum," p. 29.

46. Connaway, "Educating Catalogers," p. 43-44.

47. Ann O'Neill, "Technical Services Education for the Future," *Technical Services Quarterly* 15, no. 1/2 (1997): 9.

48. Ling Hwey Jeng, "From Cataloging to Organization of Information: A Paradigm for the Core Curriculum," *Journal of Education for Library and Information Science* 34, no. 2 (1993): 114.

49. Kathryn Luther Henderson, "Some Persistent Issues in the Education of Catalogers and Classifiers," *Cataloging & Classification Quarterly* 7, no. 4 (1987): 14. Emphasis added.

50. MacLeod and Callahan, "Educators and Practitioners Reply," p. 155-157.

51. Romero, "An Analysis," p. 210.

52. Michael Gorman, "How Cataloging and Classification Should be Taught," *American Libraries* 23, no. 8 (1992): 694.

53. Judith Hopkins, "Classification and Cataloging Education," *The Bookmark* 47 (1989): 179-82.

54. Romero, "An Analysis," p. 211.

55. Zyroff, "Cataloging is a Prime Number," p. 47-50.

56. Gorman, "library schools.com," 3.

57. Zyroff, "Cataloging is a Prime Number," p. 47-50.

58. Ibid.

59. C. Olivia Frost, "Library Studies at the School of Information," *Library Hi Tech* 16, no. 2 (1998): 97.

60. O'Neill, "Technical Services Education," p. 8-10.

61. Ibid.

62. Nancy J. Williamson, "The Importance of Subject Analysis in Library and Information Science Education," *Technical Services Quarterly* 15, no. 1/2 (1997): 68-69. Emphasis added.

63. Xu, "The Impact of Automation," p. 26.

64. "Educational Policy Statement of the Association for Library Collections & Technical Services," *ALCTS Newsletter* 7, no. 1 (1996): 7-10.

65. See Appendix 2 for the list of core competencies.

66. "Cataloging News," *Cataloging & Classification Quarterly* 7, no. 4 (1987): 167-195.

67. Sherry L. Vellucci, "Cataloging Across the Curriculum: Syndetic Structure for Teaching Cataloging," *Cataloging & Classification Quarterly* 24, no. 1/2 (1997): 44.

68. Further information on this study will be provided later in the paper.

69. Further information on this study will be provided later in the paper.

70. Spillane, "Comparison," p. 227-228.

71. See below for a fuller explanation of the differences between the studies.

72. Vellucci, "Cataloging Across the Curriculum," p. 50-54.

73. This number has decreased in more recent surveys (Spillane with 32% and Joudrey with 29% of schools offering only 1-3 courses). This may be caused by the difference in definitions.

74. See Appendix 2 for the list of core competencies.

75. Callahan and MacLeod, "Recruiting," p. 34.

76. Callahan and MacLeod, "Management Issues," p. 19.

77. Taylor, "A Quarter Century," p. 301.

78. Jerry D. Saye, "Education for Technical Services: A Summary of the Symposium," *Cataloging & Classification Quarterly* 16, no. 3 (1993): 127-133.

79. MacLeod and Callahan, "Educators and Practitioners Reply," p. 157.

80. Zyroff, "Cataloging is a Prime Number," p. 48.

81. Callahan and MacLeod, "Management Issues," p. 20-21.

82. Evans, "The Education of Catalogers," p. 50.

83. Callahan and MacLeod, "Management Issues," p. 20-21.

84. Clack, "Education for Cataloging," p. 30-35.

85. Frost, "Library Studies," p. 97.

86. Riemer, "A Practitioner's View," p. 43.

87. Romero, "An Analysis," p. 221-225.

88. Connaway, "Model Curriculum," p. 31.

89. Connaway, "Educating Catalogers," p. 43-44.

90. Clack, "Education for Cataloging," p. 30-35

91. Evans, "The Education of Catalogers," p. 50.

92. Saye, "The Cataloging Experience," p. 33-42.

93. Callahan and MacLeod, "Recruiting," p. 34.

94. Callahan and MacLeod, "Management Issues," p. 19.

95. Williamson, "The Importance of Subject Analysis," p. 68.

96. Ibid, p. 84.

97. Vellucci, "Cataloging Across the Curriculum," p. 45.

98. Spillane, "Comparison," p. 228.

99. "Cataloging News," *Cataloging & Classification Quarterly* 7, no. 4 (1994): 167-195.

100. See Appendix 1 for the list of schools included in the study.

101. Spillane, "Comparison," p. 228.

102. Ibid.

103. "Cataloging News," p. 167-195.

104. This section covers required courses in general and also contains sub-sections describing individual types of required course. Following, there is a section for elective courses. These categories are not mutually exclusive. Some courses might be placed in either category depending upon the school.

105. Vellucci, "Cataloging Across the Curriculum," p. 45.

106. Spillane, "Comparison," p. 229.

107. Ibid.

108. "Cataloging News," p. 167-195.

109. Vellucci, "Cataloging Across the Curriculum," p. 45.

110. Spillane, "Comparison," p. 229.

111. Vellucci, "Cataloging Across the Curriculum," p. 45.

112. "Cataloging News," p. 167-195.

113. Spillane, "Comparison," p. 229.

114. Vellucci, "Cataloging Across the Curriculum," p. 47.

115. "Cataloging News," p. 167-195.

116. Spillane, "Comparison," p. 229.

117. "Cataloging News," p. 167-195.

118. Spillane, "Comparison," p. 229.

119. "Cataloging News," p. 167-195.

120. Vellucci, "Cataloging Across the Curriculum," p. 49.

121. "Cataloging News," p. 167-195.

122. Spillane, "Comparison," p. 229.

123. Ibid.

124. "Cataloging News," p. 167-195.

125. Ibid.

126. Spillane, "Comparison," p. 229.

127. Vellucci, "Cataloging Across the Curriculum," p. 49.

128. "Cataloging News," p. 167-195.

129. As mentioned earlier, in a quick scan of two months of Autocat postings, 64 positions were advertised. If this rate were consistent, in one year approximately 384 cataloging positions would be advertised in this venue alone. A more structured investigation of this topic should be conducted.

130. Williamson, "The Importance of Subject Analysis," p. 84.

131. Robbins, "Educating Cataloging Librarians."

132. Clack, "Education for Cataloging," p. 30-35.

133. Evans, "The Education of Catalogers," p. 50.

134. Riemer, "A Practitioner's View," p. 43.

135. Saye, "The Cataloging Experience," p. 33-42.

136. Arlene T. Dowell, "The Two-Year Master's: Perspectives and Prospects," *Journal of Education for Librarianship* 18, no. 4 (1978): 333-334.

137. Ibid.

138. See Appendix 3 and Table 21 for a proposed fantasy curriculum.

APPENDIX 1. Schools Included in This Survey

Alphabetical by State

1. University of Alabama
2. University of Arizona
3. San Jose State University (CA)
4. University of California, Los Angeles
5. Southern Connecticut State University
6. The Catholic University of America (DC)
7. Florida State University
8. University of South Florida
9. Clark Atlanta University (GA)
10. University of Hawaii
11. Dominican University (IL)
12. University of Illinois at Urbana-Champaign
13. Indiana University
14. University of Iowa
15. Emporia State University (KS)
16. University of Kentucky
17. Louisiana State University
18. University of Maryland
19. Simmons College (MA)
20. University of Michigan
21. Wayne State University (MI)
22. University of Southern Mississippi
23. University of Missouri-Columbia
24. Rutgers University (NJ)
25. Long Island University (NY)
26. Pratt Institute (NY)
27. Queens College (NY)
28. St. John's University (NY)
29. Syracuse University (NY)
30. University at Albany (NY)
31. University at Buffalo (NY)
32. North Carolina Central University
33. University of North Carolina at Chapel Hill
34. University of North Carolina at Greensboro
35. Kent State University (OH)
36. University of Oklahoma
37. Clarion University of Pennsylvania (PA)
38. Drexel University (PA)
39. University of Pittsburgh (PA)
40. University of Rhode Island
41. University of South Carolina
42. University of Tennessee
43. Texas Woman's University
44. University of North Texas
45. University of Texas at Austin
46. University of Washington
47. University of Wisconsin-Madison
48. University of Wisconsin-Milwaukee

Excluded: University of Puerto Rico—no responses, no web pages

APPENDIX 2. ALCTS Educational Policy Statement

List of Knowledge and Skills for Catalogers
in the Area of Intellectual Access
and Information Organization

1. Knowledge of information seeking behaviors of user groups;

2. Knowledge of the activities that must be performed to provide the products and services users need;

3. Knowledge of the theory of information organization and intellectual access, including relevant national and international standards;

4. Knowledge of the theory and methods of subject analysis, including thesaurus creation, indexing, and classification;

5. Knowledge of the theory and methods for describing, identifying, and showing relationships among materials;

6. Ability to develop and apply syndetic structure and controlled vocabulary in information retrieval systems;

7. Knowledge of the theoretical basis for retrieval and how searching techniques and data structures affect precision and recall;

8. Knowledge of bibliographic relationships underlying database design;

9. Knowledge of cataloging tools and sources of bibliographic records and how to use them;

10. Knowledge of the operations of other parts of the employing organization and how they relate to providing intellectual access to information resources;

11. Ability to evaluate information retrieval systems in relation to user needs and information seeking behaviors;

12. Knowledge of basic database design and database management concepts;

13. Knowledge of principles and methods for planning and designing user-driven information retrieval systems; and,

14. Knowledge of state-of-the-art research and practice in this area.

APPENDIX 3. Proposed Cataloging Specialization Track

TABLE 21. Curriculum

Course Number	Course Name	Required?	Prerequisites
2001	Organization of Information	I	None
2400	Controlled Vocabularies & Thesaurus Construction	X	2001
2401	Indexing and Abstracting		2001
2410	Basic Cataloging: Description	X	2001
2411	Basic Cataloging: Access and Authority Control	X	2410
2420	Cataloging and Classification of Non-book Materials		2411
2421	Cataloging Internet Resources and Metadata		2411
2430	Classification Theory & Systems	X	2001
2431	Dewey Decimal Classification and Library of Congress Classification: An in-depth study		2430
2432	Subject Analysis	X	2400 & 2430
2440	Practicum	X	2411 & 2432
2445	Technical Services and Catalog Management	X	2440
2455	Special Topics: International Classification Schemes		2430
2450	Special Topics: Issues*		2432 & 2411
2460	Cataloging and Classification in School/Small Libraries	£	2001
2470	Organizing in Museums and Archives	XX	2001

I For all students   *Changes every semester
X For all Cataloging students   XX For all Archives/Museum studies students
£ For all school library students

Highlights:

- Basic Cataloging should be divided into the areas of subject work and description.

- Descriptive cataloging will be divided into a semester of description and a semester of access and authority work.

- Subject Analysis (which should be taken only after prerequisite courses on Controlled Vocabularies and Thesauri Construction and on Classification Theory and Systems) is a course focused on practical application with lab sessions required.

- Cataloging and Classification in School/Small Libraries, too, can be a "hands-on" course that will focus on the needs of schools and other small libraries.

- Classification Theory & Systems will begin with an interdisciplinary approach with topics ranging from the natural sciences to philosophy and will end with an exploration of bibliographic classification.

- An in-depth course on the Dewey Decimal and Library of Congress classification schemes can be created.

- For those interested in international librarianship, there can be a seminar exploring UDC, Colon, Bliss, and other classification systems in use around the world.

- For archives and museum students, a course in organizing in those arenas could be developed.

- Technical Services and Catalog Management will be offered to prepare students for administrative responsibilities. It may be taken only after the required practicum has been completed.

These courses are the foundation of this author's fantasy bibliographic control specialization. While it would not be practical, it would be tremendously fun.

Textbooks Used in Bibliographic Control Education Courses

Daniel N. Joudrey

SUMMARY. As part of the study reported in this paper, the usage of textbooks in bibliographic control education was also examined. This information, which is presented in the following sixteen tables (see the Appendix), was obtained by analyzing the Web sites of the 48 ALA-accredited LIS schools in the United States, excluding only the program at the University of Puerto Rico. The course description and the syllabus for each course were examined to determine the textbooks used. If a current syllabus was not available on the Web, the school's cataloging faculty was contacted by e-mail. In a few cases, telephone interviews were conducted to obtain the needed information. Data collection occurred between September 14, 2000 and February 12, 2001.

Daniel N. Joudrey, MLIS, has begun a doctoral program at the University of Pittsburgh. This paper was written to fulfill a requirement for a doctoral seminar in the organization of information held by Dr. Arlene G. Taylor (E-mail: djoudrey@mail.sis.pitt.edu).

The author wishes to thank Dr. Arlene G. Taylor, Harry M. Field, Bryan Carson, Judith Silva, Jen-Chien Yu, and Jesús Alonso Regalado for their support.

Editor's note: This paper was originally created as an appendix to Joudrey's paper "A New Look at US Graduate Courses in Bibliographic Control" (immediately preceding). The Editor considered information in the appendix important enough to stand on its own, and feared that as an appendix, it might be overlooked both by readers and indexing services. With the author's permission, therefore, the former "Appendix 4" is presented here as a separate paper.

[Haworth co-indexing entry note]: "Textbooks Used in Bibliographic Control Education Courses." Joudrey, Daniel N. Co-published simultaneously in *Cataloging & Classification Quarterly* (The Haworth Information Press, an imprint of The Haworth Press, Inc.) Vol. 34, No. 1/2, 2002, pp. 103-120; and: *Education for Cataloging and the Organization of Information: Pitfalls and the Pendulum* (ed: Janet Swan Hill) The Haworth Information Press, an imprint of The Haworth Press, Inc., 2002, pp. 103-120. Single or multiple copies of this article are available for a fee from The Haworth Document Delivery Service [1-800-HAWORTH, 9:00 a.m. - 5:00 p.m. (EST). E-mail address: getinfo@haworthpressinc.com].

From the 48 schools in this survey, it was found that 92 individual textbook titles were being used in ALA-accredited US graduate schools in the area of bibliographic control education. The total number of textbooks required for all the courses was 422 (a figure that is made up of these 92 individual titles). This averages to 8.79 bibliographic control textbooks per school or 2.12 textbooks per course. *[Article copies available for a fee from The Haworth Document Delivery Service: 1-800-HAWORTH. E-mail address: <getinfo@haworthpressinc.com> Website: <http://www.HaworthPress. com> © 2002 by The Haworth Press, Inc. All rights reserved.]*

KEYWORDS. Textbooks, cataloging education, classification, library education, bibliographic control courses

Table 1 shows the 20 highest-ranking textbooks for all of the bibliographic control courses from the current study. These texts can then be compared with the textbooks listed in Lois Mai Chan's 1987 article, the first seven of which are listed in Table 2. Chan goes on to list 26 more texts that were used in four or fewer courses.[1] Comparing the two tables, there are some similarities in the top ranking books; the notable omissions being texts not yet written at the time of Chan's article. Table 3 lists the textbooks cited in Chan's 1987 survey that do not appear in the current study.

In the remainder of this paper there is a breakdown of the textbooks used in each area of bibliographic control. Looking at Table 4: Textbooks for Required Courses, Arlene G. Taylor's *Organization of Information* is used in 22 (42%) of the 52 required bibliographic control courses (or those courses that may fulfill this type of requirement). Of all the books in this survey (i.e., for all bibliographic control courses), this textbook is used more than any other, save for *The Anglo-American Cataloging Rules, Second Edition*. The second most frequently used text in required courses is, unsurprisingly, *The Anglo-American Cataloging Rules, Second Edition*. It is used in 17 required courses (32.69%). The full list of the 31 texts used in required courses appears in Table 4, in order of usage.

The 4 textbooks used for organizing information courses are shown in Table 5. Column 3 contains the number of courses for which the text is used when including all organizing information courses. The fourth column is the number for required organizing courses only. The fifth shows the number of elective courses using the textbook. In columns four and five, the ranking for each textbook is enclosed in the parentheses after the raw number. The last column shows the percentage of organizing courses for which the text is used.

Table 6 lists the 31 textbooks used for basic cataloging courses. Unsurprisingly, *The Anglo-American Cataloging Rules, Second Edition* is in first place. Indeed, what may be more surprising is that only 31 of the 43 basic cataloging courses (72.09%) use *AACR2* or that the *Library of Congress Rule Interpretations* are not mentioned at all. Second place (39.53%) belongs to Lois Mai Chan's *Cataloging and Classification*. Ranked third is Arlene Taylor's *Wynar's Introduction to Cataloging and Classification*. The fourth slot is filled with another recent, updated edition, Saye's *Manheimer's Cataloging and Classification* (22.50%). Also in fourth, somewhat surprisingly, is *The Organization of Information* by Taylor. This is surprising only because the focus of this work is broader than traditional cataloging and classification, and is used more often in organizing courses, as seen in the preceding table.

Table 7 contains the 16 texts used in technical services courses. Unlike the other areas above, this table shows no dominant textbook being used in the area of technical services courses. The most frequently listed text is used in only four courses.

Table 8 contains the 18 textbooks used in advanced cataloging courses. Again, *The Anglo-American Cataloging Rules, Second Edition* is the highest-ranking text, being used in 65.51% of the classes. In six of the advanced cataloging courses (20.69%), the instructor assigns no textbook, using a variety of readings instead.

There are 19 textbooks used in subject courses (see Table 9). A. C. Foskett's *Subject Approach to Information* places first, being used in 60% of the subject courses. Chan's book on subject headings ranks second with four courses. Her book on the Library of Congress Classification tied for third with Thomas Mann's classic, *Library Research Models*. Fifth place is shared by Bobby Ferguson's workbook on subject analysis, Eric Hunter's *Classification Made Simple,* and *Wynar's Introduction to Cataloging and Classification* by Arlene G. Taylor. Surprisingly, Saye's new edition of *Manheimer's Cataloging and Classification* is not on the list, yet *The Anglo-American Cataloging Rules* is.

Unsurprisingly, *The Anglo-American Cataloging Rules, Second Edition* is at the top of the list of texts for descriptive cataloging courses (see Table 10). Nearly all of these courses use it; however only 40% of the courses use it in conjunction with the *Library of Congress Rule Interpretations*.

A plurality of the courses (three out of seven courses) uses no textbook at all for classification theory, relying instead on a variety of readings. Perhaps this is due to the interdisciplinary nature of classification. As can be seen from Table 11, there, too, is no definitive text for this type of course.

Of the textbooks used for teaching non-book cataloging courses, *The Anglo-American Cataloging Rules, Second Edition* and Ingrid Hsieh-Yee's recent *Organizing Audiovisual and Electronic Resources For Access: A Cataloging Guide* are tied for first place, each being used in three courses. Nancy Olson's *Cataloging of Audiovisual Materials & Other Special Materials* is in the third spot (see Table 12).

From Table 13 it is clear that textbooks for Internet resources cataloging are limited and none, so far, have taken the lead in usage. Surprisingly, Nancy Olson's *Cataloging Internet Resources: A Manual And Practical Guide* is not listed.

Those familiar with indexing education will not be surprised by the results in Table 14, which lists twelve textbooks. Lancaster's *Indexing and Abstracting in Theory and Practice* holds the first position with a substantial lead (58.97%). Mulvaney's *Indexing Books* (which focuses on back-of-the-book indexing) is in second place. It is often used in conjunction with Lancaster, Cleveland and Cleveland, or O'Connor.

There were no surprising results found in the list of the eight texts used in thesaurus construction/controlled vocabulary courses, other than the fact that both Dagobert Soergel's and F. W. Lancaster's remarkable books have been out-of-print for a number of years (see Table 15). In the list, *Thesaurus Construction and Use* by Aitchison, Bawden, and Gilchrist is ranked first. It is used in half of the eight courses. Lancaster is second with three courses and Soergel is third.

For the music cataloging course, Richard Smiraglia's two books on the subject, *Music Cataloging: The Bibliographic Control of Printed and Recorded Music in Libraries* and *Describing Music Materials: A Manual for Use with AACR2 and APPM*, are used as primary texts. For the cataloging technology courses, only two textbooks are listed for this area; each used in one of the courses. The other two courses use no textbook. The two used for Cataloging Technology are Byrne's *MARC Manual: Understanding and Using MARC Records* and Evans and Heft's *Introduction to Technical Services*.

The last two tables present all ninety-two textbooks used in bibliographic control education courses. Table 16 presents them alphabetically. Table 17 presents them by usage.

ENDNOTE

1. Lois Mai Chan. "Instructional Materials Used in Teaching Cataloging and Classification." *Cataloging & Classification Quarterly*, 7, no. 4 (1987): 134.

APPENDIX

TABLE 1. Top Twenty Texts Ranked by Usage

Author	Title	Usage
ALA	*The Anglo-American Cataloging Rules, Second Edition*	62
	No Text–Various Readings*	33
Taylor	*The Organization Of Information*	31
Taylor	*Wynar's Introduction To Cataloging And Classification*	29
Chan	*Cataloging And Classification: An Introduction*	26
Lancaster	*Indexing And Abstracting In Theory And Practice*	24
Chan	*A Guide To The Library Of Congress Classification*	9
Chan	*Library Of Congress Subject Headings: Principles And Application*	9
Furrie	*Understanding MARC*	9
Mulvaney	*Indexing Books*	9
Saye	*Manheimer's Cataloging And Classification*	9
Mann	*Library Research Models*	8
Hsieh-Yee	*Organizing Audiovisual And Electronic Resources For Access: A Cataloging Guide*	7
Svenonius	*The Intellectual Foundation Of Information Organization*	7
Cleveland & Cleveland	*Introduction To Indexing And Abstracting*	6
Foskett	*The Subject Approach To Information*	6
Gorman	*The Concise AACR2*	6
Hagler	*The Bibliographic Record And Information*	6
Maxwell and Maxwell	*Maxwell's Handbook For AACR2*	6
O'Connor	*Explorations In Indexing And Abstracting: Pointing, Virtue And Power*	6

*This heading is used throughout the tables. It indicates when no textbook at all was being used, not just when other readings were assigned. While "No text" is not a textbook, this author felt it was important to know how popular this option was with faculty and where it falls in the rankings.

TABLE 2. Chan's Top Seven Textbooks

Author	Title	Usage
ALA	*The Anglo-American Cataloging Rules, Second Edition*	10+
Chan	*Cataloging And Classification: An Introduction*	10+
Taylor	*Wynar's Introduction To Cataloging And Classification*	10+
Chan	*A Guide To The Library Of Congress Classification*	5-9
Chan	*Library Of Congress Subject Headings: Principles And Application*	5-9
Foskett	*The Subject Approach To Information*	5-9
Maxwell and Maxwell	*Maxwell's Handbook For AACR2*	5-9

APPENDIX (continued)

TABLE 3. Textbooks Cited in Chan's 1987 Survey Not Appearing in the Current Study

Author	Title
Akers	*Simple Library Cataloging*
Carpenter and Svenonius	*Foundations of Cataloging*
Comaromi	*Manual on the Use of the Dewey Decimal Classification*
Dykstra	*PRECIS: A primer*
Herdman	*Classification*
Manheimer	*OCLC: An Introduction*
Miller and Terwilligar	*Commonsense Cataloging*
Osborn, A.D.	*Serial Publications*
Osborn, J.	*Dewey Decimal Classification, 19th Edition: A Study Manual*
Rogers	*Non-print Cataloging for Multimedia Collections*
Weihs	*Non-book Materials: The Organization of Integrated Collections*

TABLE 4. Textbooks for Required Courses

Rank	Author, Title	Usage	% of Required Courses (n/52)
1	Taylor, *The Organization of Information*	22	42.30%
2	*The Anglo-American Cataloging Rules, Second Edition*	17	32.69%
3	Taylor, *Wynar's Introduction to Cataloging and Classification*	13	25.00%
4	Chan, *Cataloging and Classification: An Introduction*	12	23.08%
5	Furrie, *Understanding MARC*	5	9.62%
	Hagler, *The Bibliographic Record and Information Technology*	5	9.62%
	Mann, *Library Research Models*	5	9.62%
	Saye, *Manheimer's Cataloging and Classification*	5	9.62%
	Svenonius, *The Intellectual Foundation of Information Organization*	5	9.62%
10	Gorman, M., *The Concise AACR2*	4	7.69%
	No textbook/Various Readings	4	7.69%
12	Intner and Weihs, *Standard Cataloging for School and Public Libraries*	2	3.85%
	Maxwell and Maxwell, *Maxwell's Handbook for AACR2R*	2	3.85%
	Rowley, *Organizing Knowledge: An Introduction to Information Retrieval*	2	3.85%
15	*ALA Filing Rules*	1	1.92%
	Anderson and Perez-Carballo, *Information Retrieval Database Design*	1	1.92%
	Couch, *Information Technologies and Social Orders*	1	1.92%
	Evans and Heft, *Introduction to Technical Services*	1	1.92%
	Evans, *Developing Library and Information Center Collections*	1	1.92%
	Ferguson, *MARC/AACR2 Workbook*	1	1.92%

Rank	Author, Title	Usage	% of Required Courses (n/52)
	Ferguson, *Subject Analysis Workbook*	1	1.92%
	Fritz, *Cataloging with AACR2 and USMARC*	1	1.92%
	Harkness Connell and Maxwell (eds.), *The Future of Cataloging: Insights from the Lubetzky Symposium*	1	1.92%
	Hsieh-Yee, *Organizing Audiovisual and Electronic Resources for Access: A Cataloging Guide*	1	1.92%
	Hunter, *Classification Made Simple*	1	1.92%
	Intner and Weihs, *Special Libraries: A Cataloging Guide*	1	1.92%
	Katzer, Cook and Crouch (eds.), *Evaluating Information*	1	1.92%
	Mortimer, *Learn Dewey Decimal Classification*	1	1.92%
	O'Connor, *Explorations in Indexing and Abstracting*	1	1.92%
	Piepenburg, *Easy MARC*	1	1.92%
	Rosenfeld and Morville, *Information Architecture for the World Wide Web*	1	1.92%

TABLE 5. Textbooks for Organizing Courses

Rank	Author, Title	Usage in All Org. Courses (n = 29)	Req. Only (Rank) (n = 24)	Elect. Only (Rank) (n = 5)	% of Org. Courses
1	Taylor, *The Organization of Information*	15	14(1)	1(2)	51.72%
2	No textbook/Various Readings	5	2(7)	3(1)	17.24%
3	Hagler, *The Bibliographic Record and Information Technology*	4	4(2)	0	13.79%
	Mann, *Library Research Models*	4	4(2)	0	13.79%
5	Chan, *Cataloging and Classification: An Introduction*	3	3(4)	0	10.34%
	Svenonius, *The Intellectual Foundation of Information Organization*	3	3(4)	0	10.34%
	Taylor, *Wynar's Introduction to Cataloging and Classification*	3	3(4)	0	10.34%
	Rowley, *Organizing Knowledge: An Introduction to Information Retrieval*	3	2(7)	1(2)	10.34%
9	*The Anglo-American Cataloging Rules, Second Edition*	2	2(7)	0	6.90%
	Furrie, *Understanding MARC*	2	2(7)	0	6.90%
11	Anderson and Perez-Carballo, *Information Retrieval Database Design*	1	1(11)	0	3.45%
	Couch, *Information Technologies and Social Orders*	1	1(11)	0	3.45%
	Evans, *Developing Library and Information Center Collections*	1	1(11)	0	3.45%
	Gorman, M., *The Concise AACR2*	1	1(11)	0	3.45%
	Katzer, Cook and Crouch (eds.), *Evaluating Information*	1	1(11)	0	3.45%
	Maxwell and Maxwell, *Maxwell's Handbook for AACR2R*	1	1(11)	0	3.45%
	Rosenfeld & Morville, *Information Architecture for the World Wide Web*	1	0	1(2)	3.45%
	Rowley & Farrow, *Organizing Knowledge: An Introduction to Managing Access to Information*	1	0	1(2)	3.45%

APPENDIX (continued)

TABLE 6. Textbooks for Basic Cataloging Courses

Rank	Author, Title	Usage in Basic Cat. (n = 43)	Req. Only Basic (Rank) (n = 21)	Elect. Only (Rank) (n = 22)	% of Basic Catalog Courses
1	*The Anglo-American Cataloging Rules, Second Edition*	31	13(1)	18(1)	72.09%
2	Chan, *Cataloging and Classification: An Introduction*	17	8(2)	9(2)	39.53%
3	Taylor, *Wynar's Introduction to Cataloging and Classification*	16	8(2)	8(3)	37.21%
4	Saye, *Manheimer's Cataloging and Classification*	9	5(5)	4(4)	20.93%
	Taylor, *The Organization of Information*	9	7(4)	2(6)	20.93%
6	Furrie, *Understanding MARC*	4	2(6)	2(6)	9.30%
	Maxwell and Maxwell, *Maxwell's Handbook for AACR2*	4	1(9)	3(5)	9.30%
8	Svenonius, *The Intellectual Foundation of Information Organization*	3	2(6)	1(8)	6.98%
9	Gorman, *The Concise AACR2*	2	2(6)	0	4.65%
	Hagler, *The Bibliographic Record and Information Technology*	2	1(9)	1(8)	4.65%
	Hsieh-Yee, *Organizing Audiovisual and Electronic Resources for Access: A Cataloging Guide*	2	1(9)	1(8)	4.65%
	Intner and Weihs, *Standard Cataloging for School and Public Libraries*	2	1(9)	1(8)	4.65%
	Piepenburg, *Easy MARC*	2	1(9)	1(8)	4.65%
14	*ALA Filing Rules*	1	1(9)	0	2.32%
	Chan, *A Guide to the Library of Congress Classification*	1	0	1(8)	2.32%
	Chan, *Dewey Decimal Classification: A Practical Guide*	1	0	1(8)	2.32%
	Chan, *Library of Congress Subject Headings: Principles and Application*	1	0	1(8)	2.32%
	Ferguson, *MARC/AACR2 Workbook*	1	1(9)	0	2.32%
	Ferguson, *Subject Analysis Workbook*	1	1(9)	0	2.32%
	Fritz, *Cataloging with AACR2 and USMARC*	1	1(9)	0	2.32%
	Frost, *Media Access and Organization*	1	0	1(8)	2.32%
	Harkness Connell, *The Future of Cataloging: Insights from the Lubetzky Symposium*	1	1(9)	0	2.32%
	Intner and Weihs, *Special Libraries: A Cataloging Guide*	1	1(9)	0	2.32%
	LC Classification Outline	1	0	1(8)	2.32%
	LC, *Cataloging Concepts: Descriptive Cataloging: Trainee's Manual*	1	0	1(8)	2.32%
	Mann, *Library Research Models*	1	0	1(8)	2.32%
	Miksa, Manuscript	1	0	1(8)	2.32%
	Mortimer, *Learn Dewey Decimal Classification*	1	1(9)	0	2.32%
	O'Connor, *Explorations in Indexing and Abstracting*	1	1(9)	0	2.32%
	Olson, *Cataloging of Audiovisual Materials and Other Special Materials*	1	0	1(8)	2.32%
	Rosenfeld & Morville, *Information Architecture for the World Wide Web*	1	1(9)	0	2.32%

TABLE 7. Textbooks for Technical Services Courses

Rank	Author, Title	Usage in TS (n = 12)	Req. Only (rank) (n = 5)	Elect. Only (rank) (n = 7)	% of TS Courses
1	Evans and Heft, *Introduction to Technical Services*	4	1(3)	3(1)	33.33%
2	Gorman, *Technical Services Today and Tomorrow*	3	1(3)	2(3)	25%
	No textbook/Various Readings	3	0	3(1)	25%
4	*The Anglo-American Cataloging Rules, Second Edition*	2	2(1)	0	16.67%
	Taylor, *Wynar's Introduction to Cataloging and Classification*	2	2(1)	0	16.67%
6	Chan, *Cataloging and Classification: An Introduction*	1	1(3)	0	8.33%
	Furrie, *Understanding MARC*	1	1(3)	0	8.33%
	Godden, *Library Technical Services*	1	0	1(4)	8.33%
	Gorman, *The Concise AACR2*	1	1(3)	0	8.33%
	Intner and Weihs, *Standard Cataloging for School and Public Libraries*	1	1(3)	0	8.33%
	Johnson, *New Directions in Technical Services*	1	0	1(4)	8.33%
	Kaplan, *Planning and Implementing Technical Services Workstations*	1	0	1(4)	8.33%
	Schmidt, *Understanding the Business of Library Acquisitions*	1	0	1(4)	8.33%
	Smith and Carter, *Technical Services Management, 1965-1990*	1	0	1(4)	8.33%
	Taylor, *The Organization of Information*	1	1(3)	0	8.33%
	Wilson and Colver, *Outsourcing Library Technical Services Operations*	1	0	1(4)	8.33%

TABLE 8. Textbooks for Advanced Cataloging Courses

Rank	Author, Title	Usage in Adv. Cat. (n = 29)	% of Adv. Cat.
1	*The Anglo-American Cataloging Rules, Second Edition*	19	65.52%
2	No Textbook/Various Readings	6	20.69%
3	Chan, *A Guide to the Library of Congress Classification*	5	17.24%
4	Chan, *Library of Congress Subject Headings: Principles and Application*	4	13.79%
5	Taylor, *Wynar's Introduction to Cataloging and Classification*	3	10.34%
	Chan, *Cataloging and Classification: An Introduction*	3	10.34%
	Taylor, *The Organization of Information*	3	10.34%
8	Fecko, *Cataloging Nonbook Resources. How-To-Do-It Manuals for Libraries, no. 31*	1	3.44%
	Furrie, *Understanding MARC*	1	3.44%

APPENDIX (continued)

TABLE 8 (continued)

Rank	Author, Title	Usage in Adv. Cat. (n = 29)	% of Adv. Cat.
	Gorman, *The Concise AACR2*	1	3.44%
	Harkness Connell and Maxwell, *The Future of Cataloging: Insights from the Lubetzky Symposium*	1	3.44%
	Hsieh-Yee, *Organizing Audiovisual and Electronic Resources for Access: A Cataloging Guide*	1	3.44%
	Intner and Weihs, *Special Libraries: A Cataloging Guide*	1	3.44%
	Maxwell and Maxwell, *Maxwell's Handbook for AACR2*	1	3.44%
	Olson, *Cataloging Internet Resources: A Manual and Practical Guide*	1	3.44%
	Olson, *Cataloging of Audiovisual and other Special Materials*	1	3.44%
	Svenonius, *The Intellectual Foundation of Information Organization*	1	3.44%
	Yee & Layne, *Improving OPACs*	1	3.44%

TABLE 9. Textbooks for Subject Courses

Rank	Author, Title	Usage in Subj. (n = 29)	% of Subject Courses
1	Foskett, *The Subject Approach to Information*	6	60%
2	Chan, *Library of Congress Subject Headings: Principles and Application*	4	40%
3	Chan, *A Guide to the Library of Congress Classification*	3	30%
	Mann, *Library Research Models*	3	30%
5	Ferguson, *Subject Cataloging: Blitz Cataloging Workbook*	2	20%
	Hunter, *Classification Made Simple*	2	20%
	Taylor, *Wynar's Introduction to Cataloging and Classification*	2	20%
8	*The Anglo-American Cataloging Rules, Second Edition*	1	10%
	Bowker and Star, *Sorting Things Out*	1	10%
	Buchanan, *Theory of Library Classification*	1	10%
	Chan, Richmond, & Svenonius, *Theory of Subject Analysis: A Sourcebook*	1	10%
	Ferl and Millsap, *Subject Cataloging: A How to Do It Workbook*	1	10%
	Lancaster, *Indexing and Abstracting in Theory and Practice*	1	10%
	Langridge, *Classification: Its Kinds, Elements, Systems And Applications*	1	10%
	Mann, *Oxford Guide to Library Research*	1	10%
	Ranganathan, *Classified Catalogue Code*	1	10%
	Stone, *The LCSH Century: One Hundred Years With the Library of Congress Subject Headings System*	1	10%
	Taylor, *The Organization of Information*	1	10%
	Thomas, *Classification: Options and Opportunities*	1	10%

TABLE 10. Textbooks for Descriptive Cataloging Courses

Rank	Author, Title	Usage in Desc (n = 5)	% of Desc. Cat. Courses
1	*The Anglo-American Cataloging Rules, Second Edition*	4	80%
2	*Library of Congress Rule Interpretations*	2	40%
3	Baca, *Introduction to Metadata: Pathways to Digital Information*	1	20%
	Hudgins, Agnew & Brown, *Getting Mileage out of Metadata: Applications for the Library*	1	20%
	No text	1	20%
	Schottlaender, *The Future of the Descriptive Cataloging Rules: Papers from the ALCTS Preconference, AACR2000*	1	20%
	Taylor, *Wynar's Introduction to Cataloging and Classification*	1	20%

TABLE 11. Textbooks for Classification Theory Courses

Rank	Author, Title	Usage in Class. (n = 7)	% of Class. Courses
1	No textbook/Various Readings	3	42.86 %
2	Bowker & Star, *Sorting Things Out*	1	14.29%
	Chan, *Cataloging and Classification*	1	14.29%
	Iyer, *Classificatory Structures*	1	14.29%
	Marcella & Newton, *A New Manual of Classification*	1	14.29%
	Lakoff, *Women, Fire, and Dangerous Things: What Categories Reveal About the Mind*	1	14.29%

TABLE 12. Textbooks for Non-Book Cataloging Courses

Rank	Author, Title	Usage in Non-book (n = 7)	% of Non-book Courses
1	*The Anglo-American Cataloging Rules, Second Edition*	3	42.86%
	Hsieh-Yee, *Organizing Audiovisual And Electronic Resources for Access: A Cataloging Guide*	3	42.86%
3	Olson, *Cataloging Of Audiovisual Materials & Other Special Materials*	2	28.57%
4	ALA, *Guidelines For Bibliographic Description Of Reproduction*	1	14.29%
	Bosch, *Guide To Collecting CD-ROMs*	1	14.29%
	Ferguson, *Nonprint Materials Workbook*	1	14.29%
	Frost, *Media Access And Organization: A Cataloging And Reference Sources Guide For Nonbook Materials*	1	14.29%
	Furrie, *Understanding MARC*	1	14.29%
	Gorman, *The Concise AACR2*	1	14.29%
	Intner, *Subject Access To Films & Videos*	1	14.29%

APPENDIX (continued)

TABLE 12 (continued)

Rank	Author, Title	Usage in Non-book (n = 7)	% of Non-book Courses
	Library of Congress Rule Interpretations	1	14.29%
	Olson, *Cataloging Internet Resources: A Manual And Practical Guide*	1	14.29%
	Taylor, *Wynar's Introduction To Cataloging And Classification*	1	14.29%
	Taylor, *The Organization Of Information*	1	14.29%
	Urbanski, *Cataloging Unpublished Nonprint Materials*	1	14.29%
	No Textbook	1	14.29%

TABLE 13. Textbooks for Internet Cataloging/Metadata Courses

Rank	Author, Title	Usage (n = 5)	%
1	Hudgins, Agnew, & Brown, *Getting Mileage Out Of Metadata: Applications For The Library*	2	40%
	Baca, *Introduction To Metadata: Pathways To Digital Information*	2	40%
	No Text	2	40%
4	Hsieh-Yee, *Organizing Audiovisual and Electronic Resources for Access: A Cataloging Guide*	1	20%
	Taylor, *The Organization Of Information*	1	20%

TABLE 14. Textbooks for Indexing Courses

Rank	Author, Title	Usage in Indexing (n = 39)	% of Indexing
1	Lancaster, *Indexing and Abstracting in Theory And Practice*	23	58.97%
2	Mulvaney, *Indexing Books*	9	23.08%
3	No Textbook	7	17.95%
4	Cleveland and Cleveland, *Introduction to Indexing and Abstracting*	6	15.38%
5	O'Connor, *Explorations in Indexing and Abstracting*	5	12.82%
6	Wellisch, *Indexing from A to Z*	4	10.25%
7	Fetters, *Handbook of Indexing Techniques: A Guide for Beginning Indexers*	2	5.13%
8	Lancaster, *Vocabulary Control for Information Retrieval*	1	2.56%
	Meadow, Boyce & Kraft, *Text Information Retrieval Systems*	1	2.56%
	Milstead, *Subject Access Systems: Alternatives In Design*	1	2.56%
	Soergel, *Organizing Information Principles of Database and Retrieval Systems*	1	2.56%
	Weinberg, *Indexing: The State of our Knowledge and the State of our Ignorance*	1	2.56%

TABLE 15. Textbooks for Thesaurus Construction Courses

Rank	Author, Title	Usage in Thesaurus (n = 8)	% of Thesaurus
1	Aitchison, Bawden, & Gilchrist, *Thesaurus Construction and Use: A Practical Manual*	4	50%
2	Lancaster, *Vocabulary Control for Information Retrieval*	3	37.5%
3	Soergel, *Indexing Languages and Thesauri: Construction and Maintenance*	2	25%
4	Aitchison, *Language Web: The Power and Problem of Words*	1	12.5%
	Bowker and Star, *Sorting Things Out*	1	12.5%
	Crystal, *The Cambridge Encyclopedia of Language*	1	12.5%
	NISO, *Guidelines for the Construction, Format and Management of Monolingual Thesauri*	1	12.5%
	No textbook	1	12.5%

TABLE 16. All Textbooks–Alphabetically

Author	Title	Usage
Aitchison, Bawden, & Gilchrist	*Thesaurus Construction And Use: A Practical Manual*	4
Aitchison	*Language Web: The Power And Problem Of Words*	1
ALA	*The Anglo-American Cataloging Rules, Second Edition*	62
	ALA Filing Rules	1
	Guidelines For Bibliographic Description Of Reproduction	1
Anderson & Perez-Carballo	*Information Retrieval Database Design*	1
Baca	*Introduction To Metadata: Pathways To Digital Information*	3
Bosch	*Guide To Collecting CD-ROMs, Software And Other Electronic Publications*	1
Bowker & Star	*Sorting Things Out*	3
Buchanan	*Theory Of Library Classification*	1
Byrne	*MARC Manual*	1
Chan	*A Guide To The Library Of Congress Classification*	9
	Cataloging And Classification: An Introduction	26
	Dewey Decimal Classification: A Practical Guide	1
	Library Of Congress Subject Headings: Principles And Application	9
Chan, Richmond, & Svenonius	*Theory Of Subject Analysis: A Sourcebook*	1
Cleveland & Cleveland	*Introduction To Indexing And Abstracting*	6
Couch	*Information Technologies And Social Orders*	1
Crystal	*The Cambridge Encyclopedia Of Language*	1
Evans & Heft	*Introduction To Technical Services*	5
Evans	*Developing Library And Information Center Collections*	1

APPENDIX (continued)

TABLE 16 (continued)

Author	Title	Usage
Fecko	*Cataloging Nonbook Resources How-To-Do-It Manual*	1
Ferguson	*Nonprint Materials Workbook*	1
	MARC/AACR2 Workbook	1
	Subject Analysis Workbook	3
Ferl and Milsap	*Subject Cataloging: How-To-Do-It Manual*	1
Fetters	*Handbook Of Indexing Techniques: A Guide For Beginning Indexers*	2
Foskett	*The Subject Approach To Information*	6
Fritz	*Cataloging With AACR2 And USMARC*	1
Frost	*Media Access And Organization: A Cataloging And Reference Sources Guide For Nonbook Materials*	2
Furrie	*Understanding MARC*	9
Godden	*Library Technical Services: Operations And Management*	1
Gorman	*Concise AACR2*	6
	Technical Services Today And Tomorrow	3
Hagler	*The Bibliographic Record And Information*	6
Harkness Connell and Maxwell	*The Future Of Cataloging: Insights From The Lubetzky Symposium*	2
Hsieh-Yee	*Organizing Audiovisual And Electronic Resources For Access: A Cataloging Guide*	7
Hudgins, Agnew & Brown	*Getting Mileage Out Of Metadata: Applications For The Library*	3
Hunter	*Classification Made Simple*	2
Intner & Weihs	*Special Libraries: A Cataloging Guide*	2
	Standard Cataloging For School And Public Libraries	3
Intner	*Subject Access To Films & Videos*	1
Iyer	*Classificatory Structures*	1
Johnson	*New Directions In Technical Services: Trends And Sources*	1
Kaplan	*Planning And Implementing Technical Services Workstations*	1
Katzer, Cook & Crouch	*Evaluating Information*	1
Lakoff	*Women, Fire And Dangerous Things*	1
Lancaster	*Indexing And Abstracting In Theory And Practice*	24
	Vocabulary Control For Information Retrieval	4
Langridge	*Classification: Its Kinds, Elements, Systems, And Applications*	1
LC	*Classification Outline*	1
	Cataloging Concepts: Descriptive Cataloging: Trainee's Manual	1
	LC Rule Interpretations	3
Mann	*Library Research Models*	8
	Oxford Guide To Library Research	1
Marcella & Newton	*A New Manual Of Classification*	1
Maxwell and Maxwell	*Maxwell's Handbook For AACR2*	6
Meadows, Boyce & Kraft	*Text Information Retrieval*	1
Miksa	*Manuscript*	1

Author	Title	Usage
Milstead	*Subject Access Systems: Alternatives In Design*	1
Mortimer	*Learn Dewey Decimal Classification*	1
Mulvaney	*Indexing Books*	9
NISO	*Guidelines For Thesaurus Construction*	1
	No Text – Various Readings	33
O'Connor	*Explorations In Indexing And Abstracting: Pointing, Virtue And Power*	6
Olson	*Cataloging Internet Resources: A Manual And Practical Guide*	2
	Cataloging Of Audiovisual Materials And Other Special Materials	4
Piepenburg	*Easy MARC*	2
Ranganathan	*Classified Cataloging Code*	1
Rosenfeld & Morville	*Information Architecture For The World Wide Web*	2
Rowley & Farrow	*Organizing Knowledge: An Introduction To Managing Access To Information*	1
Rowley	*Organizing Knowledge: An Introduction To Information Retrieval*	3
Saye	*Manheimer's Cataloging And Classification*	9
Schmidt	*Understanding The Business Of Library Acquisitions*	1
Schottlaender	*The Future Of The Descriptive Cataloging Rules: Papers From The ALCTS Preconference, AACR2000*	1
Smiraglia	*Describing Music Materials*	1
	Music Cataloging	1
Smith & Carter	*Technical Services Management, 1965-1990: A Quarter Century Of Change, A Look To The Future*	1
Soergel	*Indexing Languages And Thesauri*	2
	Organizing Information	1
Stone	*The LCSH Century: One Hundred Years With The Library Of Congress Subject Headings System*	1
Svenonius	*The Intellectual Foundation Of Information Organization*	7
Taylor	*The Organization Of Information*	31
	Wynar's Introduction To Cataloging And Classification	29
Thomas	*Classification: Options And Opportunities*	1
Urbanski	*Cataloging Unpublished Nonprint Materials*	1
	Various Professional Tools	3
Weinberg	*Indexing: The State Of Our Knowledge And The State Of Our Ignorance*	1
Wellisch	*Indexing From A To Z*	4
Wilson & Colver	*Outsourcing Library Technical Services Operations*	1
Yee & Layne	*Improving OPACs*	1

APPENDIX (continued)

TABLE 17. All Textbooks–By Usage

Author	Title	#
ALA	*The Anglo-American Cataloging Rules, Second Edition*	62
	No Text–Various Readings	33
Taylor	*The Organization Of Information*	31
Taylor	*Wynar's Introduction To Cataloging And Classification*	29
Chan	*Cataloging And Classification: An Introduction*	26
Lancaster	*Indexing And Abstracting In Theory And Practice*	24
Chan	*A Guide To The Library Of Congress Classification*	9
Chan	*Library Of Congress Subject Headings: Principles And Application*	9
Furrie	*Understanding MARC*	9
Mulvaney	*Indexing Books*	9
Saye	*Manheimer's Cataloging And Classification*	9
Mann	*Library Research Models*	8
Hsieh-Yee	*Organizing Audiovisual And Electronic Resources For Access: A Cataloging Guide*	7
Svenonius	*The Intellectual Foundation Of Information Organization*	7
Cleveland & Cleveland	*Introduction To Indexing And Abstracting*	6
Foskett	*The Subject Approach To Information*	6
Gorman	*Concise AACR2*	6
Hagler	*The Bibliographic Record And Information*	6
Maxwell and Maxwell	*Maxwell's Handbook For AACR2*	6
O'Connor	*Explorations In Indexing And Abstracting: Pointing, Virtue And Power*	6
Evans & Heft	*Introduction To Technical Services*	5
Aitchison, Bawden, & Gilchrist	*Thesaurus Construction And Use: A Practical Manual*	4
Lancaster	*Vocabulary Control For Information Retrieval*	4
Olson	*Cataloging Of Audiovisual Materials And Other Special Materials*	4
Wellisch	*Indexing From A To Z*	4
Baca	*Introduction To Metadata: Pathways To Digital Information*	3
Bowker & Star	*Sorting Things Out*	3
Ferguson	*Subject Analysis Workbook*	3
Gorman	*Technical Services Today And Tomorrow*	3
Hudgins, Agnew & Brown	*Getting Mileage Out Of Metadata: Applications For The Library*	3
Intner & Weihs	*Standard Cataloging For School And Public Libraries*	3
	LC Rule Interpretations	3
Rowley	*Organizing Knowledge: An Introduction To Information Retrieval*	3
	Various Professional Tools	3
Fetters	*Handbook Of Indexing Techniques: A Guide For Beginning Indexers*	2
Frost	*Media Access And Organization: A Cataloging And Reference Source: Guide For Nonbook Materials*	2
Harkness Connell and Maxwell	*The Future Of Cataloging: Insights From The Lubetzky Symposium*	2
Hunter	*Classification Made Simple*	2

Author	Title	#
Intner & Weihs	*Special Libraries: A Cataloging Guide*	2
Olson	*Cataloging Internet Resources: A Manual And Practical Guide*	2
Piepenburg	*Easy MARC*	2
Rosenfeld & Morville	*Information Architecture For The World Wide Web*	2
Soergel	*Indexing Languages And Thesauri*	2
Aitchison	*Language Web: The Power And Problem Of Words*	1
	ALA Filing Rules	1
ALA	*Guidelines For Bibliographic Description Of Reproduction*	1
Anderson & Perez-Carballo	*Information Retrieval Database Design*	1
Bosch	*Guide To Collecting CD-ROMs, Software And Other Electronic Publications*	1
Buchanan	*Theory Of Library Classification*	1
Byrne	*MARC Manual*	1
Chan	*Dewey Decimal Classification: A Practical Guide*	1
Chan, Richmond, & Svenonius	*Theory Of Subject Analysis: A Sourcebook*	1
Couch	*Information Technologies And Social Orders*	1
Crystal	*The Cambridge Encyclopedia Of Language*	1
Evans	*Developing Library And Information Center Collections*	1
Fecko	*Cataloging Nonbook Resources How-To-Do-It Manual*	1
Ferguson	*Nonprint Materials Workbook*	1
Ferguson	*MARC/AACR2 Workbook*	1
Ferl And Milsap	*Subject Cataloging: How-To-Do-It Manual*	1
Fritz	*Cataloging With AACR2 And USMARC*	1
Godden	*Library Technical Services: Operations And Management*	1
Intner	*Subject Access To Films & Videos*	1
Iyer	*Classificatory Structures*	1
Johnson	*New Directions In Technical Services: Trends And Sources*	1
Kaplan	*Planning And Implementing Technical Services Workstations*	1
Katzer, Cook & Crouch	*Evaluating Information*	1
Lakoff	*Women, Fire And Dangerous Things*	1
Langridge	*Classification: Its Kinds, Elements, Systems, And Applications*	1
LC	*Classification Outline*	1
	Cataloging Concepts: Descriptive Cataloging: Trainee's Manual	1
Mann	*Oxford Guide To Library Research*	1
Marcella & Newton	*A New Manual Of Classification*	1
Meadows, Boyce & Kraft	*Text Information Retrieval*	1
Miksa	*Manuscript*	1
Milstead	*Subject Access Systems: Alternatives In Design*	1
Mortimer	*Learn Dewey Decimal Classification*	1
NISO	*Guidelines For Thesaurus Construction*	1
Ranganathan	*Classified Cataloging Code*	1
Rowley & Farrow	*Organizing Knowledge: An Introduction To Managing Access To Information*	1

APPENDIX (continued)

TABLE 17 (continued)

Author	Title	#
Schmidt	*Understanding The Business Of Library Acquisitions*	1
Schottlaender	*The Future Of The Descriptive Cataloging Rules: Papers From The ALCTS Preconference, AACR2000*	1
Smiraglia	*Describing Music Materials*	1
Smiraglia	*Music Cataloging*	1
Smith & Carter	*Technical Services Management, 1965-1990: A Quarter Century Of Change, A Look To The Future*	1
Soergel	*Organizing Information*	1
Stone	*The LCSH Century: One Hundred Years With The Library Of Congress Subject Headings System*	1
Thomas	*Classification: Options And Opportunities*	1
Urbanski	*Cataloging Unpublished Nonprint Materials*	1
Weinberg	*Indexing: The State Of Our Knowledge And The State Of Our Ignorance*	1
Wilson & Colver	*Outsourcing Library Technical Services Operations*	1
Yee & Layne	*Improving OPACs*	1

Where Are We and How Did We Get Here? or, The Changing Place of Cataloging in the Library and Information Science Curriculum: Causes and Consequences

Jerry D. Saye

SUMMARY. Explores factors that have influenced library and information science education over the past two decades. Emphasis is placed on cataloging instruction and particularly cataloging as a required course. Identifies the introduction of new areas of study, corresponding curricular changes, and the nature of LIS faculty as influencing the role of cataloging in the professional education of librarians. An analysis is provided of the changing perception of the importance of cataloging in professional library education programs. *[Article copies available for a fee from The Haworth Document Delivery Service: 1-800-HAWORTH. E-mail address: <getinfo@haworthpressinc.com> Website: <http://www.HaworthPress.com> © 2002 by The Haworth Press, Inc. All rights reserved.]*

KEYWORDS. Cataloging education, library schools, library school faculty, library school curricula

Jerry D. Saye is Professor, School of Information and Library Science, The University of North Carolina at Chapel Hill, Chapel Hill, NC 27599-3360 (E-mail: saye@ils.unc.edu).

[Haworth co-indexing entry note]: "Where Are We and How Did We Get Here? or, The Changing Place of Cataloging in the Library and Information Science Curriculum: Causes and Consequences." Saye, Jerry D. Co-published simultaneously in *Cataloging & Classification Quarterly* (The Haworth Information Press, an imprint of The Haworth Press, Inc.) Vol. 34, No. 1/2, 2002, pp. 121-143; and: *Education for Cataloging and the Organization of Information: Pitfalls and the Pendulum* (ed: Janet Swan Hill) The Haworth Information Press, an imprint of The Haworth Press, Inc., 2002, pp. 121-143. Single or multiple copies of this article are available for a fee from The Haworth Document Delivery Service [1-800-HAWORTH, 9:00 a.m. - 5:00 p.m. (EST). E-mail address: getinfo@haworthpressinc.com].

INTRODUCTION

In 1904, Charles A. Cutter, in the Preface to the 4th edition of his *Rules for a Dictionary Catalog*, wrote:

> Still I can not help thinking that the golden age of cataloging is over, and that the difficulties and discussions which have furnished an innocent pleasure to so many will interest them no more.[1]

Cutter's thoughts were the result of his questioning whether the Library of Congress' success with making catalog cards available to other libraries made it useful for him to prepare a fourth edition of his *Rules*. In the end he concluded that, because LC couldn't catalog everything yet nor did all libraries use LC cards, it seemed worthwhile to proceed with a new edition.

Now nearly 100 years later Cutter's words might be viewed in a different light. Is cataloging again threatened? If it is, could it be that the threat lies not so much in others providing cataloging to libraries, but rather the perception by educators in library and information science programs that cataloging is no longer a knowledge necessity for graduates of their programs?

Looking back at Cutter's musing today one might question not whether Cutter was being too pessimistic about the "golden age" having disappeared, but rather whether he was in fact very prescient. Do his words now read 100 years later apply better to the state of cataloging education?

The purpose of this paper is to assess where we are today, as well as examine what was, and posit some possible explanations for what followed. While this paper will focus on the consequences upon cataloging education, this tale may well apply now or in the future to other library specialties. Cataloging may be but the ringing bell for others.

There have been numerous laments over the years about the diminished state of cataloging education in our professional programs. This paper attempts to identify factors that may have led us to where we are at the beginning of this new century. This paper provides fact, interpretation, and opinion. The interpretations and opinions are based upon 25 years of experience teaching in cataloging at the graduate level and the observation of the changes that have occurred in our professional schools. The opinions are those of one firmly committed to teaching cataloging and its role in the library and information science education process. They also are those of a person who truly enjoys and values teaching this subject as well as seeing the enjoyment and excitement that it can provide students. This paper is not intended to be divisive, but is intended to convey the state of education as it impacts on cataloging.

THE HISTORICAL PERSPECTIVE

In the 115 years since the establishment of the first library school at Columbia College by Melvil Dewey, tremendous change has occurred in the programs that support library education. This should come as no surprise given what has happened in science, technology, and virtually all other fields of human endeavor. Dewey's library economy program was, in the words of White, "an apprenticeship school. It was designed to produce the same kind of competence as apprenticeship training but using more systematic methods."[2] Although Miksa argues convincingly that the program's lectures also included "general knowledge and principles that obviously went well beyond the 'ABCs' of library practice,"[3] Dewey's program was still strongly centered on the content covered by the library apprenticeship approach then in vogue. Library processes and routines, of which cataloging and classification were a part, accounted for "just over" 40 percent of the Columbia program's content.[4] Over the next 40 years a number of other schools established library education programs. These programs had a distribution of course content similar to that introduced by Dewey. In fact, several were directed by graduates of Dewey's program.

A very important, if not the most important event in the professionalization of library education, occurred in 1923 with the publication of the *Williamson Report*. Charles C. Williamson was engaged by the Carnegie Corporation of New York to survey the state of library education in the United States. His survey focused primarily on the 15 library schools then in operation giving only limited attention to the other modes of library education–training classes and summer schools. Curriculum was among the areas explored by Williamson. His comments on it provide useful insight into the state of cataloging in library education in the early 1920s. From data provided by 11 schools Williamson noted that "cataloguing, book selection, reference work, and classification" on average constituted nearly half of a student's time commitment. While noting that the time devoted to these subjects varied considerably among the schools, he concluded that these four subject areas were those "on which all the schools lay primary emphasis." He said that they "may well be called the heart of the curriculum.[5] A table in the *Report* of the distribution of classroom hours across the 11 schools provides even greater insight into the status of the curriculum.[6] What Williamson termed cataloging, classification and subject headings constituted, on average, 27 percent of the curriculum. Cataloging alone accounted for 15 percent. Clearly the area of cataloging and its related subjects continued to play a major role in library education nearly 40 years after the establishment of the first library school.

The most significant recommendation made by Williamson was that library education was provided best, as was true for other professions, in a professional school located within an academic institution. His recommendations and the development of accreditation standards simply stated eventually led to the configuration of accredited professional degrees we have today–graduate education in a professional school or department located within an academic institution.

As librarianship matured as a profession, the curriculum of its professional schools also matured and reflected changes in values, new definitions of library services, and the incorporation of new management principles. Several works, particularly those by Reece,[7] Wheeler,[8] Berelson,[9] and Leigh,[10] provide valuable insight into the curricular demographics of library education in the decades following the *Williamson Report*. Although most paid only passing attention to cataloging in the curriculum, Leigh made a point of noting that a cataloging course was commonly required in master's level programs.[11]

Rather than report the numerous comments made in the literature of librarianship about cataloging education over the past 80 years, it might be more informative to explore what has occurred in the somewhat more recent past. Clearly our schools have experienced tremendous change over the past 30 years. The early years of that period, the early 1970s, witnessed information science's entry into some library education programs. That, when combined with the technological changes of those three decades, had enormous impact upon the schools. Cataloging was not unaffected. How schools and cataloging education were affected by these changes is the focus of the remainder of this paper.

THE SCHOOLS

"Library schools no longer exist!" These aren't meant to be fighting words but rather are a simple statement of reality. Despite the continued use of the term "library school" in the literature and the profession in general, much to the consternation of some faculty and students, the institution that once was the library school is no more. How do we know that they no longer exist? Is there evidence to support these words?

One way that institutions communicate who and what they are and how they choose to be perceived is in the names they select to identify themselves. What has happened to the titles of the units in which our professional education programs reside is a clear indicator of dramatic change. Table 1 provides a summary of the unit title changes since 1970.

It is obvious that at the beginning of the 1970s our schools saw themselves, as they had for decades, as library science programs. By 1981, however, the introduction of information science into our programs was well underway as evidenced by the inclusion of the word "information science" in unit titles. Clearly our programs were now viewing themselves as more than just library science programs. In 1980, only one school (Syracuse) had a title that excluded the word "library" from its title. Changes in naming continued through the succeeding decade. Although by 1990 more schools had added information science to their unit title, another movement–to delete library science entirely from the unit title–began to emerge. By 2000 the trend was clearly in the direction of deletion. At that point, 29 percent of our schools no longer mentioned library science in their unit title. This simple change in a word or two of a school's title were to have long term effects on the state of cataloging education.

Changes in how schools choose to be viewed by the world outside their doors–to their universities, prospective students, graduates, fellow educators, and the profession–are indicative of monumental events that have and are taking place within our schools. Information science has

TABLE 1. Terms Used in Unit Titles

Terms*	Schools			
	1970-1971	1980-1981	1990-1991	2000-2001
Library science only	47	38	7	1
Library and information science	5	31	49	39
Library science not mentioned	0	1	3	16
Total	52	70	59	56

*Synonymous terms were included in the count, e.g., library science, librarianship, library service, etc.

been revolutionary for our programs. Most schools have integrated it into their existing ALA-accredited master's program. This integration required the introduction of new courses to support this content initiative and the revision of some existing courses. In the past decade a number of schools began to offer a master's degree in information science separate from their library science master's degree. The ALA Committee on Accreditation's 1992 *Standards for Accreditation* for the first time established standards that provided for the accreditation of information science master's degree.[12] By 2001, twelve schools had separate IS master's degrees–7 accredited by ALA and 5 where the schools did not seek IS accreditation.

Another information science related initiative also had an enormous impact on a number of schools. That initiative was the introduction of an undergraduate major in information science. Beginning in the late 1970s, but gaining momentum in the mid to late 1990s, these programs introduced a new student cohort into what had been a graduate-only student population. It also created an increased demand for additional courses to support these programs. At present only a minority of the schools (13 of 56) offer these degrees, but that number will likely increase. Although a number of schools which have information science majors have relatively small enrollment in it, the undergraduate major enrollment at several schools has increased their overall school enrollments to above 1,000 students. Other schools, while not creating information science majors, began offering information science minors. While a minor is not as dramatic in impact as the creation of an information science major on a school, it too has curricular consequences in terms of course offerings and the associated introduction of that new student group.

Change, however, is not confined to the presence of information science in the schools. Doctoral programs have also experienced dramatic change. From a handful of schools offering doctoral degrees, our profession has progressed to where slightly more than half (52 percent) of the 56 schools with ALA-accredited master's programs also have a doctoral program. This has resulted in a 43 percent increase in doctoral student enrollment since 1980. Fall of 2000 saw 735 students pursuing doctoral study in our schools.[13] Doctoral programs can have an incredible effect on schools in that they, like undergraduate programs, introduce a new student body into the school. That new student group, however, is one which has research as its primary focus. It also may modify faculty expectations of the role of research in the school, and potentially, alter the acceptance of courses that primarily focus on teaching the knowledge and skills base needed for the more applied tasks in the profession. Could this have happened to cataloging as a topic of instruction?

THE CURRICULUM

It might be asked why would schools make these changes? Weren't things just fine as they were? The library education community in the 1970s through the early 1990s witnessed something never before seen at the scale experienced then–the closure of one after another of its schools. The year 1980 saw 69 schools offering the ALA-accredited master's degree. By 2000 the number of schools offering such programs had diminished to 56. A listing of the schools which no longer have accredited master's programs reads like an obituary list of dear departed friends:

Ball State University	State University of New York at Geneseo
Brigham Young University	University of Minnesota
University of California at Berkeley	University of Mississippi
Case Western Reserve University	Northern Illinois University
University of Chicago	George Peabody University
Columbia University	University of Southern California
University of Denver	Western Michigan University
Emory University	

Even more distressing was that the closures were not confined to what might be perceived as weak programs. Rather, they encompassed the full range of schools including some of the most prestigious programs including those at Chicago and Columbia. Except for California at Berkeley all the programs in this list were victims of closure rather than a decision not to seek ALA re-accreditation.

The impact of these closures had an enormous effect not just on the programs closed, but also on the remaining schools. Library and information science education programs, as usual one of the smallest graduate programs in a university, often feel themselves in relatively weak positions at times of campus retrenchment. In 1980, our programs were still primarily library education focused. The nascent information science components offered more potential rather than strength for most. When confronted by such a situation schools did what businesses and others do. They began to follow the lead of those who had developed strategies that provided programmatic strength and healthier student enrollments. Thus over a two decade period, the development or growth of information science master's degree programs, undergraduate information science majors, doctoral programs, and other strategies were introduced to strengthen our schools. These efforts were not motivated solely for reasons of survival. Rather, they built upon the increasing role and common acceptance of the importance of information in what was becoming an electronic society.

Archives, records management and other areas of study also have been introduced in a number of schools. This has been particularly true in the last decade. These programs, complementary to library and information science, build upon our theoretical knowledge and skills base, as well as provide a new constituency for our schools. Their presence in LIS schools provides added value to courses, new information environments for our students, as well as providing additional strength to our schools.

The increased role of research within our schools can be attributed in part as the consequence of universities becoming more focused on obtaining external dollars for program support. To this can be added the desire of many faculty to explore new and exciting questions as well as obtaining additional support for their research. This increased research emphasis may have begun a shift in the orientation of the curriculum towards one that supports a discipline rather than a profession. This can have, and may already have, major consequences on courses such as cataloging. It may mean a lower perception of its importance, a change in course content toward more theoretical understanding rather than application, or the offering of a general course dealing with the theories and principles of information organization.

The changes to programmatic content, the involvement in undergraduate education, the increased research emphasis, to say nothing of efforts by universities and faculty to become engaged in interdisciplinary studies, have strengthened many of our programs within their parent universities. They have made the mission and objectives of the school more central to those of the university, thus making themselves stronger within the university.

There are curricular implications, however, when one introduces considerable amount of new content to the offerings of a school. One would imagine that the addition of new programs and new specialties has created the need for the addition of a great number of new courses to the curriculum. An examination of new courses added to curricula[14] confirms that a great number of courses have been added to curricula. Normally one would expect that this would result in greatly enlarged curricula. In fact, this hasn't occurred. Table 2 reports[15] the average number of courses listed in school catalogs over a 20 year period.

Surprisingly, the number of courses offered on average has remained remarkably stable despite the tremendous changes taking place within the schools. What has occurred is that new courses have replaced old or existing courses have been extensively revised. In some instances old courses are deleted from a curriculum and the content no longer covered. In other situations existing content is greatly revised and compressed within a course to accommodate the new content. Eventually new courses arise to fill the void left by deleted courses. These new courses provide new content for the curriculum. Many of the new courses added to curricula were information science-related and, correspondingly, a large percentage of courses deleted were library science oriented. Clearly there are implications here for cataloging.

With the changes in the offerings of our schools, and in the way in which schools choose to now identify themselves, there remain a considerable number of students who wish to become librarians. How well are these students accommodated in achieving their goal by our changing schools? Even more specifically, what is the state of instruction in cataloging for the aspiring librarian?

CATALOGING IN THE CURRICULUM

Schools of library and information science today typically offer instruction in information organization. That content might be in the form of a cataloging course or as a more general organization of information course. These courses are known under a variety of course titles.[16]

One indicator of the importance of cataloging in a curriculum, and in the perception of the importance the faculty assigns it in the preparation

TABLE 2. Number of Courses Listed in School Catalogs

Academic Year	Average Number of Courses Listed in School Catalogs
1980-1981	50
1990-1991	56
1999-2000*	56

Source: Pope 1982; Barron & Perrine 1992; Barron & Westbrook 2001.
*Most recent data available.

of a librarian, is whether a cataloging course is required of master's degree students. In the 1970s most schools required a cataloging course of those seeking that degree in library science. This is understandable given that, as we have seen, most schools viewed themselves as library schools. As such, most of their students were preparing to enter the library profession. Those changes to incorporate information science in school titles also reflected a change in career objectives of some students to work in environments other than libraries. Did this change in student career objectives affect the traditional requirement of a cataloging course for the master's degree? Table 3 illustrates the current status of cataloging or organization of information courses as a required course at the 56 schools with ALA-accredited master's programs.

For the purpose of analysis, a cataloging course was defined as a course which presented the basic principles and procedures common to cataloging work and which allowed for at least minimal proficiency in those tasks by those completing the course. An "organization of information" course was defined as a course that imparted general principles of information organization. As such, it might present some of the information taught in a cataloging course in an introductory way, but would not provide for the attainment of the "minimal proficiency" objective of a cataloging course. Courses such as abstracting and indexing were not considered organization of information courses within that definition for the former are more specific in focus. In a few instances students are required to take either a cataloging or an abstracting and indexing course. Such an "or" condition, would allow students to graduate without taking a cataloging course. As a consequence these were counted as "neither."

This table shows that fewer than half the schools (41 percent) currently require a cataloging course for the master's degree. Clearly cataloging is declining in importance as expressed through its requirement as basic knowledge needed for the degree. Many schools apparently

TABLE 3. Cataloging or Organization of Information as a Required Course

Required Course	Schools
Cataloging	23
Organization of information	21
Neither	12
Total	56

Source: 2001 school catalogs and school homepages.

feel that adequate minimal preparation is provided to their students by a more generic organization of information course. In fact, such a course can serve as an excellent introduction to a cataloging course. One might question, however, whether it is an adequate substitute for a course in cataloging for those intending to be librarians. While many might find the decline of cataloging as a core requirement distressing, there is some comfort in the knowledge that a cataloging course is offered, at least as an elective, by all schools. Most schools also have an advanced cataloging course in their curriculum, although the frequency of their offerings are unknown. Offsetting this positive note is the disturbing fact that 21 percent of our schools require neither a cataloging nor an organization of information course of their students.

One might hope that at least our leading schools are taking a strong stance on the importance of cataloging in the preparation of librarians. Those hopes, however, are not supported by the data. When the course requirements of the schools selected as the Top 10 programs[17] by *U.S. News and World Report* are examined, the requirement of a cataloging course becomes worse. Of these schools only 1 requires a cataloging course, 5 require an organization of information course, and 5 require neither. Clearly our leading schools are in the forefront of the movement away from a cataloging course requirement for the master's degree.

With the increased emphasis in many schools on an information science component, it would be understandable if the schools were reluctant to require cataloging of students, who, although part of the single master's degree program offered by the school, are seeking to develop an information science specialty rather than one in library science. Perhaps that accounts for the rise of organization of information courses as required courses rather than cataloging. This would be difficult to assess across the 56 schools without knowledge of the rationales used by the schools when making their decisions about required courses.

There are a number of schools, however, that offer a separate master's degree in library science and another in information science. At present, 12 schools (21 percent) offer these separate LS and IS master's degrees. Seven have the IS degree accredited by ALA while 5 have not sought such accreditation. One might expect that at least the schools with a separate degree specifically intended to prepare for librarianship might require students in that program to take cataloging. In fact, that expectation is not met. Five of the 12 schools require an organization of information course, 2 a cataloging course, while 5 have neither as a requirement for the LS master's degree. It would be interesting to know what has changed the perception of schools from that prevalent in the

1970s, when cataloging was deemed an essential knowledge requirement in the preparation of librarians, to its status today. Now, 30 years later, even those master's programs specifically intended to prepare students for careers in librarianship no longer view cataloging at that level of importance.

There can be no doubt that the perception of cataloging as an essential knowledge requirement for graduates of our master's programs has taken a serious decline. Although there is some exposure to cataloging, at least at its most general and theoretical level, in an organization of information course, no data are readily available of the number of students who elect to follow that course with a cataloging course. One does wonder how many students would take such an opportunity given the competition provided by other courses in our relatively short master's degree programs. Although students who have taken only an organization of information course likely possess sufficient knowledge to allow them to function as catalogers, they probably will require extensive additional education and training by their employing institution. That post-master's remedial work would, in all likelihood, be greater than that needed for students who had completed at least one course in cataloging to say nothing of those who had completed an advanced cataloging course. This also raises an additional question. How many students who have taken only an organization of information course would even apply for cataloging positions given that they did not exhibit sufficient interest in cataloging to take a cataloging course when one was available to them as an elective? And what of those students in schools where even an organization of information course is not required? Do students even take an organization of information course, let alone a cataloging course, if it is an elective? Might the status of required cataloging courses at least partially account for our shortage of catalogers?

Those involved in cataloging realize that the importance of being able to retrieve information using a library's catalog has not diminished with the advent of online cataloging, MARC records, and online catalogs. The rapid rise in importance of electronic resources, particularly the Internet, as an information source only accentuates the key role of information organization in achieving quality information retrieval. Indeed, it is ironic that concern about cataloging education and the value of cataloging has arisen at a time when another form of information organization, metadata, seems of interest to a wide range of people. Suddenly it seems that many individuals who previously had little or no interest in cataloging, or even librarianship, are now vitally involved in metadata initiatives and projects.

Could it be that the ready availability of bibliographic utilities and MARC records has had the unfortunate consequence of creating the impression that there is not much cataloging to be done and what little work remains is essentially a paraprofessional task? Granted the arrival of these support structures for cataloging have allowed cataloging staffs to be reduced over the years, but the work that remains for those in the cataloging process continues unabated. Catalogers realize that the knowledge requirements of catalogers are greater now than ever before. Unfortunately those who may hold the view that the role of cataloging is greatly diminished may be the same persons who make critical decisions about cataloging in our schools and have the most direct influence on students–the faculty.

The changes that may have lowered cataloging in the judgment of many may not lie only in their perception of the level of cataloging to be done. It may also lie in a transformation of the library profession's values. Those altered values include an increased emphasis on user services and a greater concentration of professional concern on the management of the enterprise. The profession's focus on users is to be applauded, but that attention may have been at the expense of library infrastructure activities of which cataloging is a major component. Such changes in priorities would, understandably, be reflected in decisions made about the appropriate preparation needed for the profession's entry-level degree programs. This raises two questions, however. Was it the value changes of the profession that influenced the educational programs or did the value changes in the educational programs influence the profession?

THE FACULTY

Although many things have changed in our profession, one thing that has been a constant through the years has been a tension between librarians and the profession's educators. Are educators teaching the right things? Are librarians too practice oriented? Are educators too theory based? Are faculty too removed from professional practice? Do librarians really understand what the librarians of the future really need to know? Do faculty? Questions like these aren't limited to the past few years. Rather, they and others have appeared in the literature of the field for more than 100 years.

In cataloging, although we have long had "corporate author" as a part of our work, we know that institutions don't make decisions, people do.

In schools, whether it is a change of the name of the school, changes in degree requirements, or changes in course content, those changes are often initiated by faculty and usually involve some level of faculty approval.

Curricular decisions in universities are generally decided collegially–by faculty. Are others other than faculty involved in this curricular decision-making? Is there a formal role for alumni or other practitioners to play in it? In general the answer is "no." In 1999-2000,[18] 38 schools (73 percent) had one or more of the following groups on their curriculum committees: faculty, students, staff. Only 14 schools (27 percent) included alumni or practitioners as members of those committees.[19] As a result, there is relatively little direct input from the profession into the formal curriculum decision-making, although there may be other less formal sources of input.

This approach to decision-making about the appropriate education of those desiring to be librarians can result in the decisions being made by a subset of faculty who may have had little or no contact with libraries other than as users. Has this always been the situation or have changes occurred in staffing the profession's educational programs?

Full-time library science faculty, prior to the *Williamson Report*, were most often persons who had been library practitioners. Williamson stated that two-thirds had what he characterized as "good" library work experience.[20] These educators brought to the classroom their strong commitment to the profession as well as their knowledge of its processes and needs. As unusual as it may seem today, Williamson found that only 52 percent of faculty possessed a college degree and 42 percent were teaching at the school from which they graduated.[21] The accreditation process as well as the actions of the schools to collectively improve library professional education dramatically changed the educational status of library school faculty in the decades that followed.

Although in the 1930s the University of Chicago initiated the use of faculty from a variety of disciplines in its staffing of the Graduate Library School, faculty ranks generally continued to be dominated by persons associated with librarianship. The phrase "associated with librarianship" is used because a number of faculty, although library profession oriented, held doctoral degrees in other disciplines.

The faculties of our professional schools today are well-educated academicians. Although statistical data on the demographics of library education faculty were not available in any cumulative form until the mid-1970s, data do exist from that point. In 1980, 70.8 percent of full-time faculty held doctorates, in 1991 that figure had risen to 85.6

percent and by 2001, 92.1 percent. Clearly the academic qualifications of faculty have improved tremendously.

Although the percentage of faculty holding doctorates has risen substantially, the percentage of faculty holding a doctoral degree in library or information science has remained relatively constant over the past 20 years. Table 4 reports the distribution of LIS and non-LIS doctorates from 1980 to 2001.[22]

These are relatively stable figures given the changes our schools have experienced during this period. Since 1991 the most notable difference in our faculties is subtle but has had dramatic consequences. That difference lies in the clustering of non-library and information science doctorates. In 1981, of the 174 non-LIS doctorates held by faculty, 55 were in some aspect of education, 24 in instructional technology, 20 in a literature, and 12 in history. No other field had 10 or more doctorates. In most instances, the representation of other fields was less than 3. In 1981 no doctorates were reported held by faculty in computer science or closely related disciplines. By 1991, the representation of non-LIS doctoral disciplines had changed. The 166 faculty holding such degrees continued to have education as the largest cluster with 39 persons, followed by communications and history each with 16 doctorates. Again, the remaining doctorates were distributed widely among other disciplines and professions with clustering generally under 3, but an increasing number of clusters had 4-6 faculty. In 1991, 7 faculty held computer science doctorates. By 2001 the clustering of the 226 non-LIS doctorates had changed considerably. The clusters were fewer, but the number of clusters with more than 10 faculty had increased. Table 5 displays the distribution of the largest clusters of non-LIS doctorates in 2001.[23] These clusters exhibit considerable change from those of twenty years earlier. The six doctoral fields in Table 5 constitute 57% of all non-LIS doctorates. Most noteworthy is the increase in doctorates in computer

TABLE 4. Distribution of Full-Time Faculty LIS and Non-LIS Doctorates

Doctorates	Percent		
	1981	1991	2001
Library and information science	65.9	68.3	63.1
Not library and information science	34.1	31.7	36.9

Source: Bidlack 1981; Sineath 1991, Sineath 2001.

TABLE 5. Largest Clusters of Non-LIS Doctorates of Full-Time Faculty, 2001

Discipline or Profession	Number of Full-Time Faculty
Education	37
Computer Science	28
History	22
Engineering	14
Instructional Technology	14
Communications	13
Total	**128**

Source: Sineath 2001.

science and engineering. It is likely that a number of the engineering doctorates are in aspects closely related to computer science.

No empirical data exist to support the comments that follow about changes in faculty constituency, preparation, and attitudes, so they must be viewed as solely personal observation and interpretation. Although faculty of 20 or more years ago possessed roughly the same percentage of LIS and non-LIS doctorates as faculties today, there was a distinct but subtle difference. Earlier faculties possessed a homogeneity in that, regardless of their area of doctoral study, most came to library education with a commitment to the profession. Chosen areas of doctoral study often were the result of pursuing the doctoral degree in another field as a consequence of the small number of library science doctoral programs then in existence. The presence of non-LIS doctorates was not due to a strong movement to bring other disciplines and professions into library education, although that did occur in a limited number of instances. The areas of other doctoral studies were widely scattered with few dominating. More importantly, regardless of their area of study, faculty from other fields integrated themselves into the body of library science faculty. They frequently left their research and involvement in the field of their doctoral work when becoming part of a library science faculty. It is quite different today. With the strong information science components, there is a conscious effort in many of them to bring in faculty from other fields. Although we are still attracting faculty with non-LIS doctorates into our schools in roughly the same distribution of LIS and non-LIS doctoral degrees as before, the movement toward homogenization has changed. These new faculty often are not committed to librarianship even though it is one of the programs of their school. Instead, because of the diverse nature of information science, they are brought into schools for the interdisciplinary and technological expertise they offer. Rather than integrating into the existing professions, many bring their continued involvement in their fields of study into the LIS program. While this may strengthen the IS side of the curriculum, and some aspects of the LS, it can severely weaken the LS orientation of the faculty in general. These faculty also may bring with them a values structure that may be at variance with the needs of the library profession and specifically cataloging. As a consequence, faculty homogenization no longer occurs as it had in the past, thus placing the library science values of a program in jeopardy.

The absence of homogeneity in faculties today and a greater distancing of faculty in general from the library profession may be attributable to more than just differences in distribution of non-LIS doctorates among the faculty. What of faculty who hold LIS doctorates? Have they changed also? In the early 1970s and before, faculty members who pursued a doctoral degree in librarianship had some experience in the library profession, although that experience might have been minimal. Most doctoral programs in library science had as one requirement for admission that the applicant have some minimum, often two years, of professional library experience after attainment of the MLS degree. In the intervening 30 years, requirements for admission into doctoral programs in our schools have changed dramatically. No doctoral program is known that requires any professional work experience in LIS for admission. At many schools, applicants to the doctoral program no longer need possess a maser's degree in LIS or a closely related field. Rather, many programs require a master's degree in any field as the degree for admission. Indeed, a number of programs now mandate only the bachelor's degree as the degree requirement for admission to their doctoral program.

Previously, it was relatively rare to have a student progress from master's work directly into a doctoral program. Today that path is becoming increasingly common if not the norm. Frequently, students are admitted to a doctoral program immediately upon completion of their master's work which had followed immediately upon their baccalaureate study. The result of these doctoral admission requirement changes has been the creation of a class of current and future educators holding LIS doctoral degrees who have had little, if any, experience within the profession. Can individuals with such backgrounds accurately judge the value of cataloging for prospective librarians?

There is a concern by some that changes in LIS school faculty may have resulted in a diminishment of overall respect by them for the library profession. How else do we account for the frequent reference by faculty to the "L-word" rather than the word "library?" Would one talk about something, and intentionally avoid mentioning that word, if what was being referred to was held in respect? This comment excludes the term "digital library" which seems eminently acceptable in most quarters. When the American Library Association or its officers and representatives offer criticism and suggest improvements in library and information science education, it is not unusual for those comments to be met with derision by some faculty. Even that presumes that LIS faculty pay attention to statements from ALA. Without a doubt, some ALA suggestions could be viewed as defensive and not particularly progressive. But they nonetheless are efforts by the professional community to suggest improvements in the professional education of their field. Expressions or attitudes by faculty that they, librarians, "just don't get it" are all too typical. This view implies that they, faculty, know what is needed while librarians who criticize, at best, just don't understand, and at worst, refuse to recognize that the world has changed. While all, including faculty, have a right to their opinions, such assertions are not constructive and are a disturbing indication of an increasing divide between the members of the profession and its educators.

The attitude of faculty toward librarianship is crucial for it is faculty who make curricular decisions in our schools. It is they who initially decide what courses are part of a curriculum. They decide what should be added, changed, or deleted from it. They initially decide the requirements, and thus required courses, for a degree. In making these decisions, faculty are influenced by a variety of factors. Chief among them are their perceptions of the needs of the information profession and the roles of their graduates in it. Their perceptions may be irrespective of their knowledge of the information needs of those who will work in the library profession. While one would hope that information would be available or sought of those needs, there is no mechanism to ensure that it is sought, other than a review at re-accreditation time.

School administrators and faculty also must factor into their curricular decision-making the necessity of providing an increasing array of courses to cover the ever expanding scope of library and information science. While the number of ALA-accredited LIS schools has decreased in the past 20 years, student population has increased significantly. At the same time the total number of full-time faculty has not increased proportionately. The relationship of these three key elements in LIS education is illustrated in Table 6.[24]

Although the number of schools has declined by 16 percent since 1980, student enrollment in our degree programs has increased 85 percent. At the same time, the number of full-time faculty, after a decline for a decade, has nearly reached its 1980 level. With fewer schools, there are a few more full-time faculty on average per school, but that is no panacea. Those small increases in faculty size in no way compensate for the increase in student enrollment or in the much wider range of knowledge necessary to be covered by today's curricula. Consequently, adjunct faculty and others, e.g., teaching fellows, etc., teach an increasing percentage of courses. While instructional needs can be met through their use, they are not as involved in curricular decision-making beyond the course(s) they teach. Has the change in our faculties made us more dependent on these non full-time instructional members for coverage of cataloging?

Research also has assumed a far greater role in the life of the academic. Our universities, "Doctoral/Research Universities-Extensive" through "Master's Colleges and Universities II,"[25] are placing increasing emphasis upon research. It is within these universities that our LIS programs reside. Thus faculty, like their peers in the disciplines and other professions, must meet the expectations of their parent university in order to succeed. Additionally, with an increased emphasis on research in our doctoral programs, research is where the greatest interest of some faculty resides. Research can provide a wealth of opportunities, resources and interesting questions to a professional program. It can also create serious tensions and value questions in professional schools.

TABLE 6. Relationship of Number of Schools, Full-Time Faculty and Student Enrollment

Fall Semester	Schools	Full-Time Faculty	Students*	School/ Full-Time Faculty Ratio	Full-Time Faculty/ Students Ratio
1980	67	722	9,590	1 : 11	1 : 143
1990	57	612	12,291	1 : 11	1 : 216
2000	56	708	17,773	1 : 13	1 : 317

*Students (head count) enrolled in bachelor's, master's, post-master's, and doctoral programs offered by the school. Excludes other undergraduate and other graduate students enrolled in courses in the school but not part of the school's degree programs.

Source: Learmont 1981; Hurt 1991; Saye & Wisser 2001.

Foremost among the tensions can be that of research vs. teaching. In the rewards structures of many universities faculty realize that they must give primary emphasis to research over teaching if they are to survive and prosper. Some institutions publicly deny the subjugation of teaching to research. Among academics, however, it is common knowledge that it is research and publication which are preeminent in earning tenure and promotion. Although all universities value high-quality teaching, teaching generally is not the road to professorial success. Has this emphasis upon research by faculty had a positive or negative impact on cataloging instruction? Could it have played a role in a diminished view of this essential library function?

THE BASIC QUESTION, OR, THE CONCLUSION

This paper began by asking the question in its title: Where are we and how did we get here? The journey taken by library education over the past three decades has not been without successes and consequences. It has been strongly influenced by the transfiguration of what were library schools into schools of library and information science. That transfiguration continues. Had those changes not taken place it is highly likely that the casualty roll of schools closed would have been much greater. That change, combined with increasing student enrollment and a wider array of content to address, no commensurate increase in full-time faculty, and flat growth in the number of courses offered, has had its consequences. Those consequences include library science courses and library science faculty lines being transformed or redefined to provide for the information science needs of the LIS continuum. These changes brought in new faculty with differing views and values from those of their library science faculty predecessors. For the good of the schools hard decisions had to be made. Unfortunately some of those decisions could be viewed as impacting negatively on what had been strong programs for the education of librarians. It is possible that cataloging suffered in this, perhaps disproportionately.

The necessity exists to provide a greater array of course content to a greater number of students who have a wider range of professional interests. One approach in a time of limited resources is to offer that which provides the greatest good for the greatest number of students. It is this that is believed to have had the greatest impact on cataloging instruction. Gone is the luxury of teaching a required cataloging course for a school populated by aspiring librarians. Today's schools have many who seek no such professional goal. Their needs are wider than librarianship. Accordingly, one can see where it would be attractive to require an organization of information course for all students rather than a cataloging course.

While libraries are valued by all, and particularly the academic community, programs that support only library education are not viewed as a sustainable entity within many universities. As such, the move toward embracing information science made good sense given the relationship of information science and library science. With schools unable to focus their limited resources solely upon the preparation of librarians, the courses that support the knowledge and skills acquisition of would-be catalogers have had to change. Cataloging courses have had their role in the education of librarians forever altered, never again to return to the "golden age" they once had.

In cataloging, all this occurs at a time where there is more to organize than ever before. Not only are there multiple information formats widely in use, the avalanche of electronic resources and their attendant organization tools, particularly the numerous metadata standards, have emerged–all this at a time when the remaining library specific instruction is in competition for curriculum space and student time. In all likelihood cataloging will continue its decline in the professional education curriculum. To write those words is extremely difficult for me. They seem like heresy. It goes against my professional values and seems a rejection of the very intellectual process that has been the very soul of my teaching career.

If the situation and its causes have been identified correctly, we would truly be remiss if we were to expend fruitless effort at regretting the current situation. Decrying what has occurred may give some solace to us. It allows us to collectively share our concerns and dismay with others of like-mind and can provide us the comfort of feeling not alone. Unfortunately it doesn't correct what we feel needs correction.

If libraries want well-educated and intelligent catalogers, they must identify the best graduates of our schools and take a far greater role in their preparation. It is they who must teach them the intricacies and special knowledge of our craft. This places increased responsibility on catalogers to assume that greatly increased role in knowledge-sharing that these new graduates will need in order to function effectively. Some of the problems identified in this paper related to the teaching of cataloging are not exclusive to cataloging. But those problems are the responsibility of the cataloging community to solve. It is recognized that this added responsibility accrues to libraries at the time when they too, like so many others in society, are under increased pressure to do more with less. Our schools can't, and likely won't ever again, assume some of the instructional responsibilities they once had for the preparation of catalogers. It is left to those in library practice to assume that role if future catalogers are to have the vital knowledge base needed to organize the wealth of information resources materials their users need.

The purpose of this paper has not been to ascribe blame for what has occurred to cataloging instruction, if indeed there is anything for which blame should be assigned. Rather, its focus has been to describe the events that have unfolded and interpret their effects, as objectively as possible, on cataloging instruction in our professional schools. Perhaps it has been too pessimistic. I hope so, but I think not. Clearly we cannot go back to the way things were before, nor I believe, would we want to. To point the finger at the impact of information science and its community would be fruitless and inaccurate. Information science has saved our programs, not destroyed them. Everyone has played some role in events that have occurred. There is truly no one or one thing to blame for what has occurred to library education and specifically to the education of catalogers. Would that there were a "villain" that we could all blame. What we have today are the consequences of what were perceived as good decisions made by good people. We may disagree with some of those decisions, but they are now reality. Their consequences, whether we view them as beneficial and not, have changed the very nature of what was once the library profession and is now the information profession. The future, however, is still ours to make.

ENDNOTES

1. Cutter, Charles A. *Rules for a dictionary catalog.* 4th ed., rev. Washington, Government Printing Office. (U.S. Bureau of Education. Special Report on Public Libraries, Part II), 1904, p. 5.

2. White, Carl M. (1976). *A historical introduction to library education: problems and progress to 1951,* (Metuchen, NJ: Scarecrow Press, 1976): 53.

3. Miksa, Francis L. The Columbia School of Library Economy, 1887-1888. *Libraries & culture,* 23, Summer 1988, p. 262.

4. Miksa, Francis L. The Columbia School, p. 258.

5. Williamson, Charles. *Training for library service: a report prepared for the Carnegie Corporation of New York.* (New York. The Corporation, 1923), p. 21.

6. Williamson, Charles. *Training for library service,* p. 22.

7. Reece, Ernest J. (1936). *The curriculum in library schools.* (New York: Columbia University Press, 1936).

8. Wheeler, Joseph L. *Progress and problems in education for librarianship.* (New York: Carnegie Corporation of New York, 1946).

9. Berelson, Bernard, (Ed.). *Education for librarianship.* (Chicago: American Library Association, 1949).

10. Leigh, Robert D., (Ed.) (1952). The education of librarians. In Bryan, Alice I. *The public librarian,* (New York: Columbia University Press, 1952): 299-425.

11. Leigh, Robert D., (Ed.) (1952). The education of librarians, p. 338.

12. American Library Association. Committee on Accreditation. *Standards for accreditation of master's programs in library & information studies.* (Chicago: American Library Association, 1992).

13. Saye, Jerry D. with Wisser Katherine M. Students. In E. H. Daniel & J. D. Saye (Eds.), *Library and information science statistical report 2001,* (pp. 49-233). (Reston, VA: Association for Library and Information Science Education, 2001): 68.

14. Reported in the annual editions of the *Library and Information Science Statistical Report* of the Association for Library and Information Science Education (ALISE).

15. Sources for Table 2 include: Elspeth Pope. "Curriculum." In *Library science statistical report 1982,* (pp. C-1-C-34). State College, PA: Association of American Library Schools, 1982; Daniel D. Barron & Cassandra Perrine. "Curriculum." In T. W. Sineath (Ed.), *Library and information science statistical report 1992,* (pp. 251-322). Raleigh, NC: Association for Library and Information Science Education, 1992; Daniel D. Barron & Christine Westbrook. "Curriculum." In E. H. Daniel & J. D. Saye (Eds.), *Library and information science statistical report 2001,* (pp. 235-266). Reston, VA: Association for Library and Information Science Education, 2001.

16. For the purposes of clarity, irrespective of the title used by schools for specific courses, the titles "cataloging" and "organization of information" are used throughout this paper for such courses.

17. There are 11 Top 10 programs due to a tie for the 10th position.

18. Data are available for 52 of the 56 schools.

19. Barron, Daniel D. & Christine Westbrook. Curriculum. In E. H. Daniel & J. D. Saye (Eds.), *Library and information science statistical report 2001,* (Reston, VA: Association for Library and Information Science Education, 2001): 252.

20. Williamson, Charles. *Training for library service,* p. 37.

21. Williamson, Charles. *Training for library service,* p. 37.

22. Sources for Table 4 include: Timothy W. Sineath "Faculty." In T. W. Sineath. (Ed.), *Library and information science statistical report 1991,* (Sarasota, FL: Association for Library and Information Science Education, 1991): 1-69; Sineath, Timothy W. "Faculty." In E. H. Daniel & J. D. Saye (Eds.), *Library and information science statistical report 2001.* (Reston, VA: Association for Library and Information Science Education, 2001): 1-48.

23. Source for Table 5 is Timothy W. Sineath. "Faculty." In E. H. Daniel & J. D. Saye (Eds.), *Library and information science statistical report 2001.* (Reston, VA: Association for Library and Information Science Education, 2001); 1-48.

24. Sources for Table 6 include: Carol L. Learmont. Students. In *Library science statistical report 1981,* (pp. S-1-S-72). State College, PA: Association of American Library Schools, 1981; Charlie D. Hurt. Students. In T. W. Sineath (Ed.), *Library and information science statistical report 1991,* (pp. 70-218b). Sarasota, FL: Association for Library and Information Science Education, 1991; Jerry D. Saye with Wisser Katherine M. Students. In E. H. Daniel & J. D. Saye (Eds.), *Library and information science statistical report 2001.* (Reston, VA: Association for Library and Information Science Education, 2001): 49-233.

25. Carnegie Classification of Institutions of Higher Education.

"If I Knew Then What I Know Now": UNCG LIS Graduates' Perspectives on Cataloging Education

Beatrice Kovacs
Nancy Dayton

SUMMARY. The debate over whether cataloging courses should be required has continued for many years between faculties in various 'library' schools. To gauge the value of the required UNCG cataloging course and its impact on their professional duties, graduates of the UNCG MLIS program were surveyed during the last quarter of 2001. Of the 191 respondents, whether they had positions as catalogers or not, the overwhelming majority (89%) felt that such a course is essential and should be required. *[Article copies available for a fee from The Haworth Document Delivery Service: 1-800-HAWORTH. E-mail address: <getinfo@haworthpressinc.com> Website: <http://www.HaworthPress.com> © 2002 by The Haworth Press, Inc. All rights reserved.]*

KEYWORDS. Cataloging, core competencies, cataloging curriculum, education, librarianship, research

Beatrice Kovacs, MLS, PhD in Library Science, is Associate Professor, Department of Library and Information Studies, School of Education, University of North Carolina at Greensboro, Greensboro, NC 27402-6171 (E-mail: bea_kovacs@uncg.edu). Nancy Dayton is a graduate assistant and student in the MLIS program, Department of Library and Information Studies, School of Education, University of North Carolina at Greensboro, Greensboro, NC 27402-6171 (E-mail: njdayton@hotmail.com).

[Haworth co-indexing entry note]: " 'If I Knew Then What I Know Now': UNCG LIS Graduates' Perspectives on Cataloging Education." Kovacs, Beatrice, and Nancy Dayton. Co-published simultaneously in *Cataloging & Classification Quarterly* (The Haworth Information Press, an imprint of The Haworth Press, Inc.) Vol. 34, No. 1/2, 2002, pp. 145-164; and: *Education for Cataloging and the Organization of Information: Pitfalls and the Pendulum* (ed: Janet Swan Hill) The Haworth Information Press, an imprint of The Haworth Press, Inc., 2002, pp. 145-164. Single or multiple copies of this article are available for a fee from The Haworth Document Delivery Service [1-800-HAWORTH, 9:00 a.m. - 5:00 p.m. (EST). E-mail address: getinfo@haworthpressinc.com].

145

INTRODUCTION

The Department of Library and Information Studies (DLIS), School of Education, The University of North Carolina at Greensboro (UNCG), regularly surveys UNCG MLIS graduates to identify strengths and weaknesses in the curriculum and to evaluate the program's effectiveness in preparing them for professional positions. In addition, the faculty examines competency statements by professional organizations and revises appropriate courses to provide the content expected by employers.

As part of the continuing review and assessment of the curriculum for the Master of Library and Information Studies of the DLIS, the course known as LIS 640–Organizing Library Collections was examined recently. The content of this course includes, in one semester, the introduction to organizing materials, AACR2R, Dewey Decimal Classification, Library of Congress Classification and Subject Headings, descriptive and subject cataloging, bibliographic utilities, and related matters. Naturally, none of these topics can be explored in depth; rather, the aim is to provide an introduction to the field of cataloging. Any student wishing more in-depth coursework in cataloging can enroll in the advanced courses offered at The University of North Carolina at Chapel Hill, North Carolina Central University, or any other ALA-accredited Master's program with full credit toward their degree.

Changes in the curricula of some ALA-accredited programs prompted DLIS to reexamine its curriculum. As a result of this reassessment, two questions arose:

- Should LIS 640 remain a required course, or should it be made an elective, as has occurred in many other MLIS/MLS/MS in LS programs?
- Has such a brief survey course provided sufficient background for graduates to be able to catalog effectively?

To answer these questions, a Fall 2001 survey was conducted of UNCG MLIS graduates. The results of the survey are analyzed and summarized in this report.

CURRENT PERSPECTIVES

The literature of librarianship includes many articles about the value of cataloging education, from expressing the point of view of practicing catalogers to the impressions of recent graduates regarding their entire 'library school' experience. Many of these articles are subjective in tone. Other articles provide opinions on cataloging education from authors in the field. Research conducted in cataloging education tends to focus on employer expectations, 'library school' faculty perceptions, or changes in curricula of MLIS/MLS/MS in LS programs.

Recent research articles include a study by Spillane to determine how many library schools required an introductory cataloging course in 1998 in comparison to 1986, by examining school catalogs and Web sites. She found that the number of library schools which required introductory cataloging had dropped from 43 to 31 schools.[1] In contrast, current analysis of Web sites of 56 ALA-accredited schools conducted by the authors of this article in January 2002 found that 47 of 56 library schools required some form of 'information/materials/knowledge organization' coursework, with titles from "Cataloging and Classification" (three schools) or "Introduction to Bibliographic Control" (three schools) to "Organization of Information" (nine schools), and variations of those terms. Beheshti describes an exploratory study that mapped the curricula of ALA-accredited LIS programs throughout the United States and Canada, based on clustering keywords of course titles and descriptions, and created a "concept intensity map of the subjects being presently taught in [44] LIS programs." Analyses of the clusters showed that "the main knowledge and skill based competencies" were: Technology, Management, Organization of information, Searching and database development, and ten other areas. It is interesting to note that "Organization of information," which in many schools represents the basic cataloging concepts (according to course descriptions), is the third most "intense concept covered in the curricula."[2] Romero reported on a project in which students who had completed both an introductory and an advanced cataloging course enrolled in a practicum that simulated work in a cataloging department. Evaluations by students at the end of the project showed that they developed confidence in their skills, recognized the 'connection' between theory and practice, and the value of access and cataloging standards.[3]

Opinions in the literature about library education abound. For example, Miller wrote in 1996 that one of the basic concepts she came to understand during her library studies was "that implementing the basic tenets of librarianship in a practical sense, with integrity and understanding, means lifelong self-education and the ability to adapt to change, because change is constant."[4] With regard to the changing curricula in library schools, she commented, "Older existing cataloging and classification courses have given way to information storage and retrieval course offerings." Fallis and Frické suggest that practical skills training is not appropriate in graduate level programs, and that the University of Arizona does not "offer a course that teaches students precisely how to catalog books." They further say, "Fortunately, there are other organizations (e.g., state library associations) that do provide training (e.g., cataloging workshops)."[5] One can also find articles in the literature, such as the ones by Behrend,[6] Freeborn,[7] Hu,[8] Kaplan,[9] Lange,[10] Mak,[11] and Mann,[12] that explain the basics of descriptive or subject cataloging, classification, and other matters. These articles are generally clarifications for the problems of cataloging specific materials or for organizing materials in particular collections. Finally, El-Sherbini and Klim addressed the perception of the role of the cataloging librarian[13] when they said, "Catalogers are becoming managers, teachers, and trainers of non-professionals. They manage outsourcing projects, provide quality control, and database management."

The necessity or appropriateness of cataloging education has been examined in research studies conducted by practitioners and by educators. Examples of some of the most recent reports in the literature that gauge cataloging education follow: Garrett described the value of experiential learning and field experiences as a component of cataloging instruction at the University of Hawaii.[14] Callahan and MacLeod discussed research conducted on the effectiveness of cataloging education. Their assessment suggested that close cooperation between educators and cataloging practitioners to providing "practical, hands-on experience" would provide new professionals with the skills needed for the future.[15] An electronic survey, posted to "three library listservs" by Kempe[16] yielded 21 responses from students and recent graduates. The consensus appeared to be that cataloging should be required in any MLIS/MLS/MS in LS program. Interest in the perceptions of the UNCG MLIS graduates led to the development of this research.

METHODOLOGY

A brief survey (see the Appendix) was developed, pretested, modified, and approved for use with human subjects by the UNCG Institutional Review Board in September 2001. Identifying graduates was somewhat difficult. Changes in office staff and lack of resources over the years have made it impossible to keep up with all of the people who graduated from the program. It became apparent that the DLIS had lost track of many graduates as they moved from place to place. Therefore, the determination was made to facilitate the process by verifying through various sources the names and addresses of those who had graduated. The sources included the *ALA Membership Directory 2000*, the SLA's *Who's Who in Special Libraries 2000-2001*, and a list of North Carolina school media coordinators, along with individual faculty who had kept in touch with some of the graduates. People who graduated prior to 1970 were excluded because the expectation was that they were probably retired and/or hard to find. The list of potential survey recipients was reduced from over 1,000 names of graduates since 1960 to 320 individuals who graduated since 1970.

Each person on the list was sent an envelope in which there was a copy of the survey instrument, a cover letter explaining the research, and a stamped self-addressed envelope for return of the survey. Recipients were asked to make no references that would identify themselves (anonymity was therefore guaranteed), which enabled respondents to reply honestly and truthfully. For those who might wish to refrain from answering the survey, the letter requested that they return the blank survey, to ensure that it had reached the graduate. An unforeseen difficulty arose when the Raleigh, North Carolina main postal sorting facility tested positive for anthrax, and all mail in the facility had to be decontaminated. It is unknown whether some of the surveys (or responses) were involved in the decontamination, but it is known that some mail was lost. A target of 60% was determined to be sufficient to generalize to the population of graduates of the UNCG MLIS program.

Of the 320 surveys mailed, the U.S. Postal Service returned seven as undeliverable, and 191 (60%) were returned by the recipients. Of those, three were blank, with one including a note that the recipient was retired. The remaining 188 (59%) were analyzed using Microsoft Excel.

Demographic Data

To determine whether the respondent was in a cataloging position or in some other type of job, they were asked to identify their current position and previous positions held. The current positions are shown in Table 1. Twenty-one respondents listed their job as 'Other,' including library school faculty, technical services librarians, solo librarians, and those who listed 'several of the above.' Previous positions are also shown in Table 1. Since many graduates held more than one job subsequent to graduation, the totals for previous positions are greater than the number of respondents.

TABLE 1. Positions Currently or Previously Held (n = 188)

CURRENT	TITLE OF POSITION	PREVIOUS
0	Acquisitions librarian	8
37	Administrator/Director/Manager/Head	21
4	Archives/Preservation librarian	6
3	Associate/Assistant Director	3
1	Bibliographic instruction librarian	11
0	Business officer/librarian	2
5	Cataloging librarian	19
3	Children's/Young Adult librarian	14
3	Circulation librarian	15
6	Collection management librarian	7
8	Electronic services/Systems	10
1	Interlibrary loan librarian	12
1	Outreach/Extension librarian	6
1	Public relations librarian	3
19	Reference librarian	48
3	Research librarian	6
67	School media coordinator	29
0	Serials librarian	7
5	Special collections librarian	10
21	Other	42
188	TOTAL	279

   It is interesting to note the diversity of positions held both currently and previously. Current and previous positions may affect how the respondent views the subject matter presented in LIS 640–Organizing Library Collections.
   Another demographic datum that might affect responses is year of graduation. Figure 1 shows the graduation years of respondents and identifies the years in which respondents took the cataloging course.
   UNCG MLIS graduates were also asked to identify their course instructors. Over the years, a variety of individuals taught the cataloging course: some were full-time faculty and some were adjuncts. In some cases, students were dissatisfied with the instructors, which might affect their view of the course, but otherwise would not be relevant to the study. Therefore, all comments regarding instructors, positive or negative, have been removed from this report but will be made available to the Department faculty for future assessment of available adjuncts to

FIGURE 1. Year of Graduation/Year Cataloging Course Taken (n = 188)

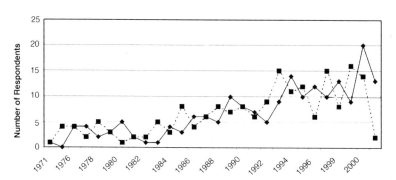

teach courses. After 1985, LIS 640 was revised to include *AACR2R*, Library of Congress Classification and Subject Headings, as well as Dewey Decimal Classification and Sears Subject Headings, bibliographic databases, and the theory of organization of materials. As can be seen by Figure 1, a majority of the respondents took the cataloging course after 1992, when the course was revised to include MARC format rather than creation of catalog cards.

The percentage of respondents who cataloged in their current or previous jobs is noted in Figure 2. Of the 72% who answered yes, 45% indicated that they had additional education for cataloging, with most of them attending workshops for specific vendor systems or for MARC format training (see Figure 3).

THE VALUE OF CATALOGING EDUCATION

It was great. Looking back, I'd have taken advanced cataloging if I knew then what I know now!

When asked whether the course assisted them in their job duties (see Figure 4), 83.5% (157) indicated that it did, no matter what their position.

Comments included: "I now know when something is wrong," "It's always good to have a grasp of cataloging procedures; it helps in searching, reference, etc.," "It made everything fall into place for me," "Even if one never uses the course information in a practical way, when you work in libraries it is still important to understand how their collections

FIGURE 2. Workplace Cataloging Experience (n = 187)

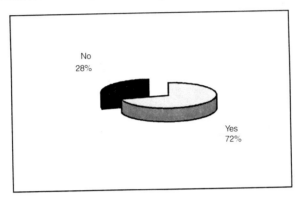

FIGURE 3. Additional Cataloging Education (n = 134)

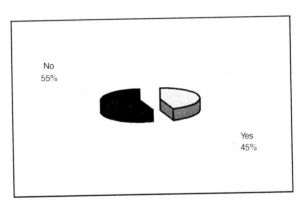

are organized," "Better understanding of catalog displays, 'tricks' for searching the catalog, advising users of materials locations, deciding a new automation as part of a library committee," and "I can't do it, but I can tell when someone who should know, doesn't."

Additional comments can be telling in terms of the naiveté of students, such as the following:

- "While it seemed one of the most boring classes at the time, it really did help."
- "As I have said to others, had it been my first course in Library Science, it would have been my last."

- "When I took the course, I was often 'lost-feeling' and felt like 'why will I need this if I can have automated cataloging.' I think the course has merit."
- "As much as I disliked the course, it did help me understand my job better. I've found at times that it helped me understand why items were placed in odd places in a collection and explain this to co-workers and the public."

Respondents were also asked to offer their opinions about whether the course should continue to be required for the UNCG MLIS program. The results, shown in Figure 5, indicate that 89% felt it should be required, 6% said that it should be offered as an elective, and 5% felt that a portion of the course should be part of the Foundations course, but the rest should be offered as an elective. One respondent, who checked 'no' to whether the course should be required, added the comment "Pay the vendor." Another said, "If you never use it, you lose it."

Some comments from the "Other" category included:

- "I'm divided on this answer. If a student wishes to work in Tech Services, absolutely. Other professional paths, I'm not so sure. It always helps to understand what all people do in making a library run."
- "Perhaps make a general overview course a requirement and make the traditional class an elective for those few students who might be interested."
- "Should be an elective for those who feel it necessary for area of specialization."
- "There probably don't need to be any required courses in the MLIS curriculum . . . If not required, LIS 640 would be the first of the core courses to become unavailable to those who wish to take it, because of insufficient enrollment. That's not a good outcome. It's a valuable course whose enrollment should not be limited to students who want to become cataloging librarians."
- "Perhaps due to automation and advanced technology the course could be combined or interwoven into another course."

On the other hand, one respondent wrote: "There should be two required cataloging courses: (1) Organization of Information Administration (an administrative, interdisciplinary approach), (2) Descriptive Cataloging (hands-on, how-to)."

Suggestions for improvement of the course ranged from offering two or more courses, beginning and advanced, to adding more information

FIGURE 4. Did the Cataloging Course Help? (n = 188)

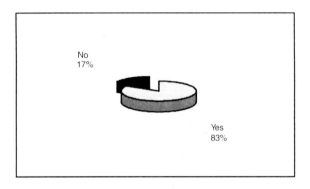

FIGURE 5. Should LIS 640 Be Required? (n = 187)

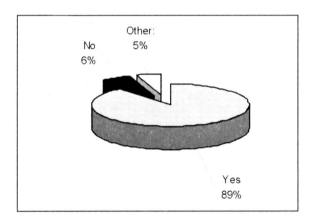

about electronic cataloging, i.e., using computerized cataloging programs and copy cataloging from bibliographic databases. Comments often followed along the lines of the current positions held by the graduates. Analysis of the responses for or against requiring the cataloging course is shown in Table 2.

Many respondents commented on their answers to this question, elaborating on their opinion with justification for keeping a traditional cataloging course as a requirement in an MLIS program. The most frequent response is that librarians need to understand how a catalog is cre-

TABLE 2. Responses by Current Job Positions (n = 188)

1. CURRENT POSITION	REQUIRE IT?	DON'T REQUIRE IT?	OTHER
Administrator/Director/Manager/Head	35	1	1
Archives/Preservation librarian	4		
Associate/Assistant Director	3		
Bibliographic instruction librarian	1		
Cataloging librarian	5		
Children's/Young Adult librarian	2		1
Circulation librarian	3		
Collection management librarian	5	1	
Electronic services/Systems	7	1	
Interlibrary loan librarian	1		
Outreach/Extension librarian	1		
Public relations librarian	1		
Reference librarian	15	2	2
Research librarian	1	1	1
School media coordinator	60	3	4
Special collections librarian	5		
Other	12	2	
Several of the above	3		1
Technical Services Librarian/Manager	3		
Total	167	11	10

ated and how to interpret records for patrons and for research. Selected additional comments are included below:

- "Even though I cannot remember details of the course, it is a *MUST*."
- "It is a necessary evil. School media people have to do all jobs so we really need instruction in everything."
- "Regardless of a person's immediate plans, you cannot know what you may consider doing later. We need librarians who are well rounded and can do it all! Not to mention librarians who can appreciate all the jobs needed!"
- "Even if we don't plan to be catalogers, we need to know the basics of how things are arranged. It makes you a better research/reference librarian!"
- "While in today's climate most materials come with LOC info, it may seem that cataloging is not as critical as it once was. I think it may be more so. Many times, I do not agree with the way it was cataloged or items in a set may be cataloged in different ways. It is good to know that I can decide where to put an item or why."

- "Because I had no previous library experience, this was a difficult course for me, but 'Cataloging' and 'Reference' were the most valuable courses I took. They gave me the basic background, or foundation, to successfully complete the other courses in the LIS curriculum. The 'Foundations' course told me I wanted to be a librarian; 'Cataloging' and 'Reference' showed me how; the remaining courses gave me additional skills that ensured success."

SUMMARY OF COMMENTS

Comments made by respondents were often insightful, humorous, or useful in determining the value of cataloging in the workplace. The authors felt that many of these comments were too valuable to be disregarded, so comments from the three positions with the greatest number of respondents (Administrators, Reference Librarians, and School Media Coordinators) are summarized.

Administrators' and Associate/Assistant Directors' Comments (n = 40)

I have observed that paraprofessionals in Technical Services can become quite proficient in locating, downloading, and adapting records for our online catalog. I still want and need a head cataloger with professional training in theory of cataloging and classification who can evaluate the tradeoffs and impact of the cataloging process becoming more rote.

Of the 40 respondents who reported their positions as either Associate/Assistant Director or Administrator/Director/Manager/Head, only one felt that cataloging and classification should be an elective, and one was uncertain whether they should be required because as an elective, the course might not have enough enrollees to be offered. The consensus of the respondents in this category was that all librarians should have a background in cataloging and classification, no matter what their position in a library. Additional comments included:

- "How can you call yourself a librarian if you can't read a catalog record and know where the information came from?"
- "As the basis for all library work, from location of material in the library to the organization of metadata in Web pages, understanding cataloging theory and rule is crucial."

- "New librarians with technical services skills are rarer [sic] and much appreciated in the 'real' world. We need to understand trends and problems, e.g., XML, shared databases, library system structures, what these systems do with tags. We need to loosen up our future hidebound catalogers while maintaining their understanding of the need for structure and discipline."

Several respondents in this category mentioned that Cataloging In Publication (CIP) is "wrong at times," requiring someone who has the proper background in theory and practice of cataloging to resolve problems with placement of materials in the collections. Also, if the library outsources the cataloging, the quality of vendor records varies. This may cause errors in the OPAC that need to be resolved. Also noted, occasionally items are acquired for, or donated to, the collections. These items may require original cataloging, since records may not exist in any bibliographic databases. Locally produced materials, for example, might not have any records for copy cataloging. If the librarians do not have the knowledge to create even short records, then access to the materials will be inhibited, errors may not be discovered, and service to patrons may be diminished.

Several stated that reference staff, serials librarians, acquisitions personnel, and indeed, all librarians needed to understand how the collections are organized and how to interpret the catalog. As stated by one respondent, "All librarians should know how and why materials are cataloged as they are. They should be able to know their collections and spot errors or mistakes that are being made by catalogers who are working either in their facilities or through outsourcing."

Reference Librarians' Comments (n = 19)

There were 19 respondents who identified themselves as reference librarians, and their comments consistently indicated that knowledge of cataloging is vital to the understanding of how library collections are organized. Most agreed that without an introduction to cataloging, a librarian would not be properly equipped to navigate the catalog efficiently or even to provide quality service to patrons, who in many cases are dependent on the librarians' expertise to guide them to the information they need. Some related comments include:

- "It is difficult to provide 'service' to patrons if you can't decipher the catalog records. You could do a passable job, but the better your understanding of the catalog, the better level of service you can provide."

- "Keep it as a basic requirement. I can't even imagine doing reference work without having had it. Cataloging is the course that teaches students the most about how library materials are organized and the rationale for that organizational scheme. It is also where we learned to decipher MARC records, use catalog records to find all sorts of info about materials that isn't apparent to the uninitiated, and figure out all of the possible subjects an item might be placed under (absolutely vital to reference librarians)."

Another prevalent theme among reference librarians' responses was the identification of cataloging as the foundation of librarianship. Many drew the conclusion that since the organization of materials is so intimately connected to librarianship as a whole, a brief education in cataloging is essential for all kinds of librarians, not just full-time catalogers. The point not to be missed is that the quality of access to a library's collection affects everyone: patrons, administration, and every librarian in between.

- "For many librarians, this will be the only exposure they have to the theories of library organization. A good librarian should be able to use this information to relate to his/her own job to help him/her do it better. I have noticed many librarians can become focused only on their particular jobs in the library. That can be detrimental to the functioning of the library as a whole. That can also keep them from helping patrons find the information they need. The MLIS curriculum should expose students to all aspects of the library. The best way we can help patrons to find information is to organize it, but if we don't organize it well or know how to use the organizational structure, then we aren't much help at all."
- "Understanding cataloging basics is *critical* to librarianship. This becomes even more true as computer technology makes searching data sets *far* more sophisticated and complex."
- "It is essential to understanding how to find materials. Even though I've never cataloged, my cataloging course has helped me with my reference work. It truly helps you understand how things are classified and why."
- "It is important for any type of librarian to understand how items are indexed or cataloged in order to better help patrons/public. I enjoyed the course and am glad I have had a chance to perform various job duties that require cataloging knowledge."

School Media Coordinators' Comments (n = 67)

> This course was one of the most relevant and directly applicable courses in my entire MLIS curriculum.

There were more school media specialists represented in the survey (making up 36% of the total responses) than any other group.

While many acknowledged that outsourcing had become the prevailing practice among school librarians, they were nonetheless quick to clarify that original cataloging is still very much a daily reality. Several pointed out that some materials, such as donated items, arrive without having been pre-processed and pre-packaged with MARC records. Many respondents also indicated that acquiring cataloging skills is particularly important in the education of a media specialist, since he/she is called on to wear many hats and perform many duties.

- "I feel the course is very important for school librarians. While cataloging is available from many companies, we still catalog many resources 'from scratch.' "
- "School libraries receive materials from various sources that will require in-house cataloging. We need an understanding of the standards and strategies for adding new materials in a logical manner."
- "It is essential to the understanding of library organization. Individual cataloging will always be needed in smaller libraries."
- "Even if librarians order items pre-processed and cataloged, I believe they still need to understand cataloging basics in order to evaluate the quality of the MARC records they receive and to be able to do some original cataloging when needed."

However, another person said, "Unsure if it was worth a full semester–a shorter course–perhaps combining it with other useful material would be more useful for media specialists since those of us using Alliance Plus catalog only about 10% of the time."

The school media specialists' responses echoed those of the reference librarians and others in that they emphasized the influence of cataloging on every position in the library. As a consequence, every librarian ought to possess a working knowledge of cataloging, or at least grasp the theories of organization that provide a context for actual library practice.

- "Every librarian should understand how items are cataloged whether he/she ever has to actually catalog or not. One can't make an educated decision about the cataloging of an item unless one knows how the system works."
- "It's difficult to imagine a library job that wouldn't need at least some knowledge about the how's and why's of cataloging."
- "Librarians need a broad understanding of cataloging, even if they never catalog. I have worked in different schools where cataloging demands varied! Not having worked in a library, I could not connect my new learning to previous knowledge. If librarians think they will never use the information learned in cataloging, but later change to areas that require the skills taught in cataloging, appropriate in-service is often non-existent or expensive."
- "I needed to know this for every job I've had."
- "Even if your job does not require cataloging, it is essential that you know the fundamentals and the process. This knowledge will help you deal with other aspects of the library."
- "Cataloging–organization–is the backbone of librarianship."

While many argued that knowledge of cataloging is useful for understanding how library collections are organized, some school media specialists who responded to the survey raised an even more interesting point, one that is too often overlooked in debates over appropriate cataloging curricula: meeting the needs of the library users. One respondent observed: "Organization is the cornerstone to accessibility. A professional librarian should be thoroughly trained in how collections are organized so that he/she can fit new acquisitions into the collection to be most easily found and utilized." Several others expressed the weight of a librarian's responsibility to catalog according to the users' needs.

- "Librarians must be aware of the need for good cataloging to provide good access to the collection. Students need to know the need for consistency. They need to know about all the options available to use for cataloging."
- "Basic knowledge of cataloging is necessary in order to understand what the new technology methods are all about. Even in today's technological age, consistent practices learned in this course are beneficial and necessary to avoid a chaotic, unorganized system, so that collection information is easily accessible to users."
- "Perhaps the most important thing I learned . . . was that how I organize my collection, or catalog my records, ought to fit my students' needs."

SUGGESTIONS FOR COURSE REVISION

The respondents made many suggestions to improve or update the cataloging course. These suggestions tended to involve several themes, as demonstrated in Table 3.

The two most frequent comments that did not directly relate to cataloging content emphasized the importance of cataloging for those who plan to seek positions in departments other than technical services. Specifically, 58 respondents commented that the cataloging course helped them understand the library collection and how it is arranged, and 41 mentioned that learning about traditional cataloging helped them understand their work, made them better reference librarians or online searchers, and is important for well-rounded librarians.

CONCLUSION

Graduates, no matter what position they hold in libraries, felt that they would not have been as effective in their jobs if they had not had the required cataloging course. The consensus among UNCG MLIS graduates is that LIS 640–Organizing Library Collections should continue to be required of all UNCG LIS students. However, they made nu-

TABLE 3. Suggestions for LIS 640 Revision (n = 184)

SUGGESTION	NUMBER OF RESPONSES
Add more information on 'electronic' cataloging	46
Stress importance of understanding MARC format	35
Provide 'field' experience and 'hands-on' with catalogers	28
Offer two courses: introduction and advanced	21
Stress importance of learning original cataloging	15
Provide exposure to various cataloging systems and how to select the best for your situation	13
Stress importance of subject authority	12
Offer 'type of library' specific cataloging courses	11
Small class size with individual attention	9
Provide more theory and less detail	8
Offer two courses: theory and practice	6
Stress importance of name and series authority files	5
Provide practice with copy cataloging from OCLC	5
Offer two courses: traditional cataloging and electronic cataloging	3
Provide more information about outsourcing	3

merous suggestions about additional or 'new' content that should be added to the course, updating material covered and adding relevance in today's technological world.

The DLIS is grateful for the many thoughtful suggestions offered by the respondents, and will assess the course structure in light of these suggestions. The authors wish to thank all those who responded to the survey for taking the time to provide such insightful and discerning comments. One respondent, in particular, seemed to synthesize the majority of opinions in the following quote (to which the authors wish they could provide attribution, but they do not know the identity of the respondent):

> People need to understand that the organization of information is more critically important now than ever, because there is so much more information out there. The world is in desperate need of our skills!

ENDNOTES

1. Jodi Lynn Spillane, "Comparison of Required Introductory Cataloging Courses, 1986 to 1998," *Library Resources & Technical Services* 43 (October 1999): 223-230.

2. Jamshid Beheshti, "Library and Information Studies Curriculum: Based on a presentation at the 27th Annual Conference of the Canadian Association for Information Science, June 9-12, 1999," <URL: http://www.gslis.mcgill.ca/beheshti/alacasi4.htm>.

3. Lisa Romero, "The Cataloging Laboratory: The Active Learning Theory Applied to the Education of Catalogers," *Cataloging & Classification Quarterly* 21:1 (1995): 3-17.

4. Marilyn Miller, "What to Expect from Library School Graduates," *Information Technology and Libraries* 15 (March 1996): 46.

5. Don Fallis & Martin Frické, "Not by Library School Alone," *Library Journal* 124 (October 15, 1999): 44-45.

6. Linda Behrend, "Access Points, Authorized Headings, and Controlled Vocabulary in the Online Catalog," *Tennessee Librarian* 51 (Fall 2000): 24-35.

7. Robert B. Freeborn, "Cataloging of the Weird: Further Examples for the 3-D Perplexed," *MC Journal* 6 (Fall 1999): electronic file available at URL: http://wings.buffalo.edu/publications/mcjrnl/v6n2/freeborn.html.

8. Jiajian Hu, "Transactional Analysis: Problems in Cataloging Chinese Names," *Illinois Libraries* 82 (Fall 2000): 251-260.

9. Allison G. Kaplan, "Standardized Cataloging Rules: An Informal Exploration for the Beginner or Faint of Heart," *Book Report* 18 (January/February 2000): 38-43.

10. Holley R. Lange, "Cataloging Maps: Getting Started," *Colorado Libraries* 25 (Spring 1999): 40-41.

11. Shiu K. Mak, "Cataloging Genealogical Materials," *Kentucky Libraries* 65 (Summer 2001): 34-36.

12. Thomas Mann, "Teaching *Library of Congress Subject Headings*," *Cataloging & Classification Quarterly* 29:1/2 (2000): 117-126.

13. Magda El-Sherbini & George Klim, "Changes in Technical Services and Their Effect on the Role of Catalogers and Staff Education: An Overview," *Cataloging & Classification Quarterly* 24:1/2 (1997): 32.

14. LeAnn Garrett, "Dewey, Dale, and Bruner: Educational Philosophy, Experiential Learning, and Library School Cataloging Instruction," *Journal of Education for Library and Information Science* 38 (Spring 1997): 129-136.

15. Daren Callahan & Judy MacLeod, "Management Issues and the Challenge for Cataloging Education," *Technical Services Quarterly* 13:2 (1996): 15-24.

16. Jeff Kempe, "New Trends in Library Education: The Attitudes of Students and Recent Graduates Towards Library School Curricula," *Mississippi Libraries* 61 (Winter 1997): 82-86.

APPENDIX. Survey of the Value of Cataloging (LIS 640–Organizing Library Collections)

Demographic Data:

1. **Current position** (check the **one** which is closest to your duties):

   ☐ Acquisitions librarian
   ☐ Administrator/Director/Manager/Head
   ☐ Archives/Preservation librarian
   ☐ Associate/Assistant Director
   ☐ Bibliographic instruction librarian
   ☐ Business officer/librarian
   ☐ Cataloging librarian
   ☐ Children's/Young Adult librarian
   ☐ Circulation librarian
   ☐ Collection management librarian

   ☐ Electronic services/Systems
   ☐ Interlibrary loan librarian
   ☐ Outreach/Extension librarian
   ☐ Public relations librarian
   ☐ Reference librarian
   ☐ Research librarian
   ☐ School media coordinator
   ☐ Serials librarian
   ☐ Special collections librarian

   ☐ Other: _____

2. Other positions you held, prior to your current position (Please check all that apply): (Same **format as Q. 1 in the original instrument**)

3. Year graduated: _____

4. Year you took cataloging (approximately): _____

5. After taking the cataloging course (LIS 640), how prepared were you to catalog materials for your collections? _____

6. Have you taken any additional courses, workshops, seminars, or other educational opportunities to update your knowledge of cataloging?
   a. ☐ Yes (If yes, please list the topics covered, briefly): _____
   b. ☐ No
   Comment: _____

7. In your work experience, has the cataloging course assisted you in conducting your job duties?
   a. ☐ Yes   b.   ☐ No   Comment: _____

8. With what you know now, what suggestions would you make about the cataloging course? (You may attach another sheet or use the back of this page.)

9. Should the course continue to be a requried course in the MLIS curriculum?
   a. ☐ Yes   b.   ☐ No   c.   ☐ Other: _____
   Please explain your response to either a, b, or c: _____

10. Is there anything else you would like to say about LIS 640: Organizing Library Collections?

Thank you for your time and input. Please **do not** put your name or identifying information on either the survey or the envelope to assure anonymity!
Please return this survey in the enclosed, stamped, self-addressed envelope.
[Please note: This instrument has been reduced from 15 questions, 5 of which refer specifically to concerns of the Department Curriculum Committee, as well as to save space for publication.]

Cataloging or Knowledge Management: Perspectives of Library Educators on Cataloging Education for Entry-Level Academic Librarians

Michelle R. Turvey
Karen M. Letarte

SUMMARY. The topic of cataloging education for catalogers and non-catalogers alike has been a perennial topic for practitioners. This follow-up study explores the views of library educators with regard to cataloging education. Twenty-three educators with primary teaching duties in reference, twenty-nine educators with primary teaching duties in cataloging and seventy educators whose primary teaching duties were in neither reference nor cataloging in ALA-accredited master's degree programs responded to a survey based on the ALCTS Educational Policy Statement, Appendix: Knowledge and Skills, Intellectual Access and Information Organization concerning the importance of cataloging competencies for all entry-level academic librarians. The survey found library educators, in general, agreed with practitioners on the listed cataloging competencies for all entry-level academic librarians. *[Article copies available for a fee from The Haworth Document Delivery Service: 1-800-HAWORTH. E-mail address: <getinfo@haworthpressinc.com> Website: <http://www.Haworth Press.com> © 2002 by The Haworth Press, Inc. All rights reserved.]*

Michelle R. Turvey is Cataloging Librarian, Duane G. Meyer Library, Southwest Missouri State University, Springfield, MO 65804-0095. Karen M. Letarte is Assistant Head of Cataloging, North Carolina State University Libraries, North Carolina State University, Raleigh, NC 27695-7111.

[Haworth co-indexing entry note]: "Cataloging or Knowledge Management: Perspectives of Library Educators on Cataloging Education for Entry-Level Academic Librarians." Turvey, Michelle R., and Karen M. Letarte. Co-published simultaneously in *Cataloging & Classification Quarterly* (The Haworth Information Press, an imprint of The Haworth Press, Inc.) Vol. 34, No. 1/2, 2002, pp. 165-187; and: *Education for Cataloging and the Organization of Information: Pitfalls and the Pendulum* (ed: Janet Swan Hill) The Haworth Information Press, an imprint of The Haworth Press, Inc., 2002, pp. 165-187. Single or multiple copies of this article are available for a fee from The Haworth Document Delivery Service [1-800-HAWORTH, 9:00 a.m. - 5:00 p.m. (EST). E-mail address: getinfo@haworthpressinc.com].

KEYWORDS. Cataloging education, competencies, academic librarians

INTRODUCTION

The library world is characterized by fast-paced change, and perhaps no other area as much as the field of cataloging. As the digital library becomes a reality, catalogers wrestle with fundamental, even existential questions. What is the nature and function of the library catalog in an increasingly digital world? Is it still desirable to create surrogates for digital objects? How will cataloging reinvent itself to address these challenges, and what skills and competencies will the new practitioners need? Seemingly in light of this existential crisis, recent articles have posed the question of whether cataloging education belongs in the graduate school curriculum.[1] Yet far from a recent debate, cataloging's place in the curriculum has been questioned cyclically since the 1920s, when those in the library field perceived a need for increased professionalism.[2]

The importance of professional education in general has come to the fore, resulting in the convening of two national American Library Association (ALA) conferences devoted to the topic: Congress on Professional Education (COPE1 and COPE2). One of the most critical issues to emerge from COPE is the concept of competencies for library education. The need for competencies, which help to define the shared professional experience, seems to lie at the heart of the profession.

Yet as ALA-accredited master's degree programs evolve to meet the changing needs of employers and graduates working in an increasingly complex information environment, the competencies within these programs are continually redefined as well. Traditionally, cataloging education has been a core element of the ALA-accredited master's degree program. At this existential crossroads for the field, do library educators still view cataloging competencies as relevant for the entry-level academic library practitioner? Do library educators and library practitioners share a common view on core cataloging competencies for today's new professionals? This follow-up study, based on an earlier study by the authors,[3] explores the perceptions of library educators on the importance of cataloging education and cataloging competencies for all entry-level academic librarians. Results are compared to those of a recent study of practitioners' views on cataloging competencies for entry-level academic librarians.

For the purposes of this paper, the term "cataloging" is broadly defined, encompassing the spectrum of intellectual activities relating to the provision of bibliographic control, from traditional cataloging and classification to the use of metadata schemata and knowledge management. Questions on specific cataloging tools and standards were included as a means of gauging the perceptions of educators as to their continued relevance given the rapid development of a variety of new standards.

The survey was based on the Association for Library Collections and Technical Services' ALCTS Educational Policy Statement.[4] The competencies included in the survey were derived from those contained in the section Intellectual Access and Information Organization, in the Appendix Knowledge and Skills. The ALCTS Educational Policy Statement[5] contains a balance of theoretical and practical technical services competencies, making it an ideal instrument.

LITERATURE REVIEW

The literature on cataloging education is varied, including a number of older studies that have not been updated or revisited. The cataloging education literature falls into five distinct groups: cataloging curriculum,[6,7,8,9,10,11] catalogers' competencies according to practitioners,[12,13,14] catalogers' competencies according to library educators,[15,16] competencies for librarians in different specialties,[17,18] and competencies for all graduates.[19,20]

The future of cataloging education is a critical issue in the brave new digital library world that all new graduates will face, whether conducting bibliographic instruction, handling vendor negotiations and contracts, or providing access to the resources themselves. Hill and Intner address the future of cataloging education, assessing the needs of the profession during the evolution of cataloging to knowledge management saying:

> It is particularly ironic that at the very moment in time that the world is poised to take advantage of a universe of new knowledge, much of it furnished to us without the burdens of having to order it, wait for fulfillment, receive, and process it, libraries hiring newly-graduated master's degree-holding librarians may lack the skilled professional staff who hold the key to managing it successfully. The reason is clear: library schools are removing cataloging

from the list of core proficiencies new professionals must acquire. Nothing could be more detrimental to successful patron service. Librarians of the future need to open the packages they have been cataloging and retrieving for decades and start describing, organizing and managing their contents. The new library collection will be global, multimedia, diverse, and only partly contained within library walls. When we have achieved a profound understanding of this new knowledge collection, we can start managing it for ours clients and our institutions.[21]

A recent study by the authors[22] explored the views of reference and cataloging practitioners on cataloging education for all entry-level academic librarians. The study revealed a high level of agreement among heads of reference and heads of cataloging in Association of Research Libraries (ARL) institutions on the continued importance of cataloging competencies (broadly defined) for all entry-level academic librarians. However, an apparent gap exists between what practitioners consider to be important knowledge for new graduates and what is contained in the curriculum. In the cataloging field, there is a definite sentiment that library schools are deemphasizing technical services, particularly cataloging, in the curriculum.[23] The literature supports this assumption, revealing a decrease in the number of required cataloging courses over the past twenty years.[24,25]

To gain a clearer understanding of the importance of cataloging education for all entry-level academic librarians, it is essential to look not only at the views of practitioners but also of library educators. Practitioners' responses, while important, must be informed by the views of those teaching and developing the curriculum within ALA-accredited master's degree programs. Library educators directly influence the perception and role of cataloging education and cataloging competencies within their individual schools.

METHODOLOGY

The ALCTS Educational Policy Statement[26] contains competencies for a variety of technical services functions, including cataloging. The survey was based on the competencies found in the ALCTS Educational Policy Statement, Appendix: Knowledge and Skills, Intellectual Access and Organization. This document includes both theory and practice, making it a balanced source of cataloging competencies. The survey on which the current study was based sought to solicit information on whether or not library educators viewed the listed cataloging competencies as important for all entry-level academic librarians.

In order to compare the views of library educators to those of the practitioners surveyed earlier, a nearly identical survey instrument was used. Only one modification was made: while respondents to the practitioner survey had been asked to identify their areas as either "reference" or "cataloging," library educators responding to the current survey specified their primary teaching duties as either "reference," "cataloging," or "other," neither primarily reference nor cataloging. As in the earlier study, an entry-level academic librarian was defined operationally as the first professional position following the receipt of an ALA-accredited master's degree. Entry-level academic librarians were targeted because the authors are most familiar with the qualifications of academic librarians.

For this study, library educators were defined as full-time teaching faculty in ALA-accredited master's degree programs. The researchers wanted to insure that all faculty who regularly teach reference or cataloging courses received surveys. Because sabbaticals, use of adjunct and doctoral teaching appointments, existence of multiple sections at some schools, and additional duties made identification of such faculty difficult, it was decided to open the survey to all full-time faculty, adjuncts, and administrators. Names were obtained from the official Web pages of each program, commonly from information found under faculty directories or the equivalent.

Letters soliciting participation were sent via e-mail to 645 library educators. In order to prevent unsolicited participation, usernames and passwords were provided within the contact e-mail. Completed surveys were returned by e-mail. Responses were then transferred into Excel for manipulation and analyzed using SPSS statistical software. Missing data was coded as such to prevent inflated figures. Of the 123 usable responses, one failed to indicate primary teaching duties. This omission brought the total number of usable responses by teaching area to 122.

Although the pool of respondents was relatively small, it was comparable to the pool of practitioner respondents in the previous study. Obtaining an accurate list of current, full-time library educators proved difficult, as many programs employ adjunct practitioners and doctoral students as instructors. A number of graduate programs included faculty from departments such as computer science or education who declined to complete the survey, citing that it was outside of their respective fields. Some administrators also declined to participate, on the basis of a lack of current, direct teaching involvement.

RESEARCH PROBLEMS

To guide the analysis of this follow-up study, the following research questions were posed. In the view of library educators:

- Is cataloging education important for all entry-level academic librarians?
- Is there a basic set of cataloging competencies that entry-level academic librarians should possess?
- Do library educators whose primary teaching responsibilities are in reference, cataloging, or neither in reference nor cataloging view the cataloging competencies differently?
- Are theory-based competencies viewed differently from practice-based competencies?
- How do the views of library educators differ from those of practitioners with respect to cataloging competencies for entry-level academic librarians?

The answers to the questions posed above have implications for the curriculum and the needs of practitioners in academic libraries now and into the future.

RESULTS

The survey, based on the ALCTS Educational Policy Statement: Knowledge and Skills, Intellectual Access and Information Organization, focused on cataloging competencies both broad and specific. For the purposes of this study, the authors adopted the broad definition of cataloging put forth by Hill and Intner, using the term to encompass the knowledge and activities of describing, indexing, classifying and providing bibliographic control.[27] In this analysis, the terms "competency" and "skill" are used interchangeably. Participants were asked to rank the importance of the competencies listed for all entry-level academic librarians, regardless of specialty, according to the following four-point scale: 1 = Essential; 2 = Important; 3 = Desirable, but not necessary, and 4 = Unimportant.

The first research question concerns library educators' perception of the importance of the listed cataloging competencies for all entry-level academic librarians. Responses for all 123 participants are summarized in Table 1, arranged as ranked by all participants from most important to least important by mean response. Table 1 shows both the mean and median level of importance for each competency. In the context of this paper, any competency with a mean response of 2.0 or lower is considered to be important to respondents. Participants appeared to agree that the majority of competencies are important for entry-level academic librarians, with all but eight of the competencies garnering mean responses less than or equal to 2.0. The range of mean responses for all competencies is relatively narrow, ranging from "the ability to read and interpret a bibliographic record in an OPAC" (mean of 1.22) to knowledge of "Library of Congress Rule Interpretations" (mean of 2.38). On the given scale, mean responses for all competencies thus fall between the categories of essential and desirable but not necessary. An examination of median responses reveals that every competency falls within the essential to important range. These results demonstrate that the respondents clearly consider the listed cataloging competencies to be important for entry-level academic librarians.

The most essential competency, with a mean response of 1.22, is "the ability to read and interpret a bibliographic record in an OPAC." The most highly ranked competencies, those with median responses between 1 and 1.5, are among the broadest and most theoretical on the list. They include:

- understanding of information-seeking behaviors of users
- knowledge of the theory of information organization and intellectual access
- knowledge of the ways in which data structures affect precision and recall
- basic knowledge of cataloging tools and
- knowledge of the MARC format.

The presence of the last two competencies in this group (with median/mean rankings of 1/1.61 and 1/1.63, respectively) is particularly interesting in the light of recent controversy over the inclusion of cataloguing education in the graduate curriculum. They are not only more specific than the other highly ranked competencies but are also more closely associated with the study and practice of the field of cataloging than are the other highly-ranked competencies. Survey respondents seem to perceive these competencies to be of continued relevance.

Competencies ranked as less important, with means greater than 2.0, include working knowledge of cataloging tools, knowledge of methods for thesaurus creation, and knowledge of specific tools and standards,

TABLE 1. Mean and Median Rankings, All Respondents

Competency	Mean	SD	Median	IQR
Ability to read and interpret a bibliographic record in an OPAC	1.22	.5679	1	0
Understanding of information-seeking behaviors of users	1.29	.6105	1	0
Knowledge of the theory of information organization and intellectual access	1.36	.6289	1	1
Understanding of the activities that must be performed to provide the products and services users need	1.49	.6711	1	1
Knowledge of the ways in which searching techniques affect precision and recall	1.55	.7488	1	1
Ability to evaluate information-retrieval systems in relation to user needs and information-seeking behaviors	1.59	.7110	1	1
Cataloging tools: Basic knowledge of	1.61	.7323	1	1
MARC format	1.63	.7841	1	1
Classification: Knowledge of theory	1.67	.7520	2	1
Knowledge of the ways in which data structures affect precision and recall	1.68	.7848	1.5	1
Knowledge of the theoretical basis for retrieval	1.69	.7589	2	1
Awareness of bibliographic utilities	1.70	.7997	2	1
Knowledge of bibliographic relationships underlying database design	1.74	.8182	2	1
Describing, identifying, and showing relationships among materials: Knowledge of theory	1.75	.7421	2	1
Subject analysis: Knowledge of theory	1.76	.7393	2	1
Library of Congress Subject Headings	1.76	.7826	2	1
Subject analysis: Knowledge of methods for	1.77	.6935	2	1
Knowledge of relevant national and international cataloging standards	1.79	.7493	2	1
Classification: Knowledge of methods for	1.83	.7651	2	1
Ability to develop and apply syndetic structure and controlled vocabulary in information retrieval systems	1.84	.7752	2	1
Library of Congress Classification	1.84	.7752	2	1
Knowledge of the basic database design concepts	1.84	.7507	2	1
Anglo-American Cataloguing Rules	1.84	.8816	2	1
Understanding the relationship of the research library's units to the provision of intellectual access to information resources	1.85	.8197	2	1
Describing, identifying, and showing relationships among materials: Knowledge of methods for	1.85	.8199	2	1
Indexing: Knowledge of theory	1.87	.7709	2	1
Understanding the relationship between classification schemes and shelf order	1.87	.8620	2	1
Knowledge of sources of bibliographic records	1.89	.8213	2	1
Thesaurus creation: Knowledge of theory	1.90	.7832	2	1
Knowledge of principles for designing user-driven information retrieval systems	1.98	.7516	2	1
Indexing: Knowledge of methods for	1.98	.7271	2	1
Cataloging tools: Working knowledge of	2.05	.8416	2	2
Dewey Decimal Classification	2.08	.8191	2	1
HTML	2.08	.8123	2	1

Competency	Mean	SD	Median	IQR
Thesaurus creation: Knowledge of methods for	2.09	.8099	2	2
Dublin Core	2.12	.7368	2	1
Knowledge of state-of-the-art research and practice in cataloging and classification	2.21	.8052	2	1
Core Record Standard	2.36	.7621	2	1
Library of Congress Rule Interpretations	2.38	.8560	2	1

such as HTML and Dublin Core. Knowledge of state-of-the-art research practice in cataloging and classification and knowledge of the Library of Congress Rule Interpretations received among the weakest ratings, with means of 2.21 and 2.38, respectively. This is not surprising, since respondents were ranking the importance of competencies for all entry-level academic librarians, not just those going into cataloging.

The second research question explores the existence of a set of cataloging competencies identified by respondents as "core" for all entry-level academic librarians. As results in Table 1 demonstrate, respondents appear to believe strongly that the competencies listed are important for academic librarians. Thirty-one of the thirty-nine competencies, or 79.5%, have means less than or equal to 2.0, suggesting that respondents consider them important or essential. These thirty-one competencies could be considered "core" in the context of this study.

Textual comments submitted by 43 respondents provide further insights into the perceptions of library educators. Some clear themes emerged from these comments. Nine of the forty-three comments (20%) suggested that knowledge of the concepts of organization of information is essential for all librarians, not just those who will work as catalogers. One respondent wrote, "I'm glad you are doing this survey. I teach reference, but tell every class that they cannot make decent reference librarians if they do not understand thoroughly the principles of organization. Indispensable!" Another stated, "I had completed the survey on the basis of 'Competencies for Entry Level Catalogers,' and then went back and re-read the instructions. When I re-coded I was surprised how few item[s] changed: mostly reversing the level of importance of theory and practice and reducing essential to important."

A second theme emerging from the written comments is that a broad understanding of these concepts, not specifically as cataloging concepts, but within the broader context of information organization, is important. Wrote one respondent, "I believe we need to dramatically shift our emphasis from 'cataloging' to organization of information which includes much, much, more than cataloging and classification." Another added, "The skills of cataloging, while still important in libraries, are not a requirement for most library and library-oriented jobs. However, the concepts of information organization are important to all information professionals."

Third, comments suggested that theoretical knowledge of the organization of information is critical. One respondent wrote, "Details and specifics of information organization are changing and variable with digital resources. This environment requires a good understanding of underlying theory for effective decision making, rather than knowledge of specific practice (although practice is always popular with employers)." Another respondent also emphasized the need for both theoretical and practical knowledge: "Even at entry level, librarians need to be equipped with theoretical and practical knowledge of database architecture, information retrieval, organization of information and information seeking behavior of library users. These issues are a significant component of the core LIS courses as well as of the daily activities of library professionals."

Respondents were asked to indicate their primary teaching areas: reference, cataloging, or other. Twenty-three of the 123 respondents identified reference as their primary area, 29 identified cataloging, and 70 identified other. One respondent did not identify an area. Table 2 shows a comparison of mean responses by teaching area, arranged from most to least important according to the perceptions of respondents who identified reference as their primary area. The data in Table 2 indicate that educators in the three groups generally agreed upon the importance of the listed competencies. The competencies for which their views differed significantly will be addressed below.

The third research question considers whether the three groups of library educators, those with primary teaching responsibilities in reference, cataloging or other (neither reference nor cataloging), viewed the competencies differently. In order to assess the differences in response, two statistical analyses were used. A one-way ANOVA was performed to analyze the variance of mean response of library educators by teaching area. The researchers hypothesized that there would be a significant difference in response between the three groups of library educators. The null hypothesis was that there would be no significant difference in the way the three groups of library educators viewed the importance of cataloging competencies for all entry-level academic librarians. With the confidence interval set at 0.95, and a p value less than or equal to 0.05, the ANOVA indicated a statistically significant difference in response between the three groups with respect to only seven competen-

TABLE 2. Mean Responses by Teaching Area

Competency	Reference Mean	Reference SD	Cataloging Mean	Cataloging SD	Other Mean	Other SD
Ability to read and interpret a bibliographic record in an OPAC	1.04 (n = 23)	.2085	1.14 (n = 29)	.4411	1.29 (n = 69)	.6440
Understanding of information-seeking behaviors of users	1.17 (n = 23)	.4910	1.38 (n = 29)	.5615	1.30 (n = 70)	.6670
Knowledge of the theory of information organization and intellectual access	1.26 (n = 23)	.4490	1.31 (n = 29)	.5414	1.41 (n = 70)	.7121
Knowledge of the ways in which searching techniques affect precision and recall	1.30 (n = 23)	.4705	1.52 (n = 29)	.7378	1.64 (n = 70)	.8171
Knowledge of the ways in which data structures affect precision and recall	1.30 (n = 23)	.4705	1.59 (n = 29)	.7328	1.80 (n = 69)	.8503
Awareness of bibliographic utilities	1.30 (n = 23)	.4705	1.69 (n = 29)	.7123	1.86 (n = 69)	.8791
MARC format	1.32 (n = 22)	.5679	1.52 (n = 29)	.6336	1.77 (n = 70)	.8710
Understanding of the activities that must be performed to provide the products and services users need	1.36 (n = 22)	.4924	1.45 (n = 29)	.5724	1.56 (n = 70)	.7544
Library of Congress Subject Headings	1.36 (n = 22)	.4924	1.59 (n = 29)	.6278	1.94 (n = 70)	.8493
Cataloging tools: Basic knowledge of	1.44 (n = 23)	.6624	1.45 (n = 29)	.5724	1.72 (n = 69)	.7837
Library of Congress Classification	1.50 (n = 22)	.5118	1.72 (n = 29)	.7019	1.97 (n = 70)	.8336
Anglo-American Cataloguing Rules	1.50 (n = 22)	.5976	1.69 (n = 29)	.7123	2.00 (n = 70)	.9780
Knowledge of bibliographic relationships underlying database design	1.57 (n = 23)	.6624	1.62 (n = 29)	.7277	1.84 (n = 70)	.8950
Subject analysis: Knowledge of methods for	1.57 (n = 23)	.7278	1.66 (n = 29)	.5526	1.84 (n = 70)	.7150
Knowledge of sources of bibliographic records	1.59 (n = 22)	.7964	1.90 (n = 29)	.8596	1.97 (n = 70)	.7980
Ability to evaluate information-retrieval systems in relation to user needs and information-seeking behaviors	1.61 (n = 23)	.6564	1.69 (n = 29)	.6603	1.56 (n = 70)	.7544
Classification: Knowledge of theory	1.61 (n = 23)	.7223	1.52 (n = 29)	.6876	1.74 (n = 70)	.7743
Classification: Knowledge of methods for	1.61 (n = 23)	.6564	1.72 (n = 29)	.5914	1.93 (n = 70)	.8396
Knowledge of the basic database design concepts	1.61 (n = 23)	.6564	1.86 (n = 29)	.7428	1.91 (n = 70)	.7754
Describing, identifying, and showing relationships among materials: Knowledge of methods for	1.61 (n = 23)	.7223	1.71 (n = 28)	.7629	1.99 (n = 70)	.8596
Knowledge of the theoretical basis for retrieval	1.65 (n = 23)	.6473	1.76 (n = 29)	.7863	1.69 (n = 70)	.7902

TABLE 2 (continued)

Competency	Reference Mean	Reference SD	Cataloging Mean	Cataloging SD	Other Mean	Other SD
Subject analysis: Knowledge of theory	1.65 (n = 23)	.6473	1.66 (n = 29)	.7209	1.81 (n = 70)	.7669
Understanding the relationship of the research library's units to the provision of intellectual access to information resources	1.68 (n = 22)	.7162	1.96 (n = 28)	.7445	1.87 (n = 68)	.8794
Indexing: Knowledge of theory	1.68 (n = 22)	.5679	1.76 (n = 29)	.7863	1.97 (n = 70)	.8160
Describing, identifying, and showing relationships among materials: Knowledge of theory	1.70 (n = 23)	.7029	1.62 (n = 29)	.6769	1.81 (n = 70)	.7856
Knowledge of relevant national and international cataloging standards	1.70 (n = 23)	.7029	1.62 (n = 29)	.6769	1.87 (n = 70)	.7787
Thesaurus creation: Knowledge of theory	1.70 (n = 23)	.6350	1.90 (n = 29)	.8596	1.96 (n = 70)	.7882
Indexing: Knowledge of methods for	1.73 (n = 22)	.6311	1.97 (n = 29)	.6805	2.07 (n = 70)	.7675
Understanding the relationship between classification schemes and shelf order	1.78 (n = 23)	.8505	1.46 (n = 28)	.7927	2.06 (n = 70)	.8493
Ability to develop and apply syndetic structure and controlled vocabulary in information retrieval systems	1.82 (n = 22)	.7950	1.86 (n = 29)	.7428	1.84 (n = 70)	.7919
HTML	1.82 (n = 22)	.6645	2.41 (n = 29)	.8245	2.03 (n = 69)	.8220
Knowledge of principles for designing user-driven information retrieval systems	1.83 (n = 23)	.6503	2.07 (n = 29)	.7987	2.00 (n = 70)	.7614
Cataloging tools: Working knowledge of	1.83 (n = 23)	.7168	2.03 (n = 29)	.6805	2.12 (n = 69)	.9320
Dewey Decimal Classification	1.86 (n = 22)	.7743	1.97 (n = 29)	.7784	2.19 (n = 70)	.8391
Thesaurus creation: Knowledge of methods for	1.87 (n = 23)	.7570	2.21 (n = 29)	.8610	2.10 (n = 70)	.8013
Dublin Core	2.00 (n = 22)	.8165	2.24 (n = 29)	.5766	2.12 (n = 69)	.7772
Knowledge of state-of-the-art research and practice in cataloging and classification	2.04 (n = 23)	.7057	2.24 (n = 29)	.8724	2.25 (n = 69)	.8118
Library of Congress Rule Interpretations	2.09 (n = 22)	.7502	2.59 (n = 29)	.6823	2.37 (n = 70)	.9352
Core Record Standard	2.18 (n = 22)	.7950	2.57 (n = 28)	.5040	2.32 (n = 65)	.8312

cies. These are shown in Table 3. A Tukey test was then performed to determine specifically which groups of educators responded differently with respect to these seven competencies.

The ANOVA and Tukey tests revealed that there was no statistically significant difference in response by teaching area for the majority (32 of 39) of the competencies. In other words, with the exception of the seven competencies shown in Table 3, library educators with primary teaching responsibilities in reference, cataloging or neither area agreed upon the importance of the competencies for all entry-level academic librarians. For the seven cataloging competencies listed in Table 3, however, the null hypothesis was rejected.

Library educators differed significantly in their attitudes towards understanding the relationship between classification and shelf order (Shelf Order), *Anglo-American Cataloguing Rules (AACR), Library of Congress Subject Headings (LCSH)*, MARC format (MARC), Library of Congress classification (LCC), HTML, and an awareness of bibliographic utilities (Bib Utilities). Table 3 summarizes the results of both the ANOVA and Tukey tests, with the final row showing the two groups whose responses differed significantly with respect to each of the seven competencies. Those teaching cataloging found an understanding of the relationship between classification scheme and shelf order (mean of 1.46) to be significantly more important than did those who teach neither cataloging nor reference (mean of 2.06). Interestingly, the difference in response on the remaining competencies occurred, for the most part, between those teaching reference and those teaching neither reference nor cataloging. Those teaching reference found that knowledge of AACR, MARC, LCSH, LCC, and an awareness of bibliographic utilities were significantly more important than did those whose duties were in other areas. In addition, those teaching reference felt that knowledge of HTML was significantly more important than did those teaching cataloging (mean of 1.82 versus mean of 2.41). With the exception of HTML, these competencies provide the foundation that supports the ability to interpret a bibliographic record in an OPAC, the competency that all groups identified as most essential. Since reference as a specialty is of necessity concerned with direct user service, it is not surprising that those teaching in this area might perceive these competencies as more important than library educators in other areas.

TABLE 3. Cataloging Competencies Viewed Differently, LIS Educators

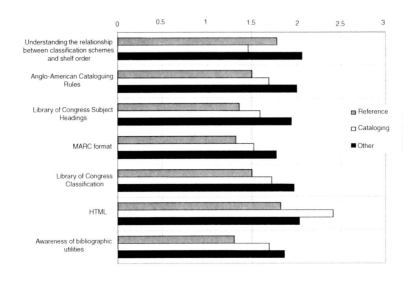

	Shelf Order	AACR	LCSH	MARC	LCC	HTML	Bib. Utilities
Ref Mean	1.78	1.5	1.36	1.32	1.5	1.82	1.3
Cat Mean	1.46	1.69	1.59	1.52	1.72	2.41	1.69
Other Mean	2.06	2	1.94	1.77	1.97	2.03	1.86
F	5.165	3.355	5.968	.041	3.615	3.874	4.324
Sig.	.007	.038	.003	3.277	.030	.023	.015
Groups	Cat vs. Other (p = .006)	Ref vs. Other (p = .05)	Ref vs. Other (p = .005)	Ref vs. Other (p = .047)	Ref vs. Other (p = .032)	Ref vs. Cat (p = .025)	Ref vs. Other (p = .011)

THEORETICAL versus PRACTICAL CATALOGING COMPETENCIES

The fourth research question examines library educators' views on theoretical versus practical cataloging competencies. Several of the competencies were presented in pairs contrasting theoretical knowledge of a concept to working or practical knowledge of it. In order to explore the question of whether or not library educators viewed the paired theoretical and practical competencies differently, a Wilcoxon signed-ranks test was performed. The confidence interval was set at 0.95, with a significant difference in response occurring only when the p value was less than or equal to 0.05. The hypothesis was that library educators would view theoretical and practical cataloging competencies differently; the null hypothesis, that there would be no difference.

There were six pairs of competencies that addressed theoretical versus practical knowledge. The six areas covered included subject analysis, thesaurus creation, indexing, classification, describing, identifying, and showing relationships among materials and cataloging tools. Of the six paired theoretical and practical competencies, library educators differed in their views on only two. Table 4 reveals significant differences in the responses of library educators with regard to thesaurus creation (p = .009) and cataloging tools (p = .000). In these two instances, the null hypothesis was rejected.

Library educators appear to believe that knowledge of the theory of thesaurus creation (mean 1.9) is significantly more important than knowledge of methods (mean 2.09). Respondents also appear to regard basic knowledge of cataloging tools (mean 1.61) as significantly more important than working knowledge (mean 2.05).

Only in these two cases did library educators differ in their views on the importance of theoretical versus practical knowledge, ranking theoretical knowledge as significantly more important. With respect to the remaining four pairs of competencies, library educators appear to view theory and practice as equally important.

COMPARISON OF LIBRARY EDUCATOR AND LIBRARY PRACTITIONER RESPONSES

The current study follows up the results of a recent study exploring perceptions of library practitioners on cataloging competencies for entry-level academic librarians. The final research question asks whether views of library educators differ from those of practitioners with respect to cataloging competencies for entry-level academic librarians. A recent study by the authors focused on the views of 120 library practitioners, including responses from 55 heads of reference and 65 heads of cataloging at ARL institutions.

In order to gain a clearer understanding of how the responses of the library educators compared with those of the practitioners surveyed previously, an independent t-test was performed on the responses of both groups.[28] The results of the t-test are shown in Table 5, which summarizes the mean responses for both groups and provides the p-values.

The researchers hypothesized that there would be significant differences in response between the two groups. An initial examination of the responses of both groups (Table 5) shows that library educators perceived a greater number of competencies to be important than did the practitioners. The educators ranked 31 of the 39 competencies as essential or important (with mean values less than or equal to 2.0), as opposed to the practitioners, who ranked 20 of the 39 competencies as essential or important.

With a confidence interval of 0.95, the t-test revealed that significant differences in response between library educators and library practitioners occurred for 22 of the 39 competencies. Bar graphs in Table 6A and 6B show the twenty-two competencies that were viewed significantly differently by educators and practitioners. This set of competencies spans the spectrum of those surveyed, including both practical and theoretical competencies as well as both conceptually broad competencies and those focused on specific tools and standards. Table 6A and 6B shows that without exception, the educators perceived the twenty-two competencies to be significantly more important than did practitioners.

DISCUSSION

The results shed new light on the debate concerning the future of cataloging education in the graduate library curriculum. Despite a perception among practitioners of polar disparity in views between library educators

TABLE 4. Theory vs. Practice Cataloging Competencies, All Respondents

Theoretical Competency	N	Mean	Practical Competency	N	Mean	Sig.
Subject analysis: Knowledge of theory	123	1.76	Subject analysis: Knowledge of methods	123	1.77	.933
Thesaurus creation: Knowledge of theory	122	1.90	Thesaurus creation: Knowledge of methods for	122	2.09	.009
Indexing: Knowledge of theory	123	1.87	Indexing: Knowledge of methods for	123	1.98	.089
Classification: Knowledge of theory	123	1.67	Classification: Knowledge of methods for	122	1.83	.055
Describing, identifying, and showing relationships among materials: Knowledge of theory	122	1.75	Describing, identifying, and showing relationships among materials: Knowledge of methods for	122	1.85	.078
Cataloging tools: Basic knowledge	123	1.61	Cataloging tools: Working knowledge of	123	2.05	.000

TABLE 5. Mean Rankings, Educators vs. Practitioners

Competency	Educators			Practitioners			Sig.
	N	SD	Mean	Mean	SD	N	
Ability to read and interpret a bibliographic record in an OPAC	122	.5679	1.22	1.11	.4058	120	.076
Understanding of information-seeking behaviors of users	123	.6105	1.29	1.48	.6349	120	.018
Knowledge of the theory of information organization and intellectual access	123	.6289	1.36	1.58	.7051	120	.009
Understanding of the activities that must be performed to provide the products and services users need	122	.6711	1.49	1.71	.7265	119	.014
Knowledge of the ways in which searching techniques affect precision and recall	123	.7488	1.55	1.53	.6208	120	.825
Ability to evaluate information-retrieval systems in relation to user needs and information-seeking behaviors	123	.7110	1.59	1.68	.7804	119	.364
Cataloging tools: Basic knowledge of	122	.7323	1.61	1.79	.8221	119	.082
MARC format	122	.7841	1.63	1.79	.8463	117	.122
Classification: Knowledge of theory	123	.7520	1.67	1.86	.7270	118	.048
Knowledge of the ways in which data structures affect precision and recall	122	.7848	1.68	1.79	.6969	120	.245
Knowledge of the theoretical basis for retrieval	123	.7589	1.69	1.87	.7839	120	.064
Awareness of bibliographic utilities	122	.7997	1.70	1.76	.7808	119	.614
Knowledge of bibliographic relationships underlying database design	123	.8182	1.74	1.88	.7003	120	.144
Describing, identifying, and showing relationships among materials: Knowledge of theory	123	.7421	1.75	1.89	.6835	120	.118
Subject analysis: Knowledge of theory	123	.7393	1.76	1.92	.7448	119	.065
Subject analysis: Knowledge of methods for	123	.6935	1.77	2.13	.7490	117	.000
Library of Congress Subject Headings	122	.7826	1.76	1.74	.7531	119	.818
Knowledge of relevant national and international cataloging standards	123	.7493	1.79	2.15	.7438	119	.000
Classification: Knowledge of methods for	123	.7651	1.83	2.15	.7265	117	.001
Ability to develop and apply syndetic structure and controlled vocabulary in information retrieval systems	122	.7752	1.84	2.10	.8135	117	.010
Library of Congress Classification	122	.7752	1.84	1.76	.6975	119	.454
Knowledge of the basic database design concepts	123	.7507	1.84	2.00	.7591	119	.095
Anglo-American Cataloguing Rules	122	.8816	1.84	2.08	.8395	119	.032
Understanding the relationship of the research library's units to the provision of intellectual access to information resources	119	.8197	1.85	1.80	.7072	118	.661
Describing, identifying, and showing relationships among materials: Knowledge of methods for	122	.8199	1.85	2.08	.6960	119	.019
Indexing: Knowledge of theory	122	.7709	1.87	2.11	.7568	119	.015

TABLE 5 (continued)

Competency	Educators			Practitioners			Sig.
	N	SD	Mean	Mean	SD	N	
Understanding the relationship between classification schemes and shelf order	122	.8620	1.87	1.79	.7719	118	.446
Knowledge of sources of bibliographic records	122	.8213	1.89	2.11	.8142	118	.041
Thesaurus creation: Knowledge of theory	123	.7832	1.90	2.21	.7436	120	.002
Knowledge of principles for designing user-driven information retrieval systems	123	.7516	1.98	2.21	.7875	120	.019
Indexing: Knowledge of methods for	122	.7271	1.98	2.35	.7224	118	.000
Cataloging tools: Working knowledge of	122	.8416	2.05	2.34	.8016	116	.008
Dewey Decimal Classification	122	.8191	2.08	2.80	.8529	118	.000
HTML	121	.8123	2.08	2.30	.8291	119	.039
Thesaurus creation: Knowledge of methods for	123	.8099	2.09	2.52	.6757	118	.000
Dublin Core	116	.7368	2.12	2.61	.8038	114	.000
Knowledge of state-of-the-art research and practice in cataloging and classification	122	.8052	2.21	2.66	.7281	119	.000
Core Record Standard	116	.7621	2.36	2.63	.8121	114	.010
Library of Congress Rule Interpretations	122	.8560	2.38	2.53	.9372	119	.189

and library practitioners, results suggest that both library educators and library practitioners believe that the listed competencies are important for all entry-level academic librarians. In fact, educators appear to believe even more strongly in the importance of the competencies, ranking most significantly more strongly than did the practitioners. Results also support the existence of a set of core cataloging competencies for entry-level academic librarians, demonstrating the usefulness and broad appeal of the ALCTS Educational Policy Statement[29] as a source for meaningful competencies for new professionals.

Perhaps the perceived gap between library educators and library practitioners is more semantic than actual, since both library educators and practitioners appear to agree on the importance of "cataloging" competencies. Comments from the educator respondents indicated the importance of a broad understanding of concepts, not specifically as "cataloging" concepts, but within the wider contexts of information organization and knowledge management. The need for broader conceptual understanding for today's graduates has been discussed within the cataloging field as well. Thomas states, "As we move into the 21st century, we must consider reorienting ourselves and rethink the way in which we provide access to information and

TABLE 6. Competencies Viewed Differently, Educators vs. Practitioners

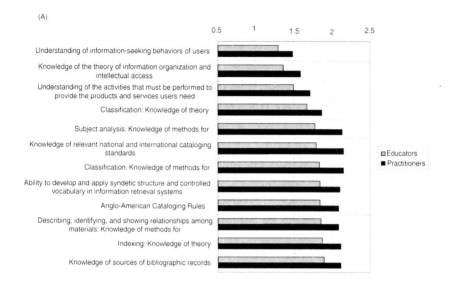

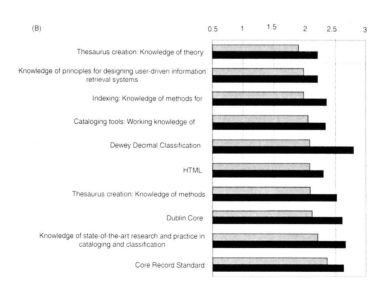

knowledge. Our familiar aids, such as AACR2, should be probed for the values and basic principles they yield."[30] But whether they are considered "cataloging" competencies or "information organization" competencies, it seems clear that both educators and practitioners strongly agree on their importance for all entry-level academic librarians.

Despite the rapid proliferation of new standards for describing bibliographic entities, the competency ranked as most essential both by practitioners and by educators is "the ability to read and interpret a bibliographic record in an OPAC." Although non-AACR, non-MARC rec- ords are becoming increasingly important to users, the library catalog is still one of the most highly useful finding aids and is likely to remain so for some time to come. Even as the scope and functions of catalogs evolve, users will continue to need librarians with the mediation skills to assist in their use.

The question that now remains is how best to equip new graduates with the knowledge necessary to function effectively in an increasingly complex information landscape, with its host of tools for resource discovery. Hill and Intner eloquently argue that,

> In order for these . . . powerful and potentially more confusing tools to be effective . . . it is essential that those who design them, those who implement them, those who customize them for a specific need, and those who input data into them have both a practical and theoretical understanding of the interrelation of all the data elements that make up the bibliographic control matrix. They must also have an understanding and appreciation of how these elements function for the internal purposes of the library, as well as how they function for the public. This kind of knowledge is not gained through a mere introduction to the concepts of the organization of knowledge.[31]

Responses of library educators and practitioners suggest that library school curricula must reflect and support the competencies put forth in this survey. Both groups appear to believe strongly in the importance of both theoretical and practical cataloging competencies for new graduates. However, these skills cannot be learned in a vacuum, but must be taught within a context that makes sense to students, balancing practical and theoretical knowledge. They must also be taught in sufficient depth for students to develop more than just a superficial familiarity with the concepts. The study of cataloging, as a logical and relevant way for students to acquire these essential competencies, must continue to hold its place as a core element of the graduate curriculum.

Though directed specifically at catalogers, Hill and Intner prescribe knowledge appropriate for any entry-level academic librarian:

> Catalogers of today need the entire arc of the pendulum, from theory to practice, and all points in between. They must have sufficient understanding of the underlying principles of bibliographic control and sufficient mastery of practice that they can apply the principles in a useful way as they attempt to provide access to a bewildering array of information resources while taking advantage of all the capabilities offered by new technologies. It is not possible to gain either a sufficient understanding of the principles or a sufficient mastery of the practice in a library education program that presents either theory or practice at the expense of the other, or that presents very little of both.[32]

CONCLUSION

Entry-level academic librarians will face a number of challenges as the catalog evolves from OPAC to information service. The number of resources available to users, particularly digital resources, continues to proliferate.[33] As the responsibility for resource description becomes more widely distributed, an understanding of the fundamental principles of cataloging as well as the broader areas of knowledge management and information organization is essential for academic librarians working in all areas of the field.

The pioneering work accomplished at the COPE1 (focusing on professional education) and COPE2 (focusing on continuing education) conferences has underscored the need for professional competencies across the field. This study confirms the importance of cataloging competencies for all entry-level academic librarians as perceived by library practitioners and library educators. Agreement between practitioners and library educators is crucial if graduates are to have the tools to overcome the challenges facing the profession. A dialogue between practitioners and library educators is vital not only to promote a set of core professional competencies, but also to pave the way for the continuing education that will fuel the success of the profession now and in the future.

REFERENCES

1. Don Fallis and Martin Frické, "Not by Library School Alone," *Library Journal* 124:17 (1999): 44-45.

2. Janet Swan Hill and Sheila S. Intner, "Preparing for a Cataloging Career: From Cataloging to Knowledge Management" (1999), *<http://www.ala.org/congress/hill-intner.html>* (March 2, 2002).

3. Karen M. Letarte et al., "Practitioner Perspectives on Cataloging Education for Entry-Level Academic Librarians," *Library Resources & Technical Services* 46:1 (2002): 11-22.

4. ALCTS, "ALCTS Educational Policy Statement" (1995), *<http://www.ala.org/alcts/publications/educ/edpolicy.html>* (March 2, 2002).

5. Ibid.

6. Desretta McAllister-Harper, "An Analysis of Courses in Cataloging and Classification and Related Areas Offered in Sixteen Graduate Library Schools and Their Relationship to Present and Future Trends in Cataloging and Classification and to Cognitive Needs of Professional Academic Catalogers," *Cataloging & Classification Quarterly* 16:3 (1993): 99-123.

7. Sherry L. Vellucci, "Cataloging Across the Curriculum: A Syndetic Structure for Teaching Cataloging," *Cataloging & Classification Quarterly* 24:1/2 (1997): 35-59.

8. Jodi Lynn Spillane, "Comparison of Required Introductory Cataloging Courses, 1986 to 1998," *Library Resources & Technical Services* 43:4 (1999): 223-230.

9. Stephen H. Peters, "Time Devoted to Topics in Cataloging Courses," *Journal of Education for Library and Information Science* 29:3 (1989): 209-219.

10. Jerry D. Saye, "The Cataloging Experience in Library and Information Science Education: An Educator's Perspective," *Cataloging & Classification Quarterly* 7:4 (1987): 27-45.

11. "CCS Task Force on Education and Recruitment for Cataloging Report, June 1986," *RTSD Newsletter* 11:7 (1986): 71-78.

12. Judy MacLeod and Daren Callahan, "Educators and Practitioners Reply: An Assessment of Cataloging Education," *Library Resources & Technical Services* 39:2 (1995): 153-165.

13. Anaclare F. Evans, "The Education of Catalogers: The View of the Practitioner/Educator," *Cataloging & Classification Quarterly* 16:3 (1993): 49-57.

14. Debra W. Hill, "Requisite Skills of the Entry-Level Cataloger: A Supervisor's Perspective," *Cataloging & Classification Quarterly* 23:3/4 (1997): 75-83.

15. MacLeod and Callahan, "Educators and Practitioners Reply," 159-160.

16. Evans, "The Education of Catalogers," p. 50.

17. Tim C. Green, "Competencies for Entry-Level Independent Information Professionals: An Assessment by Practitioners," *Journal of Education for Library and Information Science* 34:2 (1993): 165-168.

18. Ronald R. Powell and Sheila D. Creth, "Knowledge Bases and Library Education," *College & Research Libraries* 47:1 (1986): 16-27.

19. Herbert S. White and Marion Paris, "Employer Preferences and the Library Education Curriculum," *Library Quarterly* 55:1 (1985): 1-33.

20. Lois Buttlar and Rosemary Ruhig Du Mont, "Assessing Library Science Competencies: Soliciting Practitioner Input for Curricular Design," *Journal of Education for Library and Information Science* 30:1 (1989): 3-18.

21. Hill and Intner, "Preparing for a Cataloging Career."

22. Letarte et al., "Practitioner Perspectives on Cataloging Education," p. 13.

23. Hill and Intner, "Preparing for a Cataloging Career."

24. Vellucci, "Cataloging Across the Curriculum," p. 45.

25. Spillane, "Comparison of Required Introductory Cataloging Courses," p. 227.

26. ALCTS, "ALCTS Educational Policy Statement."

27. Hill and Intner, "Preparing for a Cataloging Career."

28. Letarte et al., "Practitioner Perspectives on Cataloging Education," p. 16-17.

29. ALCTS, "ALCTS Educational Policy Statement."

30. Sarah E. Thomas, "The Catalog as Portal to the Internet" (2000), 9 <*http://www. loc.gov/catdir/bibcontrol/thomas_paper.html*> (March 21, 2002).

31. Hill and Intner, "Preparing for a Cataloging Career."

32. Ibid.

33. Thomas, "The Catalog as Portal to the Internet."

Format Integration and the Design of Cataloging and Classification Curricula

Clément Arsenault
John E. Leide

SUMMARY. Cataloging is a dynamic and ever changing activity. Developments in codes and standards create a need for continuing reconsideration of the design of our curricula. Format integration, in particular, raises questions about the structure of curricula for cataloging and classification. The issues relating to differing formats of materials are not new, but the process of standardization of treatment, which was begun quite tentatively in the development of the *Anglo-American Cataloging Rules (AACR)* has blossomed to the fore in the ensuing years. This paper examines the historical context of the integration of formats before addressing

Clément Arsenault, is Professeur adjoint, École de bibliothéconomie et des sciences de l'information, Université de Montréal, C.P. 6128, succursale Centre-ville, Montréal (QC) H3C 3J7 Canada (E-mail: clement.arsenault@umontreal.ca). <http://mapageweb.umontreal.ca/arsenec>. John E. Leide is Associate Professor, Graduate School of Library and Information Studies, McGill University, 3459 McTavish Street, Montreal (QC) H3A 1Y1 Canada (E-mail: innl@musicb.mcgill.ca).

[Haworth co-indexing entry note]: "Format Integration and the Design of Cataloging and Classification Curricula." Arsenault, Clément, and John E. Leide. Co-published simultaneously in *Cataloging & Classification Quarterly* (The Haworth Information Press, an imprint of The Haworth Press, Inc.) Vol. 34, No. 1/2, 2002, pp. 189-201; and: *Education for Cataloging and the Organization of Information: Pitfalls and the Pendulum* (ed: Janet Swan Hill) The Haworth Information Press, an imprint of The Haworth Press, Inc., 2002, pp. 189-201. Single or multiple copies of this article are available for a fee from The Haworth Document Delivery Service [1-800-HAWORTH, 9:00 a.m. - 5:00 p.m. (EST). E-mail address: getinfo@haworthpressinc.com].

189

the continuing arguments that maintain that all types of materials should be treated in an introductory course as opposed to those that assert that format issues should not be covered in any depth in an introductory course. A design for an integrated, but not exhaustive, treatment of formats in an introductory course with more detailed coverage included in advanced courses is proposed. *[Article copies available for a fee from The Haworth Document Delivery Service: 1-800-HAWORTH. E-mail address: <getinfo@haworthpressinc.com> Website: <http://www.HaworthPress.com> © 2002 by The Haworth Press, Inc. All rights reserved.]*

KEYWORDS. Format integration, nonbook cataloging, cataloging education, cataloging curriculum

INTRODUCTION

Format integration poses philosophical and practical problems for the teaching of cataloging. This paper addresses issues related to the teaching of cataloging for a variety of formats and types of documents. More specifically, it develops a series of arguments that will help the reader find appropriate answers to the question: "Should education for cataloging of all types of materials be combined?" In other words, "Does format integration imply curricular integration for the teaching of cataloguing for various media?" In this paper the terms "type of materials" and "format" are used interchangeably to represent any category of information resource that share a similar physical form (i.e., books, maps, microforms, etc.), publication pattern (i.e., periodicals, loose-leaf publications, etc.), type of content (i.e., music scores, images, etc.) or that have any other common bond (i.e., "foreign" language materials, etc.).

As library collections increasingly tend to include ever larger proportions of material published in non-traditional formats (e.g., non-book, non-print, non-text), and as more and more content is available in an array of different formats and media, the question of whether or not an introductory graduate-level course in cataloging should cover all types of material becomes increasingly important to curricular design of library schools as well as expectations for entry-level catalogers in most institutions. At its origin, the question is related to the "practice versus theory" dilemma, which has been debated with much force in the literature over the years by such authors as Ranganathan,[1] Morehead,[2] Ryans,[3] Nelson,[4] Luther Henderson,[5] Young,[6] Intner,[7] Clayden,[8] MacLeod and Callahan,[9] and Romero.[10]

OVERVIEW OF THE QUESTION

As the structure of *AACR2* suggests, the majority of the theoretical concepts underpinning the practice of cataloging and organization of information generally can be dissociated from format. Concepts are, for the most part, not format-dependent, that is, they transcend physicality or publication pattern. In theory, Part I, chapter 1 and Part II of *AACR2* cover all the basic concepts of access and description for any form or type of document, with the possible exception of the concept of seriality, which is covered in chapter 12. At an abstract level, one need not consider format or even refer to any physical form–or, in the case of electronic documents, non-physical form–to explain the theoretical concepts. It is perfectly feasible to simply and generically talk about "documents," "objects," or "information resources" at an abstract level to explain fundamental concepts such as access, description, authority control, and subject analysis. Subject analysis theory has also been focused on content rather than form, and most of the theoretical concepts covered in verbal subject access and classification extend over various types of material.

Much has been written on the value of cataloging as a core subject in the field of library and information science (Goodell;[11] Kovacs;[12] Gorman;[13] Jeng;[14] Connaway[15]). Cataloging is often perceived as being too "mechanical" and too "skill oriented" to belong in a graduate program and learning cataloging is often thought to consist solely of going through a highly convoluted drill. This perception is a major factor in the perennial debate over adopting either a more theoretical or a more practical approach in the design of a graduate level introductory course (Clack 30).[16] Over the years, the value of theory-based instruction for cataloging has been increasingly recognized. Although one approach might be preferred over the other by certain instructors or curriculum designers, there seems to be consensus that both the theoretical and the practical bases are valuable and are needed to ensure a thorough understanding of the subject (Ryans;[17] Clayden;[18] MacLeod & Callahan;[19] Romero[20]). As theory is induced from practice and, in turn, helps in assessing and validating the practice, establishing strong parallels between the two is unquestionably essential. Still, the worth of teaching the practice of cataloging at a graduate level is recurrently being questioned, since, as we know, the professional information specialist is, more than ever, expected to work in a situation where supervision, planning and management, rather than actual cataloging, will take the largest part of his or her time. Nonetheless, it is unrealistic to believe that knowledge can only be acquired through theory. A good exposure to practice is often a very efficient way for students to acquire the theoretical notions that form the base of the field of organization of information. In the same way that an image is said to be worth a thousand words, a well-designed practical assignment may also be worth a thousand abstract models. Putting theory to practice is also a good way to test if the theory really has been fully absorbed and understood, and as Saye[21] puts it: "the real meaningful learning occurs as students attempt to apply that which the instructor has presented." The study of theory detached from practice is like trying to learn everything about nothing. Proof of the theory lies in its application; the exceptions prove the rule.

Arguably, as practice changes and varies more than theory–i.e., both over time and within different environments[22]–our ultimate goal is to communicate the theoretical concepts, for once these are well actualized, they provide students with sufficient freedom to apply them in a variety of environments.[23,24] This does not necessarily mean, however, that teaching should be devoid of practical examples and concrete applications. It is not only possible, but also highly desirable to strike a balance between the two.[25] Also, instructors should keep in mind that graduates coming out of school into the current job market will very often be asked, in their first appointment, to perform some form of cataloging. Having had some exposure to the practical side of cataloging, either in the classroom or in labs, makes students feel confident that they can at least get started without too many problems and apply their hands-on experience to new situations. If they have been exposed to a certain amount of practical work, graduates can state that they have done some cataloging, which is probably better than saying that "in theory" they know how to do it. Of course practice in the classrooms or in labs is no substitute for on-the-job training and experience, but it might make a critical difference in success when applying for an entry-level position.

If practice is an important and essential part of teaching cataloging, document format is indeed an issue that should be addressed. What is to be gained, in terms of the theoretical base, from examining all the peculiarities of various formats? Is there a role for format in teaching cataloging and, if so, what should be emphasized or de-emphasized? Should all formats be taught all at once in an integrated manner, or is there a minimal set that would be necessary to support the basic theoretical concepts? Furthermore, even though issues related to format may be important, do they belong in an introductory-level course or could they be treated in one or more advanced courses? This paper will look at some of the issues related to physical format, the content versus carrier dilemma, publication patterns (seriality), special materials (music, government publications, law/legal documents, multimedia, sacred scriptures), and "foreign" languages, and will analyze the merits of integrating these types of materials in a basic graduate-level cataloging course or handling them in a separate course.

HISTORICAL AND CURRENT CONTEXT

In the first edition of the *Anglo-American Cataloging Rules,* published in 1967, there was a concerted effort to address issues related to the processing of non-traditional materials, as the standard included rules for the treatment of several kinds of media. *AACR* did not, however, provide a fully integrated approach, and many felt that non-traditional materials were treated "as second class citizens in the world of books."[26] Furthermore, the standard was rebuffed by some communities, most notably the map collection librarians[27] who felt that the newly emerging standard was not detailed enough to fully address their needs. It was not before 1978, with the publication of the second edition of the *AACR (AACR2)* which fully integrated all media "according to a single bibliographic pattern" (Intner[28]), that the standard became more widely accepted throughout the bibliographic community at large. The proliferation, within the past two decades, of multiple format-specific international standards for bibliographic description *(ISBDs),* and, the merging of the various MARC bibliographic formats into a single format applicable to all types of materials in the mid 1990s further contributed to a more integrated and homogeneous treatment of all types of information resources, and in the fading of boundaries among formats. The direct consequence of this was an increase in the importance of non-traditional materials in library collections, at least in terms of access, and the integration of bibliographic records for a multitude of materials, including moving images, sound recordings, archives, electronic resources, etc., in a single bibliographic file, the catalog.

The intensification of electronic publishing, notably through the Internet, and the emergence of multimedia information resources, within the past six or seven years, has increased the breach between the information (i.e., the intellectual content) and its carrier. Since the content of any given work is in theory a stable entity, while its carrier may take many forms and change over time, it has been proposed that rule 0.24 of *AACR2,* which establishes that the physical form is the starting point for the creation of bibliographic records, be reversed to give precedence to content, which would produce a more stable model for bibliographic control.[29] In today's dynamic and fluid environment, content and access to that content are increasingly important, while the form the content takes seems to be more and more relegated to the back burner, so to speak. The medium is no longer the message.

With the ever-increasing importance of non-traditional formats and their amalgamation within our collections and catalogs, catalogers are more and more likely to have to handle a diverse assortment of materials. One could argue that it is therefore necessary to cover all types of materials in an integrated manner to ensure that students are able to process them all consistently and equally. On the other hand, as content and its accessibility, rather than format, becomes the focus of our concerns, the case for teaching at a more conceptual level and de-emphasizing format also seems to be valid. These two approaches are presented in the next section.

OPINIONS

Arguments for Integration

The need to include instruction for the cataloging of non-book materials in the graduate library and information science (LIS) curriculum is undeniable and has long been recognized by most academic institutions.[30] The graduating student who has some knowledge of how to organize information published in electronic and other media or in "foreign" languages will be especially well equipped to face today's job market. In cataloging departments of many large institutions, responsibilities are often assigned by language and format; descriptive cataloging of monographs is usually performed by non-professionals, while non-book and foreign language materials are often processed by professional catalogers, due to the added complexity related to the treatment of these items. Furthermore, as boundaries among formats tend to fade, and as more and more content tends to transcend format, today's professional cataloger is increasingly called upon to handle a wide variety of different types of material. In order to echo today's reality, it might appear essential that treatment of non-print be covered as comprehensively as treatment for traditional print material. In addition, since most theoretical concepts in cataloging are not format-dependent, it might be preferable not to emphasize specifically any format in particular, and to illustrate the theory with examples taken from a variety of types of material. If all types of material are integrated in one course, it may be easier to establish parallels among them and illustrate what elements are format-dependent and format-independent. Integrating formats in one course may also help to weaken the enduring partiality for print, so that non-print materials are no longer considered as second-class material.

Arguments Against Integration

On the other hand, one could also argue that format issues should not be covered in any depth in an introductory course. Different formats may only confuse the student for minimal returns as most of the key concepts are not format dependent–hence the importance of *AACR2* chapter 1. The cataloging course is often dreaded by many students,[31] who may be somewhat mystified and disconcerted by cataloging because it is unlike anything they have been exposed to before; so it is a good idea to keep things as simple as possible at first. It is possible to simplify the introductory course by illustrating all basic concepts with a single well-known format such as printed books. Using printed monographs to teach cataloging is the simplest solution because they are easy to observe, handle and obtain, and they do not require any specific or technological knowledge. Their content is easily accessible and no special apparatus is required. This is not the case with many non-book materials such as computer files, recorded music or videorecordings. Most rules and cataloging tools were originally designed for books. Other formats often require the use of special guidelines and specialized tools, and are also prone to many rule interpretations. These specialized tools often require a good understanding of the basic general tools because they usually build upon the basic rules designed for print material. Using a single format, such as printed monographs, is sufficient to form a good basis to cover all elementary concepts.

A first course in cataloging, if well designed, could introduce students to the essential theoretical concepts to allow them to inductively extrapolate to other forms of documents. It is probably preferable to spend more time on making sure the underlying theory is well absorbed than on spending time explaining the idiosyncrasies pertaining to every format, for "the power of generalization through *induction* is that we can then use the general laws to draw conclusions about cases not yet observed."[32] A quick explanation of the structure of Part I of the *AACR2* standard will often be sufficient to allow students to extrapolate from the concepts acquired from chapters 1 and 2 to their applications in chapters 3 to 11.[33]

It might be more appropriate to use certain formats, and certain types of documents to introduce and illustrate more advanced concepts, or to elicit the importance of certain fundamental concepts, in a follow-up course. For instance, one could use music scores, sound recordings, foreign language works or sacred scriptures to introduce or reinforce the concept of uniform titles. Printed or recorded music and motion pictures and videorecordings could be used to engage students on a more in-depth reflection on the concept of authorship. Musical works could also be used to introduce the rather unusual Class M from the *Library of Congress Classification (LCC)*, which gives precedence to format rather than subject.[34] Peculiarities related to subordination in the formulation of corporate headings could be examined with government publications. Foreign language works can be used to alert students to the difference between language of document versus language of catalog and heighten their awareness of English language bias. Loose-leaf publications, electronic resources such as Web pages, and periodicals can be used to illustrate the concepts of seriality, and analytics, and edition versus version issues. Moving images (film, videorecordings and disks) are especially useful to initiate a reflection in the concept of a work, the content versus carrier issue, as many of these works are issued on multiple supports. The distinction between form and genre subject access is also of special concern for moving images. Realia, photographs and archives could be used to elaborate issues related to published versus unpublished works, single copies versus collections, as well as the concept of enhanced titles. Cartographic materials can be used for exploring class G (from *LCC*) with its unique citation order and a rather peculiar class number construction pattern for maps and atlases.[35] Maps are also good examples to initiate a reflection on the difference between the treatments of text versus image. Other specific aspects, such as rules for the formulation of geographic name and subject headings could also be introduced at that time.

In an advanced class, one could also introduce alternative or parallel codes and tools for different formats (*Rules for Archival Description (RAD), Encoded Archival Description (EAD)*, the Library of Congress *Map Cataloging Manual*, etc.) as these are usually meant to be used in conjunction with the more traditional tools and tend to discuss more advanced concepts. This does not mean that we should not encourage students' to develop a critical approach toward traditional standards for description, access and analysis such as *AACR2* and *LCSH* from the beginning.

A Modest Proposal

Some fifteen years ago, Jerry Saye remarked that the "topics to be covered in the basic cataloging course have not changed enormously over the past half century."[36] This statement still holds valid today. The basic topics of description, authority work, and subject analysis (through subject heading systems and classification schemes) are still relevant in today's context, though the process and substance may have changed somewhat. One of the joys of teaching cataloging is that the questions remain the same; only the answers change. The introductory cataloging course should be used primarily to cover the theoretical concepts associated with the basic topics, with enough depth and flexibility to meet the needs of the largest proportion of students, those who want to be catalogers—or who may end up working as catalogers—and those who do not, but who nonetheless still need to understand the principles of organization of information. These principles can be exemplified in a variety of contexts and with a variety of tools. Using "traditional" cataloging tools (*AACR, MARC, LCSH, DDC, LCC*, bibliographic utilities, etc.) in a library setting is a viable option as it is an excellent application model that is well documented and easily understood. It is sufficiently comprehensive to provide a wide array of situations and concrete examples to provide some practical hands-on experience that will prove valuable to many students. Evidently, ensuring that all the basics are covered in a single course does not leave much time for too many digressions; it is difficult to conceive of an introductory course that could adequately cover all the above-mentioned material and include the many format-specific details, special rules and exceptions[37,38]. As mentioned before, many non-print materials require the use of format-specific codes and guidelines in addition to the *AACR* rules. For the neophyte, the *AACR* standard is dense enough *per se*. It seems more important to lay a sound foundation in the introductory course and to cover format-specific codes and guidelines in an advanced course. Students should be encouraged to develop a critical approach toward *AACR2* even in an introductory course, but covering alternative codes, guidelines and rule interpretations in advanced courses could allow time to evaluate the adequacy of *AACR* and the need for more precise codes, guidelines and interpretations.

It would be counterproductive and unrealistic to overload the introductory course just to claim that all formats have been covered. It would be equally inappropriate to exclude non-traditional formats when examples from a specific format would be especially appropriate to explain or reinforce a basic concept (for instance, using music to explain the principles of uniform titles). If non-traditional formats are covered in advanced courses, it will be easier to introduce more advanced MARC features such as format definitions that are expressed through control fields 006, 007 and 008. An introductory course should emphasize and explain the fundamental structure of *AACR2* and the relationships among the various chapters to enable students to extrapolate from the basic principles, but it need not cover all the details of each chapter. "If we want to learn anything, we mustn't try to learn everything."[39] What is essential is that students thoroughly understand the structure of *AACR2*, the content versus carrier issues, and which things are format-dependent and which are not. An introductory course in cataloging is just the first step on the road of life-long learning. We must lay a solid foundation for inductive learning for advanced courses, on-the-job-training, and independent study. If class size is sufficiently small, instructors could also consider allowing students who express an interest in a specific format to cover it as a special project.

CONCLUSIONS

Current developments in format integration have renewed the discussions of the content and organization of introductory courses in cataloging and classification.

On one hand, there are those who argue that there is an undeniable need to include instruction for the cataloging of non-book materials in the basic curriculum. Libraries are increasingly collecting and cataloging materials in diverse formats and the boundaries between formats have begun to fade. Format integration establishes a theoretical structure that can be applied to all types of materials, and the current shift of focus from container to content supports the view that if all types of material are integrated in one course, it may be easier to establish parallels among them and weaken the enduring partiality for print.

On the other hand, there are those who argue that format issues should not be covered in any depth in an introductory course, because different formats may only confuse the student. It is possible to simplify the introductory course by illustrating all basic concepts with a single well-known format. Other formats often require the use of special guidelines and specialized tools, which require a good understanding of the basic general tools. Using a single format is sufficient to form a practical basis for further study in advanced courses and life-long learning.

Each of these views fails to capture the complex realities of cataloging and classification, which presents most students with a brave new world that is a symbiotic blend of theory and practice. An introductory course can only lay a basic foundation. It would be counterproductive and unrealistic to overload the introductory course just to claim that all formats have been covered. It would be equally inappropriate to exclude non-traditional formats when examples from a specific format would be especially appropriate to explain or reinforce a basic concept. What is essential is that students thoroughly understand the structure of *AACR2*, the content versus carrier issues, and which things are format-dependent and which are not. An introductory course in cataloging is just the first step on the road of life-long learning.

Courses beyond an introductory course could focus on one or more specific topics:

- Advanced cataloging (more in-depth look at theoretical concepts)
- Non-print materials (if time and interest permit all "other" formats may be treated in a number of "advanced courses")
- Seriality
- Foreign languages
- Subject access

Cataloging and classification is most often taught in special courses. Nevertheless, issues, techniques, and tools can be considered in other courses in the curriculum (type of library courses, and advanced information storage and retrieval courses, as well as those dealing with users and the sociology and politics of information). Music librarianship, Law librarianship, Map librarianship and Theological librarianship are particularly concerned with special types of materials. Courses in archival studies must necessarily deal with the unique demands of the archival context, as do those in information and knowledge management. Courses in materials and services for children and young adults in public and school libraries can provide additional opportunities for further exploration of issues in cataloguing and classification, particularly with respect to educational and instructional technologies.

The issues of format and cataloging and classification are as old as library and information science itself, and the design of curricula for graduate-level programs is a never-ending process.

ENDNOTES

1. S. R. Ranganathan. "Imaginary battle within library science." In *Theory and Practice of Abstracting. Developments in Classification. Technique of Teaching Documentation*, vol. 1, 432. (Bangalore, India: Documentation Research and Training Centre, Indian Statistical Institute, 1968).

2. J. Morehead. "Toward a resolution of theory and practice." Chap. 5 in *Theory and Practice in Library Education: The Teaching-Learning Process*, 107-20. (Littleton, CO: Libraries Unlimited, 1980).

3. C. C. Ryans. "Academicians views on the role of theory in the cataloging curriculum." *Catholic Library World* 51:9 (1980): 395-401.

4. J. R. Nelson. "Cataloguing theory and practice in nineteenth century Australian libraries." *Cataloguing Australia* 12:3 (1986): 18-38.

5. K. Luther Henderson. "Some persistent issues in the education of catalogers and classifiers." *Cataloging & Classification Quarterly* 7:4 (1987): 5-26.

6. J. B. Young. "The teaching of cataloging: education or training." *Cataloging & Classification Quarterly* 7:4 (1987): 149-63.

7. S. S. Intner. "Cataloging practice and theory: what to teach and why?" *Journal of Education for Library and Information Science* 30:4 (1990): 333-36.

8. J. Clayden. "Theory versus practice in cataloging education: some Australian experiences." *Journal of Education for Library and Information Science* 36:3 (1995): 230-38.

9. J. MacLeod & D. Callahan. "Educators and practitioners reply: an assessment of cataloging education." *Library Resources and Technical Services* 39:2 (1995): 153-65.

10. L. Romero. "The cataloging laboratory: the active learning theory applied to the education of catalogers." *Cataloging & Classification Quarterly* 21:1 (1995): 3-17.

11. J. Goodell. "The future of cataloging as a core subject." *Education for Librarianship: Australia* 5:2 (1988): 93-97.

12. B. Kovacs. "An educational challenge: teaching cataloging and classification." *Library Resources and Technical Services* 33:4 (1989): 374-81.

13. M. Gorman. "How cataloging and classification should be taught." *American Libraries* 23:8 (1992): 694-97.

14. L. H. Jeng. "From cataloging to organization of information: a paradigm for the core curriculum." *Journal of Education for Library and Information Science* 34:2 (1993): 113-26.

15. L. Connaway "A model curriculum for cataloging education: the library and information services program at the University of Denver." *Technical Services Quarterly* 15:1/2 (1997): 27-41.

16. D. H. Clack. "Education for cataloging: a symposium paper." *Cataloging & Classification Quarterly* 16:3 (1993): 30.

17. Ryans. "Academicians views," p. 399.

18. Clayden. "Theory versus practice," p. 237.

19. MacLeod & Callahan. "Educators and practitioners reply: an assessment," p. 164.

20. Romero, L. 1995. "The cataloging laboratory," p. 5-7.

21. J. D. Saye. "The cataloging experience in library and information science education: an educator's perspective." *Cataloging & Classification Quarterly* 7:4 (1987): 35.

22. Ryans. "Academicians views," p. 396.

23. Young. "The teaching of cataloging," p. 160-61.

24. Intner. "Cataloging practice and theory."

25. Ryans. "Academicians views," p. 396.

26. S. Massonneau. "Bibliographic control of audiovisual materials: opportunities for the 1980s." *Catholic Library World* 51:9 (1980): 384.

27. H. L. P. Stibbe. *Cartographic Materials: A Manual of Interpretation for AACR2.* (Chicago: American Library Association, 1982): vii.

28. S. S. Intner. "Equality of cataloging in the age of AACR2." *American Libraries* 14:2 (1983):p. 102.

29. L. C. Howarth. "Content versus carrier." In *The Principles and Future of AACR: Proceedings of the International Conference on the Principles and Future Development of AACR,* ed. J. Weihs. (Ottawa: Canadian Library Association. 1998): 148-157.

30. C. O. Frost. "Teaching the cataloging of non-book media." *Journal of Education for Librarianship,* 19:1 (1978): 38-39.

31. Saye. "The cataloging experience," p. 27-28.

32. G. M. Weinberg. *An Introduction to General Systems Thinking.* (New York: Wiley, 1975): p. 36.

33. Saye. "The cataloging experience," p. 34.

34. L. M. Chan. *A Guide to the Library of Congress Classification.* 5th ed. (Englewood, CO: Libraries Unlimited, 1999): 322.

35. Chan. *A Guide to the Library of Congress Classification,* p. 216-27.

36. Saye. "The cataloging experience," p. 33.

37. Saye. "The cataloging experience," p. 34.

38. E. Green Bierbaum. "Teaching the cataloging of three-dimensional objects." *Journal of Education for Library and Information Science* 29:1 (1988): 6.

39. Weinberg, G. M. 1975. *An Introduction to General Systems Thinking,* p. 105.

Cataloging and Metadata Education:
Asserting a Central Role
in Information Organization

Ingrid Hsieh-Yee

SUMMARY. This paper describes challenges in organizing digital resources, the role of cataloging in such an effort, forces that threaten the future of cataloging, and responses from the field. It identifies ten issues for consideration when one designs a future cataloging education program. A model program providing four levels of expertise is presented to illustrate that future cataloging education will have a broader scope, incorporating metadata and various aspects of information organization. The program shows that LIS programs can meet different market demands to cover cataloging and metadata topics adequately to help students and ensure the central role of the profession in future information organization. *[Article copies available for a fee from The Haworth Document Delivery Service: 1-800-HAWORTH. E-mail address: <getinfo@haworthpressinc. com> Website: <http://www.HaworthPress.com> © 2002 by The Haworth Press, Inc. All rights reserved.]*

KEYWORDS. Cataloging, metadata, cataloging education, metadata education, digital resources, information organization

Ingrid Hsieh-Yee is Associate Professor, School of Library & Information Science, Catholic University of America.

[Haworth co-indexing entry note]: "Cataloging and Metadata Education: Asserting a Central Role in Information Organization." Hsieh-Yee, Ingrid. Co-published simultaneously in *Cataloging & Classification Quarterly* (The Haworth Information Press, an imprint of The Haworth Press, Inc.) Vol. 34, No. 1/2, 2002, pp. 203-222; and: *Education for Cataloging and the Organization of Information: Pitfalls and the Pendulum* (ed: Janet Swan Hill) The Haworth Information Press, an imprint of The Haworth Press, Inc., 2002, pp. 203-222. Single or multiple copies of this article are available for a fee from The Haworth Document Delivery Service [1-800-HAWORTH, 9:00 a.m. - 5:00 p.m. (EST). E-mail address: getinfo@haworthpressinc.com].

FORCES IMPACTING CATALOGING
AND CATALOGING EDUCATION

Over the years educators and practitioners have examined cataloging education by analyzing course offerings,[1,2,3,4] reviewing course content,[5,6,7,8] discussing trends,[9,10,11,12] and describing teaching philosophy and strategies.[13,14,15,16,17,18] These studies reflect their efforts to be responsive to changes in the information environment. Such efforts, unfortunately, have not resulted in greater emphasis on cataloging. Instead, the number of library and information science (LIS) programs requiring cataloging courses has decreased,[19] and a 2001 study found that only seven of 45 programs studied have integrated Web resources into cataloging courses.[20]

This situation may be related to the fact that the necessity of cataloging has been called into question by information professionals, especially the cataloging of digital resources. In 1991 Mandel proclaimed "Cataloging must change!" and urged catalogers to pay more attention to subject analysis and less to descriptive cataloging.[21] That call for providing data to support user access intensified as the need to organize Internet resources efficiently and effectively becomes more urgent.[22,23,24,25,26,27] Critics of cataloging lamented the complexity of cataloging standards and practice and found them too cumbersome, costly, and inadequate for organizing resources that are dynamic, unstable in location, heterogeneous, massive in volume, and varying in quality.[28,29,30,31,32]

Many in the cataloging community, however, have concluded that cataloging principles can be applied to digital resources[33] and that it is worthwhile to catalog important Internet resources for users because such efforts add value to the resources by collocating materials, facilitating access, and saving time.[34,35,36,37] Many also realize the need to change cataloging standards and practice to allow catalogers to handle digital resources more efficiently.[38,39,40]

The organization of information has changed dramatically in recent years. In addition to the challenges posed by digital resources, two powerful forces confront cataloging. First, cataloging standards are in direct competition with newer metadata schemes for being the standards for document representation. Developers in various disciplines have designed their own metadata schemes to facilitate the organization and access of information in their fields–Text Encoding Initiative,[41] Encoded Archival Description,[42] FGDC[43] are prime examples.[44,45] This trend will continue and more discipline-based schemes are likely to be developed.[46] An even greater challenge is posed by metadata schemes such as Dublin Core (DC) that are generic, simple, and easy to understand. The value of Dublin Core has been enumerated,[47,48] various projects have implemented the scheme with success,[49] tools such as DC-Dot[50] and systems such as CORC[51] are in place to support rapid DC record creation, and catalogers have successfully integrated diverse collections by mapping original metadata onto Dublin Core elements.[52]

While some declared "Cataloging must change!"[53] others suggested a new model for cataloging,[54] and some believe that the relationship between cataloging record and metadata can be complementary. To be effective and efficient in organizing resources in digital and other formats, future OPACs are likely to draw on the strengths of cataloging and metadata[55] and records may be produced at different record levels depending on the importance of the resources they represent.[56] Some practitioners pointed out that some form of collaboration between catalogers, publishers, vendors, and even users in creating metadata would benefit all parties involved.[57,58,59]

Another strong force impacting cataloging comes from new technologies and tools for organizing digital resources. Search engines show the strengths and limitations of full text searching. The CORC project demonstrates the ease of harvesting data for quick record creation by machines and the potential of automatic assignment of subject terms.[60,61] The INFOMINE system illustrates how designers struck a balance between cataloging and minimal indexing to describe digital resources and provide multiple access options.[62] XML's potential for managing Web resources were discussed.[63] Prototypes have been developed from technology for Web citation analysis (ResearchIndex),[64] concept mapping (Oingo),[65] and visualization (Visual Net and WebBrain).[66] The Open Archive Initiative shows promise in harvesting and sharing metadata across digital collections in the National Science Digital Library Program[67] and e-print archives,[68] suggesting a feasible solution for interoperability. It's clear that the contribution of machines to information organization has increased and the roles of humans in the process of information organization have changed.

In response to these challenges there are several efforts to design cataloging education for the 21st century. The Library of Congress Conference on Bibliographic Control (2000) set out to explore ways to control Web resources more effectively and efficiently, and developed an action plan that includes items on cataloging education:

5.1 Address educational needs through improved curricula in library and information science schools and through continuing education for cataloging practitioners by: promoting consensus on determination of "Core Competencies"; devising training in the two areas of "Mind set and values" and "Managing operations"; developing Toolkits; and identifying other mechanisms to meet these needs.

5.3 Promote the use and understanding of standards for describing Web resources through education, targeted outreach, etc.[69]

Under the leadership of the Association for Library Collections and Technical Services (ALCTS) and support of the Association for Library and Information Science Education (ALISE), efforts are underway to develop a model curriculum for cataloging and metadata education. Library and information science (LIS) educators' responses so far include discussions of new cataloging curriculum strategies,[70,71] a Delphi study of metadata experts' views on how metadata ought to be covered in the LIS curriculum, and a survey on practitioners' perspectives on metadata education.[72] Practitioners conducted surveys of the extent to which Web resources were included in cataloging course descriptions[73] and on the core cataloging competencies needed by entry-level academic librarians.[74]

CATALOGING EDUCATION IN THE DIGITAL WORLD

The impact of these forces on cataloging leaves LIS educators with a major challenge: How do we develop a cataloging education plan that will prepare a new generation of information professionals who will demonstrate the relevancy and centrality of our profession in the digital world? Such a plan requires us to consider the following questions in the context of a digital environment.

- What is cataloging? What are the purposes of cataloging?
- What are the functions of the catalogs?
- How is cataloging related to metadata?
- What roles will LIS graduates play in the organization of information?
- What should be the objectives of future cataloging education?
- What should be covered and to what extent?
- How much theory should we cover?

- Should we offer cataloging in separate units or integrate cataloging topics into the curriculum?
- How much hands-on experience is needed? How important is it for students to have a digital environment to practice the creation and management of digital resources?
- How do we prepare students to take a proactive role in shaping the future of information organization?

What Is Cataloging? What Are the Purposes of Cataloging?

With the proliferation of digital resources and increasing reliance on technology, we need to broaden the definition of cataloging beyond traditional cataloging practices. The purposes of cataloging have always been to facilitate users' discovery, selection, and access to information resources. These objectives can be accomplished through cataloging standards and rules, indexing policies, metadata schemes and other methods for organizing information. Cataloging can mean applying cataloging rules to organize a video collection, developing metadata standards for a collection of heterogeneous resources, or other similar activities. To ensure a future for the profession, cataloging needs to address issues related to information organization and cover various methods, practices, and standards of information organization. As a result, cataloging education of the future will have a broader scope and examine information organization in various information environments, including libraries, museums, corporate information centers, and so on. It may be more precise to refer to such education as cataloging and metadata education.

What Are the Functions of the Catalogs?

As libraries and information centers include resources of various formats in their services, cataloging needs to cover many formats well. To address the special nature of electronic resources better, a new chapter 9 of the *Anglo-American Cataloging Rules* was published in 2001, and a new chapter 12 on serials is in the works to deal with the seriality nature of some publications. But cataloging is more than just rules. It is about the organization of information for access. Catalogs have been a trusted tool by which users find quality resources for their information needs. By including the catalog resources of diverse formats and data elements that can enhance access and facilitate management of resources, we will ensure a major role for the profession in the digital world. The objectives of the catalog and the required data elements were specified by Cutter who laid out the finding, collocating, and relating functions of the catalog[75] and by "Functional Requirements for Bibliographic Records" which updates Cutter's terminology and identifies data elements needed to support users in finding, identifying, selecting, and acquiring or obtaining information.[76] These ideas continue to be valid and can serve as principles for information organization in the digital environment. As the information universe continues to expand, it is essential that students of cataloging keep these principles in mind so that they know how to adapt in a changing information environment.

How Is Cataloging Related to Metadata?

Discussions of cataloging and metadata tend to treat the two concepts as separate entities and present a dichotomy that is not always present. Different types of metadata serve different functions–resource discovery, authentication, preservation, access, and so on. But metadata and cataloging share the common objectives of controlling information resources, managing them and facilitating access to them. Gorman recommended that resources be cataloged at different levels according to their importance to users, including a level that may employ Dublin Core.[77] Reynolds also pointed out the value of a hierarchy of record levels and the benefit of having metadata-based cataloging records.[78] In the digital world the key words are collaboration and cooperation. Because no one single group will be able to control all the important digital and non-digital resources in the world, the ability to work together and to leverage existing knowledge and various types of information infrastructure will be critical for information access and management.[79]

What Roles Will LIS Graduates Play in the Organization of Information in the Digital World?

Playing the role of reference librarians, our graduates may assist users in using cataloging/metadata records to find what they need. Similar to catalogers, they may be responsible for the creation and maintenance of cataloging/metadata records for resources in one format or in various formats. In a more challenging role, they may be given the task to integrate diverse collections into a system, thus facing the problems of reconciling multiple record standards and resolving interoperability issues. In a more technical capacity, they may be tasked with the development of a metadata scheme and the implementation of that scheme to organize a digital collection. As they gain more experience, they may become managers of metadata projects.

What Should Be the Objectives of Future Cataloging Education?

What do students need to know to function well in the digital world? The objectives of future cataloging and metadata education are to prepare students well for the roles specified above, depending on their interests and aspiration. For those interested in user services, an understanding of how information is organized and what tools are available for discovery and access to resources is critical. For those aspiring to organize information resources, a firm grasp of principles, the big picture as well as the details, is essential. They also need to know the importance of understanding users' information behavior and information use and to develop the ability to apply cataloging principles, practice, and standards to various settings and situations.

What Should Be Covered and to What Extent?

While traditional cataloging education covers rules, standards, and practice, the popularity of the Internet and the reality of how people seek information there remind us that those involved in the organization of resources need to keep in mind users, their information needs, their information use, and the attributes of information resources. Panelists at the "Reconceptualizing cataloging" program organized by OCLC in January 2002 explained changes brought about by the move from print to digital format, discussed the importance of understanding users' needs and information use, illustrated why the context of information use is valuable to users, and described users' input in generating metadata.[80] Figure 1 and Figure 2 present two models of catalogs to illustrate what students need to know to create records for each type of catalog.

The catalogs in Figure 1 serve as a bridge between users and information resources. They contain representations of various types of information resources, and users interact with them to find the desired resources. Catalogs of this type support searching by surrogates, and current online catalogs follow this model. The focus of the catalogs is to provide accurate resource descriptions (including descriptive details and subject information) to facilitate user access to information resources. To create this type of catalog, students need to become familiar with cataloging rules, standards, tools, and procedure.

In Figure 2 the catalogs continue to be a link between users and various types of information resources, and users interact with them to find desired information. But the scope of the catalogs has expanded to in-

FIGURE 1. Catalogs As the Bridge Between Users and Information Resources

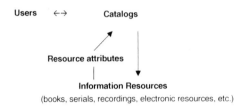

clude information on users, user needs, information use, the context of information use, and information resources (including attributes of these resources and data needed for their use and management). Lynch pointed out that there are three common approaches to searching in the digital environment: by surrogates, by socially-based data such as reviews and citations, and by content-based computational techniques such as full text searches.[81] The catalogs proposed in Figure 2 will support the first two types of searches. The importance of information use and the context of use has been noted,[82] but has not been implemented in available OPACs. A close example of this type of catalog is Amazon.com, which incorporates user reviews, purchasing patterns and user profile to facilitate searching and browsing. To create this type of catalog, students will need to understand users, their needs, their use of information, the context of information use, the attributes of information resources and data needed to manage and use them, in addition to cataloging rules, standards, tools, and procedure.

It's true that students preparing to work in the first type of environment can also benefit from the knowledge students interested in the second environment must obtain, but they may not be able to apply that knowledge in the first environment very much because the procedures for record creation are usually well established. The second model is potentially more useful because it is user-centered and decisions on what to include in a record are based on an understanding of the user community and the information behavior of its members. This model can be applied to a variety of disciplines and situations.

It is conceivable to introduce the first model, and then broaden students' understanding with the second model. As for the specifics of what topics to cover, that will vary by the level of education desired. Details are presented later in the sample program section.

FIGURE 2. New Scope of Catalogs

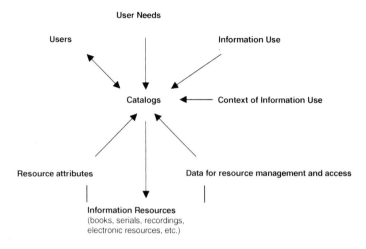

How Much Theory Should We Cover?

The tension between theory and practice in cataloging education has a long history. But some practitioners do appreciate theory[83] and the coverage of theory has received more support from practitioners in recent years.[84] Since digital technology is changing rapidly and new formats may be introduced anytime, it is important for students to have a firm grasp of the theory of cataloging, authority control, subject analysis, subject headings, thesaurus, and classification. With such background they will find it easier to apply the fundamentals of cataloging to the organization of information resources in any format.

Should We Offer Cataloging in Separate Units or Integrate Cataloging Topics into the Curriculum?

Both approaches are desirable. Cataloging and metadata related topics that can help students function well in the digital world ought to be integrated into the curriculum, whereas topics that are more appropriate for students who are interested in a career in information organization can be offered in separate units for in-depth coverage. For example, the concepts of cataloging and metadata should be integrated into courses on digital libraries and collection development, while Dublin Core or

Text Encoding Initiative can be studied in depth in courses on the organization of digital resources. This view is similar to the syndetic structure recommended by Vellucci[85] and was endorsed by metadata experts in a Delphi study.[86]

How Much Hands-On Experience Is Needed? How Important Is It for Students to Have a Digital Environment to Practice the Creation and Management of Digital Resources?

The amount of hands-on practice depends on the level of education desired. For awareness-level courses, a small amount of hands-on practice or a demonstration may be sufficient. But for students preparing for a career in cataloging, a fair amount of practice will be necessary for them to qualify for entry-level positions. As for students interested in managing resources in digital and other formats, much hands-on practice in digitizing, encoding, and indexing resources will deepen their understanding of the process of organizing such resources and increase their confidence. Most metadata experts in a Delphi study on metadata agreed that a digital environment in which students can practice the creation and management of digital resources would be very helpful, and some of them suggested LIS programs pool their resources to create such an environment collaboratively.[87]

How Do We Prepare Our Graduates to Take a Proactive Role in Shaping the Future of Information Organization?

Values, knowledge, skills, and confidence are needed to accomplish this objective. If students develop an appreciation for information organization, have a solid foundation in cataloging principles and basics, understand issues related to the organization of information, and have enough experience to become confident, they will be eager to take part in discussions of information organization as professionals. To stay relevant and central in the organization of digital resources we need to prepare more graduates for this role.

A SAMPLE PROGRAM FOR CATALOGING AND METADATA EDUCATION

Many topics can be covered in future cataloging and metadata education. A sample program is sketched below to illustrate the possibilities. Cataloging and metadata education can be offered at four different levels. There are many other courses students may need to take to be fully prepared for a career in a particular area. For example, to be a digital library manager, students will need some knowledge in systems in addition to the courses described below.

Level I. General-Awareness Level

Intended audience: This level is designed for students who do not plan to be involved in information organization after graduation. They may be interested in collection development, reference services, management or other functions.

Objectives

- To understand how information is created, reviewed, disseminated, organized, and used.
- To learn the methods of information organization, including the principles and practice of indexing, abstracting, cataloging, database creation, and Web site design.
- To understand the role of cataloging and metadata in information organization and clarify the relationship between them.

Sample Topics

- Overview of cataloging and metadata, including why and how cataloging and metadata records are created, how to make use of them, and how to interpret them.
- Introduction to standards such as *AACR* and Dublin Core.
- Introduction to authority control, subject analysis, controlled vocabulary (subject headings and classification), and the effects of controlled vocabulary on information retrieval.
- Discussions of bibliographic utilities and the MARC format.
- Demonstrations of an opac, a database system, and a well-known metadata project such as CORC.

A course like this is designed to provide students with a general understanding of how information is organized and what tools can help them function well as information professionals. This course could be offered in LIS programs as a required introductory course.

Level II. Knowledge and Skills for Entry-Level Cataloging Positions

Intended audience: This level is designed for students planning to pursue a career in cataloging or planning to become a metadata librarian.

Objectives

- To obtain the knowledge and skills for descriptive cataloging and subject analysis.
- To understand the purposes of cataloging and metadata.
- To have hands-on practice in creating cataloging and metadata records, using the CORC system and Dublin Core tools.
- To obtain the knowledge and ability to place metadata in a larger ontology of knowledge management methods.[88]

Sample Topics

- Information cycle, scholarly communication, methods of information organization.
- Principles of cataloging and functions of the catalog.
- Metadata: types, functions, development of metadata schemes, hands-on practice in Dublin Core, metadata crosswalk, project examples.
- Relationship between cataloging and metadata.
- Descriptive cataloging: standards and practice.
- Authority control, subject analysis, subject headings, classification systems: theory and practice.
- Bibliographic networks, OPAC, MARC, and metadata-based cataloging.

This course reflects an expansion of a traditional cataloging course. It covers traditional cataloging topics and metadata topics in sufficient depth for students to function well as beginning catalogers while at the same time being capable of moving between standard cataloging practice and metadata, and being able to address basic metadata issues intelligently. The challenge in teaching such a course lies in allocating enough time to cover each topic well.

Level III. Advanced Cataloging Knowledge and Skills

Intended audience: This level is designed for students who plan to become cataloging experts or metadata specialists.

Objectives

- To become familiar with the cataloging of materials in several formats such as sound recordings, videos, and electronic resources.
- To have in-depth knowledge of subject headings and classification systems.

- To know the history, semantics and structure of two metadata schemes and their strengths and limitations.[89]
- To obtain the knowledge and ability to place metadata in a larger ontology of knowledge management methods.[90]
- To know the strengths and limitations of using cataloging and metadata for controlling resources in any format.

Sample Topics

- Principles of cataloging and their application to electronic resources.
- Cataloging of materials in various formats.
- Knowledge of LC subject headings and LC classification system.
- Practice in creating MARC and Dublin Core records in CORC.
- Preparation of guidelines for using a metadata scheme.
- Interoperability, crosswalk, and integration of diverse collections.
- Metadata projects and evaluation issues.

This course builds on the Level II course to provide more in-depth coverage of issues related to cataloging and metadata. The intent is to provide students with the knowledge and skills to assume leadership in managing future cataloging and metadata efforts.

Level IV. Expert Knowledge in Cataloging and Metadata

Intended audience: This level is designed for students who expect to be responsible for organizing resources in various formats in various types of information environments.

Objectives

- To understand several current approaches for organizing Internet resources and the strengths and limitations of each.
- To understand issues critical to organizing a collection for remote access.
- To develop a framework for organizing a digital collection.
- To understand and use metadata standards such as Dublin Core, Text Encoding Initiative (TEI), and Encoded Archival Description (EAD).
- To have hands-on practice in CORC, and with database design and DTD design.

- To know the applications of metadata sets by various information professionals.
- To know how to identify areas for metadata development, and to have the ability to develop metadata sets, implement them, and evaluate their effects on information access.[91]
- To understand the process of implementing a metadata project, including needs assessment, project management, metadata scheme adaptation, and so on.

Sample Topics

- Methods for organizing Internet resources.
- Framework for organizing Internet resources.
- Metadata: types, functions, analysis of metadata projects.
- SGML, DTD, XML.
- Dublin Core, TEI, EAD.
- Hands-on practice with CORC, Dublin Core, TEI, and EAD.
- Development of metadata sets.
- Implementation of metadata projects.
- Evaluation of metadata projects.

This course deals with issues of information organization in library and other settings. It focuses on metadata schemes and their implementations. It also discusses the applications of cataloging related topics such as resource description, authority control, subject analysis, and classification in metadata projects. The goal is for students to obtain the knowledge and skills to implement and manage metadata projects and prepare them to serve as a bridge between the library community and other communities that use metadata. This course, when combined with a hands-on metadata implementation project, will enable our graduates to assert a central role in information organization in the digital world.

CONCLUSION

To meet the demands of the digital world, future cataloging and metadata education will need to expand to include metadata and information in digital and any new formats. The ten issues discussed in the paper provide a framework for the sample curriculum for cataloging and metadata education. The proposed plan shows that LIS programs can offer cataloging and metadata education at four levels. The course at the general awareness level will give students a basic understanding of cataloging and metadata, enable them to make good use of cataloging and metadata records, and develop an appreciation of the roles of cataloging and metadata in information organization.

The second level of education calls for expansion of current cataloging courses. Since information resources in various formats will be provided in libraries, traditional cataloging standards and practice will continue to be relevant. But as digital information proliferates, the effort to organize them will intensify and catalogers need to be well prepared to remain relevant and central to this effort. In addition to subjects typically covered in cataloging courses, students need to have a broader perspective of information organization, to understand how metadata relate to cataloging, and to know how to make use of metadata to organize resources. These subjects can be covered in cataloging courses designed to prepare students for entry-level cataloging positions.

In the third course level students will learn to catalog resources in various formats while becoming more immersed in metadata applications. At the fourth level students who aspire to be metadata experts will learn to consider various issues related to organizing a collection for remote access, develop an information architecture for resources, analyze metadata projects, develop metadata sets, and examine the process of implementing a metadata project. Such a course, if combined with hands-on experience in project implementation, will prepare students well for the organization of any resources.

This series of four courses plus a project implementing metadata provides a full range of options for students. Students may start with the general awareness course and continue on to the next level. If they are inspired to do more with metadata after the second level, they can take courses at the next two levels or take either the third or the fourth level course. The final hands-on project is designed to complement the level four course. It would be ideal to have an environment for students to practice creating a digital collection and manage it. If that turns out to be not feasible, an alternative is to seek partners with local digital library projects and arrange for students to be involved in aspects of the projects. Students' field experience in this case will be limited but still valuable.

A major challenge in offering these courses is time. Instructors will need to manage time well to cover the large number of topics. Furthermore students may not be able to take four or five courses in one subject area when a typical master's degree program requires 12 courses. But if a student intends to pursue a career in information organization, the sample series described in this paper should prepare that student well. Another challenge in teaching cataloging and metadata is the misperception that cataloging is a rule-based subject that has become increasingly irrelevant in the digital environment. One way to counter this is to design a curriculum that will provide relevant knowledge, promote values of information services, help students appreciate information organization, help them develop communication, cooperation, and problem-solving skills, and motivate them to keep on learning about information organization. These types of educational experiences can be embedded into the courses sketched above.

The popularity of the Internet, changes in publishing and scholarly communication, and users' reliance on digital resources result in an information environment that often seems chaotic. While users can retrieve some information from search engines, many have experienced information overload and some have experienced difficulty assessing the authenticity or authority of the resources found on the Internet. Catalogs can serve as an effective portal to the Internet so long as we know how to retain its strengths and learn to apply the principles of cataloging to organize digital resources using cataloging standards or metadata schemes.[92] Our profession's involvement in information organization will determine its relevance in the digital world. A cataloging and metadata education plan like the one presented will prepare graduates to meet different market demands and ensure the central role of the profession in future information organization.

ENDNOTES

1. Francis Miksa, "Cataloging Education in the Library and Information Science Curriculum," in *Recruiting, Educating and Training Cataloging Librarians*, S. Intner and J. S. Hill, eds. (New York: Greenwood Press, 1989): 273-297.

2. Jerry D. Saye, "The Cataloging Experience in Library and Information Science Education: An Educator's perspective," *Cataloging & Classification Quarterly* 7, no. 4 (1987): 27-45.

3. Roxanne Sellberg, "The Teaching of Cataloging in U.S. Library Schools," *Library Resources and Technical Services* 32 (January 1988): 30-42.

4. Sherry L. Vellucci, "Cataloging Across the Curriculum: A Syndetic Structure for Teaching Cataloging," *Cataloging & Classification Quarterly* 24, no. 1/2 (1997): 35-59.

5. Saye, "The Cataloging Experience," p. 27-45.

6. Desreta McAllister-Harper, "An Analysis of Courses in Cataloging and Classification and Related Areas Offered in Sixteen Graduate Library Schools and Their Relationship to Present and Future Trends in Cataloging and Classification and to

Cognitive Needs of Professional Academic Catalogers," *Cataloging & Classification Quarterly* 16, no. 3 (1993): 99-123.

7. Taemin Park, "The Integration of Electronic Resources into Cataloging Instruction in the LIS Curriculum," *The Serials Librarian* 41, no. 3/4 (Spring 2002): 57-72.

8. Vellucci, "Cataloging Across the Curriculum," p. 35-59.

9. Doris H. Clack, "Education for Cataloging: A Symposium Paper," *Cataloging & Classification Quarterly* 16, no. 3 (1993): 27-37.

10. McAllister-Harper, "Analysis of Courses," p. 99-123.

11. Vellucci, "Cataloging Across the Curriculum," p. 35-59.

12. Park, "Integration of Electronic Resources," 57-72.

13. Lynn S. Connaway, "A Model Curriculum for Cataloging Eduation: The Library and Information Services Program at the University of Denver," *Technical Services Quarterly* 15 (1997): 27-41.

14. Michael Gorman, "How Cataloging and Classification Should be Taught," *American Libraries* 23 (Sept. 1992): 694-697.

15. Ingrid Hsieh-Yee, "Organizing Internet Resources: Teaching Cataloging Standards and Beyond," *OCLC Systems & Services* 16 (2000): 130-143.

16. Ling Hwey Jeng, "From Cataloging to Organization of Information: A Paradigm for the Core Curriculum," *Journal of Education for Library and Information Science* 34 (1993): 113-26.

17. Jerry D. Saye, "The Organization of Electronic Resources in the Library and Information Science Curriculum," *OCLC Systems & Services* 17 (2001): 71-78.

18. Kirsten Strunck, "About the Use of 'Functional Requirements for Bibliographic Records' in Teaching Cataloguing," *International Cataloguing and Bibliographic Control* 29, no. 4 (2000): 68-70.

19. Jodi Lynn Spillane, "Comparison of Required Introductory Cataloguing Courses, 1986-1998," *Library Resources & Technical Services* 43 (1999): 223-30.

20. Park, "Integration of Electronic Resources," 57-72.

21. Dorothy Gregor and Carol A. Mandel, "Cataloging Must Change!" *Library Journal* 116 (Apr 1, 1991): 42-47.

22. Gregor and Mandel, "Cataloging Must Change!" p. 42-47.

23. Daniel Dorner, "Cataloging in the 21st Century–Part 2: Digitization and Information Standards," *Library Collections, Acquisitions, & Technical Services* 24 (2000): 73-87.

24. David M. Levy, "Cataloging in the Digital Order" (1995). Available at: *http://www.csdl.tamu.edu/DL95/papers/levy/levy.htm.*

25. Clifford Lynch, "Searching the Internet." (1997). Available: *http://www.sciam.com/0397issue/0397lynch.html.*

26. Norm Medeiros, "The Effects of Digitalization on Libraries: A Cataloger's Perspective," *OCLC Systems & Services*, Vol. 15 No. 1, p. 5.

27. Norman Oder, "Cataloging the Net: Can We Do It?" *Library Journal* 123, no. 16 (1998): 47-51.

28. Ron Chepesiuk, "Organizing the Internet: The 'Core' of the Challenge," *American Libraries* 30, no. 1 (1999): 60-63.

29. Carl Lagoze, "Business Unusual: How 'Event-Awareness' May Breathe Life Into the Catalog?" (2000). Available at: *http://lcweb.loc.gov/catdir/bibcontrol/lagoze_paper.html.*

30. "Nordic Metadata Project Final Report" (1998). Available at: *http://linnea.helsinki.fi/meta/nmfinal.htm.*

31. Regina Romano Reynolds, "Partnerships to Mine Unexploited Sources of Metadata," (2000). Available at: *http://lcweb.loc.gov/catdir/bibcontrol/reynolds_paper.html*.

32. Roy Tennant, "The Art and Science of Digital Bibliography," *Library Journal* 123, no. 17 (1998): 28, 30.

33. Carl A. Mandel and Robert A. Wolven, "Intellectual Access to Digital Documents: Joining Proven Principles with New Technologies," *Cataloging & Classification Quarterly* 22, no. 3/4: 25-42.

34. Michael Gorman, "Metadata or Cataloging? A False Choice," *Journal of Internet Cataloging* 2, no. 1 (1999): 5-22.

35. Diane I. Hillmann, " 'Parallel Universes' of Meaningful Relationships: Envisioning a Future for the OPAC and the Net," *Cataloging & Classification Quarterly* 22, nos. 3/4 (1996): 97-103.

36. Oder, "Cataloging the Net," p. 47-51.

37. James R. Veatch, "Insourcing the Web," *American Libraries* 30, no. 1: 64-67 (1999).

38. F. H. Ayres, "Time for a Change: A New Approach to Cataloguing Concepts," *Cataloging & Classification Quarterly* 28, no. 2 (1999): 3-15.

39. Dorner, "Cataloging in the 21st Century," p. 73-87.

40. Sarah E. Thomas, "The Catalog as Portal to the Internet." (2000). Available at: *http://lcweb.loc.gov/catdir/bibcontrol/thomas_paper.html*.

41. Text Encoding Initiative (TEI Home Page). Available at: *http://www.tei-c.org/*.

42. EAD Home Page. Available at: *http://lcweb.loc.gov/ead*.

43. FGCD Metdata. Available at: *http://www.fgdc.gov/metadata/metadata.html*.

44. Priscilla Caplan, "International Metadata Initiatives: Lessons in Bibliographic Control," (2000). Available at: *http://lcweb.loc.gov/catdir/bibcontrol/caplan_paper.html*.

45. Jean Hudgins, Grace Agnew, and Elizabeth Brown, *Getting Mileage out of Metadata: Applications for the Library* (Chicago: American Library Association, 1999).

46. Sherry L. Vellucci, "Metadata," *Annual Review of Information Science and Technology* 33 (1998): 187-222.

47. Caplan, "International Metadata Initiatives."

48. Norm Medeiros, "Making Room for MARC in a Dublin Core World," *Online* 23, no. 6 (1999): 1-5. Also available at: *http://www.onlineinc.com/onlinemag*.

49. Dublin Core Metadata Initiative. Available at: *http://dublincore.org/*.

50. DC Dot-Dublin Core Generator. Available at: *http://www.ukoln.ac.uk/metadata/dcdot*.

51. CORC Home Page. Available at: *http://www.oclc.org/corc/*.

52. Metadata Implementation Group, "Dublin Core Data Dictionaries." Available at: *http://www.lib.washington.edu/msd/mig/datadicts/default.html*.

53. Regina Reynolds, "Physical to Digital: Winds of Change" (presented at "Reconceptualizing Cataloging," New Orleans, Louisiana, Jan. 2002). Also available at: *http://www.oclc.org/events/videoondemand/symposium/*.

54. Lagoze, "Business as Usual."

55. Thomas, "Catalog as Portal."

56. Reynolds, "Partnership to Mine."

57. Amira Aaron, "Vendor Partnerships For Bibliographic Control." (2000). Available at: *http://lcweb.loc.gov/catdir/bibcontrol/aaron_paper.html*.

58. Cindy Cunningham, "Metadata in Post E-commerce" (presented at "Reconceptualizing Cataloging," New Orleans, Louisiana, Jan. 2002). Also available at: *http://www.oclc.org/events/videoondemand/symposium/*.

59. Reynolds, "Partnership to Mine."

60. C. Jean Godby and R. Reighart, "Terminology Identification in a Collection of Web Resources," *Journal of Internet Cataloging* 4, nos. 1/2 (2001): 49-65.

61. Thom B. Hickey, "CORC: A System for Gateway Creation," *Online Information Review* 24, no. 1 (2000): 49-53.

62. Julie Mason et al., "INFOMINE: Promising Directions in Virtual Library Development," *First Monday* 5, no. 6 (June 2000). Available at: *http://www.firstmonday.dk/issues/issue5_6/mason/index.html*.

63. Norm Medeiros, "*XML and the Resource Description Framework: The Great Web Hope*," *Online* 24, no. 5 (2000): 37-40.

64. See, for example, ResearchIndex. Available at: *http://citeseer.nj.nec.com/cs*.

65. See, for example, Oingo Meaning-Based Search. Available at: *http://www.oingo.com/*.

66. See, for example, Visual Net, available at: *http://www.map.net/* and WebBrain.com, available at: *http://www.webbrain.com/html/default_win.html*.

67. Carl Lagoze, "Peer-to-Peer Sharing of Metadata" (presented at "Reconceptualizing Cataloging," New Orleans, Louisiana, Jan. 2002). Also available at: *http://www.oclc.org/events/videoondemand/symposium/*.

68. Richard E. Luce, "The Open Archives Initiative: Interoperable, Interdisciplinary Author Self-Archiving Comes of Age," *The Serials Librarian* 40, no. 1/2 (2001): 173-182.

69. "Bibliographic Control of Web Resources: A Library of Congress Action Plan." (Revised December 19, 2001). Available at: *http://lcweb.loc.gov/catdir/bibcontrol/actionplan.html*.

70. Hsieh-Yee, "Organizing Internet Resources," p. 130-143.

71. Saye, "Organization of Electronic Resources," p. 71-78.

72. Ingrid Hsieh-Yee, "A Delphi Study on Metadata: Curriculum Implications and Resaerch Priorities" (presented at the annual meeting of the American Society for Information Science and Technology, Washington, D.C., Nov. 2001).

73. Ingrid Hsieh-Yee, "A Delphi Study on Metadata."

74. Karen M. Letarte et al., "Practitioner Perspectives on Cataloging Education for Entry-Level Academic Librarians," *Library Resources & Technical Services* 46, no. 1 (2002): 11-22.

75. Charles A. Cutter, *Rules for a Dictionary Catalog*, 4th ed. (Washington, DC: GPO, 1904).

76. *Functional Requirements for Bibliographic Records, Final Report*. Edited by IFLA Study Group on the Functional Requirements for Bibliographic Records. (Munchen: K.G. Saur, 1998).

77. Gorman, "Metadata or Cataloging?" 5-22.

78. Reynolds, "Partnership to Mine."

79. Clifford Lynch, "The New Context for Bibliographic Control In the New Millennium." (2000). Available at: *http://lcweb.loc.gov/catdir/bibcontrol/lynch_paper.html*.

80. "Reconceptualizing Cataloging" (a panel presentation held in New Orleans, Louisiana, Jan. 2002. Presenters included Regina Reynolds, Carl Lagoze, David Bearman,

and Cindy Cunningham.) Available at: *http://www.oclc.org/events/videoondemand/symposium/*.

81. Lynch, "New Context."

82. David Bearman, "The Metadata of Cultural Stuff" (presented at "Reconceptualizing Cataloging," New Orleans, Louisiana, Jan. 2002). Also available at: Lynch, "New Context."

83. Shela S. Intner, "Cataloging Practice and Theory: What to Teach and Why?" *Journal of Education for Library and Information Science* 30 (1990): 333-336.

84. Vellucci, "Cataloging Across the Curriculum," 35-59.

85. Ibid.

86. Hsieh-Yee, "Delphi Study."

87. Ibid.

88. Ibid.

89. Ibid.

90. Ibid.

91. Ibid.

92. Thomas, "Catalog as Portal."

On Teaching Subject Cataloging

Arlene G. Taylor
Daniel N. Joudrey

SUMMARY. The authors, Professor Arlene G. Taylor and her doctoral student, Daniel N. Joudrey, discuss their approach to teaching subject cataloging in the graduate library and information sciences (LIS) program at the University of Pittsburgh's School of Information Sciences. This essay discusses the authors' thoughts on the importance of subject cataloging in graduate LIS education, the theory versus practice debate, goals, class work, grading, making it concrete to the students, ordering topics in the courses, separating subject analysis from descriptive cataloging, and concerns for the future.

In the not too distant past, library schools considered the teaching of *Dewey Decimal Classification* and *Library of Congress Subject Headings* to be totally adequate preparation for graduates to function subject-wise in their chosen profession. As time has moved on we have gone through periods in which even these were considered unnecessary "because keyword searching is better than subject headings" and "classification is only a location device." The complexities of the current world of subject access (or lack thereof), however, demand that a more complex and thorough approach be taken. *[Article copies available for a fee from The Haworth Document Delivery Service: 1-800-HAWORTH. E-mail address: <getinfo@haworthpressinc.com> Website: <http://www.HaworthPress.com> © 2002 by The Haworth Press, Inc. All rights reserved.]*

Arlene G. Taylor, PhD, is Professor, School of Information Sciences, and Daniel N. Joudrey, MLIS, is a PhD student, both at the Department of Library and Information Science, School of Information Sciences, Pittsburgh, PA 15260.

[Haworth co-indexing entry note]: "On Teaching Subject Cataloging." Taylor. Arlene G., and Daniel N. Joudrey. Co-published simultaneously in *Cataloging & Classification Quarterly* (The Haworth Information Press, an imprint of The Haworth Press, Inc.) Vol. 34, No. 1/2, 2002, pp. 223-232; and: *Education for Cataloging and the Organization of Information: Pitfalls and the Pendulum* (ed: Janet Swan Hill) The Haworth Information Press, an imprint of The Haworth Press, Inc., 2002, pp. 223-232. Single or multiple copies of this article are available for a fee from The Haworth Document Delivery Service [1-800-HAWORTH, 9:00 a.m. - 5:00 p.m. (EST). E-mail address: getinfo@haworthpressinc.com].

KEYWORDS. Subject cataloging education, cataloging education, subject analysis

IMPORTANCE FOR ALL LIBRARIANS
TO UNDERSTAND SUBJECT ACCESS

In a profession that often seems to devalue technical services functions, it is important to acknowledge cataloging (especially subject cataloging) as a skill that is important to all aspects of librarianship. In general, there is overall agreement among the recent bibliographic control education articles on the topic of the universality of cataloging skills.[1] Zyroff stresses this, pointing out that familiarity with cataloging skills provides an "in-depth perspective on the structure of information,"[2] and she notes that learning to use controlled vocabulary also assists in searching and retrieval, necessary skills for all librarians. Nancy J. Williamson writes in a 1997 article that understanding the process of subject analysis is important for all librarians since subject analysis is all about retrieval:

> Locating information by subject is one of the fundamental approaches to all information-seeking. It is essential that *all* information professionals have a basic knowledge of the principles of subject analysis and an understanding of their application in indexing and retrieval in online systems of various kinds.[3]

With these points in mind, it is only reasonable to state that all librarians must have a basic understanding of and must possess basic skills in bibliographic control. Lack of understanding of controlled vocabulary and classification lead to less effective reference services, collection development, and, needless to say, cataloging.

THEORY vs. PRACTICE

Over the years, there has been a great deal of debate as to whether library school programs should focus on theory or practice. In the area of bibliographic control, this debate seems ever present in the literature. Everyone has an opinion and each opinion finds its own place on the continuum between the two extremes. In the bi-level approach to teaching subject cataloging that we, the authors, use here at the University of

Pittsburgh (a general, basic level course, followed by more specific, advanced-level courses), we believe that both points of view must be well represented. Neither theory without practical skills nor practical skills without a firm grasp of the theoretical foundations is helpful for new library professionals. It is the job of educators, with a responsibility to the profession, to ensure that students understand not only the "how" of cataloging, but also the "why." We feel our approach to subject cataloging education represents a healthy balance. It is a practical approach that is grounded in theory.

Catalogers in the field have been known to complain about the lack of emphasis on the tools of cataloging in library schools. We believe this is short-sighted. In larger libraries paraprofessionals have very successfully learned to follow the rules and use the tools in the cataloging process, misleading some administrators into thinking that they can save money by not hiring professionals for any cataloging position. However, in our experience, when these paraprofessionals decide to get the MLIS degree and come to school thinking they already know cataloging, we find that they know one way of doing things very well but are shocked to learn that there are other ways of doing the same thing. In addition, they often do not know *why* things are done. In smaller libraries the one or two professionals in the system have to understand the "whys" in order to determine such things as which rules can be circumvented for the sake of time without significantly harming the retrieval process. Such decision-making ability is not born from slavish learning of rules and tools.

GOALS FOR THE COURSES

In Organizing Information, the basic level course that we teach at the University of Pittsburgh's School of Information Sciences (SIS), all students are expected to have a basic understanding of the tools, common systems, vocabulary, concepts, processes, and the place of subject access in the information organizing process. It is not expected that the students finishing this course are qualified to be catalogers. This course is a general introduction to the topic of organizing information in a variety of information settings. It may be a foundation for later cataloging courses, but it is not in itself a cataloging course.

In the advanced courses students have more time to explore the issues involved in providing access to information. SIS offers two advanced-level master's courses that particularly address cataloging:

Descriptive Cataloging, and Subject Analysis. On completion of these courses, the students are still not catalogers, but a more in-depth understanding of the processes, concepts, tools, and systems should be in place. In the following paragraphs we discuss the particular implications of the teaching of subject analysis-related topics.

MAKING IT CONCRETE

In the introductory course, Organizing Information (a required course for all library science students), the students are exposed to the basic theories of subject access to information. This is followed up with in-class exercises and formal assignments in order to make the theory more concrete. Over the years, we have come to discover that theory alone is difficult for the students to grasp. It is only with some practical skill-building exercises that it becomes "real."

The advanced courses in the program are built upon the teachings of the earlier course. They are taught assuming a basic level of understanding on the part of the students. As the advanced courses have the general Organizing Information course as a prerequisite, each student *should* understand the basics for the various ways in which subject access is provided. [The word "should" in the proceeding sentence is emphasized because this is not always the case. There are times when students have forgotten the material from the previous course or never understood the material in the first place. Sometimes some students who struggled in the introductory course go on, against all logic, to take one of the advanced courses. It can be a great source of frustration for high-achievers to deal with students who ask questions about material covered in the introductory-level course. While it is important to give every student the opportunity to succeed, it should be without detriment to the students who have worked hard to master the materials of the earlier course. "Remedial" questions can take up a great deal of class time if it is allowed.]

The Subject Analysis course that follows the introductory course goes into greater detail in the theoretical foundations, principles, and practices of the process of subject analysis, the *Library of Congress Subject Headings* (LCSH), *Dewey Decimal Classification* (DDC), and the *Library of Congress Classification* (LCC). Each unit in this course includes in-class exercises, workbook problems, and formal, graded assignments. These help to strengthen the students' understanding of the theories discussed in class. This course also introduces students to a number of other subject heading schemes, thesauri, and classification schemes, although there is not time for real practice using these other tools.

SEPARATING SUBJECT ANALYSIS
FROM DESCRIPTIVE CATALOGING

One of the ways that we handle the teaching of advanced coursework at the University of Pittsburgh is to separate the teaching of subject analysis from that of descriptive cataloging. While all of these topics are covered in the basic Organizing Information course, the topics have been divided into two advanced level courses. This has been done to allow for greater depth in exploring these topics. It gives the students the opportunity to spend more time working on the principles and usage of subject headings and on individual classification schemes. In a single, one-semester, cataloging and classification course, there is just too little time to fully explore all of the concepts adequately. DDC, LCC, and LCSH alone take nearly an entire semester to cover, but when you also want the students to be familiar with *Medical Subject Headings* (MeSH), Bliss, Colon Classification, the *Art & Architecture Thesaurus* (AAT), and other schemes, you have no time left to cover description, access and authority control. Our solution has been to create the two courses, and it has worked well.

We do understand that there are benefits in teaching descriptive cataloging and subject analysis together as parts of a single process. We believe, however, that the students benefit more by having a deeper understanding of each process and that they can adequately put the pieces from the two courses together on a conceptual basis.

ORDER IN WHICH THE TOPICS ARE INTRODUCED

When teaching subject cataloging, it is helpful to order topics so that each unit builds upon the preceding unit. In Organizing Information we first approach subject access after discussing history, description, access, and authority control. The first topic discussed is the subject analysis process. This unit includes discussions of Cutter's objects for the catalog, the purpose of subject analysis, the steps in subject analysis, the concept of exhaustivity, and concepts to look for in the analysis process. Subject analysis is then followed by verbal subject access systems in which we discuss the general principles of controlled vocabulary, specific problems in creating controlled vocabulary, issues of translating concepts into index terms, the differences between subject heading lists, thesauri, and ontologies, along with examples of each. Once verbal subject access is complete, we begin work on classification theory and concepts. These discussions are followed up with examinations of DDC and LCC. Students are also required to complete formal, graded assignments on subject analysis, on controlled vocabulary, and in using both classification systems, in addition to in-class exercises. The history of subject access tools is also covered, but in an earlier history unit.

The advanced Subject Analysis course, as we have said, assumes a mastery of the material taught in the basic course. It begins with an exploration of subject analysis, albeit a more in-depth exploration than that undertaken in the beginning-level course. This discussion is supported with subject analysis practice. The students are required to analyze several information packages and provide aboutness statements and hierarchies for each information package.

Because in real life cataloging, subject headings are usually determined before classification, we start with LCSH after covering subject analysis. Due to the complex nature of the Library of Congress Subject Headings, three to four weeks are spent discussing the principles, procedures, and application of subject headings. Form/genre is discussed as a concept, and an attempt is made to distinguish such access from topical subject access. Time is spent teaching the students to use the resources available to them (e.g., the *Subject Cataloging Manual: Subject Headings, Free Floating Subdivisions,* etc.) to create properly constructed subject heading strings. They are also instructed in how to write a properly constructed, viable subject-heading proposal. The LCSH unit is the longest unit in the semester-long course. It is generally the most difficult for students, as the procedures of subject heading work can be confusing and, at times, seemingly contradictory. Sorting through *Subject Cataloging Manual: Subject Headings,* H1095, alone can take a substantial amount of time. Students are required to provide sets of subject headings, correctly coded as if going into a MARC bibliographic record, for the information packages that they analyzed at the beginning of the course.

After the unit on LCSH, the students begin their study of classification systems. One of the first things to note is that we use different approaches to teaching classification in the basic course and in the advanced course. In Organizing Information, the students are required to understand the basics of classification theory and some broad classification concepts. However, when it comes to practical exercises, they are limited only to number deconstruction. It is not required for students at that level to be able to build complex notations. They can achieve the necessary level of understanding by deconstructing notations instead. In the Subject Analysis course, however, we do expect the students to build notations. They must build at least 50 notations during the units on classification with the possibility of more if they are so inclined.

In the advanced subject course we begin study of classification with Dewey. In general, the students do tend to have more difficulties with the DDC's procedures for number building than they do with the LCC equivalents. Many students lose their place when adding from other parts of the DDC schedules or when using the literature tables. The LCC unit is by far less stressful for the students than the units on DDC and LCSH. Having it later in the term serves to give the students a breather just when other courses are becoming heavier. It also serves to boost their confidence to have a unit that is easier to grasp. The DDC and LCC classification units are constructed similarly. Students examine the principles and practices of the classification scheme, participate in numerous in-class exercises, and provide complete call numbers for the information packages with which they have been working throughout the course. The goal of these units is to help the students to create sound, well-constructed classification numbers. In addition to creating the classification notations, the students are required to create Cutter notations for the items and to code the call numbers as they would for a MARC bibliographic record. After the units on classification, the students study the MARC classification format and issues and problems in subject cataloging. These units generally consist of lectures and discussion. During the final class sessions, each student is required to make a thirty-minute presentation (length varies depending upon the number of students in a particular class) on a subject access system less frequently encountered in the United States.

CLASS WORK

The Organizing Information course is taught both as an on-campus course and as a Web course. Material covered with the two methodologies is the same. Required readings are taken from a number of sources and are designed to supplement the textbook with more detail.[4] Recommended readings are suggested for the purpose of providing more in-depth coverage of topics that may be of particular interest to a student. PowerPoint presentations with notes are used to cover basics and principles. Handouts of examples illustrate principles. In the on-campus class, the PowerPoint presentations and handouts can be gone over and discussed face-to-face. In the Web version, it is up to the students to retrieve the documents from the Web, to absorb them, and to ask questions about what they do not understand. There is a Discussion Board for the purpose of discussion and questions. In-class exercises (called practice exercises for the Web version) assist in the process of applying theory to practice. For example, students may have a thesaurus building exercise in addition to the classification notation deconstruction exercises already mentioned.

Various tools for subject analysis can be demonstrated in class. These include the Library of Congress' "Classification Plus" CD-ROM system; OCLC's online cataloging system (including WebDewey, which can be used for automatic suggestions of DDC notations for Web resources, in addition to its being used to determine the meanings of DDC notations); Web sources for MARC data; subject authority records from various sources; and other resources for controlled vocabulary such as the Getty Web site for the AAT,[5] the National Library of Medicine Web site for MeSH,[6] and the ontology *WordNet*.[7] While tutorials have been designed for some of these for the Web version of the course, we have found that these tools need to be demonstrated in a face-to-face component (conducted for one weekend during a term) of the Web course.

For the advanced course, class work is much the same. There are required and recommended readings, PowerPoint presentations, handouts of examples, demonstrations of tools, and many, many more in-class exercises.

GRADING ISSUES

In Organizing Information, grading is not very difficult. The assignments reflect the students' level of knowledge and their abilities as well as the instructor's expectations for the course. Much of the work is designed to be as objective as possible. Classification number deconstruction is a fairly obvious example. The deconstruction is correct or it is not. The rules were followed or they were not. The instructions were followed or they were not. Another example is the students' assignment on controlled vocabulary in which the students are asked to compare four systems of vocabulary control (e.g., compare the same concept in *LCSH, Sears List of Subject Headings, Art & Architecture Thesaurus,* and *WordNet*). The assignment is designed to allow the students to display their mastery of the principles and concepts of the verbal subject access systems discussed in class. In grading the assignment, the principles are discussed intelligently and with understanding or they are not.

Grading the assignments in the advanced course is not as easy. Due to the greater depth of study and the nature of the exercises, the answers are less obvious and sometimes have room for interpretation. That said, while there may be no "right" answer, there definitely can be wrong answers. In Subject Analysis, students are required, for their graded assignments, to analyze several information packages, assign appropriate, well-constructed subject headings, and appropriate, well-constructed classification and cutter notations (all of which should be encoded for the MARC format). These assignments are based on a conceptual analysis agreed upon by the entire class. The students are all working from the same aboutness statement for each item. This allows the students' answers to be compared with each other and with the answers determined by the instructor. By comparing all of these answers, the grading can be more consistent.

Each portion of the assignment can be judged on several criteria. The subject headings, for example, can be graded on whether the student followed the rules, on the level of specificity, on the co-extensiveness of the headings, on whether they were coded correctly, and, of course, on whether or not they make sense. By having an agreed upon analysis and by asking the question, "Is the information package really *about* Subject Heading X?" it is easier to determine whether the student completed the assignment adequately.

For the DDC and LCC portions of the assignments, one can look at whether the notations were built correctly. One can examine whether the students followed the rules and the tables of preferences, whether the notation has an appropriate level of specificity, whether or not the student made logical choices, and whether the coding is correct. Finally, one needs to determine if the notations reflect the subject headings and the aboutness statements better than any other notations. While these are not quite as objective as in the basic level course, they are criteria on which one can generally grade fairly and accurately.

CONCLUSION

This is our basic approach to teaching subject cataloging. At times, it is tempting to think about simpler approaches or the good old days, but those times are over. It may also be tempting to downplay the importance of subject access, with the notion that keyword searching will re-solve all our problems. That time is not here yet (and it may never be). In this "Information Society," we live in a complex world, where infor-mation retrieval is not just a walk to the card catalog or a stroll on the Internet. We have a variety of information formats, a variety of retrieval tools, and a variety of standards (or non-standards) in play. Our infor-mation world is cluttered, messy, and oft-times frustrating. Subject ac-cess, controlled vocabulary, and classification are still important and are grossly underutilized.

At this juncture, we want to encourage cataloging educators to re-main vigilant. In this time of increasing reliance on Internet search en-gines and keyword access and, apparently, a waning appreciation for precision in searching, it is more important than ever that we instill in our students an understanding of the necessity, importance, benefits, and joys of subject access to information.

ENDNOTES

1. For a review of the recent literature, see Daniel N. Joudrey's "A New Look at US Graduate Courses in Bibliographic Control," *Cataloging & Classification Quarterly*, 34, 1/2 (2002): 59-101.

2. Ellen Zyroff, "Cataloging is a Prime Number," *American Libraries* 27 (1996): 47-48.

3. Nancy J. Williamson, "The Importance of Subject Analysis in Library and Infor-mation Science Education," *Technical Services Quarterly* 15, no. 1/2 (1997): 68-69. Emphasis added.

4. The textbook used for the introductory course is: Arlene G. Taylor, *The Organi-zation of Information* (Englewood, CO: Libraries Unlimited, 1999).

5. Getty Information Institute. "The Art & Architecture Thesaurus Browser." *http://www.getty.edu/research/tools/vocabulary/*.

6. National Library of Medicine. "Free MEDLINE" *http://www.ncbi.nlm.nih.gov/entrez/query.fcgi*.

7. "WordNet." *http://www.cogsci.princeton.edu/~wn/*.

Education for Authority Control:
Whose Responsibility Is It?

Rebecca L. Mugridge
Kevin A. Furniss

SUMMARY. Educating librarians to perform authority work and catalog maintenance involves formal education in library school and both on-the-job and in-service training. However, the path from library school graduate to authority control librarian is neither direct nor self-evident. The authors surveyed the membership of the AUTOCAT electronic discussion group to determine how librarians learn the theory and practice of authority control and catalog maintenance; strategies that would make authority control easier to learn; levels of educational responsibility involved for the library schools, individual librarians and their employers; and how librarians value authority control. The survey results show that an ongoing collaboration among librarians, employers and educators is needed to refine and simplify the process of authority control education. *[Article copies available for a fee from The Haworth Document Delivery Service: 1-800-HAWORTH. E-mail address: <getinfo@haworthpressinc.com> Website: <http://www.HaworthPress.com> © 2002 by The Haworth Press, Inc. All rights reserved.]*

KEYWORDS. Cataloger education, authority control, catalog management, library school courses

Rebecca L. Mugridge is Head of Cataloging Services, Pennsylvania State University Libraries (E-mail: rlm31@psu.edu). Kevin A. Furniss is Cataloging/Systems Support Librarian, William Howard Doane Library, Denison University (E-mail: furniss@denison.edu).

[Haworth co-indexing entry note]: "Education for Authority Control: Whose Responsibility Is It?" Mugridge, Rebecca L., and Kevin A. Furniss. Co-published simultaneously in *Cataloging & Classification Quarterly* (The Haworth Information Press, an imprint of The Haworth Press, Inc.) Vol. 34, No. 1/2, 2002, pp. 233-243; and: *Education for Cataloging and the Organization of Information: Pitfalls and the Pendulum* (ed: Janet Swan Hill) The Haworth Information Press, an imprint of The Haworth Press, Inc., 2002, pp. 233-243. Single or multiple copies of this article are available for a fee from The Haworth Document Delivery Service [1-800-HAWORTH, 9:00 a.m. - 5:00 p.m. (EST). E-mail address: getinfo@haworthpressinc.com].

233

INTRODUCTION

Because authority work is such an integral part of cataloging, it is important to understand how librarians learn about the concepts and practice of authority control and authority work. It is the authors' premise that there is little formal education of catalogers in the area of authority control, and that the majority of catalogers learn about authority control on the job, rather than in library school. If this is the case, there are significant implications for both the librarians and the libraries that hire them.

DEFINITIONS

We were interested in how librarians learn about both "authority work" and "authority control." We define authority work as the intellectual effort that is spent during the cataloging process of establishing or selecting the correct form of heading to be used in a cataloging record. Authority control is defined as the work that is done, post-cataloging, in order to maintain the integrity of the catalog. Both require a basic understanding of all or most of the following:

- Application of *AACR2R* and related Library of Congress Rule Interpretations (LCRIs)
- Problems faced in catalogs such as split files, blind references, data migration errors, typographical errors (some very common ones), tagging errors, indicator errors, subfield coding errors
- Determining which errors have an impact on the ability of users to access records and which do not
- How to prioritize projects based on the impact that they will have on the catalog
- Where to find answers (e.g., MARC format for authorities, Subject Cataloging Manual, *AACR2R*, authority file)
- Automated authority control within an Online Public Access Catalog (OPAC)
- Authority control vendors and the services they offer
- Resources that can be used to identify errors in and updates to the catalog (e.g., Cataloging Service Bulletin, LC weekly lists, list of common typos to look for).

LITERATURE REVIEW

A search of the literature revealed that little has been published about how librarians learn about authority work, much less about authority control as we have defined it. This is surprising considering that "Developing authority files for cataloging" is considered to be one of the common competencies required of librarians who work in technical services, according to Rehman, who writes about competencies in all areas of library science in *Preparing the Information Professional*.[1] Taylor reports that in the library science program that she attended, much time and attention was given to the subject of authority control, although "the process did not seem to have a name then."[2] Connaway, in a study of what a model curriculum for cataloging education should include, concludes that "cataloging education should include both theory and practice,"[3] but does not address authority control specifically. Vondruska reminds us that continuing education is required in all areas of librarianship, including authority control, reporting that "the adoption of new terminology in subject headings as reflective of new concepts requires continuing learning."[4] Presumably this would apply to changes in subject terminology, and the inevitable changes to the related subject headings that cause authority control librarians so much ongoing catalog maintenance work.

SURVEY

In an effort to understand how librarians learn about authority control, the authors sent a survey to AUTOCAT: Library cataloging and authorities electronic discussion group that is distributed to well over 3,000 list members. The survey included the following questions:

Question #1. How did you learn about authority control? Place an 'x' beside any that apply to you.

Library school course
On the job training
   As a librarian
   As a paraprofessional
Manuals (e.g., MARC format for authorities)
Locally-written documentation
Articles in library literature

Attending workshops or conferences
From someone you worked with
Clack's *Authority control: principles, applications and instructions*
Burger's *Authority work: the creation, use, maintenance, and evaluation of authority records and files*
NACO training
SACO workshops
ILS documentation
Other (please describe)?

Question #2. What would you do to make authority control easier to learn?

Question #3. What responsibilities should be assumed by

  a. the library school
  b. the employer
  c. the individual

Question #4. Please comment on what you see as the value of authority control.

RESULTS

The survey generated 49 respondents, which were organized by type of library as follows:

Academic librarians 26
Public librarians 13
Special librarians 8
Uncertain 1

Question #1

On the job: 50
    As a librarian 38
    As a paraprofessional 12
Manuals 35
Articles in library literature 25
Workshops/Conferences 25
Someone you worked with 23
Library school course 18

NACO workshop 11
Locally-written documentation 8
Burger's *Authority work: the creation, use, maintenance, and evaluation of authority records and files* 7
Clack's *Authority control: principles, applications and instructions* 4
SACO workshop 4
ILS documentation 4
Other
    Internship in Cataloging 2
    Ghikas' *Authority control: the key to tomorrow's catalog* 1
    Drabenstott's *Subject authorities in the online environment* 1
    AUTOCAT 1
    Internet searching 1

It is clear from these results that the great majority of practicing authority control librarians learned about authority control on the job rather than in library school. Of the 18 respondents who indicated that they had learned about authority control in library school, many included qualifying comments such as "in general terms," "it was mentioned in my cataloging class, but we did not study it in any detail," "small part of cataloging core course," "was probably mentioned, but did not sink in," and "vaguely." One respondent indicated that she had learned about authority control in a library technician program, not in a graduate program.

The second question in the survey, "What would make authority control easier to learn," received a wide range of responses. Nine respondents thought that workshops and training were the best ways to make authority control easier to learn. Suggestions along these lines included making a Web-based tutorial available, with introductory information about *AACR2R* as well as the most important entities in setting authority control standards (Joint Steering Committee for the Revision of the Anglo-American Cataloguing Rules (JSC), the Library of Congress (LC), LC's Cataloging Policy and Support Office (CPSO)), and such projects as the Program for Cooperative Cataloging (PCC) and its authority control components (NACO and SACO). Several respondents specifically mentioned well-organized workshops sponsored by local library networks that they had attended as being particularly helpful. Several suggestions were made to have workshops covering authority control similar to the way the Serials Cooperative Cataloging Training Program (SCCTP) covers serials cataloging. Five respondents specifically identified local or regional workshops as being particularly needed in their respective geographic areas.

Ten respondents thought that authority control would be easier to learn if it were taught in library school, many pointing out that library schools should be covering the basic concepts of authority control. Two respondents recommended that library schools offer an entire course in authority control, particularly for those students planning on entering the cataloging field after graduation.

Another ten respondents thought that it would make it easier to learn authority control if the logic and theory of authority control were studied in a systematic way. It is clear from some of these answers that respondents were talking not just about authority control from the database management point of view, but about authority work during the course of cataloging (e.g., establishing form of entry). Responses along this line included "start from the philosophical basics," "study the logic," and "teach more of the theory of AACR2 access points." One person pointed out that sometimes the concepts behind authority records are difficult to learn, such as how uniform title and series authority records are related.

Many of those who responded along the lines of "study the theory" also indicated that seeing the effects of authority control in an actual catalog would help one learn authority control. One person wrote that "a lot of reading from texts and library literature to understand the theory of authority control and then even more actual work in a catalog to see the positive results of authority control and the negative results of ineffective or nonexistent authority control" would help one learn about authority control. Another wrote that authority control should be "taught hand in hand with sessions on access." Another wrote "look at mock-up 'dirty' OPAC displays that demonstrate how several forms of a heading existing side-by-side prevent the patron from accessing all material by a certain author or on a certain subject." Others emphasized how important it is to have hands-on experience to truly understand the effects of authority control. Several comments along this line included: "There is no way to learn without hands-on experience within a particular catalog and cataloging environment," "Show examples of what happens when there is no authority control and then show the comparisons with authority control," and "You need a catalog to work in. It's really difficult to see how it all works and why it matters without a fully functional catalog."

Five of the respondents pointed out that authority control would be easier to learn if there were better documentation, several of them calling for making all relevant documentation and manuals available from a centralized Website. Other ideas included doing authority control regularly (2), working with someone knowledgeable (1), and more standardization (of authority control rules, presumably) (1).

Five respondents discussed how the various integrated library systems affect one's ability to learn and practice authority control. One wrote, "Part of the problem with teaching au[thority] control is that systems are not able to do what the card catalog did for collocating, so in addition to learning what au[thority] control is, each individual must also incorporate that into the ILS [Integrated Library System] capabilities and pitfalls." Another wrote, "I frankly think the task is pretty hopeless. We might have a chance if the developers of ILS systems understood authority control and constructed systems that followed the standards. As it is, the librarian has to master the intricacies of the work itself (no mean task) and fight the ILS s/he happens to be using." A third wrote, "there is nothing easy about understanding authority control, or the way it is implemented in various library systems." While most respondents acknowledged that learning authority control concepts is challenging, such as one who wrote, "I'm not at all sure there is an easy way to learn authority control," this was by no means unanimous. One wrote, "I'm not sure how to answer this, since I did not find the basic concepts difficult to learn."

Overall, the responses to the question "What would make authority control easier to learn" were evenly divided among four responses:

1. Well-organized workshops or other training opportunities, preferably at the local level
2. Coverage of authority control in library school cataloging courses, possibly offering courses covering just authority control
3. Using either "live" or "mock-up" OPACs to illustrate examples of catalog indexes with and without authority control, and other "hands-on" practice
4. Studying the theory and logic of authority control.

We found it interesting to observe how these ideas are further developed by respondents' answers to the third question in our survey, which dealt with who would assume which responsibilities for teaching authority control to prospective or current catalogers.

Question #3 of our survey was broken down into 3 parts, and the responses to each part will be examined separately. The first part was "What responsibilities should be assumed by the library school?" The responses to this question were overwhelmingly similar, with 32 saying that the responsibility of the library school lies in teaching the fundamental theory and concepts of authority control. One respondent wrote that the "library school should give a student a sound foundation for the theory of authority work." Another wrote, "The school should teach the theory, history, and provide the justification for authority control (present the studies demonstrating its value)." Other typical responses included: "The basic principles and philosophy should be taught," "The theory at least, and an introduction to the tools used," "Teach the principles," and "Good fundamentals."

Six respondents said that library schools should provide some hands-on practice. This could be in the form of practice exercises, or instruction in searching the national authority files through OCLC or RLIN.

Five respondents specifically called for authority control to be taught in either its own course or as an integral part of cataloging courses.

Finally, three responses were negative in nature, indicating that library schools could not teach authority control: "They've given up; they're hopeless," "They barely teach cataloging nowadays, let alone authority work," "They haven't really taught it in the past and probably won't be teaching it in the future."

The responses to the question "What responsibilities should be assumed by the employer" were also very much in agreement. The employer is responsible for providing in-house training, according to 24 of our respondents. The employer should "realize that on-the-job training is needed" and "should be sure that every cataloger has training in authority control." Some respondents make the point that even if a cataloger has had authority control training or experience, he or she will still need to receive "adequate training in authority control as instantiated in the library's ILS."

Eighteen of the survey's respondents made the point that employers need to communicate their support for authority control activities in general. There were two common points made here. The first was that the library should encourage authority control work by making it library policy, writing it into procedures, establishing goals, and supporting continuing education in the area of authority control. The second common theme concerned time spent on authority control. Typical comments included "Allow time to do it." One statement in particular summed up this sentiment: the responsibility of employers lies in "creating an environment where the time spent on authority work is valued."

Support by employers of continuing education activities was mentioned by ten of the respondents. This generally fell into three areas: financial support, time off to attend continuing education opportunities, and encouragement to participate in continuing education opportunities. Typical of these comments is the statement that the employer should "encourage and support professional development."

Twelve of the respondents indicated that the employer should provide appropriate documentation and resources to support authority control activities. This should include reference works, well-written documentation, NACO documentation when appropriate, and a mentor or resource person when possible.

Finally, one respondent indicated the difficulty in answering this question because of the differing abilities of libraries of various sizes to direct resources towards authority control.

The third part of question three was "What responsibilities should be assumed by the individual?" Twenty-one respondents stated that individuals should be making an effort to keep up with issues related to authority control in general. One typical response was "The professional cataloger has an obligation, I think, to stay well-informed and up to date on issues involving authority control." Another wrote that "The individual should take the time to develop his/her own knowledge." Along these lines, nine respondents specifically mentioned professional reading as being the responsibility of the individual, and three mentioned reading AUTOCAT, the cataloging and authorities electronic discussion list.

Thirteen respondents mention that individuals should attend conferences and workshops; several make the point that it may be necessary for an individual to use personal funds to pay for some of the professional development opportunities. Seven people assert that authority control should be done regularly so that librarians maintain a comfort level with it and expand their skills.

The responses to Question #4 reveal unsurprisingly that those who participate in authority control activities recognize the value of the work. There were many comments to the effect that without authority control, we would have chaos in our catalogs. Many compared the catalog without authority control to the current state of the Internet and the difficulties of finding pertinent information through that medium.

CONCLUSION

We can draw some conclusions from the results of this simple but revealing survey.

First, most librarians learn about authority work and authority control on the job. Those that are exposed to it in library school often receive only a cursory or basic examination of the subject. There is a perceived lack of hands-on practice available in library school. The implications of this are that most employers will have to either send new librarians to workshops to get them aware of and comfortable with the authority control concepts and practices that they need to understand in order to do their job, or they have to provide the training in-house in the form of a mentor or locally-produced documentation. Whichever option is used, it is clear that significant resources, financial and otherwise, will have to be spent to provide new employees with basic competencies.

Second, it is essential that workshops at the regional level be available to librarians responsible for authority work. Small libraries often cannot afford to send employees to national conferences where they could take advantage of the many programs and workshops available about authority work. Therefore, regional workshops or conferences are the only recourse available to them.

Third, library schools should review their course offerings and consider offering courses in authority work, or at the very least, make sure that it is covered in advanced cataloging courses. Consideration should also be given to providing significant hands-on experience for students who are seriously considering pursuing cataloging as a career.

Fourth, employers of librarians responsible for authority work must recognize: (a) they will need to invest in continuing education activities for their employees; and (b) they will have to allow their employees to use work time to enhance their knowledge and understanding of current authority practice.

Finally, librarians responsible for authority work must recognize that it is necessary to maintain their own current awareness of trends in authority control and cataloging. This will involve spending time reading the appropriate material, quite possibly one's own time, and will also most likely involve spending one's own money on workshop or class fees.

We hope that our findings will serve as a catalyst for library educators to collaborate with theorists and practitioners to improve education in authority control and authority work. Theories of information organization need a more thorough integration into practice to improve the quality of both our catalogs and our catalogers.

ENDNOTES

1. Sajjad ur Rehman, *Preparing the Information Professional* (Westport, CT: Greenwood Press, 2000): 131.

2. Arlene G. Taylor, "A Quarter Century of Cataloging Education," in *Technical Services Management, 1965-1990*, ed. Linda C. Smith and Ruth C. Carter (New York: The Haworth Press, Inc., 1996): 300.

3. Lynn Silipigni Connaway, "A Model Curriculum for Cataloging Education: The Library and Information Services Program at the University of Denver," *Technical Services Quarterly*, 15, no. 1/2 (1997): 32.

4. Eloise M. Vondruska, "Continuing Education and Technical Services Librarians: Learning for 1965-1990 and the Future," in *Technical Services Management, 1965-1990*, ed. Linda C. Smith and Ruth C. Carter (New York: The Haworth Press, Inc., 1996): 313.

What Else Do You Need to Know?
Practical Skills for Catalogers and Managers

Janet Swan Hill

SUMMARY. Catalogers and those who manage cataloging operations need a broader practical knowledge base than can be reasonably acquired in library schools, especially since the availability of cataloging coursework in library schools has decreased over time. This paper is written from the perspective of a manager of cataloging operations, and considers the kinds of skills, education and training needed for both catalogers and managers. It concentrates primarily on library specific education, computer, and communication skills, and suggests how such skills can be acquired and maintained. *[Article copies available for a fee from The Haworth Document Delivery Service: 1-800-HAWORTH. E-mail address: <getinfo@haworthpressinc.com> Website: <http://www.HaworthPress.com> © 2002 by The Haworth Press, Inc. All rights reserved.]*

KEYWORDS. Cataloging education, technical services education, continuing education, competencies

Janet Swan Hill is Associate Director for Technical Services, University of Colorado, Boulder Libraries.

Editor's note: This is based on a paper originally delivered to the Michigan Library Association's Technical Services Roundtable's 2000 annual meetings, on the assigned topic of "Practical Skills for Technical Services." The paper itself was originally titled "Mick Jagger Was Right." Because it was revised to fit into this volume, after all other papers had been submitted and read by the author/editor, many of the references in it are to other papers in this collection.

[Haworth co-indexing entry note]: "What Else Do You Need to Know? Practical Skills for Catalogers and Managers." Hill, Janet Swan. Co-published simultaneously in *Cataloging & Classification Quarterly* (The Haworth Information Press, an imprint of The Haworth Press, Inc.) Vol. 34, No. 1/2, 2002, pp. 245-261; and: *Education for Cataloging and the Organization of Information: Pitfalls and the Pendulum* (ed: Janet Swan Hill) The Haworth Information Press, an imprint of The Haworth Press, Inc., 2002, pp. 245-261. Single or multiple copies of this article are available for a fee from The Haworth Document Delivery Service [1-800-HAWORTH, 9:00 a.m. - 5:00 p.m. (EST). E-mail address: getinfo@haworthpressinc.com].

INTRODUCTION

Although I still think of myself as a cataloger, it's been more than twenty years since I actually cataloged anything. That's how long I have been managing either cataloging or technical services operations. During that time I have been responsible for hiring catalogers and for overseeing technical services activities, and although life for catalogers and cataloging managers was much simpler in the 1970s and 1980s, it didn't take a very perceptive person to notice even then that catalogers and managers needed to know a great deal more than we learned in library school.

When I consider what the knowledge base of a cataloger must be these days, and the resources available to them to attain it, I am irresistibly reminded of the Rolling Stones song, whose refrain tells us that "You Can't Always Get What You Want . . . But if you try . . . sometimes you just might find . . . you get what you need." What I *want* is for library schools to offer a complete education for cataloging, so that new librarians could bravely march into a cataloging position, knowing that they knew enough to get by in the job while continuing to learn more, without being an undue burden on the library they are working for. Unfortunately, it is depressingly obvious that library schools not only can't supply what I want, but they have no intention of doing so. This means that all librarians involved with cataloging are placed in the position of trying their best just to get what they need.

This paper addresses two different kinds of knowledge and skills that people involved in bibliographic control need. The first are those that are specific to cataloging and technical services, which reasonable people might think they would be able to acquire through earning a library degree. The second group includes non-technical services specific skills that are useful for survival and success in a cataloging operation, but which a reasonable person wouldn't necessarily expect to acquire with the library degree.

LIBRARY SPECIFIC SKILLS

A long time ago, well before there were organized courses of library instruction, most of what people who were identified as librarians did were what we would today consider technical services activities, centering around acquiring, describing, organizing, and maintaining inventory control over materials. A little more than a century ago, when

Melvil Dewey formed the first library school, technical services topics formed the largest part of the curriculum, and nobody got out of library school without knowing how to catalog.

Technological and organizational advances were made and adopted, and changed how library work was done. Most seemed to affect technical services more than the rest of the library. Things like typewriters and mimeograph machines, and Library of Congress cataloging cards, and later on, computers and shared databases, contributed to decreasing the time required to do cataloging and related operations. Each advance made it simpler to separate work that was clerical from work that required professional judgement, so the number of support staff as a portion of all those engaged in cataloging activities grew. Partly in answer to these developments, and partly in answer to mistaken and hopelessly optimistic and unrealistic assumptions about what the developments in technology would lead to, the proportion of time devoted to cataloging in the library school curriculum also decreased. Even so, well past the first half of the last century, cataloging and related topics continued to occupy a sizeable portion of the curriculum, and it was still true that every librarian emerged from library school knowing how to catalog.

Then came 1967. The *Anglo-American Cataloging Rules* were published, the Ohio College Library Center was incorporated, and the MARC format for bibliographic data was approved for use. The significance of these developments was not at first fully understood. *AACR* was looked at as just a more rational set of cataloging rules. MARC was a mystery to many, and for a time seemed to be touted mainly as a means of making catalog cards available faster and more cheaply. OCLC was seen as an interesting regional experiment that might possibly someday be duplicated elsewhere. But although people might not have realized that the synergistic interplay of these three tools would revolutionize bibliographic control worldwide, they were nevertheless fairly quick to conclude that rules that were easier to understand, combined with a means of computerizing catalog cards would make cataloging easier and faster, and thus reduce the need for catalogers.

In 1969, when I was getting my library degree, I was required to take two cataloging courses, and took three. There was, however, very little else in the curriculum that was related to cataloging or technical services. Technical services issues formed only a minor part of the management courses, and about half of the serials course. The library automation course was actually focused on public services activities, such as computer assisted instruction.

By the mid 1980s, most library schools offered at most two catalog-ing courses, and the first was increasingly not a cataloging course *per se*, but was instead a kind of "cataloging appreciation course," sporting a name like Introduction to the Organization of Knowledge. In some schools, not even those courses were required.[1] This diminution of at-tention might have escaped my notice, except that as the head of a cata-loging department in a large library, I often needed to recruit catalogers. In the late 1970s and early 1980s, my job postings for entry level posi-tions called for a "substantial concentration of cataloging-related courses," and typically attracted over 100 applicants.[2] By the middle of the 1980s, we were forced to drop the requirement for a concentration of cataloging coursework, because our pools of applicants had dwin-dled alarmingly, and we increasingly received applications from people whose single cataloging class was all that their school offered.

Things haven't improved in the intervening years. Look at library school catalogs on the Web today, and you'll see very limited course of-ferings in cataloging or in any aspect of technical services. There may be one or two cataloging courses, a course in indexing and abstracting, and possibly a course in library automation. A few schools offer a seri-als course and there are a handful of courses in technical services man-agement offered across the country.

Library school faculty will tell you that they are not in the business of training. They are in the business of education. They will tell you that their role is to introduce students to the principles and the issues and the basics of librarianship, and to teach prospective librarians how to learn, so that they can learn throughout their career. They'll say that they can't possibly give training in library specific procedures, and that librarians will get their training on the job.

There is much merit to these assertions about the role of library schools, but there is unfortunately a vast wilderness between learning basic principles and learning library specific procedures. As for getting training on the job, in large libraries there may well be personnel who can provide the training that's needed, but most libraries are small. Many newly-degreed librarians find themselves working as the only cataloger, or as the head of cataloging, or even as the only person doing all of technical services. Meanwhile, library schools seem not to have realized, or not to want to acknowledge the fact that most librarians will find themselves in jobs where there is nobody to teach them but them-selves. It's my guess that, in part, this is because schools may be peo-pled by faculty whose library experience (if any) was in large libraries, and in part because things have changed. In the past there would have been more than one librarian in cataloging departments. Entry level cat-alogers would have taken a position where they could be trained and have their work overseen by someone with experience before they moved to a position of greater responsibility themselves.

I believe that it is not too strong a statement to say that library schools have abrogated their responsibility to educate catalogers and technical services managers. I believe this can be partially attributed to a mis-taken belief that technical services activities are now, or soon will be, automated, clerical, and passé. It is no doubt also significantly due to environmental and political factors affecting the schools themselves, which Saye has effectively outlined in his paper.[3] Perhaps the schools' own realization that they are doing what may be an increasingly less sat-isfactory job in preparing people for cataloging positions contributes to the fervency with which they explain why they can't or shouldn't do more. In any case, neither the beliefs nor the environment are easily sus-ceptible to change. Practitioners can and should attempt to inform and to exert influence in their profession,[4] but they should understand that such efforts are for the long term, and will have almost no immediate impact.

In a shorter timeframe catalogers and those who manage cataloging operations have to do what's in their power to make up for the education and training that library schools don't provide. There are many ways to go about it, and many sources of education, but in order to take advan-tage of them, it's necessary first to recognize that pursuing such training is not only worthwhile, it's essential. Catalogers and cataloging manag-ers must realize that a library school education is insufficient to every-body's needs, not just catalogers', and that even if people did emerge from school richly educated, things are moving so fast that there will al-ways be the need to update information and skills. Having realized this, managers then have to allow themselves and those who work for them the time to pursue that training and education, and they must be willing also to support it with money. They have to encourage actively an over-all culture that assumes that every librarian (and every paraprofessional for that matter) will need to continue her/his education on an ongoing basis, and the culture mustn't yield to excuses such as "I'm too busy."

Papers elsewhere in this volume describe many different types of continuing education opportunities. Intner, for instance, mentions pro-fessional conferences and regional institutes, as well as the library's bibliographic network or automation vendor. She further observes that library schools often offer special seminars, institutes and courses.[5] Consortia and associations may offer workshops both on- and off-site.

Projects in which a library may be involved, such as the Program for Cooperative Cataloging described by Hixson and Garrison[6] or the Colorado Digitization Project described by Kreigsman[7] may offer training for those purposes. Videoconferencing is becoming more common, and may be used within a library school program[8] or through an association. From time to time there may be training offered on the Web.[9,10] There are manuals. There's professional reading. There are electronic discussion lists.[11] There is networking and schmoozing at conferences. At some point in their careers, catalogers will probably need to avail themselves of nearly all of these types of continuing education.

NON LIBRARY SPECIFIC SKILLS

In addition to the knowledge and skills that are specific to cataloging and technical services, there are numerous skills which may be of great practical use to catalogers and those who manage bibliographic control operations, which are not specific to library work, and which a reasonable person, therefore, would not expect to be able to acquire in library school. The skills fall into four general categories: computer skills, communication skills, management and personal skills, and personnel skills. Although many will be useful to anyone engaged in cataloging operations, some are more critical to managers. There are more such skills than can be reasonably covered in any detail in a paper of this type, so I have chosen to concentrate on computer skills and communication skills, first discussing what kinds of skills may be useful, and then in general terms covering how to go about acquiring them. A list of personnel-related skills and issues, prepared for the Michigan Library Association presentation upon which much of this paper is based, is included as an Appendix to this paper.

Computer Skills

I learned to type in 9th grade in a mandatory typing class, and at that time (1963) it was regarded as unusual to require typing to be taught to all students. Some years later, when ALA's Resources and Technical Services Division (RTSD)–the precursor to today's Association for Library Collections and Technical Services (ALCTS)–awarded its Margaret Mann Citation to Lucia Rather, Rather reminisced in her acceptance speech about being grateful to her parents for having encouraged her to do whatever she wanted, and for having assumed that she could succeed at whatever that was. She noted ruefully, however, that her father used to tell her that "A girl can be anything she wants, so long as she never learns how to type."[12]

My how things have changed. Typing is a life skill now, and children are learning to type on computers at about the time they are learning to write. Having a rudimentary knowledge of computers appears to have become a life skill on a par with typing. Increasingly, college students are required to have their own computers, and to use them routinely in coursework. Library school students, even though they tend to be older than other graduate students, may be required to demonstrate a certain competence with computers prior to admission, and they too will likely be expected to use computers in a variety of ways in their coursework, especially if they are enrolled in a distance education course.[13,14,15,16] There is a vanishingly small number of positions in libraries that do not involve considerable interaction with computers for most aspects of the job, and unless it be in a very small library, virtually none of these jobs is in cataloging. Not all that many years ago, if the system went down, or you were having trouble with your computer, you could find other things to do, but these days, when something like that happens, you might as well go for a walk, or go home.

Basic Computer Skills

There are several categories of computer skills useful in cataloging. To start with, essentially all catalogers need to have a level of basic comfort with computers, and to be able to do things like turn the thing on and off; do warm and cold reboots; change basic defaults; navigate from one program to another, and one window to another; copy, delete, upload and download files; find files that you have somehow lost; print; do simple troubleshooting; install some kinds of software; back things up. Two skills that only a few years ago might have fallen into the "also possibly nice to know" category, but which now can be regarded as basic are comfort and skill with e-Mail, and with searching and using the World Wide Web. There may still be some older employees who grew up professionally without learning these things, and to whom they are still foreign, but that generation will soon be retiring, and in the meantime, those librarians must be encouraged to incorporate use of these tools into their routines.

Software for Library and Technical Services Specific Needs

Younger catalogers may find it difficult to believe, but it was once enough to be able to use OCLC on a gargantuan and dedicated OCLC terminal. Those days are long gone. Now catalogers need to use a variety of computer applications, usually on a single workstation. They need to know their way around the bibliographic network software and the local automation system(s). They should be able to use Websites or software of vendors. They should be competent to use various online learning resources and tools, such as the local system's online manual, or the LC Cataloger's Desktop; they should be ready to utilize, as appropriate, manuals, instructions, tipsheets, and policies of the consortia to which their institutions may belong, projects in which they may be participating, and of other libraries with which they may not be associated, but which may nevertheless have useful information on their Websites. Some catalogers may need to know a great deal about such things as file transfer protocols, about writing database loaders, monitoring database loads, and changing defaults, coding, and displays in their automated systems.

Software and Applications Not Library Specific

Beyond library related tools there are many kinds of multipurpose computer applications that range from essential to very useful to just "nice," all depending on the particular job. These may include: word processing; spreadsheets; statistics packages, including graphing; citation software; desktop publishing, including graphics and organization charts; calendars, including personal digital assistants (PDAs) and perhaps calendars jointly maintained; Web page design, HTML; project tracking; chat groups, Web boards and other mechanisms for enabling group project collaboration; presentation software and hardware.

Acquiring the Skills

Many catalogers and cataloging managers are already heavy users of these types of software, but there are still people who don't use them, and still those who are intensely uncomfortable with them. As we think about how to get or provide instruction in computer applications, or to provide training that itself involves using computers, it's important to recognize the difference between those individuals who might be termed early adopters, late adopters, and resisters. It's important also to recognize the difference between those who approach computers with a disposable camera outlook, wanting and expecting operations to be uncomplicated, reliable, and transparent with few options, and those who approach computers with a Nikon mindset, accepting with equanimity and perhaps even enjoying a process that is complex, full of options and pitfalls, and which requires manipulation. It makes a difference in what kind of instruction will work best, and in what kind of goals should be set and how much monitoring of progress may be needed.

In past decades, when use of such tools was not common, and none of it was actually essential, it was possible to rely on the early adopters and the self-starters to puzzle things out for themselves, and to seek training on their own. That's no longer either possible or fair. While librarians will increasingly come to their jobs already experienced with many of these kinds of packages, many do not. And whether they come with experience or not, it is inevitable that the software they are familiar with now will be upgraded or replaced, and entirely new applications will be introduced.

Just as there are many avenues for pursuing continuing education for library specific skills, there are many sources for computer and software instruction. There are classes offered in local high schools, community colleges, colleges, or your own institution. There are commercially offered classes, either by the software vendors or other organizations. There are Web courses. There is individual instruction from understanding and knowledgeable co-workers, or your organization's "designated guru." You can ask your kid for help. There are print manuals from the manufacturer. There are online manuals, which tend, unfortunately, to be much less detailed than print manuals. There are third party manuals, such as the "X For Dummies" books, which many people find easier to use and understand than ones that come from the vendor. Finally, there is practice and play. Most people can't learn a computer program in the abstract, or with a made-up project. They need to use the program–to find a project that needs to be done, and plunge in.

This brings me to what may be the most important computer-related skill of all–learning how to learn. Computer software is rarely completely intuitive. There aren't many software packages that are so transparent that users can sit down and start working with them right away. There is always a learning curve. The more different types of software a person becomes familiar with, however, the less steep the learning curve will be, because in the process of learning about *this* program, or *that*, a person learns about things that software packages tend to have in common, and about how to explore, how to play, and how to use manuals. But as noted before, it's necessary to realize that the time it takes to acquire skills is worth it, and that it's also false economy to begrudge the money that training may take. Catalogers and cataloging managers can't afford to resent the time it takes, or to worry about how much faster they might do the job by hand, or using the current method. Continuing to use the current method will waste more time in the long run than taking the time to stumble through the learning process.

Communication Skills

Communication skills are not something usually stressed for those who embark upon a cataloging career. They are nevertheless important because of the increasing degree to which all library work is interconnected. Where once catalogers could make decisions about the catalog more or less independently, and non-catalogers could be almost proud of how little they knew about cataloging issues, nowadays virtually everything any library staff member does, everything s/he touches, decides, or devises, has a vital impact on somebody else's work.

The importance of effective communication is amplified by the relative dearth of catalogers in libraries these days, and by how little most other people who make it through library school learn about cataloging. Things that seem second nature to a cataloger, steps that a cataloging manager may blithely skip past in explanations, may be bewildering to someone whose career has been in reference. Because we all learn our jobs bit by bit, we can be unaware of how much we know, and how much others probably don't. When I was a college freshman, I took calculus. The proofs in my textbook often showed steps 1, 2, 3, followed by a long gap, then 17, 18, and a gay little sentence that chirped, "the intervening steps are intuitively obvious." Not to me they weren't. Cataloging can be like calculus to those who don't do it for a living. Intervening steps are not intuitively obvious. When catalogers communicate about their work to someone whose experience is not the same as theirs, they need to supply those missing steps, no matter how self-evident they may seem.

Cataloging departments have a reputation of being havens for social misfits and hermits–of being the place where people who can't deal with people are sent. Most catalogers energetically reject this stereotype, but there is a kernel of truth to it. Many catalogers are not the world's most gregarious people, being happy in their own company, and deriving satisfaction from working quietly doing good work. Many catalogers therefore may not have developed the knack of talking easily to small or large groups. In written communication they may be terse, and assume a greater level of knowledge on the part of their readers than actually exists. These are weaknesses that can be addressed by taking some cues from our public services colleagues.

The Reference Interview

We all hear about "the reference interview" in library school as something that's needed by public services librarians, but reference interviews may be another life skill for us all. More and more often I find myself doing a reference interview with my mother. She asks me a question, and I find myself having to ask *her* questions to discover what she's talking about and what kind of answer she's looking for. I need to find out the context in which she's asking the question. I need to find out why she thinks that I will know the answer. I need to find out how she is defining her terms, and I often discover that she's using terms in a way that she thinks I use them. I need to find out what she's already tried, what she already knows, and how she's going to use the answer. I often have to try out a few half-answers and assess the results–judging from her reaction whether I'm getting warmer or colder–and then I refine my response based on those results. The people at work are not nearly so likely to have the faith in us that our mothers do, but they need the same kind of personal attention.

Know Your Audience

Catalogers and managers often need to communicate either orally or in writing with library management, co-workers and colleagues from all over the library, working groups and governing boards. These groups and individuals may sometimes be allies of cataloging, and sometimes enemies. More often they fall somewhere in the middle. In order to get a point across, to obtain and convey necessary information, or to elicit co-operation, it's necessary to match the message to the audience, and be clear and persuasive. If the nature, viewpoint, and knowledge of the audience are misjudged, there is a risk of answering a question that wasn't asked, of using as a clincher something that means nothing whatsoever to the audience, or using something that actually alienates them.

Listening

Finding out about the audience, what it knows, what it wants, what it understands, requires listening, and listening is another skill to be developed. Some years ago the director of a library at which I was head of cataloging was concerned about the cost of original cataloging, and seemed to think that the problem lay in searching. He thought that if we did our work better, the hit rate would improve and we would have less original cataloging to do. After several years of explaining, providing statistics, and conducting experiments, I finally realized the problem was that the director thought there was copy available for everything. He hadn't made the connection that in order for there to be copy for something, someone has to catalog it, and that if no other library has the item, no one else will. Once I really listened, I realized that the question he wanted answered was not the one he was asking, and only then could I provide him with an answer that satisfied him.

Be a Little Entertaining

It's easy to be over-earnest in telling people about cataloging work and organizational needs, and to lard memoranda and presentations with statistics and complex sentences, and lots of detail, and thereby lose the audience, or put it to sleep. Not everything lends itself to entertainment, but sometimes just a good choice of examples can brighten an otherwise dreary explanation and disarm the audience. There are plenty of absurd subject headings or amusing authors' names to put into examples, as well as examples that may have special significance to a particular audience. It's worth finding them.

Storytelling

Another valuable user services skill is storytelling. By drawing comparisons to things that may be familiar, stories (for example the story about my mother and the reference interview) and analogies can help those who know little about some issue to understand it. I once delivered a talk called cataloging as baseball, and another that compared recent developments in authority control to the history of figure skating. I once managed to get across to someone the distinction between cost and value by talking about buying a leather jacket on sale. It's interesting to note how much more readily people may pick up on a point, and how much more firmly they may hang onto it, if it is delivered in an analogy or story. Stories also break down the barriers between the presenter and the audience. They are a kind of sharing that can soften an otherwise harsh content. Moderation, of course, is important. A little storytelling goes a long way. If you make all of your points through analogy or stories, you can end up with a paper, memorandum or presentation that is light on content, diffuse, difficult to follow and perhaps, that gives the impression of not being serious.

Acquiring the Skills

As with continuing education in library specific subjects and computer skills, the first step in becoming more accomplished in communication is realizing that it matters. Managers can recruit for effective communicators. Oral and written communication skills can be written into job postings and incorporated into the search and interview processes. Search committees can pay attention to how candidates write cover letters and organize CVs, and to anything that the candidate may have published. During interviews, oral communication ability can be assessed in small and large groups, and through a required presentation.

Such tactics, however, only apply to new recruits. Everyone else should be encouraged to make an effort at improving communication skills and practicing them as if they matter. This involves accepting editing and rewrites as a fact of life; accepting that grammar, syntax, punctuation, and spelling matter; using available spellcheckers and grammar checkers, while knowing when to ignore their advice; trying to identify in others' writing or presentations, what holds interest, what causes the mind to wander, and what kinds of things elicit rejection; asking others to comment on drafts; reading everything aloud; rehearsing and timing even very small presentations.

Help in listening, public speaking, and writing can be found through classes, workshops, and seminars offered both locally and at greater distances. A number of self-help books is also available. But learning about communications, especially written communication, is a challenge. Most of us assume that by the time we've gotten out of a graduate program, we ought to know how to write, and how to speak, but the sad fact is that this isn't true. I'm a manuscript reviewer or on the editorial board of a number of journals, and I am often saddened and appalled at the organizational and writing skills displayed. Similarly, I'm often astonished at the degree to which people will express themselves utterly mysteriously or incomprehensibly in meetings.

People who have received postgraduate degrees generally assume that knowing how to write and speak is a "base skill." They may be more reluctant to take time, spend money, take classes, ask for help, or practice writing or speaking than they would be to spend the same time or money to learn about some software package. This is unfortunate, because communication is a job skill too, just like knowing how to use a computer. Cataloging can sometimes be a hard enough sell all by itself. Catalogers and cataloging managers need to use all the tools they can to help make that sale.

CONCLUSION

The most practical skill of all for both catalogers and those who manage cataloging operations is knowing how to learn. The most critical thing to remember is that learning is essential, and since it's essential, it deserves support. Learning requires time and commitment, and it may require money. In a time of budgetary restraint, getting the most out of what we have becomes imperative, and making sure that everyone is adequately equipped through education and training is one way of achieving it. As tempting as it may be, none of us can afford to make a habit of saying, or allowing those whose work we manage to say "Oh, I'll figure that out tomorrow," or, "I don't have the time for it now." Responsible management must foster an atmosphere and a habit of constant learning, because the skills that catalogers have today won't carry them through their careers. They'll only carry them through today. That oughtn't be a scary thing. It ought to be exciting. It ought to be fun. And if it's hard to think of it as fun, just remember Mick Jagger. "You can't always get what you want. But if you try, you can get what you need."

ENDNOTES

1. "CCS Task force on Education and Recruitment for Cataloging Report, June, 1986" *RTSD Newsletter* (11:7) 1986, pp. 71-75.

2. This was at Northwestern University Library, whose applicant pool was probably enhanced by its location in a major metropolitan area in the center of the country, in a state served by–at that time–four ALA accredited library school programs.

3. Jerry D. Saye, "Where Are We and How Did We Get Here? or, The Changing Place of Cataloging in the Library and Information Science Curriculum: Causes and Consequences," *Cataloging & Classification Quarterly*, 34, 1/2 (2002): 121-143.

4. Consider activities such as the following: Get involved in your professional organizations, including those committees that address education for librarianship. Write to your own library school (if it still exists) and tell them how you feel about the preparation they are providing for new graduates, and how it matches with your needs. Remind them that the fantasy of being able to learn on the job is just that–a fantasy–in small libraries. Look at their course catalog, and ask where their students learn about managing cataloging. Write to the library schools from which you've gotten recent hires, and tell them where the schools succeeded, and where they missed the boat. Tell them how you feel about having to provide a couple of years of training for a cataloger who was supposed to have been a qualified professional when you hired them. Do research. Write. Publish. When the accreditation standards come up for revision, watch for the invitation to comment, and then comment.

5. Sheila S. Intner, "Persistent Issues in Cataloging Education: Considering the Past and Looking Toward the Future," *Cataloging & Classification Quarterly*, 34, 1/2 (2002): 15-29.

6. Carol G. Hixson and William Garrison, "The Program for Cooperative Cataloging and Training for Catalogers," *Cataloging & Classification Quarterly*, 34, 4 (2002): 355-365.

7. Sue Kreigsman, "Catalog Training for People Who Are Not Catalogers: The Colorado Digitization Project Experience," *Cataloging & Classification Quarterly*, 34, 4 (2002): 367-374.

8. Elaine Yontz, "When Donkeys Fly: Distance Education for Cataloging," *Cataloging & Classification Quarterly*, 34, 4 (2002): 299-310.

9. Robert Ellett, "An Evaluation of the Effectiveness of OCLC Online Computer Library Center's Web-Based Module on Cataloging Internet Resources Using the Anglo-American Cataloging Rules and MARC21," *Cataloging & Classification Quarterly*, 34, 4 (2002): 311-338.

10. Anna M. Ferris, "Cataloging Internet Resources Using MARC21 and *AACR2*. Online Training for Working Catalogers," *Cataloging & Classification Quarterly*, 34, 4 (2002): 339-353.

11. Judith Hopkins, "The Community of Catalogers: Its Role in the Education of Catalogers," *Cataloging & Classification Quarterly*, 34, 4 (2002): 375-381.

12. Paraphrased from memory from Rather's acceptance remarks for the Margaret Mann Citation.

13. Gertrude S. Koh, "Innovations in Standard Classroom Instruction," *Cataloging & Classification Quarterly*, 34, 4 (2002): 263-287.

14. Judith L. Aulik et al. "Online Mentoring: A Student Experience at Dominican University," *Cataloging & Classification Quarterly*, 34, 4 (2002): 289-292.

15. Kate Harcourt and Susan M. Neumeister. "Online Distance Learing with Cataloging Mentors: The Mentor's Viewpoint," *Cataloging & Classification Quarterly*, 34, 4 (2002): 293-298.

16. Yontz. "When Donkeys Fly: Distance Education for Cataloging," 299-310.

APPENDIX A

Personnel Issues for Technical services:
Strategies, Skills, and Mysteries

(Originally prepared to accompany a breakout session following the delivery of the paper upon which this paper is based.)

Personnel issues are often complex, frustrating, mysterious, intractable, and worst of all, unavoidable. Most technical services librarians will at some point be in a supervisory, management, or administrative position, yet the training that most librarians receive in dealing with personnel issues is minimal.

The purpose of this session is discussion. We have no set agenda. We will discuss whatever you want to discuss. The following list of personnel issues is provided only as a means of suggesting possible topics for discussion.

Recruiting

- Position descriptions–writing them, adhering to them, how detailed
- Other duties as assigned–how much of the job, when does it violate the classification
- Setting the qualifications–how much is in your power, what's reasonable, how detailed
- Required vs. Preferred–what's the difference, what are the consequences
- Evaluation tools–evaluating the applications, weights, phoned reference interviews
- The interview–how long, how involved, who sees, what do you ask, presentations
- Repost or settle–consequences of "settling," rethinking the position
- Diversity issues

Evaluation

- Quantitative measures–inadvertent biases, unexpected consequences, waffle room
- Subject vs. Objective–the nature of the beast
- Judging Behavior–when is behavior a legitimate measure
- Upward evaluations–who participates, confidentiality, usefulness
- Narrative vs. Checkoffs and numbers
- Tenure review, Peer review
- Retention review–when to fish, and when to cut bait

Supervising

- Training–in house, one on one, delegated, self-directed, external, what's job related
- Who is in charge
- Supervisor's rights
- Counseling
- Grievances
- Reasonable Accommodations for physical impairments
- Disciplinary/Corrective actions

Job Options

- Enrichment
- Working above the classification level

- Overtime, Compensatory Time
- Job Sharing
- Flextime
- Flexplace

Communications/Management Style

- Open door vs. chain of command
- Getting the word out–how, to whom, when, how much
- Consultation, Consensus, Fiat
- Delegation

Innovations
in Standard Classroom Instruction

Gertrude S. Koh

SUMMARY. Describes the characteristics of contemporary students in library schools, their experiences and expectations, and how they shape the goal of cataloging courses. Reviews historical innovations in cataloging instruction. Defines the nature of "cataloging" courses in the curriculum. Presents samples of innovations used in standard classrooms for teaching and learning a core-course and one of the elective "cataloging" courses. Focuses on how and why online mentor catalogers are incorporated in the teaching and learning of one particular course (Metadata for Internet Resources, at Dominican University Graduate School of Library

Gertrude S. Koh, PhD, is Professor, Graduate School of Library and Information Science, Dominican University.

[Haworth co-indexing entry note]: "Innovations in Standard Classroom Instruction." Koh, Gertrude S. Co-published simultaneously in *Cataloging & Classification Quarterly* (The Haworth Information Press, an imprint of The Haworth Press, Inc.) Vol. 34, No. 3, 2002, pp. 263-287; and: *Education for Cataloging and the Organization of Information: Pitfalls and the Pendulum* (ed: Janet Swan Hill) The Haworth Information Press, an imprint of The Haworth Press, Inc., 2002, pp. 263-287. Single or multiple copies of this article are available for a fee from The Haworth Document Delivery Service [1-800-HAWORTH, 9:00 a.m. - 5:00 p.m. (EST). E-mail address: getinfo@haworthpressinc.com].

263

and Information Science). Discusses how and in what ways collaborative teaching with expert practitioners in cataloging online at remote sites contributes to the education of future librarians. *[Article copies available for a fee from The Haworth Document Delivery Service: 1-800-HAWORTH. E-mail address: <getinfo@haworthpressinc.com> Website: <http://www.HaworthPress.com> © 2002 by The Haworth Press, Inc. All rights reserved.]*

KEYWORDS. Innovations for cataloging education, online mentor catalogers, distance education, collaboration with practitioners, teaching cataloging, educating catalogers

INTRODUCTION

"A library is not worth anything without a catalog–it is a Polyphemus without any eye in his head."[1] This remark made by the British historian, Thomas Carlyle, compares a library that has no catalog to Polyphemus, the Cyclops who imprisoned Odysseus during Odysseus' wanderings home from the Trojan War. To escape Polyphemus' grasp, Odysseus blinded the Cyclops. Without a catalog, users are blind to what is in a library's collection. The catalog is the window through which users search and see the logical structure and interconnectedness in a collection. What form the catalog takes–book, card, or online–is immaterial, so long as it allows effective use of the library's resources. The importance of the catalog requires the librarian responsible for its contents–the cataloger–to have an excellent education and broad knowledge.

This paper will explore innovations for standard classroom cataloging instruction, especially in the use of online mentors for the course Metadata for Internet Resources. Strictly defined, an innovation is something unprecedented, entirely new, but it can be argued that there is no such thing as educational innovation, because it is impossible for a teacher to work in a vacuum. However ingenious her teaching pedagogy, it must arise out of her own previous experiences and the experiences of others in the profession. In order to demonstrate how the author's innovations in standard classroom instructions have arisen out of her own previous experiences and the experiences of others in the profession, the author begins by highlighting some historical innovational trends and issues in teaching cataloging.

HISTORICAL PERSPECTIVE ON INNOVATIONS IN CLASSROOM INSTRUCTION

Since 1950, a recurrent theme has echoed through the literature of the profession regarding education for cataloging, and that is the importance of the users' point of view. Hazel Dean expounded on this topic in 1949,[2] believing that a change from teaching mere skills and techniques would allow the cataloger to assume a more vital role in library service. Thirty-seven years later, in 1987, Lizbeth Bishoff continued this reasoning by declaring: "Catalogers . . . must be trained to consider how a user will search for particular information. Catalog librarians must be risk takers. They will be challenged by the dynamic nature of today's libraries into taking calculated risks in developing new library services–risks based on their knowledge of today's information demands . . . and most importantly, the library user."[3] Ellen Zyloff advanced cataloging as "a prime number" in serving users, noting that "A cataloger's mind-set is crucial to the establishment and oversight of information organization and is key to successful access. The intellectual framework of reference is based on the intellectual framework of cataloging."[4]

Cataloging had an important place in the first library school organized by Melvil Dewey in 1887, at Columbia College in New York. Dewey's curriculum, which was steadfastly practical, established the characteristics of library education for its first period of development, which lasted until the mid-1920s. In 1926 the Graduate Library School of Chicago was established to emphasize research, and set the stage for the second period of library education, which lasted until the mid-1960s. This period incorporated a theoretical approach to cataloging and ushered in cataloging research in the form of catalog use studies, and the study of issues related to subject access and principles underlying access points. Influenced by the availability for purchase of prepared catalog cards from the Library of Congress and H.W. Wilson, cataloging coursework was narrowed in scope to entry preparation rather than system making, and it also addressed management of cataloging. Margaret Mann's textbook, arising from a revision of cataloging instruction at the University of Michigan, incorporated description, classification, and assignment of subject headings into one course. Initially published in the 1930s, this work was widely used until the early 1950s. The American Library Association (ALA) standards for accreditation for library school programs set the stage for the most recent period of library education, from the mid-1960s to the present, a period that has been characterized by an increasing emphasis on cataloging principles.[5] The curriculum envisioned by the standards is to include: emphasis on the significance and function of the subjects taught; stress on understanding and ability to apply basic principles and methods; and currency with trends in library development and professional education.[6] Catalogers who would be flexible, adaptable, and knowledgeable were sought, as exemplified by Frederick Wagman's comments in 1951.[7]

Under the leadership of Thelma Eaton, the University of Illinois offered two types of cataloging instruction in three sequential courses: a practical introductory course to cataloging and classification, and two advanced courses encompassing studies in historical developments and critical examination of present practices.[8] E. J. Humeston's survey in 1950 reported that more than half of the respondents from thirty-five accredited programs were placing more emphasis on principles and theories of cataloging, organization and administration of catalog departments, and understanding the use of the card catalog.[9]

The revised accreditation standards of 1971 reflected changes in the profession. The curriculum of library schools was designed to stress understanding of principles and to respond to current trends in library development and professional education. The ALA mandated that the curriculum should be reviewed and revised constantly, and be receptive to innovation and that library schools have access to a collection of multimedia resources, computer services, and facilities for independent study using current technology and equipment.[10]

In response to technological advances such as those being implemented throughout the profession, competency in data processing technology, and systems analysis began to be demanded. Robert M. Hayes documented the response to this demand with a table that listed technological courses offered at thirty-five library schools. He profiled the approach to technology at the University of California, Los Angeles, which offered four courses: the first introduced the principles of systems analysis and data processing; the second examined data processing applications to library operations with emphasis on computer programming; the third investigated systems analysis; and the fourth was a seminar in system design and information handling.[11] Herbert Landau commented on the necessity for librarians to become database managers, stating that a librarian " . . . is really . . . an expert in the organization, storage, retrieval and use of information, regardless of what storage medium and level of mechanization are applied to it."[12] Landau believed that the librarian must become an innovator in database management or he risks losing control of the library to those outside the profession.

Betty Brown reported on a mixture of traditional and new topics in the cataloging curriculum in order to prepare knowledgeable, adaptable cataloging librarians for an automated environment. The first course stressed techniques and practices of classification and descriptive cataloging. The second emphasized the Library of Congress Classification scheme, subject headings, and non-book materials. A third group of courses offered history, philosophy and theory of cataloging and classification and technical processing, and automated control of library collections.[13] In 1987, Mary Biggs and Abraham Bookstein surveyed forty-five faculty members in ALA accredited programs to discover what constituted a high-quality master's program. Sixty-two percent of respondents named faculty research and publishing activity as the most important criterion.[14] Stephen Peters' 1987 survey of basic and advanced cataloging courses found that the traditional topics of corporate headings, monographic description, and personal author headings were taught in all basic classes, and that the MARC format was also covered. The advanced level included instruction in bibliographic utilities and authority control.[15]

According to a 1987 paper by Jerry Saye, topics to be studied in cataloging courses had not changed much in fifty years, except for the addition of computer-related topics. His essentials for an introductory course included descriptive cataloging, access points, subject headings, Dewey Decimal Classification (DDC), Library of Congress Classification (LCC), MARC format, searching on a bibliographic utility, and treatment of non-book materials. An advanced course would cover descriptive cataloging, Library of Congress Rule Interpretations (LCRIs), MARC formatting, additional classification work, input and editing on a bibliographic utility, and serials cataloging, all with an emphasis on problem solving and initiative. For cataloging specialists, Saye recommended courses in management of technical services, systems analysis, database management, library automation, abstracting and indexing, theory of classification, collection development, government publications, serial publications, online searching, and history of the book.[16]

Sheila Intner[17] stated that we cannot expect students to know something if we do not teach it, even though all librarians must commit to a career-long obligation to keep up with their field. She promotes WYTIWYG (What You Teach Is What You Get) in theory and practice to define the substance of a curriculum to be covered in a beginning course. She identifies her pedagogy with the acronym SERA (Stimulation, Experimentation, Resolution, Analysis). SERA involves small groups of student-catalogers seeking potential solutions to intellectually challenging problems, selecting alternatives and defending them under the guidance of a teacher who helps them analyze the solutions. Intner finds SERA a strategy well-suited to teaching cataloging concepts and issues. Her proposals, SERA and WYTIWYG, are presented in order to set new goals and objectives for coursework in cataloging, and to help educate "unintentional" cataloging librarians.

In short, historically, there has been a steady flow of innovations in standard classroom cataloging instruction, and much has been described in the professional literature. Most innovations have focused on course content, including core course content, reshaping course content to incorporate new developments, especially technological ones, and adding other related courses. It is apparent that cataloging has become more complex since 1950 and demands broader knowledge of a greater variety of subjects and issues. In the 21st century, library science programs must provide proper education, imbued with information technologies, including the Internet Web world. Janet Swan Hill[18] believes that library schools deserve their share of criticism for the lack of well-trained, creative catalogers available today because of their de-emphasis of cataloging courses. Roxanne Sellberg and James Rush think that cataloging courses should become a specialty in the second year of a master's program, so that catalogers have time to study relevant theory and practical problem solving.[19] Other authors believe that librarians must possess a positive attitude toward information technologies and a determination to use them effectively to improve library service. Now and then, internship programs (albeit general without a cataloging focus) are reported.[20]

Despite the technological advancements adopted by our profession, library education literature curiously lacks contributions describing library educators' innovative ways of using technology to bring "real world" cataloging to the classroom. Seldom is there discussion of effective pedagogy in delivering course content in collaboration with seasoned expert practitioners, or of how successful delivery can be achieved by using the most advanced technologies available today.

THE CONTEXT FOR INTRODUCING INNOVATIONS IN CATALOGING EDUCATION

Students

Innovations described in this paper are the author's adaptive responses to the changing professional graduate school environment, to student expectations and experiences, and to the context of the information world created by technological advancements. Students' expectations and experiences are largely shaped by their use of the Internet and the number of computers in the workplace and homes. Increasingly, students come equipped with expanded vocabularies and skills in Web crawlers, SGML, HTML, and XML. The Internet, Web pages, e-mail, and computers are taken for granted as part of many people's lives, work, and leisure. Today's students come with the experience of learning from each other, and working together on homework problems and special assignments, and in surfing the Web. Many of them routinely spend hours engaged in discussions in chatrooms and using e-mail. Having grown up with technology, they are comfortable relying on it to connect them to the information they need. Teaching should utilize these familiarities and tap into their experience with a collaborative approach to working, learning, and even entertainment.

Yet students are increasingly less homogeneous in age, experiences, backgrounds, ethnicities, interests, subjects, and career aspirations. At least half of a typical student body in most graduate library education programs is composed of adult learners who have been away from school for several years. Recognizing adult learners' different stages of cognitive development and their affective learning styles as described by Michael Carpenter,[21] can help educators provide "cataloging" as a cornerstone of excellent information service. Adult learners' cognitive domain ("those objectives which deal with the recall or recognition of knowledge and the development of intellectual abilities and skills")[22] is accomplished by achieving the affective domain objectives. Applied to library science, this means understanding how and why professional intellectual decisions at the input (cataloging) stage affect the outcomes of information retrieval and system management.

Library education will need to teach students about metadata, crosswalks, information architecture, authentication, and authorization, as well as about such things as online multimedia course packs, customized textbooks, video conferencing, telecommuting, digital cash, and DVDs, because libraries will be involved with them all. Libraries will need to make decisions about such things as how to select materials for digitization and how to handle conversion. They will need to decide how to integrate physical and digital collections, how to provide an integrated tool for users by tapping into other domains' metadata initiatives, and how to maintain and preserve all the resources and reservoirs of integrated tools, both analog and digital.

Approach to Cataloging

Students expect all the tools librarians use to be as easy to use as Internet search engines. Students may not see the difference between Amazon.com and a library catalog. Taking advantage of the expectations and experiences that students bring with them is important. It is a goal of the author's Organization of Knowledge class, one of three core courses at the Dominican University Graduate School of Library and Information Science, for students to see that there are many different traditions of handling information needs. Archives, museums, businesses, libraries and other cultural institutions use finding aids, database management systems, Internet search engines, bibliographies, indexes, catalogs, and other tools in different ways to suit their own requirements. In the context of describing Internet Web resources, significant metadata schema from a variety of domains (DC, TEI, EAD, GILS, ONIX) are studied. The changing landscape for metadata schema on the Web and the juxtaposition of the librarian's responsibility and ethics for competing metadata schema in any library provides a complex, yet realistic context of the information world for students to consider and study. What values and solutions their profession purports to add to the information world at large are fervently thought through and examined. All of these explorations segue to discussion of the traditional library catalog and of professional responsibilities for organizing knowledge.

The author's response to today's tension within the graduate school curriculum environment has also shaped the innovations she uses in various "cataloging" courses. She defines cataloging broadly as the entire process of making knowledge systems, akin to Francis Miksa's bibliographic systems.[23] The courses in cataloging and classification in particular present a tremendous tension, since these are the first areas of curriculum that are directly impacted by technological advancements, just as the first impact of technological advancements in any library is usually felt in the cataloging department.

The nature of the tension created in the curriculum for cataloging, however, is different from that in library technical services, where tension created by technological advancements becomes a positive force when technical services operations are improved, and technological advancements (computing, storage and telecommunications) make cataloging and classification more productive and economical. Miriam Drake, writing on economics regarding technological innovation and organizational change, states that:

Most libraries have reduced the size of their catalog departments as they have realized the economies of shared cataloging. Some libraries have outsourced cataloging to book vendors and other agencies. The need to catalog electronic resources and to make them available creates a demand for catalogers and indexers who can add value to records by adding metadata and descriptions of intellectual content. The decision to enhance records is difficult because it involves expenditure and reallocation of resources by the library. Users do not pay directly for more effective access, so the gain is difficult to measure.[24]

Reduction of cataloging workload in the library, or reallocation of library personnel resources is often misinterpreted in library schools as reduction in the intellectual content future librarians need. If the gain of more effective access is difficult to measure in the library, convincing library school faculty how teaching effective access is directly related to effective organization is often a monumental curriculum task to measure. Faculty advising in building any individual student's cohesive program plays a critical role in dissipating the direct link of cataloging courses to cataloging positions. It takes a "village" of gifted faculty to educate potential catalogers and future librarians who will treasure cataloging functions. What effective access via effective organization means in terms of professional responsibility and ethics is difficult to measure and to achieve in a curriculum.

Cataloging Substances in Layers

As subjects to teach, cataloging and classification have not only remained as challenging as ever before, but as a result of technological advancements, they have become even more complex, and can be regarded as involving layers of decisions, arranged in tiers representing areas of concern that range from narrow and specific to very broad. The following are some of the tiered layers to be addressed in cataloging courses:

- Library catalog records (i.e., knowledge records) with intellectual components (AACR, subject headings, classification)
- System making for the library catalog (public catalog, shelflist, and authority file)
- System maintenance (file structure and database management systems)

- MARC as metadata
- Interconnections of intellectual contents in MARC
- Automated indexing achieved via MARC tagging
- Relevancy in the new landscape of metadata schema on the Web
- Local file systems and their integration in national and international networks (automation systems, OPACs, bibliographic utilities)
- Prioritizing values added; value added via controlled vocabulary in particular

The basic underpinning components for knowledge organization (bibliographic description, choice of access points, heading formulation, authority control, classification, and system design for the catalog) are the same as they were prior to library automation, and are used in the creation of three basic related files–public catalog, shelflist, and authority file.[25] In electronic format, the logical relation of these files and components are invisible. Coursework must aid students in conceptualizing their interconnections. One exercise might be to illustrate the power of classification through the notion of an electronic classified catalog.

MARC has served as the vanguard cooperative framework for library automation projects and vendor systems. It is the first layer of complexity imposed on intellectual decisions reached through cataloging. Understanding how MARC is constructed and indexed helps information professionals understand search and retrieval. For instance, MARC field tags 1xx, 6xx, 7xx, etc., are usually indexed and the xxs in these field tags indicate the types of headings (replacing xx with 00 indicates a personal name type, 10 a corporate body, etc.). With the ubiquitous keyword searching experiences with which students come to the classroom, these complicated MARC tags seem silly, unless two value added services can be demonstrated: (1) the significant difference in search results produced by phrase searching, and (2) the same results corroborated by meaningful collocation provided by headings and classification. Studying how automatic indexing with added values of phrase searching and collocation relates directly to searching and to the quality of search results must be in any core cataloging course.

The MARC encoding scheme with its leaders, directory, variable fields, control fields, fixed fields, etc., dates back to the mid-1960s, almost three decades prior to the Web revolution on the Internet. As the format upon which libraries have standardized, it has successfully conveyed the semantic content essential to human-machine communication and system-to-system communication. The library profession's success in delivering intellectual content via MARC has involved unceasing innovation. For instance, recently MARC DTD (document type definition) in SGML (Standard General Markup Language) as well as in XML (Extensible Markup Language) has been developed to signal the advancement of MARC to the Web world. It is essential for students to have an ownership understanding of how MARC is deployed in an automated environment, how and what is automatically indexed and searched according to the way MARC represents the intellectual contents, and therefore, what contents are searchable. To claim students' ownership understanding, the connections between the intellectual contents, indexing and searchability of contents, requires study and examination of MARC deployment as the evidence in action. OCLC's WorldCat offers an opportunity for such study. Studying how automatic indexing of natural language is the same in the WorldCat and Internet search engines, and how automatic indexing of controlled vocabulary via authority control adds value to library catalogs, is vitally important for students, who will be our colleagues in a year or so. Learning that the intellectual contents in WorldCat are derived from *AACR2R,* subject heading lists (LCSH, MeSH, AAT, Sears, etc.) and classification schema (DDC, LCC, UDC, etc.) will assist catalogers in making correct and useful decisions and will contribute to the role and value that we, the professionals, add to natural language.

EXAMPLES OF SOME CLASSROOM INNOVATIONS

The Core Course

The Organization of Knowledge course, one of three core courses offered at the Dominican University Graduate School of Library and Information Science, is a survey of principles, concepts, methods, and systems. Innovations employed are collaborative and provide creative learning experience via (1) self-instruction for searching the WorldCat via OCLC PRISM, which teaches individual students the basics of various modes of searching in about 30 minutes; (2) small group assignments which build on individuals' self-instructed experience to learn the three decision actions in any search: the match, the mis-match, and the no-match; (3) small group assignments to focus on descriptive cataloging; (4) small group assignments in analyzing, selecting and evaluating search results; and (5) small group assignments of searching some defined set of problems in WorldCat in OCLC PRISM and in OCLC FirstSearch in order to demonstrate the interrelationships of PRISM and FirstSearch as well as the use of Boolean operators. Two results of the assignments are a single team report on their self-selected experience, and a creative oral presentation by each small group, focusing on one type of learning experience to share with their peers. Self-selected and self-driven, the assignments ensure students' active learning. Students learn not only to teach the course content to each other by reinforcing what has been discussed in the class meetings and in the readings, but also to share their learning by collaboration.

The Elective Course

In the elective course of Cataloging and Classification, each student's portfolio is the final required report. Since the purpose of this course is to provide the student with specific practices in the routines and procedures of descriptive cataloging and subject analysis, this is the foundation course for those who want to build in-depth knowledge, including those who prepare to work as professional catalogers and classifiers. Theoretical focus is balanced with specific applications and decisions, which are grounded on reasoned practical considerations, based on solid discussion and writing on at least some of the principles and issues connected with those practices. Theory, principles, and concepts that are not coupled with application examples are not meaningfully incorporated into the students' knowledge purview. Students' active learning through applying theory, principles, and concepts instills understanding of complex interconnections in either designing or applying a system of bibliographic control. Students' active learning means that they experience the creation of a catalog record by applying the necessary tools, thus becoming not just practitioners, but practitioners who think critically to improve and lead the advancement in the art of cataloging.

Students in this class want individual mentors but cannot have them. Each student desires individual attention for all the questions and detailed decisions regarding particular examples cataloged. In addition to the specific example-oriented questions, which often elicit endless follow-up questions, two additional issues make individual mentoring impossible. The first is the need to have the same work in hand for students and mentors, because the principle that the chief source of information for the item in hand must be examined is critically important. The second issue is that since all types of materials are dealt with, connecting students with practicing catalogers who have certain necessary expertise is daunting, even impossible. One of the course projects does require that students visit at least two professional catalogers and one non-cataloger, but other courses, such as Practicum and Independent Study provide more opportunity for tapping into the expert knowledge of practicing catalogers in-depth.

A student portfolio is used to assess how theory, principles, and concepts are melded with practical applications and what students have learned by reflecting, reviewing, and discussing the themes for each class meeting. The portfolio is intended to promote student ownership of their learning. This is preferable to their worrying about test scores which, especially in cataloging and classification, are only indirect indicators of learning. The portfolio for the course is not all inclusive, and is instead a "selection portfolio." Each student prioritizes and reflects on what they have learned in each class meeting and via their respective assignments. The creation and organization of a selection portfolio mirrors the need for prioritizing the many competing tasks that a cataloger will face in real life. Demonstrating individual learning in this way places the focus on actual achievements and on what students can do with their knowledge and skills, not simply on whether knowledge has been acquired.

ONLINE MENTOR CATALOGERS

The course Metadata for Internet Resources is a seminar style course that provides a comprehensive and practical understanding of cataloging Internet resources–from selection and collection management to cataloging/classification and catalog maintenance. The course also explores complements and alternatives to MARC/*AACR2* cataloging, including Dublin Core, TEI headers, EAD, GILS, VRA/CC, ONIX, and Web pages. Through the study of the underlying concepts of these approaches and their implementations, the course pushes the boundaries of new technology applications by exploring and examining automated metadata record creation, subject analysis, and classification.

Rationale

From the inception of this course, the author seized the opportunity to collaborate with expert catalogers who are explorative (instead of definitive) in seeking solutions, are cataloging Internet resources, and are willing to invest in the next generation of librarians. Critical to success of this course, which offers the opportunity to collaborate with expert catalogers at various sites, are: (1) availability of the same Web resources both to students on campus and mentors at remote sites, thus upholding the catalogers' axiom of "cataloging the item in hand" (something that is only possible because the cataloging targets are Internet resources); (2) WebBoard technology that facilitates uploading catalog records with precision and accuracy; (3) WebBoard technology that provides a collaborative learning environment; (4) confirmation of classroom learning in the real world, bridging theory and practice; (5) encouragement and positive rallying by mentor coaching; (6) the importance of experts' perspectives which are grounded in substantial experience in cataloging and classification; and (7) contact with professional mentor catalogers who are risk-takers in exploring solutions.

The most important rationale for having mentor catalogers on the WebBoard is the creating of a collaborative learning environment for everyone enrolled in the course. A discussion forum is created and maintained between an individual student and their respective mentor cataloger. This forum is open, however, for other members in the class to "listen in," further enhancing learning for everyone. The WebBoard discussion between individual students and their mentor catalogers thus extends classroom study and discussion. How much a student learns is influenced by his desire to learn, because each student must catalog four Web resources selected according to some personally arrived at library selection criteria, but any student can effectively catalog and classify many times that number of Web resources by examining other students' selections and related cataloging records.

The confirmation of classroom learning by real world catalogers is an unnerving and yet exhilarating experience for both students and instructor. In many ways, there is a great deal of trepidation in creating a WebBoard encounter for a prospective "novice" and "the expert" (to use the terms of Dreyfus and Dreyfus in *Mind Over Machine*).[26] Although Dreyfus and Dreyfus were discussing the human skill acquisition process[27] in terms of the attempts of computer scientists to create intelligent machines, the process applies here in terms of different attainment levels of knowledge. As Dreyfus and Dreyfus stated, the distinction between the detached rule-following beginner and the involved intuitive expert is crucial. This author finds that describing these five stages of knowledge and skill acquisition serves a useful purpose for students, especially when they are impatient or discouraged with their creation of catalog records that do not reflect the application of their understanding of the principles, concepts, methods, and tools. Students readily recognize these five stages of knowledge and skill acquisition as different levels of knowledge and experience attainment for cataloging and classification, and they are willing to identify themselves as "the novice" in their creation of catalog records.

Model for Decision-Making Steps

Once they accept themselves as novices, each student approaches cataloging in a series of delineated steps of decision making. Separating the intellectual decisions they need to make before relating their content decisions to the appropriate MARC tags is initially a groundbreaking realization for most students, who may at first believe that MARC determines record contents as well as coding, instead of understanding that MARC is an encoding scheme for intellectual contents that are dictated by other standards. The realization that the intellectual contents may be encoded not only in MARC but also in any number of other encoding schema such as DC, TEI, or ONIX opens students' eyes to new opportunities and challenges to what professional value they can offer.

Accepting the simple logical steps involved in cataloging is a quiet relief for beginners. Recognizing the beginning step, that involves the eight descriptive areas and application of ISBD (International Bibliographic Description) punctuation, as one of the most common bibliographically sensible decisions, provides students a sense of control over cataloging. Thereon, how these areas and ISBD punctuation are found in and applied from the first part of *AACR* paves the road for analytical and critical thinking in building a series of intellectual decisions. Students are more comfortable with the second step: relating the description to access points. Grounding their decisions on cataloging access points rationally means honing their analytical and critical ability to understand their needs in view of information users, who are unseen, and to apply the second part of *AACR* to design a file system. The importance of subject access in accommodating users' unknown item searches brings out a new dimension of professionalism from these future librarians. They realize their unique professional opportunities and challenges to contribute value through authority control, providing headings and all appropriate access points for users. Recognition of a meaningful file design in a library catalog that integrates all types of information resources, including those that are not inter-shelvable or physically browseable, takes students to a new level of understanding of classification.

Understanding the design of the file system in view of information needs is the third logical step. Internalizing the system design for user access to individual catalog records provides students a deeper sense of professionalism. Intertwined with system design is the fourth step, which leads to understanding of MARC bibliographic and authority formats. This step involves examination and study of various aspects of MARC, including fields that are not addressed by or related to *AACR* contents. The fifth step involves subject access. Understanding the rationale for subject access points, including classification numbers, involves a deeper intellectual content reservoir and a more complex set of decisions, taking students beyond simple analytical and critical thinking ability. Students may examine and compare currently available systems, including various OPACs, utilities and Internet search engines. Some students begin to read research on classification, or to formulate research questions concerning subject approach. They begin to see the value that their profession can add even in this age of high technology.

The mentors' expert eyes appear to see the "whole picture" of the entire record and yet still see the connections of parts to the whole and interrelationships among the parts. I call this expert analysis, production and evaluation of every element in a MARC catalog record, the top to bottom approach. Top to bottom is the expert's way of creating a MARC catalog record. Whether fixed fields are given at the top of a work form or at the bottom of a screen, expert catalogers tackle and solve problems by seeing connections intuitively. Seemingly effortlessly, mentors analyze and evaluate students' recording of intellectual decisions in the variable fields. Their ability to make connections between intellectual contents in variable fields and in coded data is uncanny. Their proficiency in making corrections to the intellectual content in a professional manner with positive tone has been consistent. What students and mentor catalogers have exhibited in the deployment of their skills and knowledge through this process confirms Dreyfus and Dreyfus' five stages of knowledge and skill acquisition[27]–(1) Novice, (2) Advanced beginner, (3) Competent, (4) Proficient and (5) Expert.

Cataloging as a Science and as an Art

What is daunting for the instructor is making sure that students learn to document decisions instead of creating catalog records intuitively, or whimsically based on seeing similar catalog records "somewhere," and yet learn to appreciate cataloging as an art. Students who can observe cataloging as a science (in terms of precision and accuracy), and at the same time as an acquired art (in terms of intuition and analysis) can be motivated to cultivate their knowledge further. On the other hand, instructors must ensure that expert catalogers (the artists) will remember their first years as beginning catalogers, and will translate their intuitive solutions in terms of evidential decisions based on documents and experienced rationale.

Mentor coaching enhances the theory and applications discussed in class. Students' perceptions of the mentors' input as "correct" is the hook for mentoring and the key to WebBoard mentoring success. Students make connections between concepts and methods explained by the instructor in class when their mentor catalogers make similar comments specifically directed to the students' own work. This coaching often provides more practical and grounded rationale than classroom study or discussion, because of its connection to a concrete example record of the student's own creation.

For those who are interested in technical services and cataloging in particular, the mentor contact may also provide an important opportunity for future professional networking. Students are delighted to associate mentors' names with writings they have read, studied, cited, and reflected upon. Sometimes this networking occurs in the semesters following the course, as mentor catalogers extend their help when former mentees call upon them for assistance.

In class, the various philosophical approaches to cataloging, and the four types of catalogers (legalistic, bibliographic, perfectionist and practical) are discussed, with reference to Osborn:[28] the legalistic person makes no decision unless a rule is cited; the bibliographic person catalogs every item as if it is rare and describes every detail; the perfectionist demands perfection and permanent solutions or does not catalog at all; the practical cataloger exercises judgment within boundaries. After mentoring by catalogers concludes, at about the 3rd quarter of the semester, students have become confident in applying standard cataloging tools, and are less "evidentiary," that is, less likely to require all the specific rules, documentary evidences, etc., and they are able to embrace "the practical cataloger" as the type needed to catalog Internet resources. *AACR2R* does not always provide an exact answer or rule for electronic resources; the resources are not rare, and the impermanence of Web resources argues against perfectionism. They see that rules provide the basis for all cataloging, but are only good if they provide value; that it is important to know both the particulars and the principles. The practical cataloger is more aware of adding value without getting bogged down in details. The author actively promotes the value of being pragmatic as well as philosophical.

Mentoring Profile

The author has used various ways to identify potential mentors, including personal knowledge of and contacts with mentors at meetings; previous knowledge of mentors by their publications; and professional colleagues' recommendations. What is required of mentor catalogers are: cutting edge involvement with Internet resources issues; actual cataloging experience with Internet resources; commitment to and interest in cataloging; personality traits as instructors; responding to and nurturing students' interests; coaching students in creating catalog records; being available for a specified two week period; and signing up and using the WebBoard for discuss and instruction. Table 1 shows the sustained involvement of mentors over the years, and the ratio of mentors to students.

All mentors who have participated at least once have volunteered for succeeding courses. When they have been unable to continue because of conflicting professional commitments, they ask to remain in the pool, and have invariably recommended potential mentors to replace them. Some mentors have limited their participation to specific areas, such as serials or cartographic materials. Mentors' biographic profiles include any stipulations such as traveling commitments, or unavailability at certain times during the mentoring period of two weeks. The three original mentors have continuously participated whenever the course is offered. They have enhanced library education enormously by their generous sharing of expert knowledge and experience, and by the professional contribution of their personal time and care.

The fact that individual mentor catalogers have the flexibility to manage their time has been a key to the success of this innovative collaboration. As distinct from teaching in a classroom or giving a lecture, cataloger mentors can respond to students' questions or examine their catalog records when they find time during off-work hours, in the evenings or on weekends. Mentors' average turn-around response time during weekdays is a couple of hours, and the seemingly instant replies have often surprised and impressed students. The manner of mentor response has varied: (1) links provided to additional Web resources and sites for students to check and study; (2) suggestions in direct response to each part of students' catalog records; (3) narrative response to students' questions; (4) narrative discussion and suggested solutions and

TABLE 1

Mentoring Profile

	Sum98	Sp99	Sp00	Fall00	Fall01
1. Ruth B. R.	x	x			
2. Rick B.	x	x	x		
3. Diane B.	x	x	x	x	x
4. Patricia D.				x	x
5. Brad E.				x	x
6. William G.	x	x	x	x	x
7. Kate H.				x	x
8. Wayne J. (serials only)	x	x	x	x	
9. Mary L. (cartographic materials only)				x	x
10. Sue N.	x	x	x	x	x
11. Jackie S.					x
Number of students enrolled:	20	9	5	23*	7

*17 at St Catherine site and 6 at Dominican site

(Only the initials of the individual mentors' surnames are provided in this table for this article, in lieu of getting their individual permission for inclusion.)

alternatives to students' inquiries; and (5) attachment of mentors' own catalog records that contain highlighted corrections. Their responses have been surgically sharp, and consistently professional, clear, accurate, up-to-date, objective and to the point.

The WebBoard has proved to be a suitable technology to enhance both precision communication, and for the type of discourse of rationales necessary for learning cataloging. The nature of communication on the WebBoard reflects the progression of students' learning. The major initial focus is accuracy and precision in such matters as punctuation, spacing, capitalization, and other details. MARC tagging of variable fields, subfields, and indicators falls into the next group of discussion topics, followed by discourse on interconnections in the MARC fixed fields, initially 008, then 007 and 006. Students' final reckoning of the fixed fields' dependency on the intellectual content of knowledge records is heightened by students' understanding of the need for appropriate selection of certain MARC bibliographic formats that further influence searching protocols and eventual search results. Checking the appropriate authority file for the necessary headings and establishing the main, added, and subject headings intensify the final stages of mentoring. Suggestions and discourse on classification open up insightful and spirited class discussion on classification theory for the Web world.

As shown in Table 1, the WebBoard facilitated one "virtual class" discussion and learning environment for students who were enrolled in two different sections of the same course taught at two different institutions (St. Catherine College in Saint Paul, Minnesota, and Dominican University in River Forest, Illinois) at two different locations in two states and two time zones: The presence of remote cataloger mentors online via the WebBoard enhanced the sense of a unified class. Mentoring and students' learning went on seamlessly. Students utilized their cataloger mentors on the WebBoard while the instructor commuted between the two campuses. The WebBoard made variations of physical location and differences of time zones invisible and resolved the variance of physical location.

Preparation for Students

The success of the remote cataloger mentoring of individual students depends on the success of planning and managing the WebBoard. Some of the following points call for routine, consistent and constant management: (1) setting up and organizing the WebBoard; (2) getting every mentor's agreement to be available during the designated two week period; (3) getting students ready to select appropriate Web resources; (4) assuring students that no course grading is based on their cataloging records; (5) making sure that students understand the purpose of mentors' participation; (6) ensuring that students formulate catalog records in MARC; (7) getting individual students' records posted on the WebBoard on time; and (8) managing and monitoring the WebBoard communication between the mentors and mentees.

Planning–course schedule planning in particular–is the key to this type of collaboration. At what point in the course schedule this activity takes place must be planned precisely so that the two weeks the mentors agree to be available coordinates with the class syllabus, exactly. In this aspect of schedule planning, two points are critically important. The first is the preparation of course content, making sure that students, most of whom have never cataloged anything prior to the course, have sufficient cataloging background to be able to receive meaningful mentoring. For most beginning catalogers, including these students, the simple experience of writing down cataloging information in black and white is terrifying. Since the thrust of the course is metadata schema, students explore comprehensive and practical cataloging of Internet resources, including alternatives (Dublin Core, TEI headers, EAD, GILS, VRA/CC, ONIX, metadata, and Web pages). Time available for traditional cataloging and MARC consists of only one-third of the course. Understanding traditional cataloging and MARC is tantamount to discussion and understanding of metadata and Web resource management. Cataloging Web resources by Dublin Core elements as a group in class early in the semester is followed by individual experience. By using Dublin Core elements, students get experience of and instructor's feedback on the description of the four Web resources of their choice. The instructor's evaluation is on the students' general report on their experience in using Dublin Core elements, rather than on the resulting records. The Dublin Core experiences are intended to abate students' terrifying feeling of writing down cataloging information in black and white. Moving beyond this, because students initially post their catalog records with great trepidation, a select group of Internet resources is collaboratively examined and studied together. Small groups of two or three students work on the selected Web resources in class and present a single team catalog record per resource. In small groups students debate, exchange and test their solutions and respective documentation. Each group presents and defends its solutions to their peers, further generating insights and challenges to cataloging problems.

The second critical preparation for the class is the practice of generous sharing and collaboration with critical and analytical eyes—a hallmark of catalogers and cataloging. The instructor must build a collaborative working environment in which students are willing to share what they know, to tell their stories, to discuss their problems and test their solutions. This preparation involves ensuring that each one understands and studies that every decision made should be grounded on a rationale derived from collective experience and agreement (cataloging tools) instead of whimsical personal likings. Students are often imbued with competition since they are used to grading by curves. The notion of "competition in collaboration," when everyone may excel or fail, is a difficult one to accept. Often critical and analytical examination of a student's cataloging work by the instructor is negatively interpreted, with some students even feeling humiliated. From the onset, therefore, it is essential that everyone knows that catalog records created and discussed on the WebBoard are not evaluated for grades. What is evaluated is each student's two-page report on cataloging principles, issues, and unique/difficult decision-making points. In addition, the report requires their reflection on mentors' input in relation to their work (catalog records, tools used, assigned readings) and classroom lectures and discussions. The instructor's ability to create and maintain a collaborative working spirit for the course paves the eventual push and energetic inspiration for the WebBoard mentoring.

One of the most precious learning results that students gain is the abatement of this feeling of humiliation when they make some little mistake. Each student comes away saying that their cataloging work is okay (sometimes feeling that their work is pretty darn good), although they all know there is a lot more to learn. A gigantic leap takes place during the mentoring period of two weeks. Reassurances and affirmations communicated by mentors mean the most to individual students. Another important learning result imparted by mentors is the confirmation of what students have learned in the classroom. Bridging academe to real world experts is accomplished quickly and solidly when mentors participate. Finally, there is greater understanding of the intellectual components of cataloging and their complex connections. Learning to catalog and make complex connections is eased by the WebBoard technology that abates ambiguities. The simultaneous viewing of all necessary details in catalog records in relation to cataloging tools used and the Web resources further provides the connection and makes possible fuller conceptual learning. Expansion beyond and extension to classroom learning is achieved by students' active learning, when they are engaged in individual consultations with the respective mentors or when they actively "listen in" on other consultations going on in the WebBoard.

CONCLUSION

In summary, a steady flow of innovations in standard classroom cataloging instruction has historically filled the professional literature. Most of the innovations reported, however, have focused on course contents. The full implications of technologies and the Internet Web in particular demand problem definition, value prioritization, and linear and yet creative problem solving skills for librarians. Organizations as well as individuals must be educated in the impact on information retrieval of the way information is organized, especially in the Web world. Employers should encourage librarians to participate in educating their future colleagues, by acquiring and maintaining necessary skills through continuing education, reading, attendance at conferences and on-the-job experience. The results are good library service and satisfied library patrons.

Often, libraries where good prospective cataloger mentors may work look upon internships in cataloging as too expensive an investment, impeding production and draining resources without any reciprocal return from interns to offset the investment of time. Yet cataloging job notices from these libraries frequently require beginning catalogers to have cataloging work experience. Students are often puzzled or discouraged by this paradox, and ask for opportunities to work with experienced catalogers. Full implementation of technologies at libraries, especially network technologies, provide an opportunity to take advantage of a small group of select cataloging mentors to work with protégées who are interested in cataloging. Network technology, therefore, especially the Internet, may fill the chasm between practitioners and academe.

Seldom in the library education literature is there discussion of effective pedagogy for delivering course content in collaboration with seasoned practitioners (cataloging experts), or of how successful delivery can be achieved by using the advanced technologies available today. Innovations in delivering course contents online collaboratively with practitioners are possible only when the goals and objectives of the courses in cataloging are readdressed and well formed, as presented and posited by Michael Carpenter.[29] The goal of the core cataloging course is appreciation of the role a catalog and the cataloging function play in a library. I echo Lubetzky's thought on cataloging as a subject for library schools:

> In a library school whose objective, as that of a professional school, is to cultivate not only practitioners but also thinkers and critics of the art, not only followers but also leaders of the profession–librarians who will not only carry on but also advance the art of the profession–in such a school it is proper to treat the subject of cataloging not as a how-to-do-it routine outlined in so many rules, but rather as a problem in the methodological system to facilitate the exploitation of the library's resources by its users.[30]

Innovations in delivering cataloging courses online in collaboration with cataloging experts are natural outcomes within these newly set goals and objectives.

REFERENCES AND NOTES

1. Seymour Lubetzky, "On Teaching Cataloging," *Journal of Education for Librarianship* 5 (Spring 1965): 255.

2. Hazel Dean, "Is Cataloging a Vanishing Profession?" *Journal of Cataloging and Classification* 5 (Winter 1949): 41.

3. Lizbeth Bishoff, "Who Says We Don't Need Catalogers?" *American Libraries* 18 (September 1987): 694-696.

4. Ellen Zyroff, "Cataloging Is a Prime Number," *American Libraries* 27, no. 5 (May 1996): 47-50.

5. Francis Miksa, "Cataloging Education in the Library and Information Science Currriculum," *Recruiting, Educating and Training Cataloging Librarians: Solving the Problems*, edited by Sheila S. Intner and Janet Swan Hill. (New York: Greenwood Press, 1989). (New Directions in Information Management): 273-297.

6. "Standards for Accreditation," *ALA Bulletin* 46 (February 1952): 48.

7. "Training for Cataloging," *Journal of Cataloging and Classification* 7 (Spring 1951): 27-28.

8. Thelma Eaton, "Preparing Catalogers at the University of Illinois," *Journal of Cataloging and Classification* 7 (Spring 1951): 33-37.

9. E. J. Humeston, Jr., "Teaching Cataloging Today: A Survey," *Journal of Cataloging and Classification* 7 (Spring 1951): 37-41.

10. "Revised Standards for Accreditation," *American Libraries* 2 (October 1971): 959-961.

11. Robert M. Hayes, "Data Processing in the Library School Curriculum," *ALA Bulletin* 61 (June 1967): 662-669.

12. Herbert B. Landau, "Can the Librarian Become a Computer Data Base Manager?" *Special Libraries* 62 (March 1971): 118.

13. Betty Martin Brown, "Curriculum: Acquisitions and Cataloging," *Drexel Library Quarterly* Vol. 3 (January 1967): 84-91.

14. Mary Bigg and Abraham Bookstein, "What Constitutes a High-Quality M.L.S. Program? Forty-Five Faculty Members' Views," *Journal of Education for Library and Information Science* 29 (Summer 1988): 28-46.

15. Stephen H. Peters, "Time Devoted to Topics in Cataloging Courses," *Journal of Education for Library and Information Science* 29 (Winter 1989): 209-219.

16. Jerry D. Saye, "The Cataloging Experience in Library and Information Science Education: An Educator's Perspective," in *Education and Training for Catalogers and Classifiers*, ed. Ruth C. Carter (New York: The Haworth Press, Inc., 1987), p. 27-45.

17. Sheila S. Intner, "Response to Change: New Goals and Strategies for Core Cataloging Courses," *Recruiting, Educating and Training Cataloging Librarians: Solving the Problems*, edited by Sheila S. Intner and Janet Swan Hill. (New York: Greenwood Press, 1989). (New Directions in Information Management): 227-243.

18. Janet Swan Hill, "Staffing Technical Services in 1995." In *Library Management and Technical Services*. (New York: The Haworth Press, Inc., 1988): 87-103.

19. Roxanne Sellberg, "The Teaching of Cataloging in U.S. Library Schools." *Library Resources and Technical Services* 32 (January 1988): 30-42.

20. Francis R. St. John. *Internship in the Library Profession*. Chicago: American Library Association, 1938. Rice-Lively, Mary Lynn. "A Model for an Academic Library and Library School Mentor/Protégé Program," *College & Research Libraries News*. (March 1991): 163-4.

21. Michael Carpenter, "Making Cataloging Interesting," *Recruiting, Educating and Training Cataloging Librarians: Solving the Problems*, edited by Sheila S. Intner and Janet Swan Hill. (New York: Greenwood Press, 1989). (New Directions in Information Management): 169-186.

22. Benjamin S. Bloom, ed. *Taxonomy of Educational Objectives: The Classification of Educational Goals. Handbook 1: Cognitive Domain*, by a committee of college and university examiners. (New York: David McKay Company, 1956, reprinted 1965): 7.

23. Francis Miksa, "Cataloging Education in the Library and Information Science Curriculum," *Recruiting, Educating and Training Cataloging Librarians: Solving the Problems*, edited by Sheila S. Intner and Janet Swan Hill. (New York: Greenwood Press, 1989). (New Directions in Information Management): 273-297.

24. Miriam A. Drake, "Technological innovation and organizational change revisited," *Journal of Academic Librarianship* v. 26 no 1 (Jan. 2000) p. 53-9.

25. Sheila S. Intner and Janet Swan Hill, eds. *Recruiting, Educating and Training Cataloging Librarians: Solving the Problems*. (New York: Greenwood Press, 1989). (New Directions in Information Management). No author in this book disputes the necessity for the intellectual contents in knowledge records of a library catalog. No author in this book disputes any of the course content.

26. Hubert L. Dreyfus, and Stuart E. Dreyfus. *Mind Over Machine*. (New York: Free Press, 1986).

27. For a fuller explanation of these stages, see the table on page 50 in Hubert L. Dreyfus and Stuart E. Dreyfus. *Mind Over Machines*. New York: Free Press (1986).

28. Osborn, Andrew D. "The Crisis in Cataloging." (in Foundations of Cataloging: A Sourcebook. Edited by Michael Carpenter and Elaine Svenonius.) (Littleton, CO: Libraries Unlimited, 1985): 90-103.

29. Michael Carpenter, "Making Cataloging Interesting," *Recruiting, Educating and Training Cataloging Librarians: Solving the Problems*, edited by Sheila S. Intner and Janet Swan Hill. (New York: Greenwood Press, 1989). (New Directions in Information Management): 169-186.

30. Seymour Lubetzky, "On Teaching Cataloging," *Journal of Education for Librarianship* 5 (Spring 1985).

Online Mentoring:
A Student Experience
at Dominican University

Judith L. Aulik
Holly Ann Burt
Michael Geeraedts
Elizabeth Gruby
Bongjoo Moon Lee
Anita Morgan
Corey O'Halloran

SUMMARY. This paper explores the online learning experience of seven students in the Graduate School of Library and Information Science at Dominican University. In a class entitled *Metadata for Internet Resources*, the students developed a distance learning relationship with professional catalogers. Student assignments included posting bibliographic records on the WebBoard[TM] for mentor input. In an online exchange, the mentors responded by posting their suggestions for improving student records. The interaction between students and mentors is discussed, as is the educational value of distance learning. *[Article copies available for a fee from The Haworth Document Delivery Service: 1-800-HAWORTH. E-mail address: <getinfo@haworthpressinc.com> Website: <http://www.HaworthPress.com> © 2002 by The Haworth Press, Inc. All rights reserved.]*

Judith L. Aulik, BS, MS, PhD, Holly Ann Burt, BS, MDiv, Michael Geeraedts, BA, MSEd, MLIS, Elizabeth Gruby, BA, MA, Bongjoo Moon Lee, BA, MEd, Anita Morgan, BA, MLIS, and Corey O'Halloran, BA, were all students in the class "Metadadata for Internet Resources" offered at the Graduate School of Library and Information Science at Dominican University in 2001 at the time this was written.

[Haworth co-indexing entry note]: "Online Mentoring: A Student Experience at Dominican University." Aulik. Judith L. et al. Co-published simultaneously in *Cataloging & Classification Quarterly* (The Haworth Information Press. an imprint of The Haworth Press. Inc.) Vol. 34, No. 3. 2002. pp. 289-292: and: *Education for Cataloging and the Organization of Information: Pitfalls and the Pendulum* (ed: Janet Swan Hill) The Haworth Information Press, an imprint of The Haworth Press. Inc., 2002. pp. 289-292. Single or multiple copies of this article are available for a fee from The Haworth Document Delivery Service [1-800-HAWORTH. 9:00 a.m. - 5:00 p.m. (EST). E-mail address: getinfo@haworthpressinc.com].

KEYWORDS. Mentoring, distance education, cataloging education, Internet resource cataloging

In the class, *Metadata for Internet Resources*, we gained a comprehensive and practical knowledge of cataloging Internet resources. From selection and collection management to cataloging and classification to catalog maintenance, we learned about MARC tags, *AACR2* and subject headings. In addition, we learned about other cataloging alternatives such as Dublin Core, EAD, GILS, ONIX, TEI headers, and VRACC.

An assignment for the course was for each of us to choose four Internet-accessible resources, one in each of the following categories: a Website, a single Web page, a collection of non-textual objects, and a single non-textual object. Using these Internet resources we began our bibliographic description by applying the *Dublin Core Metadata Element Set, Version 1.1: Reference Description*. After in-depth practice with Dublin Core, we used these same Internet resources and began original cataloging in full bibliographic description. Our cataloging tools included the online campus-only access *Cataloger's Desktop*, which featured *Classification Plus*, *Anglo-American Cataloging Rules*, Second Edition (1998 Revisions with Amendments, 1999-2001) and *MARC21 Format for Bibliographic Data*.

To gain greater perspective from this assignment, our instructor for *Metadata for Internet Resources* provided us with the opportunity to work with professional catalogers as mentors. Through the use of the class WebBoard™ we were introduced to eight cataloging professionals from distance learning institutions. Currently working in various cataloging positions in North America, they volunteered their time and skills to correct our bibliographic records. Each mentor posted a biographical sketch on the class WebBoard™. From this, we chose the mentor that best suited our own individual interests, and thus, we began our distance learning experience.

Our class WebBoard™ had restrictions that allowed access to only the students in class, our instructor and the mentors. For a two-week period, we posted our bibliographic records on the class WebBoard™ for the mentors and our classmates to see. Using the MARC21 work form for electronic resources, we provided access points, subject headings, main and added entries, variable data fields, and variable control fields. Not only did we tag these four Internet resources in MARC format, but we also cited each tag's corresponding rule according to *AACR2* to show how we arrived at our bibliographic descriptions.

Most of us selected an Internet serial or a Web page rather than a visual resource for our initial posting. By posting this one record, we received feedback from our mentors before we began our bibliographic description on the other three Internet resources. Later we posted the remaining three records after correcting the initial record and learning from our mistakes. The value of the class WebBoard™ was that all students in the class could look at each other's records to see how they were cataloged, and the mentor's response to the records.

If a posted record was improperly tagged or the record displayed an error concerning the relevant rule for *AACR2*, the mentor would suggest a correction and explanation. Suggestions by mentors included checking the OCLC authority file for accuracy, making sure to use the $u in the 856 tag for the URL, and proper use of capitalization in subject headings. At the outset, students were apprehensive about receiving visible criticism; however, the replies and suggestions made by the mentors assisted everyone in the class. The number of times each posting was read was generated on the WebBoard™, but the students were not privy as to who was reading each post.

Because each mentor worked with different students on different Internet resources, the student/mentor interactions varied. Some students experienced a time lapse between posting a record and the mentor's response. This was sometimes caused by a student taking more time to post a record due to lack of experience in bibliographic description. Other times it was the mentor who had work-related conflicts or whose available WebBoard™ time did not correspond with the student's needs. Mentors tended to work evenly Monday through Thursday, while students worked mostly on the weekends. Other times there was difficulty with the WebBoard™ technology. Aside from these remedial issues, the students were in agreement on the benefits of distance learning.

By providing the opportunity to ask questions as they arose during the creation of bibliographic records, the mentors served as a sounding board for free thought. Receiving a response from the mentors gave impetus to new questions and provided deeper understanding of how bibliographic description works. An advantage of the WebBoard™ approach was that it was a timesaver in class for the students and instructor. By using the class WebBoard™ all student records could be opened in class for us to examine. Utilizing the students' online Internet resources and the WebBoard's bibliographic descriptions provided well-focused questions and answers.

Mentorship using Internet communication was an essential part of the course *Metadata for Internet Resources*. In autumn 2001, an unfortunate juxtaposition of national events and campus construction rendered distance learning more vital than had been anticipated. All students agreed that the interchange with mentors through the WebBoard™ was valuable.

The mentorship experience gave us the opportunity to network with real-world professional catalogers *outside* the classroom. They provided insight into how bibliographic description is often intuitive and subjective within the cataloging world of objective rules. In addition, the mentors served to verify what was being taught in the classroom. Their ease and expertise at offering corrections reinforced our textbook-learning that translated into an applied and practical science. Another opportunity this mentorship program can offer is the potential for a continued relationship for professional growth and development for students.

Online Distance Learning with Cataloging Mentors: The Mentor's Viewpoint

Kate Harcourt
Susan M. Neumeister

SUMMARY. Cataloging experts from across the United States were asked to critique assignments from students enrolled in Professor Gertrude Koh's classes at the Graduate School of Library and Information Science at the Dominican University in River Forest, Illinois through the use of an Internet bulletin board (WebBoard™, O'Reilly & Associates, Inc.). This paper examines the mentors' perspective on teaching cataloging and their experience in teaching future colleagues via the WebBoard. *[Article copies available for a fee from The Haworth Document Delivery Service: 1-800-HAWORTH. E-mail address: <getinfo@haworthpressinc.com> Website: <http://www.Haworth Press.com> © 2002 by The Haworth Press, Inc. All rights reserved.]*

KEYWORDS. Mentoring, distance education, cataloging education, Internet resource cataloging

INTRODUCTION AND BACKGROUND

This paper reports on the experiences of the authors Sue Neumeister and Kate Harcourt, who have been mentoring students in Professor Gertrude

Kate Harcourt is Assistant Head, Original and Special Materials Cataloging, Butler Library, Columbia University. Susan M. Neumeister is affiliated with the Acquisitions Department, University at Buffalo Libraries.

[Haworth co-indexing entry note]: "Online Distance Learning with Cataloging Mentors: The Mentor's Viewpoint." Harcourt, Kate, and Susan M. Neumeister. Co-published simultaneously in *Cataloging & Classification Quarterly* (The Haworth Information Press, an imprint of The Haworth Press, Inc.) Vol. 34, No. 3, 2002, pp. 293-298; and: *Education for Cataloging and the Organization of Information: Pitfalls and the Pendulum* (ed: Janet Swan Hill) The Haworth Information Press, an imprint of The Haworth Press, Inc., 2002, pp. 293-298. Single or multiple copies of this article are available for a fee from The Haworth Document Delivery Service [1-800-HAWORTH, 9:00 a.m. - 5:00 p.m. (EST). E-mail address: getinfo@haworthpressinc.com].

Koh's cataloging classes since the summers of 1998 and 2000 respectively. Initially called "Internet Resources Cataloging and Access Management," the class has evolved with the changing times and is currently called: "Metadata for Internet Resources." From the beginning, the experience and guidance of experienced professional electronic resource catalogers has proved to be a valuable addition to the classroom.

The Dominican University's WebBoard was used as the tool for online conferencing for the class to enable mentors and students to share information quickly and easily. We were able to post messages directly to the WebBoard conference and to attach files to our messages. Although neither of us had used a WebBoard before, after we had read an overview of the WebBoard structure that Professor Koh sent through email to all mentors, we found that navigating through the WebBoard was quite simple, and after brief examination, each "button" link was found to be essentially self-explanatory. Although first time posting can be intimidating, some of the stress was removed by the WebBoard's ability to allow re-reading messages and spell checking responses before sending and posting them.

Before each semester began, Professor Koh would inform the mentors as to what would be involved in the current distance learning project. Typically a project would include critiquing a few catalog records during a one-week period, utilizing the distance education method (WebBoard). She would provide the starting and ending dates she had set for the project and asked the mentors to inform her if they were available for another week afterward in case students had additional questions.

Individual students chose mentors based on biographies sent to Professor Koh. Prior to the start of each semester, Professor Koh would update these biographies, by asking the mentors if there were any changes to incorporate in their biographical information.

Professor Koh provided the mentors with the Web address (URL) for the class WebBoard. It was necessary for participants to register themselves on the WebBoard each semester in order to assure that only those students and mentors who registered could participate in the conferencing.

Class lectures and discussions that took place at The Dominican University provided an overview on cataloging Internet resources, starting with description. Students were expected to take what was learned in class and develop a catalog record for each of two Internet resources they chose by applying and citing *Anglo American Cataloging Rules*, 2nd ed. revised, *Cataloging Internet Resources: A Manual and Practical Guide*, and USMARC. Professor Koh made sure that the mentors understood that for most of her students, this was their first cataloging experience and their first formal cataloging course, although they had all completed one required introductory course in "Organization of Knowledge."

In order to make the mentoring of each student individually manageable, and to facilitate providing answers to student questions, Professor Koh created each of the mentor's names as separate conferences under "Mentoring by Catalogers." Students would then post drafts of the records for their selected Internet resources to the "conference" of the mentor they had chosen. These records were thus made available on the WebBoard for input and critiquing by the mentor. In addition to posting their records, students also asked questions along the way concerning problems they encountered while cataloging these resources. Mentors were instructed to respond to students on the WebBoard.

MENTOR'S ROLE

There are many challenges facing mentors who are, after all, practicing catalogers rather than educators. Mentors must make the effort to provide constructive criticism of the students' work and incorporate affirmative, positive reinforcement. Because there is no face-to-face interaction through the WebBoard, mentors need to take the time to provide feedback and well thought out responses that will properly evaluate and reinforce the strengths of their students' cataloging. It was difficult at times, for instance, to judge whether our comments were fully understood, because we lacked the obvious visual cues and had to depend on our students being brave enough to say when they did not understand us.

Too much information in a Web environment can also be problematic. We tried to be concise, use short, coherent statements and ask direct questions. Sometimes we would write several responses dealing with different concepts for the same record rather than send one complex analysis. This allowed us to create discussion threads on topics of particular interest or difficulty.

We reviewed each record carefully looking for an understanding of the process of organizing information, application of the specific rules for electronic resources and an awareness of users' searching behavior. It was a challenge at times to step back from looking for every miscoded indicator, and evaluate instead whether a student had in fact grasped fundamental principles of information science. We also provided links and citations for reference tools so that our students could learn more about a particular cataloging rule or MARC field.

THINGS TO CONSIDER

The following illustrate some of the aspects of long distance mentoring that have had to be dealt with and resolved based on experience gained through repeated offering of the class.

Technology

Every working environment is not technologically equivalent. A perfect example was Sue Neumeister's first semester of mentoring. Students would post their catalog records as file attachments using the version of Word that came with Microsoft Office 95. The University at Buffalo Libraries where Sue worked, however, were still in the process of converting to Microsoft Office 95 and there was only one workstation in technical services that had the necessary software. Sue had to go to that workstation to view and download the attached file, save it in the earlier version of MS Word, and then take it back to her own work area. When recruiting new mentors, a message from the instructor outlining the technological requirements necessary to participate is essential.

Instructor's Role

Telling mentors ahead of time exactly what the assignment will be maximizes the learning experience for the students, and makes the mentors more effective. There were times, for example, when some students included more description in their catalog records than others, including such things as fixed field information, call numbers, and subject headings. Some students did authority work, others did not. Early in the mentoring program, some cataloged two sites, others only one. We didn't know if the students providing less information were being negligent, or if the students including more information were trying to gain extra credit. A clear understanding of the objectives and expectations at the beginning helps to avoid misunderstandings later.

At the inception of the program, during the summer of 1998, mentors were scarce and the class size was large. That first semester, some mentors had four students in the "Internet Resources Cataloging and Access Management" class. Later experience has shown that to be fair to the students, a maximum of two students for each mentor per semester would be ideal. Sometimes the course has been offered in a regular semester consisting of 14 weeks and other times it has been offered in an executive format over six weeks. In the executive format, everything seems to be intensified in a short amount of time. If you mentored more than two students in this shorter format, it was really a challenge, and required very quick response. By the time Kate Harcourt came on board in 2000, the workload, while intense, was manageable.

BENEFITS FOR MENTORS

We both found that mentoring sharpened our cataloging skills as we would check and double-check the rules as part of reviewing our students' records. Mentoring also gave us an opportunity to work with electronic resources that may be unfamiliar to those of us in academia, such as community information Websites. In a few instances, we were able to help Professor Koh by calling her attention to relevant digital projects at our institutions. Using the WebBoard also gave us a glimpse of some of the challenges our public services colleagues are grappling with as they design online reference services and chat rooms.

CONCLUSION

We always had a stimulating experience when we mentored. In some cases, it was a learning experience for us as well as for the students, as we just tried to keep one step ahead of them. Distance learning mentoring has some problems, but on the whole it is a good way to get different perspectives on ways to catalog. Through contact with practicing catalogers as mentors, Professor Koh's students learned early on about cataloger's judgment. They not only learned to reinforce their position by citing rules and examples, but they also realized that there are frequently valid alternative ways to catalog the same item. The field of cataloging, especially with Internet resources, is constantly evolving and, as mentors, we need to stay current with those changes if we are to train our future colleagues properly.

Professor Koh emphasized to the mentors that the cataloging exercises done by their students represented the very first time that most of them had ever cataloged anything, and that it took a lot of courage for them to post their catalog records for us to critique. As mentors, we hoped that through positive feedback and encouragement, their apprehensiveness would fade. It was rewarding to watch students' confidence grow even in the short time we served as mentors. We only regret that we may never know how many students went on to choose careers in cataloging.

After each semester, Professor Koh extended her sincere appreciation for our generous participation and for incorporating our mentoring in our busy daily schedules. In return, we would like to thank her for providing this innovative way of teaching and giving us the opportunity to help shape tomorrow's catalogers.

When Donkeys Fly:
Distance Education for Cataloging

Elaine Yontz

SUMMARY. Distance education–a mode of course delivery in which the teacher is geographically separated from the students and in which that separation is mediated by technology–is increasingly used in LIS programs. This paper covers advantages and drawbacks of distance education for cataloging, argues that the possibilities outweigh the disadvantages, summarizes current educational research on distance education, and offers a list of elements that may help educators and students to take full advantage of the possibilities. *[Article copies available for a fee from The Haworth Document Delivery Service: 1-800-HAWORTH. E-mail address: <getinfo@haworthpressinc.com> Website: <http://www.HaworthPress.com> © 2002 by The Haworth Press, Inc. All rights reserved.]*

KEYWORDS. Distance education, cataloging education

INTRODUCTION

On top of the file cabinet in my office sits a stuffed donkey, Eeyore, from Winnie the Pooh. My Eeyore is wearing a silvery halo and white wings.

Elaine Yontz is Associate Professor, Master of Library and Information Science Program, Valdosta State University, Valdosta, GA.

[Haworth co-indexing entry note]: "When Donkeys Fly: Distance Education for Cataloging." Yontz, Elaine. Co-published simultaneously in *Cataloging & Classification Quarterly* (The Haworth Information Press, an imprint of The Haworth Press, Inc.) Vol. 34, No. 3, 2002, pp. 299-310; and: *Education for Cataloging and the Organization of Information: Pitfalls and the Pendulum* (ed: Janet Swan Hill) The Haworth Information Press, an imprint of The Haworth Press, Inc., 2002, pp. 299-310. Single or multiple copies of this article are available for a fee from The Haworth Document Delivery Service [1-800-HAWORTH, 9:00 a.m. - 5:00 p.m. (EST). E-mail address: getinfo@haworthpressinc.com].

I acquired Eeyore during the second semester in which I taught a Web-delivered course. During the first such semester, I had announced loudly to anyone nearby that I would teach via the World Wide Web again when donkeys sprouted wings and flew to the moon. I thought I needed something tangible to remind me of the irony of my former adamancy, so I found Eeyore at Toys "R" Us and asked my student assistant to devise a way for the donkey to have wings. She got the assignment in October 1998 and was able to find an angel costume meant for a pet dog, so we had the perfect halo and wings (see Figure 1).

The irony is compounded by the fact that as of Fall 2001 I am helping to create a new MLIS program in which 24 of the 40 required semester hours are expected to be Web delivered. I have gone from stark opposition to "distance education," particularly for cataloging, through a conviction that like it or not, it's here and must be made to work, to emerge as truly heartened by the possibilities that distance education offers for strengthening education for cataloging.

I will discuss the advantages and drawbacks of distance education for cataloging, argue that the possibilities outweigh the disadvantages,

FIGURE 1

summarize current educational research on distance education, and offer a list of elements that may help us to take full advantage of the possibilities.

DEFINITION AND CURRENT PRACTICE

In this article the phrase "distance education" will mean coursework in which the teacher is geographically separated from the students and in which that separation is mediated by technology. The most commonly used technologies at this writing (April 2002) are interactive television, also called interactive video, and the World Wide Web. Instruction via the World Wide Web can be done through freestanding Web pages or via Web-accessible information mounted within course delivery software packages such as WebCT or Blackboard.

The extent to which teacher and students are separated in time can vary greatly. Some interactive video courses require that students gather in a studio at the same time each week and be taught by a teacher in another location. In these situations, teacher and students can see and hear each other via screens and phone lines. Some Web delivered courses require that students sign on and interact with the teacher and other students via their desktop computers at simultaneous predetermined times, using such tools as chat software, audio software, or interactive white boards. In some courses, a limited amount of required face-to-face meeting time is combined with "anywhere anytime" Web-delivered content. In contrast, Web delivered courses can be entirely "asynchronous," with course content and assignments posted for the students to access at times of their choice. At the University of Southern Mississippi, the School of Library and Information describes three "modes of instruction" for distance education courses (see Table 1).[1]

A look at some of the cataloging courses offered as distance education in U.S. library schools during 2001/02 gives a glimpse of the diversity in course offerings. In the Fall of 2001, the University of Arizona offered "Knowledge Structures I"[2] in asynchronous online format. At the University of Oklahoma, students in Norman and Tulsa attended the same "Organization of Information" class via interactive video in Fall 2001.[3] At the University of South Carolina, students can take Indexing and Abstracting via interactive video in Spring 2002.[4] Florida State University's "Information Organization"[5] course is an example of one that requires weekly synchronous time at the student's personal computer, as do courses offered by the University of Tennessee.[6] "Cata-

TABLE 1. Modes of Instruction

There are three modes of instruction, two online, that have been designed to provide flexibility: Interactive Video Network (IVN), Online and Hybrid, as explained briefly below.

IVN	Hybrid	Online
• Requires regular class attendance at night • Students use video and audio telecommunications to interact with each other and the instructor • IVN Sites are located throughout the state of Mississippi	• Requires intermittent class attendance in Hattiesburg on Saturdays • Students use the Internet to communicate with each other and the instructor • Students must have their own ISP or access to a computer with Internet access and current Web browsers, and a working knowledge of computers	• NO regular class attendance • Students interact with the instructors and each other on course sites on the Internet • Students must have their own ISP or access to a computer with Internet access and current Web browsers, and a good working knowledge of computers • Students must be able to work independently

Source: *Modes* 2001.

loging and Classification II"[7] in the University of Illinois's LEEP program combines synchronous and asynchronous Internet instruction with one required on-campus session. A course in the "Web Institute" option at the University of North Texas combines an intensive four-day weekend on campus with online instruction for the rest of the semester.[8] Texas Woman's University[9] plans to offer courses in cataloging and in technical services through their LIFE program, which combines Web-based learning with three intermittent Saturday classes. The University of Arizona plans Knowledge Structures II[10] as a combination of online instruction and two on-campus meetings.

This snapshot indicates that distance education is actively being used to teach both beginning and advanced classes in cataloging and the organization of information and that a variety of delivery options are being employed. Most of these courses include a synchronous requirement, and about half of them include a limited amount of in-person class time.

Some Advantages of Distance Education

- *The same teacher can reach more students.* A teacher can reach students in disparate locations, making learning available in otherwise inaccessible places.

- *Education becomes possible for more students.* Many potential librarians will not undertake an MLS degree unless they can do so with minimal disruption to employment and family responsibilities. Distance education provides them with such an option.
- *Geographic stumbling blocks are minimized for students and teachers.*
- *Distance courses are popular with many students.* Though some of the students I taught at the University of South Florida preferred traditional courses, it was also true that Web-delivered courses typically were fully enrolled within a few days of registration and that additional sections of these courses were often added as a result of student demand.
- *Travel time and energy is saved for students and teachers.* This time and energy can be invested in course work.
- *Distance education can improve teaching.* As one colleague said, "Distance education made me a better teacher. It made me plan further ahead and integrate more technology into my classes. I had to be more organized and prepared for class sessions."
- *Learning over distance can be less passive for students.* A teacher who teaches both live and online classes remarked recently, "The students who take the online version learn more because they are required to interact with the material more closely." A student can "vegetate" in a live class and get away with it much more easily than in an online class. In an online discussion, student contributions are archived and can be evaluated for both participation and content.
- *"Visiting Experts" from other locations can be more easily utilized.*

Some Disadvantages

- *Distance education is not ideal for all students.* Some students are much better suited to distance learning than are others. As Threlkeld and Brzoska, explain, "Adults who are most likely to complete courses using distance technology have a cluster of important characteristics, such as tolerance for ambiguity, a need for autonomy, and an ability to be flexible. In contrast, those who are more likely to drop out tend to prefer a great deal of structure, face-to-face lectures, and the opportunity to interact with the instructor."[11]

- *Equipment needs and difficulties become factors.* The machines must be available, and they must work. For interactive video courses, students and teacher may be dependent on persons from outside the school for such services as unlocked doors and functioning equipment. To take an online course, a student needs access to a computer and must be or become relatively adept at using it.
- *Nonverbal communication is diminished or eliminated.* In a face-to-face interaction, such indicators as facial expression, body stance, and tone of voice do most of our communicating. In most e-mail or chat situations, these helpful attributes are missing. One teacher of online courses said, "I can't look into their eyes and see that they're not getting it." This reduced communication means that . . .
- *The teacher's ability to make instantaneous adjustments is diminished.* Most classroom teachers, particularly experienced ones, evaluate hundreds of verbal and nonverbal cues from students and respond by making spontaneous adjustments. This possibility is eliminated or lessened when students and teacher are not together.
- *Teaching over distance takes more time* than teaching a traditional class. Mechanisms for creating sustainable faculty workloads in the face of this reality have not yet solidified.

RESEARCH ON EFFECTIVENESS

Most of the research done to date on the effect of mode of delivery on teaching effectiveness has found either "no significant difference" or increased performance in distance students. Barbara Lockee summarized the conclusion of many educational researchers when she said,

> The delivery mode we know for a fact does not impact the learning. It's the design of the instruction that impacts the learning, and also what the students bring to the instructional situation. Instead of comparing, say, our online multimedia-authoring course to the face-to-face course, we would look to see that our distance learners are achieving our intended outcomes no matter how they're getting it.[12]

Thomas L. Russell's 1999 bibliography *The No Significant Difference Phenomenon*[13] reports on 355 pieces of research that support the contention that mode of delivery does not determine student learning. Russell's work is supported by a Web site that offers selected entries from the book and information about relevant studies identified after the book was published. Russell's collection includes a 1926 dissertation that compared a correspondence course to an in-person counterpart and numerous studies of non-interactive television teaching, interactive video, and online courses. These studies repeatedly show comparable results when comparing student achievement.

Russell's Web site titled "Significant Difference"[14] chronicles studies that do show a significant difference when comparing modes of course delivery. The number of studies listed here is much lower than in Russell's book and on the "No Significant Difference" site, perhaps because the "Significant Difference" site is described as "under construction."[15] The most striking fact about the "Significant difference" bibliography, however, is that usually when a difference was found, the students taught via distance education did better. Of twenty-three instances in which a significant difference in student achievement was found, distance education students outperformed their traditionally educated peers in twenty-two of them. A study by Nesler et al.[16] found that nursing students in a distance program outscored traditionally educated students in two measures of professional socialization and noted that internships and other experiences in the workplace were important factors in socialization. Six of the nine studies that found a significant difference in student satisfaction report that satisfaction was lower among the distance students.

Threlkeld and Brzoska, in their review of distance education research, concur that when media for teaching are compared, " . . . the most common outcome is 'no significant difference' between mediated and face-to-face instruction,"[17] but they also assert that differences among students deserve more attention in research studies. They point out that the strong advantages which distance education offers non-traditional students will probably make their satisfaction rates high in comparison with other types of students.[18] In regard to synchronous versus asynchronous interaction, their analysis shows little to no effect on student achievement, but does note that some students prefer to have a synchronous option, when even those same students took minimal advantage of the option. "There is little empirical evidence to support the current drive for live and interactive instruction, although this type of distance learning seems to be preferred by many students. What does seem to be very important is support for the distant learner. Students want and need rapid feedback from instructors as well as access to library resources and other supporting materials."[19]

DISCUSSION

Since my first experiences with distance teaching, I have been reluctant and have tended to express my reluctance in doubts that distance delivery can be effective. The preponderance of research that indicates otherwise has forced me to revise my thinking on this point. Part of the explanation for my discomfort may be in teachers' strong tendency to teach the way we were taught. Too, perhaps I'm falling prey to the usually mistaken notion that "the good old days" were very different and much better than today.

A main concern of mine is the possibility of teaching attitudes from a distance. I have always assumed that I help to dispel the myths about catalogers by being lively and reasonable in class and have been skeptical that such affective attributes can be communicated through a computer screen. However, a former online student reports that she was constantly aware of my "indomitable spirit" and another student reports that, "Oh yes, my friend had you as an online teacher, and he loved it. He talks about you all the time." These admirers are people I have never, to my conscious knowledge, even seen. At first I thought they must be hallucinating to imagine that they know me at all–is this how Brad Pitt sometimes feels, I wonder? On the other hand, who am I to be suspicious of this process, particularly when I have no personal experience as an online student? Perhaps my reluctance to believe that distance education can work has more to do with the fact that I want to teach the way I was taught than it has to do with reality.

When I teach a site-based class in the evening to people who have worked all day, then fought urban traffic to drive to class, it sometimes seems that the exhausted students are "distant," even though they are physically present. To channel their energy into coursework and thought rather than travel and frustration looks like a good idea in those moments.

The question of "how well this works" almost doesn't matter. However well it works or doesn't, it's here. The possibility that distance education offers for creating librarians who would not otherwise pursue the field and the attractiveness of the advantages to students insure that distance education will be used in LIS education for the foreseeable future. Cataloging is the intellectual foundation of librarianship, the work that makes all other activity within the profession possible. This body of knowledge must be transmitted to the next generation. The wise warrior conserves her energy for winnable battles. I want to focus my energy on making distance education for cataloging work as well as it can. If I cannot beat them, I will take them over in the service of my own goals. My main goal is to see our precious enterprise continue.

The studies that suggest lower student satisfaction in distance education classes point out the need to maximize aspects that may increase satisfaction. Timely communication from the instructor, assignments that encourage student-to-student interaction, and synchronous options all look like good ideas.

The study that showed successful socialization of distance nursing students is especially heartening for a professional specialization like ours. Socialization is an area that deserves careful attention from distance educators in library science. Nesler et al.'s 2001 conclusions that workplace experience and practica advance socialization invite the suggestion that we should encourage our distance students to get as much hands-on experience in libraries as possible. Tours, interviews with practitioners, volunteering, paraprofessional work, and internships for credit are approaches that can be considered. These experiences are particularly important for students who have little background in libraries and can be used to help those who have more extensive previous experience to broaden their perspectives. When possible, these experiential activities should have a curricular tie in order to increase student motivation. In other words, if the student gets academic credit or a grade for it, he or she is more likely to do it.

HOW TO DO IT WELL

The features below will help me to mine the advantages and ameliorate the drawbacks of distance course delivery. I include them here as a reminder to myself and as a list you might use as you seek to identify quality distance learning opportunities for your employees or yourself.

- *When students have a choice of modes of delivery, encourage them to evaluate their suitability as distance students.* One self-assessment tool is "Are distance learning courses for me?"[20]
- *Include an interview assignment.* In my classes, both live and distance, students have an assignment in which they must meet a live technical services librarian. The assignment includes interview questions and suggested language to be used in the initial phone call. Such an assignment can be carried out wherever the student lives and has the added advantage of strengthening the student's place in the local library "scene."

- *Encourage student involvement in professional organizations, conferences, and workshops.* Require it as a curricular assignment if practical.
- *Share my own experiences.* Make succinct "personal stories" part of the class lectures, whether in person or on screen.
- *Use "visiting experts."*
- *Use pictures and sound when possible.*
- *Be responsive to students' needs to communicate.*

  - Respond to student questions promptly.
  - Hold online office hours.
  - Consider using the phone. A colleague was a great help to one of her distance students when she responded to an anguished e-mail by phoning the student at home immediately.

- *Encourage student-to-student networking.*

  - Provide a chat room in online courses.
  - Use discussion questions.
  - Look for ways to incorporate collaborative projects.

- *Acquaint students with the wider world of cataloging.* Assign exploration of such resources as the PCC Web pages and the AutoCat archives.

CONCLUSION

As I finish writing this article in the Spring of 2002, I am teaching a basic cataloging course in online, asynchronous format at Valdosta State University.[21] To my surprise, I have enjoyed it so far. I am grateful that I enjoy writing, because a large part of my time has been spent creating verbal explanations to supplement the texts. The use of internal links offers intriguing possibilities for designing explanations of technical details. The amount of time required to prepare and teach the course is a concern, but I am hopeful that I will learn time-saving techniques as I gain more experience. The University of Southern Mississippi plans to teach cataloging totally online in the Fall of 2002.[22,23]

For those who want to learn more about distance education, the works of Barry Willis are particularly recommended. His Web-accessible "Distance education at a glance"[24] is a good beginning point. Christine Jenkins' "The LEEP experience: An instructor's perspective"[25] provides an online window into life as a teacher or a student in a distance-education program. A useful way to see what various schools are offering is to monitor their Web pages, which can be efficiently located via the Directory maintained by the ALA Office for Accreditation.[26]

Distance education for cataloging can work as well or better than traditional teaching. The new technologies offer strong advantages in our quest to extend the reach of library education in general and cataloging education in particular. We have been offered a valuable tool for educating the next generation, and we have a professional obligation to take full advantage of this potential.

ENDNOTES

1. "Modes of Instruction." University of Southern Mississippi School of Library and Information Science [*http://www-dept.usm.edu/~slis/SLISonline.htm#modes*]. Accessed 25 March 2002.

2. Anita Sundaram Coleman. "Knowledge Structures I." University of Arizona School of Information Resources & Library Science [*http://www.u.arizona.edu/~asc/kshome.html*]. Accessed 25 March 2002.

3. Danny P. Wallace. "LIS 5043: Organization of Information." University of Oklahoma School of Library and Information Studies [*http://facultystaff.ou.edu/W/Danny.P.Wallace-1/5043fall2001.htm*].

4. "SPRING, 2002 Class Schedule." University of South Carolina College of Library and Information Science [*http://www.libsci.sc.edu/Schedule/spring2002.htm*]. Accessed 25 March 2002.

5. Marcella Genz. "LIS 5703: Information Organization." Florida State University School of Information Studies [*http://slis-one.lis.fsu.edu/courses/Fall2001/common/infoView/index.cfm?cID=fa01_5703*]. Accessed 25 March 2002.

6. "2002 Online (Distance Education) Spring Schedule." University of Tennessee School of Information Sciences [*http://www.sis.utk.edu/spring02ol.htm*]. Accessed 25 March 2002.

7. Ellen Crosby. "LIS 408 LE Cataloging and Classification II." University of Illinois at Urbana-Champaign Graduate School of Library and Information Science [*http://leep.lis.uiuc.edu/spring02/LIS408LE/index.html*]. Accessed 25 March 2002.

8. William E Moen. "Introduction to Information Organization: SLIS 5200." University of North Texas School of Library and Information Sciences [*http://courses.unt.edu/SLIS5200Resources/Spring2002/Welcome/WebInstituteIfoPageSp2002.htm*]. Accessed 25 March 2002.

9. "LIFE: Learning in Flexible Environments Program." Texas Woman's University School of Library and Information Studies [*http://www.libraryschool.net/programs/lifeprog.htm*]. Accessed 25 March 2002.

10. Anita Sundaram Coleman. "Knowledge Structures II." University of Arizona School of Information Resources & Library Science [*http://www.u.arizona.edu/~asc/ks2index.html*]. Accessed 25 March 2002.

11. Robert Threlkeld and Karen Brzoska. Research in distance education. In Barry Willis (Ed.), *Distance Education: Strategies and Tools.* Englewood Cliffs, NJ: Educational Technology Publications, 1994: 54.

12. Barbara B. Lockee. "What Matters in Judging Distance Teaching? Not How Much It's Like a Classroom Course." Interview by Dan Carnevale. *Chronicle Daily News*, 21 February 2001 [*http://chronicle.com/free/2001/02/2001022101u.htm*]. Accessed 26 March 2002.

13. Thomas L. Russell. "The No Significant Difference Phenomenon: As Reported in 355 Research Reports, Summaries and Papers." North Carolina: North Carolina State University, 1999.

14. Thomas L. Russell. "Significant difference." TeleEducation New Brunswick [*http://teleeducation.nb.ca/significantdifference/*]. Accessed 16 April 2002.

15. Russell. "The No Significant Difference Phenomenon." TeleEducation New Brunswick [*http://teleeducation.nb.ca/significantdifference/index.cfm*]. Accessed 16 April 2002, par. 2.

16. M. S. Nesler, M. B. Hanner, V. Melburg, and S. McGowan. "Professional Socialization of Baccalaureate Nursing Students: Can Students in Distance Nursing Programs Become Socialized?" *Journal of Nursing Education* 40 (7): 293-302.

17. Threlkeld and Brzoska. Research in distance education. p. 50-51.

18. Threlkeld and Brzoska. Research in distance education. p. 42.

19. Threlkeld and Brzoska. Research in distance education. p. 62.

20. "Are Distance-Learning Courses for Me?" College of DuPage Center for Independent Learning [*http://www.cod.edu/dept/CIL/CIL_Surv.htm*]. Accessed 25 March 2002.

21. Elaine Yontz,. "MLIS 7300: Cataloging and Classification." Valdosta State University Master of Library and Information Science Program [*http://books.valdosta.edu/mlis/liscat.html*]. Accessed 25 March 2002.

22. Dorothy Elizabeth Haynes. E-mail to author, 13 December, 2001.

23. "Tentative Schedule of LIS Courses available via Distance Learning: Summer 2002, Fall 2002, Spring 2003." n.d. University of Southern Mississippi School of Library and Information Science [*http://wwwdept.usm.edu/~slis/DistanceLearning 2002_03.htm*]. Accessed 25 March 2002.

24. Barry Willis. "Distance Education at a Glance." University of Idaho Engineering Outreach [*http://www.uidaho.edu/evo/distglan.html*]. Accessed 26 March 2002; Barry Willis, ed. *Distance Education: Strategies and Tools.* (Englewood Cliffs, NJ: Educational Technology Publications 1994); Barry Willis. *Distance Education: A Practical Guide.* (Englewood Cliffs, N. J., Educational Technology Publications, 1993); Barry Willis. *Effective Distance Education: A Primer for Faculty and Administrators.* (Fairbanks: University of Alaska, 1992).

25. Christine Jenkins. "The LEEP Experience: An Instructor's Perspective." University of Illinois at Urbana-Champaign Graduate School of Library and Information Science [*http://leep.lis.uiuc.edu/demos/jenkins/*]. Accessed 26 March 2002.

26. "Directory of Accredited LIS Master's Programs." American Library Association Office for Accreditation [*http://www.ala.org/alaorg/oa/lisdir.html*]. Accessed 26 March 2002.

An Evaluation of the Effectiveness of OCLC Online Computer Library Center's Web-Based Module on Cataloging Internet Resources Using the Anglo-American Cataloging Rules and MARC21

Robert Ellett

SUMMARY. In January 2001, the OCLC Institute released its first online learning course, *Cataloging Internet Resources Using MARC21 and AACR2.* This research investigated whether participants using this Web-based tool would gain experience equivalent to that of librarians who are already proficient in the skill of cataloging Internet resources. A pre-course/post-course comparison of test results of librarians not experienced with cataloging Internet resources indicated an increase of 35 percent (from 51 to 86 percent) of the correct answers after taking the Web-based course. The group experienced with cataloging Internet resources answered an average of 71 percent of the questions correctly. *[Article copies available for a fee from The Haworth Document Delivery Service: 1-800-HAWORTH. E-mail address: <getinfo@haworthpressinc.com> Website: <http://www.Haworth Press.com> © 2002 by The Haworth Press, Inc. All rights reserved.]*

Robert Ellett is Catalog Librarian, Joint Forces Staff College, Norfolk, VA. He is also a doctoral candidate at Nova Southeastern University's Graduate School of Computer and Information Sciences.

The author wishes to thank Steven D. Zink, PhD, for reading an earlier draft of this article and suggesting improvements.

[Haworth co-indexing entry note]: "An Evaluation of the Effectiveness of OCLC Online Computer Library Center's Web-Based Module on Cataloging Internet Resources Using the Anglo-American Cataloging Rules and MARC21." Ellett, Robert. Co-published simultaneously in *Cataloging & Classification Quarterly* (The Haworth Information Press, an imprint of The Haworth Press, Inc.) Vol. 34, No. 3, 2002, pp. 311-338; and: *Education for Cataloging and the Organization of Information: Pitfalls and the Pendulum* (ed: Janet Swan Hill) The Haworth Information Press, an imprint of The Haworth Press, Inc., 2002, pp. 311-338. Single or multiple copies of this article are available for a fee from The Haworth Document Delivery Service [1-800-HAWORTH, 9:00 a.m. - 5:00 p.m. (EST). E-mail address: getinfo@haworthpressinc.com].

KEYWORDS. Web-based training, cataloging Internet resources, OCLC Institute, distance education

Although librarians use many Internet-based databases as research tools, the concept of using Web-based technology for a library training instrument is a relatively new idea. Beagle surveyed the literature and discovered only a small number of articles dealing with the use of Web-based training tools in libraries.[1] The OCLC Online Computer Library Center (henceforth referred to as OCLC) is a well-known non-profit organization providing systems that connect libraries worldwide. The OCLC Institute released its first Web-based training product, *Cataloging Internet resources using MARC21 and AACR2* in January 2001. Throughout this study, the term "Internet resources" is used to describe any electronic information resources accessible through a wide-area network. This OCLC initiative is an important step in introducing librarians to two new frontiers: Web-based training environments and the cataloging of Internet resources.

The OCLC product is designed for librarians, paraprofessionals, and library school students who catalog or plan to catalog Internet resources according to the principles of the *Anglo-American Cataloging Rules, 2nd ed. rev.* and MARC21. The Web-based course has no admission requirements or prerequisites other than a basic knowledge of monographic cataloging rules. Its content and instructional design were developed jointly by OCLC-affiliated and network trainers at SOLINET, Amigos, and NELINET (which are regional networks affiliated with OCLC), OCLC trainers and staff, along with Steve Miller, head of the Monographs Dept. at the University of Wisconsin-Milwaukee. The Web-based course contains 28 interactive lessons that provide immediate feedback. System requirements for using the Web-based tutorial are Internet connectivity with browser capabilities of Internet Explorer at 5.0 or higher. Netscape Navigator was tested but evidenced problems with handling Java script. The tutorial is accessible 24 hours a day, seven days a week. Both OCLC members and non-members can purchase the tutorial.

The question that remains unanswered is whether this Web-based tutorial will meet its objectives of teaching the user to catalog Internet resources. No studies have been conducted to test its effectiveness. The central research question here is whether participants using this tool will gain knowledge equivalent to that of librarians already proficient in the skill of cataloging Internet resources. A secondary question is whether librarians not previously exposed to cataloging of Internet resource training perform better after completing the Web-based course.

BRIEF LITERATURE REVIEW

This study involves two relatively new phenomena–Web-based instruction and tutorials and the cataloging of Internet resources. Both of these issues have been debated in the literature and a proper review of these topics will form a basis for the current study.

Web-Based Training

Web-based training (WBT) has proliferated in today's educational environments. WBT in the United States generated over $197 million in revenue in 1997. Predictions call for the figure to exceed six billion dollars by 2002.[2] The 1999 Computer Based Training (CBT) Report published by Inside Technology Training reported that 54 percent of respondents to a study of chief executive officers of major U.S. companies indicated that their companies deliver training or facilitate learning via the World Wide Web.[3] Virtually every major university and college now offers some Web-based courses. Barley[4] accounts for this trend in increased Web-based instruction by discussing the growing need for professional post-graduate education in today's digital world. The workplace has changed to a knowledge-based structure. In fact, according to John Chambers, the CEO of Cisco Systems, "The next big killer application for the Internet is going to be education. Education over the Internet is going to be so big it is going to make e-mail usage look like a rounding error."[5]

Likewise, the World Wide Web (WWW) is revolutionizing activities in libraries, which now commonly deliver bibliographic instruction in the form of Web-based tutorials. WBT offers many advantages over more traditional methods of instructional delivery. It reduces travel costs associated with workshops and conferences, as institutions have no need to pay for airline tickets, hotel rooms, rental cars, and meals for employees who attend these training programs. Driscoll[6] cites average cost savings of $1,500 per employee per year by using WBT. Driscoll also observes that conferences and workshops requiring travel time also impose opportunity costs, revenues that are lost as a result of the employee being out of the office. Consequently, in businesses, profits suffer as sales figures are reduced. In libraries, however, a different opportunity cost is more common. The employee is not in the office to perform his or her function so other employees must either step in and assist or the workload will become backlogged.

Another advantage of reducing travel is that many employees, especially those with families, prefer not to travel. They are happier employees when they are not required to leave their families to benefit from training opportunities. Hall's[7] research indicates that the actual time required as measured by computer averages about 50 percent that of instructor-led programs.

Another benefit to employers choosing WBT methods is the consistency of instructional delivery. Often speakers in a traditional classroom may present different versions of the same lectures. With WBT, employers can be assured that their staff members receive exactly the same instruction and information.[8] WBT, unlike training produced on a CD-ROM, is easily updated if changes are required. Changes can be made on the server which stores the program and everyone, even worldwide users, can access the update.[9] In today's economy, many organizations have experienced downsizing or adopted flatter management structures. Libraries have often suffered economic shortfalls and budget cuts. In these organizations, outside travel may be almost unavailable because the employees not traveling must often do the work of those dismissed or not replaced for a variety of reasons.

A chief advantage of WBT over CBT is that the former can be accessed by a variety of different operating systems including Windows, Macintosh, or Unix environments without requiring additional software. The program is authored once and can be delivered over the Internet or even the company intranet. Users can proceed through a training program both at their own pace and as Hall[10] indicates "at their own place." The training program can be accessed at the time of need and only as much as needed, a situation referred to as "just in time and just enough training."

The Effectiveness of Web-Based Training

Although distance education in the form of WBT has revolutionized the field of education, the question of whether WBT techniques are as effective as traditional classroom or face-to-face instruction still remains. Although the answer may at first seem quite obvious, ironically few studies have been conducted that investigate the issue. Some educational researchers deem such a comparison of traditional classroom instruction versus WBT almost impossible because of methodological flaws. For example, if one instructor creates or moderates a Web-based course and another instructor teaches in a traditional classroom setting, it would be difficult to determine whether outcome differences were due to the different instructors or to the use of the technology medium, even if the same instructor taught both groups. There is often a bias as the instructor has invested additional time and effort in creating the technology medium used in the Web-based course. Hall, Watkins, and Ercal[11] mention another problem in studies of WBT. It is often impossible to assign students to Web-based classes randomly, unlike physical classroom courses, as both pragmatic reasons and self-selection biases frequently occur.

Nevertheless, several arguments favor additional Web-based instructional effectiveness studies. Evaluation is needed on WBT given its current popularity and growth as mentioned above. The studies cited below are mentioned here because they are well-known within the educational community and comprehensive in their approaches.

WBT Effectiveness Studies

Schutte (1998):[12] In the fall 1996 semester, 33 students in the social statistics course at California State University-Northridge were randomly divided into two groups. One group was taught in the traditional classroom setting, while the other group was taught via the World Wide Web. The same instructor taught and monitored both groups. Each group was given the same assignments, mid-term examinations, and final examinations. The Web-based group did meet in the traditional classroom setting for the mid-term and final examinations. Results indicate that the virtual students scored an average of 20 points higher on the mid-term and final examinations. These differences are highly statistically significant. The results also indicated that the virtual students communicated more with fellow students. The virtual students also indicated that they had more flexibility and a greater understanding of the material. Thus, the data indicated that virtual interaction produced better results. Schutte notes that since the virtual students were unable to ask questions of the instructor in a face-to-face environment, they communicated more with their fellow virtual students. Schutte hypothesizes that this collaboration manifested its effect in better test scores.

Jones (1999):[13] The purpose of Jones's study was to replicate the Schutte 1998 study. The participants were 89 students enrolled in two sections of an introductory statistics course at Texas A&M University (Corpus Christi campus). One class was again taught in the traditional classroom setting, while the other was taught via the World Wide Web. Unlike Shutte's 1998 study, in Jones's study, students were not randomly divided between the classes. Instead, students registered for their chosen class during registration. The same instructor taught the classes with the same course content, assignments, and examinations. Jones's results indicated that the students who enrolled in the Web-based course were "somewhat more mature students." The Web-based class members were statistically significantly older than the students in the traditional classroom. Jones reported that the Web-based group's test scores on the final examination averaged six points higher than those of the traditional classroom group.

Kiser and Toreki (1997):[14] In the fall 1996 semester, Kiser and Toreki used TopClass, a software program designed to manage the delivery and support of training over the Internet. TopClass delivers information and quizzes via the World Wide Web. Its features include email, discussion lists, Web delivery of course information, and quizzes. The program was used by 128 students enrolled in an introductory chemistry class. Participation with the Web-based TopClass software was strictly voluntary. Not only were students' comments about TopClass positive, but also results from this study showed very strong correlation between use of TopClass optional quizzes and overall performance in the course. The extra effort and studying by the students who used TopClass increased their level of achievement in the course.

White (1999):[15] White divided a group of 40 students, enrolled in a communications technology class, into a volunteer Internet section (16 students) and a traditional classroom setting (24 students). All of the students in the Web-based section were required to subscribe to a class listserv on which written lectures were available to them. The lecture notes included images and graphics as well as links to other Internet sites for further reading. Students in both sections took the examinations in the same classroom at the same time. White concluded that Web-based instruction was as effective as classroom instruction as far as the graded assignments in the course were concerned. The two groups did not significantly differ on scores from the midterm and final examinations.

Wideman and Owston (1999):[16] Wideman and Owston's study constitutes one of the largest and most comprehensive comparisons of Web-based versus traditional instruction. The study included 1,099 students in Web-based courses, 2,467 students in correspondence courses, and 2,003 students in traditional classroom courses. These researchers compared student performance in the three instructional modes

(Internet-based, correspondence, and traditional classroom instruction) at Atkinson College during the spring 1998 semester. Student grades from Internet-based courses held between the fall 1996 semester and the fall 1998 semester were compared to grades for the same courses offered in both correspondence and traditional classroom settings. Statistical analysis revealed that there were in fact significant differences among performances within the three instructional modes. An analysis of the data from this study indicated that students in the correspondence courses scored significantly lower than those in the other two modalities. Internet-based instruction and traditional classroom instruction did not significantly differ. However, when only final examination scores were considered, the students taking Internet-based courses performed significantly better than both the correspondence students and the students in the traditional classroom courses. Wideman and Owston did note a statistically significant drop-out rate in the Internet-based courses compared to the other two modalities. The students in this study were randomly assigned to the various instructional modalities. There may be various student characteristics that would influence student grades. For example, those deemed capable may have been motivated students who were more likely to have a computer and to be more knowledgeable about its use. The students may have been more willing to try a new format of course delivery. The students' motivation or computer competence could have influenced the results.

It can be concluded from these Web-based course effectiveness comparative studies that learner variables play an important role in the selection of and performance in Web-based courses. Often the students who select Web-based courses have more computer competence, are more mature or older, and have better academic records in the form of higher grade point averages. The most significant factor to influence student satisfaction with Web-based courses was the level of structured collaboration and active learning occurring within the course.

CATALOGING OF INTERNET RESOURCES

In the library world, the Internet has brought both great excitement and grave concern over the future of the library as an entity. Within the library community of catalogers, there is a debate over whether Internet resources should be cataloged and put into local online public access catalogs.

To Catalog or Not to Catalog Internet Resources

Many librarians cite Internet resource characteristics such as poor organization, lack of stability, and variable quality that make those resources poor candidates for inclusion in online catalogs. The issues of why Internet resources should be cataloged, how they should be cataloged and even who should catalog them have inspired debates within the library literature for several years. Baruth has even challenged the notion that Internet resources belong in online catalogs as resources for library users.[17] Baruth contends that the online public access catalog or OPAC is not the ideal place to store or organize Internet resources. One of the first questions tackled is the ability to keep the catalog current amidst ever-changing Web sites. Ellett responds to this argument by pointing out that librarians, specifically catalogers, have always had a backlog of catalog maintenance problems. In the days of the card catalog, the situation was even worse. Lost and discarded items, title changes, and other maintenance duties are all part of the cataloging department's work. The argument not to include Internet resources in the online catalog because they change or "die" is flawed because print resources change too.[18]

Many authors (Baruth;[19] Banerjee;[20] Dillon and Jul[21]) note the instability of Internet resources as a factor contributing to cataloging difficulty. Internet resources are sometimes described as "moving targets."[22] Banerjee discusses several reasons why Internet resources are difficult to describe. One is that print resources can be examined as a whole because they were intended to be used in a linear fashion. On the other hand, Internet resources, in hypertext environments, allow users to read documents in a sequence best suited to their needs. Another is that it is often difficult to identify what is being cataloged. Relationships between the files often depend on how the user reads the electronic document.[23]

Banerjee also indicates that many users prefer the full-text indexing provided by search engines.[24] Johns poses a similar question and asks whether including Internet resources in the online catalog is redundant given the multitude of Internet search engines. This argument is quickly countered by evidence of what search engines actually do index.[25] Kassel delves into the issue of whether search engines that claim to index all Internet information in fact do. Kassel's analysis of the HotBot search engine suggests that often search engines index only about one-half of the documents available on the Internet. In April 1998, it was reported that there were about 320 million Web pages on the

Internet. Kassel found that only 200 million pages were actually searchable.[26] Thus, it is a myth to assume that Internet search engines index the entire World Wide Web. Commercial databases index some of the Web, but often their services are not available without a fee.

"Cataloging the Internet" has sometimes been interpreted as cataloging every resource or Web page resident on the Internet. It is widely agreed, however, that no attempt should be made to catalog all the resources available on the Internet.[27] That feat would be akin to trying to purchase all the materials listed in *Books in Print*. The goal of teaching librarians to catalog Internet resources is not so that they will duplicate Internet search engines. On the contrary, collection development of Internet resources is an important facet of librarianship that has been well noted by other authors, including Ellett,[28] Weber,[29] Jul[30] and Gerhard.[31]

Dillon and Jul discuss the concept of ownership versus access. The introduction of Internet resources into a library catalog begins to change the fundamental definition of library access. Library collections have now expanded to include both materials libraries own and those they can access. Collections also include items physically stored in the library and those available remotely for use.[32]

Gerhard describes several advantages to including Internet resources in library online catalogs. The first and foremost reason given is that library users are increasingly becoming Web-savvy searchers who now expect the library to provide the same types of material found by search engines. Gerhard, however, points out that these search engines are limited, often having difficulty locating and retrieving a specific known item Web site. The research quality of search engine results has also been questioned. Gerhard also presents another very interesting issue in the cataloging and inclusion of Internet resources in the local catalog: territoriality. The decision to include Internet resources in the online catalog must involve not only the cataloging department but also other areas such as reference, collection development and acquisitions.[33] Ellett presents a strategy involving several library departments and their roles in increasing the inclusion of Internet resources in the library collection.[34] Lam discusses the issue of why Internet resources should be cataloged but also the issues of what to select for cataloging and how to catalog it, which are problems in the library cataloging environment.[35]

Another issue in this debate is whether current cataloging tools such as the machine-readable cataloging (MARC) format and the *Anglo-American Cataloging Rules, 2nd ed, rev. (AACR2R)* should be used to catalog Internet resources. Taylor discusses five problem areas in the cataloging of Internet resources. One problematic question is whether a particular Internet resource is a monograph or a serial. Internet sites often change, so are they all to be considered as serials? That issue can be resolved with the inclusion of "static" and "dynamic" destinations in cataloging records. Defining the most stable source for the title also may be difficult, although *AACR2R* clearly states that catalogers should use the title screen as the chief source. The question of whether the Internet resource is a new edition is also an issue.[36] Olson states that if there is any change in intellectual content, in programming language, or operating system, the item is a new edition. Typically, only words or phases such as "edition," "update number," "revision," etc., constitute the call for an edition statement. Whether the terms "last revised <date>" or "updated <date>" indicate the presence of a new edition is still a matter for debate. Arguments over whether all Internet resources are published and require publication data (place of publication, publication date) are still prevalent.[37] Finally, Taylor questions the rule of "3" in *AACR2R* which states that if more than three personal authors or corporate bodies are intellectually responsible for the work, then the main entry for the work is to be under title, and an added entry is made for the first named personal or corporate author.[38] Taylor fails to mention that catalogers can and should use judgement in creating additional access points as long as such exercise of judgment does not erode the consistency produced by the use of the cataloging code (*AACR2R*, Rule 0.9).

Nevertheless, many librarians who believe that Internet resources do belong as a format in online catalogs must deal with other issues. Although it has already been argued that library users benefit from the addition of Internet resources in online catalogs, that inclusion does not come without costs. Libraries that choose to catalog Internet resources may need to divert staff resources from other projects thus creating opportunity costs. Cataloging Internet resources does not, however, incur any physical processing costs because of the very nature of the format.[39]

One of the most compelling arguments for cataloging Internet resources is that many paper resources are now available only as digital documents on the Internet. Not only is it often easier to publish documents on the Internet, it is usually less expensive. The cost incentive seems to drive many publishers and agencies to publish solely on the Internet because paper prices have skyrocketed. A recent illustration of why it is critical to begin cataloging Internet resources is the Government Printing Office (GPO), whose Federal Depository Library Program (FDLP) found in a 1996 study that permanent public access to its documents was needed to ensure that the information was permanently and continually available to the public. The GPO has, in recent years, increased the number of titles it disseminates electronically. For instance, in fiscal 1999, 46 percent of new titles, and in FY2000, over one half of the titles were disseminated only in electronic format. In May 2000, the House Appropriations Committee passed H.R. 4516 that cut the GPO FY2001 budget by 11 percent as more titles are being planned for electronic distribution only.[40] The cataloging of these Internet resources will, in essence, replace the cataloging of the printed documents that will no longer be published in that form.

Cataloging Internet Resources Studies

Dillon and Jul describe several cataloging projects undertaken by OCLC as a means to apply cataloging methods to Internet resources and relate their experience.[41] An OCLC Office of Research study during 1991-92 had attempted to resolve the issue of whether to catalog such resources. Results from the 1991-92 OCLC Internet Resources Project indicated that catalogers had some difficulty in determining basic bibliographic information from a collection of test files. Their difficulties were attributed to a lack of experiences in cataloging computer files and serials, a failure to adhere to the experiment's guidelines, and technical problems. Recommendations from that study were favorable to the cataloging of Internet resources. The creation of machine-readable cataloging records (MARC) for remotely accessible electronic data was encouraged. This early study also suggested monitoring the use and effectiveness of records created for providing descriptive information and access. The project concluded that with only a few modifications USMARC computer file format and *AACR2* Chapter 9 could be used to catalog Internet resources.[42] It was also recognized that the current cataloging code, *Anglo-American Cataloging Rules*, 2nd ed., would need further expansion to reflect the characteristics of this new format.

The necessity to link bibliographic records directly with remote resources was also recognized at this early stage. In response to that finding, OCLC and the Library of Congress (LC) jointly sponsored a proposal to create a new MARC field 856, "Electronic Location and Access." The 856 field now accommodates the explicit encoding of additional electronic location and access information.

The OCLC Intercat Project, which ended March 31, 1996, concluded that standard cataloging practices could be applied to Internet resources and that the implementation of the 856 field was a very important step in relating the Internet resource to its bibliographic description in the library online catalog.

Numerous studies have been conducted to investigate the feasibility of cataloging Internet resources using the traditional cataloging tools of *AACR2* and MARC. Neumeister found that it was difficult to determine whether the Internet resource would be considered as a monograph or a serial. In the study at the University of Buffalo libraries, the question of cataloging entire Web sites or just individual pages was raised. Even determining what data elements should be recorded as the title of the resource was an issue here. Neumeister indicated that further education and workshop training was needed to discuss these concerns. Collaborative procedures and examples were subsequently published.[43]

Thus it can be seen that both the areas of Web-based training and cataloging Internet resources for inclusion in library OPACs present new challenges and spark new debates that can be resolved only by further study and analysis.

PROJECT DESIGN AND IMPLEMENTATION

To measure the tool's effectiveness, the OCLC Institute, along with its development partners, commissioned the present research study, which was designed to include professional librarians (holders of Master of Library Science degrees) who are current OCLC cataloging members. The research design of this study called for posting calls for participation from the following cataloging electronic lists:

1. AUTOCAT (Cataloging and Authorities Listserv)–3,302 members as of February 1, 2001
2. INTERCAT (Listserv of catalogers of Internet resources)–1,907 members as of February 1, 2001
3. CORC-L (Listserv of Cooperative Online Resource Catalog participants)–1,078 members as of February 1, 2001
4. MILCAT-L (Electronic list of 22 catalogers moderated by the author in military institutions)–22 members as of February 1, 2001

The call requested participants from two groups. The first included librarians who use OCLC for cataloging services but had not cataloged Internet resources. This group is henceforth referred to as the inexperienced group. These participants had to have had familiarity with the use of Anglo-American Cataloging Rules (*AACR2*) and Machine-Readable

Cataloging (MARC21). Participants in that group were asked to use the Web-based tutorial that takes approximately 16 hours to complete. Participants were given free access to this Web-based tutorial and asked to complete the program of study between February 15, 2001 and April 15, 2001. Before being given access to the Web-based product, participants were asked to take a pretest developed by the author that sought to measure comprehension of the concepts found in the Web-based course. The pretest was returned by February 15, 2001. After participants completed their review of the Web-based course (after April 15, 2001), they were given a posttest (also developed by the author) to measure the effectiveness of the Web-based course as a learning tool.

The call for participants also requested librarians who had experience in cataloging Internet resources. That group, henceforth referred to as the experienced group, consisted of librarians who are OCLC cataloging members familiar with *AACR2R* and MARC. Each attended a workshop or course dealing with the cataloging of Internet resources. Those participants acted as the control group and were not given access to the Web-based course. The experienced group took the same posttest instrument, which was administered between April 1 and 15, 2001.

The Web-based course uses software produced by Click2Learn, Inc. and contains multiple choice practice questions and tests to monitor comprehension within each lesson. The pretest and posttest did not contain multiple-choice questions. Instead, the pretest instrument consisted of four Internet resource screen captures and a list of short-answer questions designed to test knowledge and comprehension better than multiple-choice questions in which the answers are frequently guessed. The posttest included six Internet resource examples. The pretest and posttest also contained a section in which the participants were asked to indicate errors found in various MARC sample entries concerning Internet resources.

Data analysis was performed on the pretest and posttest of the inexperienced group participants and comparisons were made between the posttest of the inexperienced group participants and the test results of the experienced group.

Before the pretest and posttest, Jay Weitz, OCLC Senior Database Consultant, volunteered to review the instruments created by the researcher to provided suggested answers. He had originally reviewed the Web-based cataloging course for cataloging content accuracy. His participation was designed to help prevent researcher bias by ensuring that the researcher would not be providing responses to the questions in the study instruments that he created.

Testing Environment

The inexperienced group received the pretest instrument by February 10, 2001 and returned it with answers to the researcher by February 15, 2001. As soon as the researcher received the completed pretest from the inexperienced group, the authorization number and password for the course were sent in an email message. As the participants emailed the completed pretests, posttests, and tests, the name of each participant was recorded and the participant's test given a number. The name of the participant was removed from the answer sheet and replaced with a number to ensure impartiality of grading results by the researcher. All of the pretests, posttests, and tests were evaluated with the answers provided by Jay Weitz. When answers differed significantly from Weitz's, the researcher contacted Weitz for validation that a particular answer was permissible according to the rules of *AACR2* or MARC21. The pretest consisted of several short-answer questions, totaling 100 points. The posttest also consisted of several short-answer questions, totaling 115 points.

The inexperienced group participants were given approximately two months to complete the Web-based course. They were instructed not to review the pretest materials. The posttests were given as the inexperienced group participants emailed the researcher and reported that they had completed the course. All of the inexperienced group participants completed the posttest between April 10 and 20, 2001. The participants were asked to take no more than three days to complete the posttest and not to use the Web-based course itself, any cataloging tools, any materials (including notes) taken from the course, or any other source of help such as a colleague for assistance. All but one of the participants in the inexperienced group completed the posttest within a three-day period. One participant completed the posttest in five days.

PROJECT OUTCOMES AND RESULTS

Participant Demographics

During the period of February 1-10, 2001, 111 librarians volunteered to be inexperienced group participants. Less than 12 percent (13 participants) of the applicants for the inexperienced group were accepted. Those not selected had already attended a workshop or course on cataloging Internet resources, had experience in cataloging Internet resources, or worked at an institution that was a Cooperative Online Resource Catalog (CORC) participant. CORC is OCLC's newest Web-based catalog containing bibliographic records of Internet resources.

The inexperienced group population included those with cataloging experience ranging from two to 20 years with an average of 7.8 years experience. Eleven (85 percent) of the 13 participants had experience with cataloging formats other than books. The type of library or institution in which the inexperienced group participants were employed also varied. Participants worked in academic libraries (eight participants or 62 percent), public libraries (four participants or 31 percent), and a special library (one participant or 7 percent).

All 13 applicants for the experienced group were selected. The experienced participants' cataloging experience ranged from two to 23 years with 8.5 being the average. Eleven (85 percent) of the experienced group were CORC participants. Nine (69 percent) had taken courses or attended workshops on the cataloging of Internet resources. Most worked in academic libraries (11 or 85 percent). One (7.5 percent) worked in a public library as a cataloger and one (7.5 percent) worked in a special library. The experienced group was not given access to the OCLC Web-based course on cataloging Internet resources. They took the same posttest instrument given to inexperienced group participants. The experienced group participants completed the test instrument from April 1-20, 2001. Most of the experienced group participants (11 or 85 percent) completed it within three days. All agreed not to seek any assistance from information sources such as cataloging tools or manuals, Web sites, or discussions with colleagues.

Organization of the Course

The Web-based course itself is divided into three main parts. The first part of the course is designed to introduce the student to the online course and discusses system requirements of the equipment needed. It also lists the various online desktop learning aids such as Internet resources recommended as supplementary material for the course. Finally, this part of the course recommends various navigational tips such as opening computer windows and maximizing and minimizing other screens. This part did not contain any practice exercises or test exercise, but was given purely as informational instruction. The first section did not deal with the subject content of the course. Figure 1 displays an outline of the course components.

FIGURE 1. Outline of Web-Based Cataloging Course Curriculum

Part 1		Getting Started
Part 2		Guided Tour through Two MARC Records
Part 3		Interactive Lessons
	Section 1	MARC Leader and Control Fields
	Section 2	Title and Statement of Responsibility
	Section 3	Edition Statement
	Section 4	Computer File Characteristics
	Section 5	Issue Designation for Serials (forthcoming in next release)
	Section 6	Place, Publisher, and Dates of Publication
	Section 7	Series Statement
	Section 8	(Bibliographic) Notes
	Section 9	Electronic Location and Access (MARC Field 856)
	Section 10	Main and Added Entries
	Section 11	Headings and Classification

Analysis of Aggregate Test Results

Concerning the pretest, the participants in the inexperienced group answered 51 percent of the questions correctly. The highest individual score on the pretest was 67 percent, the lowest was 32 percent. In the ten sections of Part 3 of the course, the lowest aggregate score was 17 percent on Section 4–the Edition Statement. The highest aggregate score was achieved on Part 3 Section 11–Subject Headings and Classification. On the posttest for the inexperienced group, the highest individual score was 97 percent, the lowest was 72 percent. Within the ten sections of Part 3, the lowest aggregate score was 47 percent achieved in Section 4–Edition Statement. The highest score (100 percent) was achieved on Part 3 Section 7–Series Statement.

The highest individual score for the entire test in the experienced group's results was 90 percent, while the lowest score was 37 percent. In the ten sections of Part 3, the lowest aggregate score was 46 percent achieved on Part 3 Section 4–Edition Statement. The aggregate score of Part 3 Section 6–Publication Data was also low at 47 percent. The highest aggregate score (87 percent) for the experienced group participants was achieved on Part 3 Section 7–Series Statement. In contrast, the inexperienced group posttest takers answered an average of 86 percent of the questions correctly. The highest individual score on the posttest was 97 percent, while the lowest score was 77 percent. Figure 2 compares the average aggregate scores for each of the test measurements arranged by course section.

Analysis of Course Section Test Results

Part 2–Guided Tour

The second part of the course is entitled, "Guided Tour through two MARC records for Internet resources." This section discussed the similarities and differences in cataloging print resources and Internet resources. The objectives included learning in which ways cataloging Internet resources is the same as cataloging print resources according to *AACR2* and MARC21 as well as the differences between the two formats.

The section also explained how Internet resource cataloging could vary based on the type of Internet resource being cataloged. The course compared and contrasted bibliographic data elements in a record for an electronic book and an online Web service. This section seemed particularly helpful if a participant had some background or experience in monographic cataloging, as all should have, since basic cataloging experience is a requirement for this course. This section used real MARC record examples and data in a MARC tag comparison of records. The inexperienced group score on this part of the course increased from pretest to posttest, and the posttest score for the group averaged 19 percent-

FIGURE 2. Aggregate Average Scores Arranged by Section in Course

Course Section	PRETEST (Inexperienced Group)	POSTTEST (Inexperienced Group)	TEST (Experienced Group)
Part 2	45%	93%	74%
Part 3–Section 1	21%	82%	68%
Part 3–Section 2	65%	92%	80%
Part 3–Section 3	36%	72%	77%
Part 3–Section 4	17%	47%	46%
Part 3–Section 6	62%	70%	47%
Part 3–Section 7	58%	100%	87%
Part 3–Section 8	39%	86%	70%
Part 3–Section 9	48%	80%	52%
Part 3–Section 10	55%	82%	73%
Part 3–Section 11	69%	85%	77%

age points higher than scores of the experienced participants. Figure 3 compares the aggregate average test scores for this part.

Part 3 Section 1–MARC Leader and Control Fields

Section 1 dealt with introducing the MARC leader and control fields that are designed to help in describing additional aspects of Internet resources not described elsewhere in the record. This section also sought to help the student judge whether an Internet resource were an online system or service. It explained the differences between static and dynamic monographic resources and why this distinction is important in cataloging. Interestingly, the authors of the Web-based course indicate to the student that this lesson may in fact be the most difficult section to comprehend and apply, and course instructions recommended reviewing other lessons first returning to this lesson later. Indeed, judging from the results of the inexperienced group pretest, this was the most difficult lesson to master. From the pretest to the posttest, the inexperienced group improved 61 percent. Experienced participants scored 14 percentage points lower than the posttest takers. Figure 4 compares the results. Several of the inexperienced participants commented about the need for a "cheat sheet" while coding fixed field data fields. Such a "cheat sheet" would be a list of appropriate codes to be applied to the various MARC tags.

FIGURE 3. Comparison of Test Results: Part 2

Inexperienced Group Pretest	45%
Inexperienced Group Posttest	93%
Experienced Group 2 Test	74%

FIGURE 4. Comparison of Test Results: Part 3 Section 1–MARC Leader and Control Fields

Inexperienced Group Pretest	21%
Inexperienced Group Posttest	82%
Experienced Group 2 Test	68%

Part 3 Section 2–Title and Statement of Responsibility

The inexperienced group participants also improved in Section 2 from the pretest to the posttest, with scores increasing an average of 27 percent. The experienced group scored on average 12 percentage points lower than the posttest inexperienced group. Figure 5 compares scores within this course section in which key questions included what constituted the title and variant title access as well as what elements were permissible as part of the statement of responsibility. Although some judgment was allowed in determining the title proper of the resource, variant title had to be recorded for full access. The question, "According to *AACR2R*, what is the chief source of information for Internet resources?" elicited some interesting responses. Some of the participants commented that *AACR2R* does not address Internet resources, even though Chapter 9 (Computer Files) of *AACR2R* specifically uses the term "remote computer file" and Internet resources are defined as remote computer files. This section also dealt with the use of the general material designator (GMD). Several of the inexperienced participants did not realize that "computer file" was the only authorized GMD.

Part 3 Section 3–Edition Statement

Section 3 is the only one in which the experienced group participants scored better than the inexperienced group posttest participants. Figure 6 compares the scores. From the pretest to the posttest, the inexperienced group participants doubled their average score. However, the experienced group participants still scored five percentage points higher than the posttest takers. What constitutes an edition statement in the cataloging records for Internet resources was a central question. In monographic cataloging, the presence of words such as "updated" or "revised" usually signals the existence of a new or different edition of the work. That rule does not apply to the cataloging of Internet re-

FIGURE 5. Comparison of Test Results: Part 3 Section 2–Title and Statement of Responsibility

Inexperienced Group Pretest	65%
Inexperienced Group Posttest	92%
Experienced Group 2 Test	80%

sources, which obviously confused some of the study participants. Although Internet resources such as Web sites frequently use the term "last updated" or "last revised," those terms do not usually constitute information that should be entered in the MARC field 250 edition statement area.

Part 3 Section 4–Computer File Characteristics

This section dealt with describing the nature of the Internet resource as "computer data," "computer program(s)," and "computer program(s) and data." These three choices are the only valid possibilities for the 256 MARC field according to *AACR2R* and MARC21. In the test answers, the participants supplied a variety of incorrect responses. The comparison of pretest to posttest scores shows a 30 percent increase. The experienced group test takers scored only one point on average lower than the posttest inexperienced group. Figure 7 displays a comparison of the test results.

Part 3 Section 5–Issue Designation for Serials (Forthcoming in Next Release)

This section will be added in a future release of the course and was not evaluated in this study.

FIGURE 6. Comparison of Test Results: Part 3 Section 3–Edition Statement

Inexperienced Group Pretest	36%
Inexperienced Group Posttest	72%
Experienced Group Test	77%

FIGURE 7. Comparison of Test Results: Part 3 Section 4–Computer File Characteristics

Inexperienced Group Pretest	17%
Inexperienced Group Posttest	47%
Experienced Group 2 Test	46%

Part 3 Section 6–Place, Publisher, and Dates of Publication

Data for the test results in this area indicates that from the pretest to the posttest, scores increased an average of eight percentage points. This is the area where the inexperienced group exhibited the least amount of improvement between the two test instruments. Problem areas in this section included choosing the correct publication date for the resource. Although many Internet resources included current or very recent dates, these dates were not appropriate for the 260 subfield c MARC field. That field requires that the beginning date of publication be entered. Often the participants were unaware of the beginning publication date and/or how to record that information in the MARC field. A comparison of the average test scores for this section is in Figure 8.

Part 3 Section 7–Series Statement

The inexperienced posttest takers again scored better on average than the experienced participants. The comparison in Figure 9 reveals that the posttest takers scored 42 percentage points higher than on the pretest. In this section of the test instruments, there were only one or two questions dealing with series statements. The posttest takers scored 13 points higher than the experienced. The central issue in this section was what constitutes series statements. The same principles that govern the recording of a series statement for printed monographs apply to Internet resource cataloging.

FIGURE 8. Comparison of Test Results: Part 3 Section 6–Place, Publisher, and Dates of Publication

Inexperienced Group Pretest	62
Inexperienced Group Posttest	70%
Experienced Group 2 Test	47%

FIGURE 9. Comparison of Test Results: Part 3 Section 7–Series Statement

Inexperienced Group Pretest	58%
Inexperienced Group Posttest	100%
Experienced Group 2 Test	52%

Part 3 Section 8–(Bibliographic) Notes

This section introduced the objective of learning the required and recommended bibliographic notes in the cataloging of Internet resources. The students in the inexperienced group had to learn which bibliographic notes were required and in what sequence. For example, a source of title note is always required when cataloging Internet resources. The score of the inexperienced group from pretest to posttest increased an average of 47 percentage points. The posttest group also scored an average of 16 percentage higher than the experienced participants. Figure 10 illustrates the differences in the scores of the two groups.

Part 3 Section 9–Electronic Location and Access (MARC Field 856)

This section focused on instruction about the 856 MARC field that contains as one of its components the uniform resource locator (URL) or the Internet address of the resource. The inexperienced posttest group again improved, in this case, by 42 percentage points. The inexperienced posttest group outscored the experienced group test takers by 28 percent. Figure 11 presents the comparison of figures.

FIGURE 10. Comparison of Test Results: Part 3 Section 8–(Bibliographic) Notes

Inexperienced Group Pretest	39%
Inexperienced Group Posttest	86%
Experienced Group 2 Test	70%

FIGURE 11. Comparison of Test Results: Part 3 Section 9–Electronic Location and Access (MARC Field 856)

Inexperienced Group Pretest	44%
Inexperienced Group Posttest	80%
Experienced Group 2 Test	52%

Part 3 Section 10–Main and Added Entries

Participants were instructed in the application of *AACR2R* Chapter 21 (Choice of Access Points) in this section. The same rules for choosing access points for printed monographs apply to the cataloging of Internet resources. On average from pretest to posttest, the inexperienced group participants improved by 27 percentage points. The inexperienced group posttest takers scored an average of nine points higher than the experienced participants. The role of cataloger's judgement also applies to this section. The participants' rationale for choosing main and added entries was accounted for in this section. Figure 12 shows the comparison of scores.

Part 3 Section 11–Headings and Classification

This section of the course was rather brief and general, dealing only with the application of subject headings and classification schemes in general. There was no instruction in specific classification schemes or subject headings lists. The participants mentioned that this section of the course should be expanded for students using the *Library of Congress Subject Headings, Library of Congress Classification Schedules, and the Dewey Decimal Classification* schedules. Only one question from the pretest and the posttest addressed the content of this section. The inexperienced group posttesters' scores increased by 16 percentage points, which was eight points higher than the average score of the experienced group participants. In Figure 13, the average section scores of each test are given.

CONCLUSIONS AND RECOMMENDATIONS

From the examination of the test scores for the pretest and posttest groups, it can be concluded that the inexperienced group participants had

FIGURE 12. Comparison of Test Results: Part 3 Section 10–Main and Added Entries

Inexperienced Group Pretest	55%
Inexperienced Group Posttest	82%
Experienced Group 2 Test	73%

FIGURE 13. Comparison of Test Results: Part 3 Section 11–Headings and Classification

Inexperienced Group Pretest	69%
Inexperienced Group Posttest	85%
Experienced Group 2 Test	77%

a positive learning experience. The OCLC Institute's first venture into the world of electronic learning or e-learning was a success, judging purely from the examination of the test results. In all but one of the sections of the course, the inexperienced group participants who were initially inexperienced in the cataloging of Internet resources scored higher than the experienced group participants who were self-identified experienced catalogers of Internet resources. The comments from the inexperienced group participants after taking the Web-based course were also overwhelmingly positive. The participants praised the advantages of e-learning courses over traditional classroom instruction, several of them citing factors such as "no fear, no pressure" and being able to use the course whenever and wherever they chose. The ability to review course content at a later date was also a chief advantage mentioned repeatedly.

The participants made several recommendations about the course, however, which should be considered. Several called for the course to use other than multiple-choice questions to evaluate performance. Likewise, several suggested that a graded test at the end of the course would be a helpful evaluative tool. Perhaps this test, which would apply the concepts learned in the course, could be graded by OCLC personnel and returned to the students with appropriate feedback. The participants also commented in favor of having an online course moderator. The participants indicated that they appreciated the researcher's presence and ability to answer questions during the online course. One wrote the suggestion, "OCLC needs an instructor like you to answer cataloging questions" and another wrote concerning the researcher, "Thanks for your encouraging emails. I felt better being able to email you." Still another participant wrote, "I always felt connected with your e-mails."

These comments are not unusual for students in online learning environments. In fact, Salmon proposes a five-step process to electronic moderating or e-moderating.[44] The first stage involves providing access to the course and encouraging or engendering motivation for the students to take the course. Online socialization is another goal. The use of technology should encourage a level of networking, which begins to build an online community of people who feel they are working together at common tasks. When participants feel comfortable with the online customs and the technology used, they move to the mode of contributing knowledge. The role of the e-moderator is to encourage these discussions. This comfort level leads to the third stage, which is information exchange. The students need interaction with both the course and other people. In the fourth stage, knowledge construction, the participants interact with each other as online conferences develop. In this environment, participants are liable to learn as much from one another as from the course material.[45] Salmon reports that with this interaction, highly productive collaborative learning may develop. In the final stage of e-moderating, development, the participants become responsible for their own learning through some computer-mediated opportunities. Critical thinking skills are a valuable byproduct in this stage.[46]

Given the participants' comments about the researcher and his role in this study, there are several recommendations for improving the OCLC Institute Web-based courses. An OCLC staff member should be assigned to monitor or moderate the online course. Currently, OCLC has a mechanism in place with which the participants can contact OCLC personnel about technical issues such as connection and software browser compatibility. The OCLC staff member assigned to the course should be very familiar with the content of the course, be able to answer content-related questions, and add a human dimension to the course. Since the course is available to the participants for only one year from the date of purchase, this OCLC staff member could also encourage the online students to complete the course in a reasonable time. Another recommendation for the online course would be to create an electronic list in which the course participants could offer suggestions and pose questions about the cataloging of Internet resources to each other. The participants could discuss both the examples used in the course and real-life examples from their work environments.

In evaluating the research design of this study, several recommendations can also be presented. The question of knowledge retention has been raised. Will the inexperienced group participants remember knowledge gained from the course at a later date? This point is especially relevant for those participants who do not plan to begin cataloging Internet resources shortly after they complete the course. Does this Web-based course foster long-term memory and application? Another recommendation would be to have some expert other than OCLC personnel provide suggested responses to the posttest, which could eliminate or lessen any research methodology bias. Another recommendation would be to give participants a pretest in order to ensure that the experienced group genuinely did comprise experienced catalogers of Internet resources. The assumption was made that volunteers for the experienced group were, in fact, experienced Internet resource catalogers, but some of the test results cast doubt on that assumption.

The purpose of the OCLC Institute's Web-based course was to provide both new knowledge to inexperienced catalogers of Internet resources and a refresher course for experienced catalogers. Given the performance of the inexperienced group participants in the test instrument, it is logical to assume that even the experienced group participants would benefit from participating in the online course. Another recommendation would be to encourage the experienced group participants to use the Web-based course and complete another student instrument. Testing more participants would also assist in further validating these research results.

The value of e-learning in the cataloging environment requires further study and research. The OCLC Institute's new product has assisted in forging a path in this uncharted area. This Web-based course is a well-designed beginning to the process of asynchronous education in library cataloging departments.

ENDNOTES

1. Beagle, D. "Web-based learning environments: Do libraries matter?" *College & Research Libraries*, 2000: 367-377.

2. Driscoll, M. "Web-based training in the workplace." *Adult Learning* 10(4) 1999: 21-25.

3. Boisvert, L. "Web-based learning: The anytime anywhere classroom." *Information Systems Management* 17(1) 2000: 35-40.

4. Barley, S.R. "Computer-based distance education: Why and why not." *Education Digest* 65(2) 1999: 55-59.

5. Mccright, J. S. "Cisco's Chambers elearning will help 'control our destinies.' " *PC Week News*, 1. 1999, November 16. Retrieved December 20, 2001, from the World Wide Web: http://www.zdnet.com/filters/printerfriendly/0,6061,1018192=54.00.html.

6. Driscoll, M. "Web-based training," p. 21-25.

7. Hall, B. *Web-based training cookbook*. (New York: Wiley, 1997).

8. Driscoll, M. "How to pilot Web-based training." *Training and Development* 52(11) 1998: 44-49.

9. Hall, B. *Web-based training cookbook*.

10. Hall, B. *Web-based training cookbook*.

11. Hall, R. H., Watkins, S. E. & Ercal, F. *The Horse and the Cart in Web-Based Instruction: Prevalence and Efficacy.* (New Orleans, LA: American Education Research Association. (ERIC Document Reproduction Service No. ED 443 425), 2000).

12. Schutte, J. G. "Virtual teaching in higher education: The new intellectual superhighway or just another traffic jam?" 1998. Retrieved December 24, 2001, from the World Wide Web: http://www.csun.edu/sociology/virexp.htm.

13. Jones, E. R. *A comparison of a web-based class to a traditional class.* (San Antonio, TX: Society for Information Technology & Teacher Education. (ERIC Document Reproduction No. ED 432 286), 1999).

14. Kiser, R. & Toreki, R. (1997). *Efficacy of TopClass software in CHE 105-001. 1997.* Retrieved December 24, 2001, from the World Wide Web: http://www.chem.uky.edu/misc/topclasssurvey.html.

15. White, S. E. *The Effectiveness of Web-based instruction: A case study.* (St. Louis, MO: Central States Communication Association and the Southern States Communication Association. (ERIC Document Reproduction Service No. ED 430 261), 1999).

16. Wideman, H. & Owston, R.D. *Internet-based courses at Atkinson College: An initial assessment.* 1999. Retrieved December 24, 2001, from the World Wide Web: http://www.edu.yorku.ca/csce/tech99_1.html.

17. Baruth, B. "Is your catalog big enough to handle the Web?" *American Libraries* 31(7) 2000: 56-60.

18. Ellett, R. O. "Internet search engines giving you garbage? Put a 'CORC' in it: The implementation of the Cooperative Online Resource Catalog." *The Christian Librarian* 44(2) 2001: 46-53.

19. Baruth, B. "Is your catalog big enough," p. 56-60.

20. Banerjee, K. "Describing remote electronic documents in the online catalog: Current issues." *Cataloging & Classification Quarterly* 25(1), 1997: 5-20.

21. Dillon, M. & Jul, E. "Cataloging Internet resources: The convergence of libraries and Internet resources." *Cataloging & Classification Quarterly* 22(3/4) 1996: 197-238.

22. Olson, N. B. (Ed.). *Cataloging Internet resources: A manual and practical guide.* (2nd ed.). (Dublin, OH: OCLC, 1997.) Also retrieved December 24, 2001, from the World Wide Web: http://www.oclc.org/oclc/man/9256cat/toc.htm.

23. Banerjee, K. "Describing remote electronic documents," p. 5-20.

24. Johns, C. "Cataloging Internet resources: An administrator's view." *Journal of Internet Cataloging* 1 (1), 1997: 17-23.

25. Johns, C. "Cataloging Internet resources," p. 17-23.

26. Kassel, A. "Internet power searching: Finding pearls in a zillion grains of sand." *Information Outlook* 3(4) 1999: 28-33.

27. Lam, V. "Cataloging Internet Resources: Why, What, How." *Cataloging & Classification Quarterly* 29(3) 2000.

28. Ellett, R. O. "Internet search engines giving you garbage?" p. 46-53.

29. Weber, M. B. "Factors to be considered in the selection and cataloging of Internet resources." *Library Hi-Tech* 17(3) 1999: 298-303.

30. Jul, E. "Cataloging Internet resources: An assessment and prospectus." *The Serials Librarian* 34(1/2) 1998: 91-104.

31. Gerhard, K. H. "Cataloging Internet resources: Practical issues and concerns." *The Serials Librarian* 32(1-2) 1997: 123-137.

32. Dillon, M. & Jul, E. "Cataloging Internet resources," p. 197-238.

33. Gerhard, K. H. "Cataloging Internet resources," p. 123-137.

34. Ellett, R. O. "Internet search engines giving you garbage?" p. 46-53.

35. Lam, V. "Cataloging Internet resources: Why, what, how." *Cataloging & Classification Quarterly* 29(3) 2000: 61.

36. Taylor, A. G. "Where does AACR2 fall short for Internet resources?" *Journal of Internet Cataloging* 2(2) 1999: 43-50.

37. Olson, N. B. (Ed.). *Cataloging Internet resources: A manual and practical guide.* (2nd ed.). Dublin, OH: OCLC, 1997. Also retrieved December 24, 2001, from the World Wide Web: http://www.oclc.org/oclc/man/9256cat/toc.htm.

38. Taylor, A. G. "Where does AACR2 fall short," p. 43-50.

39. Ellett, R. O. "Internet search engines giving you garbage?" p. 46-53.

40. Coggins, T. L. "Print no more: *U.S. Code, Code of Federal Regulations,* and the *Federal Register.*" *Virginia Lawyer* 49(3) 2000: 53-55.

41. Dillon & Jul. "Cataloging Internet resources," p. 197-238.

42. Dillon, M. "Assessing information on the Internet: toward providing library services for computer-mediated communications: results of an OCLC Research Project." *Internet Research* 3(1) 1993: 54-69.

43. Neumeister, S. M. "Cataloging Internet resources: A practitioner's viewpoint." *Journal of Internet Cataloging* 1(1) 1997: 23-45.

44. Salmon, S. *E-Moderating: The Key to Teaching and Learning Online.* London: Kogan Page, 2000.

45. Rowntree, D. "Teaching and learning online: a correspondence education for the 21st century?" *British Journal of Educational Technology* 26(3) 1995: 205-215.

46. Salmon, S. *E-Moderating.*

Cataloging Internet Resources
Using MARC21 and *AACR2*:
Online Training for Working Catalogers

Anna M. Ferris

SUMMARY. This article endorses the use of Web-based instruction for cataloging education as represented by OCLC's online course, *Cataloging Internet Resources Using MARC21 and AACR2*. This type of instruction is particularly useful to working catalogers (professional and paraprofessional alike) who cannot spare the time or the expense to attend workshops and seminars in order to receive training in the latest developments in the field. The OCLC course also paves the way for a new standardized program of online cataloging education that will be tailored for working catalogers at all levels of expertise and that will offer specialized, yet convenient, training in a wide variety of formats. *[Article copies available for a fee from The Haworth Document Delivery Service: 1-800-HAWORTH. E-mail address: <getinfo@ haworthpressinc.com> Website: <http://www.HaworthPress.com> © 2002 by The Haworth Press, Inc. All rights reserved.]*

KEYWORDS. Web-based training, cataloging Internet resources, OCLC Institute, distance education

---

Anna M. Ferris is Monographic Cataloger, University of Colorado Libraries, Boulder, CO.

[Haworth co-indexing entry note]: "Cataloging Internet Resources Using MARC21 and *AACR2*: Online Training for Working Catalogers." Ferris, Anna M. Co-published simultaneously in *Cataloging & Classification Quarterly* (The Haworth Information Press, an imprint of The Haworth Press, Inc.) Vol. 34, No. 3, 2002, pp. 339-353; and: *Education for Cataloging and the Organization of Information: Pitfalls and the Pendulum* (ed: Janet Swan Hill) The Haworth Information Press, an imprint of The Haworth Press, Inc., 2002, pp. 339-353. Single or multiple copies of this article are available for a fee from The Haworth Document Delivery Service [1-800-HAWORTH, 9:00 a.m. - 5:00 p.m. (EST). E-mail address: getinfo@haworthpressinc.com].

INTRODUCTION

"Learn everything you can about Internet resources!" This has been the most consistently repeated advice offered to me since I became a cataloger over three years ago. It is very practical advice since, as catalogers, we cannot ignore the impact the Internet has had on every aspect of our daily routine in the library. Intent on heeding this advice, I sought out what was currently available and discovered several options for catalogers wanting to learn about Internet resources cataloging: (1) the literature on the subject is abundant; (2) educational workshops/seminars are repeatedly being offered throughout the country; and (3) *Cataloging Internet Resources Using MARC21 and AACR2*,[1] an online course specifically designed to teach the basics of cataloging web resources, had recently been introduced by the Online Computer Library Center (OCLC) in December of 2000. After reading the literature, and not being able to attend a workshop, I chose to sign up for the online course and completed it within two months. I will summarize the content of *Cataloging Internet Resources Using MARC21 and AACR2* (CIRMA) and discuss why Web-based instruction can become a viable and convenient way for working catalogers to learn about recent changes in cataloging procedures.

LITERATURE REVIEW

The library literature over the past few years has provided many enlightening articles for catalogers who seek to stay apprised of the latest developments in Internet resources cataloging. So many articles on the subject have appeared that Weiss and Carstens[2] (2000) have observed, "the Internet [has] monopolized much of recent cataloging literature." The *Journal of Internet Cataloging*, which first appeared in 1997, was developed for the purpose of presenting the latest research in this area. Many noteworthy articles have addressed the reasons why accessibility to Internet resources is important and offer suggestions on how this should be accomplished.[3]

While these articles help clarify many unfamiliar issues pertaining to Internet resources cataloging, few of them address specifically how working catalogers are taught to catalog these new resources. Two articles make passing reference to this. Kristin H. Gerhard refers to the initial process of introducing Internet cataloging to her Technical Services department at Iowa State University:

> Initially, we decided that cataloging Internet resources should be handled by MLS catalogers only . . . Once cataloging these titles becomes somewhat routine, we hope to pass the copy cataloging of some serials on to serials copy catalogers.
>
> It should be said at the outset that none of the catalogers involved . . . had extensive experience cataloging items on the Internet, including the Electronic Resources Coordinator. We needed to learn how to catalog these resources . . . The catalogers as a group learned to catalog Internet resources by cataloging them. Nancy Olson's manual for Internet cataloging was particularly useful, as was the CONSER *Cataloging Manual*. The collegiality of discussion that took place in this process was a significant factor in our progress.[4]

In the course of her discussion of the initiatives taken by Central Technical Services at the SUNY Buffalo Libraries, Diane Ward makes a brief remark about how their catalogers are taught:

> Training flows through the catalogers working with electronic resources; they are encouraged to attend conferences and workshops and to discuss approaches with colleagues in order to hone the craft of cataloging. Sources such as AUTOCAT . . . supplement and enhance emphasis on cataloging principles. Additionally, staff at all levels were trained by peers and also through University Libraries-sponsored classes . . .[5]

Yvonne W. Zhang provides the most in-depth article with her appraisal of a workshop held on September 18, 1998 at Occidental College in Los Angeles, California, which was presented by Greta de Groat (Stanford University) and Steve Shadle (University of Washington).[6] According to Zhang, the workshop was organized into three parts: general issues, MARC tagging, and cataloging related issues. Forty-three participants were offered "an incredible amount of information in a relatively short time." The workshop included hands-on exercises covering various aspects of Internet resources cataloging as well as theoretical issues ranging from Web sites 'change frenzy' to details such as what qualifies to be coded as the second indicator 2 for field 856.

This is one example of the many programs and workshops designed to introduce developing standards for Internet resources cataloging which are being offered throughout the country. De Groat and Shadle continue to present the workshop described above and Nancy Olson, as of this writing, is scheduled to present a 4-day "Cataloging Electronic

Resources" workshop in Lakewood, Colorado (October) as well as in Jacksonville, Florida (November) in 2001.[7] In addition, one successful initiative, the Serials Cataloging Cooperative Training Program (SCCTP),[8] has been developed by the CONSER division of the Library of Congress to offer a standardized program of training for serials catalogers regardless of their level of expertise. Their newest course, "Electronic Serials Cataloging Workshop," is scheduled for release in April of 2002 to coincide with the publication of the revised Chapter 12 (Serials) of the *AACR2*. Much research and manpower has been committed to the SCCTP to promote a better understanding of serials cataloging despite limited–even declining–demand.

In the case of Internet resources cataloging, the relationship between educational resources and demand is quite different. The availability of training programs is inadequate for the growing number of catalogers in need of immediate training. A new educational opportunity currently being offered for working catalogers promises an effective means of satisfying this demand.

THE IMPORTANCE OF CATALOGING INTERNET RESOURCES

There is a variety of reasons why Internet resources cataloging has suddenly become a pressing issue. (Many of these reasons are reiterated at length in the aforementioned literature.) For catalogers, the essential motivation goes beyond concern about the immeasurable rate of growth or the rampant disorganization of the Internet, it has more to do with our professional vocation. Our basic job function has always involved bringing order to chaos. We do this by maintaining our institutions' most vital link to information access, the library's catalog. The following issues represent a cataloger's rationale for including Internet resources in the library's catalog:

Use the Library's Catalog–It Works!

In a paper dealing primarily with educational resources, D. Grant Campbell offers an excellent justification for continuing to draw from the "tradition of rich, detailed cataloging procedures" to integrate these newer resources into the library's catalog rather than setting them apart in a separate index. For Campbell, the catalog is more than an organized list of documents. It is unique because it provides access to selected documents; it offers descriptions of these documents in enough detail to inform researchers whether they are relevant to their search; it offers consistency in its use of a standard bibliographic formula for description which is familiar to researchers; and it provides an unequivocal link between the bibliographic record and the document it represents. But, the most important feature of the library's catalog is that "it is more accessible than ever before: it can be reached easily from a great distance by anyone with an Internet connection . . . it provides a gateway to the electronic resources themselves . . . [with] the added advantage of being a discriminating gateway: more discriminating than many Web-based search tools."[9]

Internet Resources Add Depth to the OPAC

By including Internet resources into the library's catalog, we extend its usefulness and make it a truly integrated tool of information delivery. While Internet resources basically represent another form of publishing, they are remarkable for the diversity of formats in which they are accessed (online library systems, software programs, electronic bulletin boards, census data, videogames); their modes of access (WWW, Gopher sites, FTP sites); and assorted manifestations (bibliographic, representational, interactive multimedia). The public access catalog is greatly enhanced by the addition of these types of electronic media resources.

Patrons Expect to Find Internet Resources in the Catalog

Every new academic year brings a more sophisticated breed of researcher. As adept at creating Web sites as they are at navigating them, these researchers expect nothing less than timely–even instant–access to pertinent Internet resources through our public access catalog. Needless to say, the more demanding these patrons become, the keener our colleagues at the reference desk will be to make sure we provide the essential link to these Web resources.

While the above points help to justify the cataloger's rationale for including Internet resources in the library's catalog, there would be inevitable consequences to acting upon this rationale. Implementing these measures would have major repercussions for catalogers.

Every Cataloger Will Need to Share in the Task

Since the growth of Internet resources is potentially limitless, catalogers will come to realize that their workflow will increase in proportion to this growth. Consequently, the need to learn how to catalog these resources will become even more critical. What is more, catalogers will no longer have the option of writing off certain resources because they happen to fall outside of their area of specialization, say, in format, language or subject expertise. Internet resources will increasingly supplant a large part of what has already been published in many of these areas. Proficiency in Internet resources cataloging will therefore become a requisite skill for all catalogers regardless of their status as technical staff or professional librarians.

Consider the Cleanup!

An added consideration concerns the revision and clean up of incorrect records for Internet resources which have been added to the cooperative cataloging databases. Until recent approval by the Joint Steering Committee for the Revision of the *Anglo-American Cataloguing Rules* (JSC), the standards for the cataloging of Internet resources (found in *AACR2*, Chapter 9) had not been officially prescribed. But while guidelines have been available for years, such as *Cataloging Internet Resources: A Manual and Practical Guide*[10] edited by Nancy B. Olson or the CONSER manual, flawed records for Internet resources are still being created by catalogers who have had little or no authoritative specialized training. This may account for the number of records found in OCLC and RLIN that do not conform to the basic standards recommended in the guidelines. A quick perusal of computer file records in these databases will turn up inconsistencies in the application of even the simplest rule: how to use the general material designator. The task of cleaning up these flawed records will become the responsibility of catalogers who have received formal training on how to apply the approved standards. As more catalogers learn to apply these standards, we should expect to see more reliable records for Internet resources, comparable to PCC records for bibliographic items.

The above-mentioned issues represent important reasons why catalogers are seeking to learn about Internet resources. But not all catalogers are in the situation where our most essential function–remaining active agents of information delivery–has been conveniently realized. In reality, many libraries have not yet resolved to include Internet resources in their catalogs. Few catalogers can claim to work for institutions where breakthrough projects in cataloging are encouraged, or where the time and financing to attend cataloging seminars and workshops is readily available. Still, the need to learn about Internet resources remains a compelling one.

THE OCLC INSTITUTE'S ONLINE LIBRARY LEARNING SERIES

The OCLC Institute, a non-profit, educational division of OCLC, has taken the needs of catalogers into consideration. They have embarked on a major effort to provide educational opportunities for catalogers who must be prepared for the demands made on their professional expertise. The first course offering of its Online Library Learning (OLL) Series was announced in December of 2000.

Cataloging Internet Resources Using MARC21 and AACR2 (CIRMA) is a true product of the Internet–it was digitally born. Lacking an exact, corresponding print version, it is a particularly good example of the type of "cybergenre" Shepherd and Watters[11] (1998) call "novel" and "spontaneous." Simply stated, here is a resource, in a genre all its own, which was designed, exists and is accessible exclusively on the World Wide Web.

Its closest print-format relative is the OCLC document edited by Olson, *Cataloging Internet Resources* (CIR), which is not an educational course per se but rather a set of guidelines on how to apply the *Anglo-American Cataloging Rules* for bibliographic description while cataloging Internet resources. There are similarities shared by CIRMA and CIR. Besides having the common objective of providing current guidelines for Internet resources cataloging, they are complementary in other ways:

- both deal exclusively with the description of remotely accessed computer files
- both incorporate established standards: *AACR2*, 2nd ed. (Chapter 9); *International Standard Bibliographic Description for Electronic Resources; OCLC MARC* formats; and OCLC's *Bibliographic Formats and Standards,* 2nd ed.
- both acknowledge that certain rules and terms are currently undergoing revision

Of the dissimilarities, the following are the most significant:

- Fixed field codes are an important part of CIRMA, not CIR
- Serials cataloging is discussed in CIR, not CIRMA
- Selection criteria are addressed in CIR, not CIRMA
- CIRMA gives more details on MARC tags 260 (Publication) and 650 (Subj. Headings)
- CIR gives more details on MARC tags 856 (Access) and 5XX (Notes)

DESCRIPTION OF THE COURSE

Parts 1 and 2 of the course (see Appendix A) outline basic orientation information and give a helpful comparison of the MARC records for two versions of Olson's *Cataloging Internet Resources*: one record for the print version (books format), the other for the electronic version (computer file format) available on the World Wide Web. Part 3, the central part of the course, consists of 28 lessons in 11 sections each of which corresponds to a specific MARC tag and *AACR2* rule. Throughout the course, links are available to learning aids and reference resources. Direct email contact to OCLC's network support staff is also provided.

Any lesson can be accessed at any time. Each lesson follows the same pattern: objectives, illustrative examples, practice test questions and final test questions. All test questions are interactive multiple choice or true/false questions. The choice of answer triggers a statement which relates to the correctness or incorrectness of your response.

The initial six lessons (Section 1) are the most challenging segment of the course. They provide valuable guidelines on the Leader and Control Field codes which are not easily mastered without repeated scrutiny. These codes determine record types (Leader/06), bibliographic levels (Leader/07), types of computer files (008/26), etc. Illustrative examples of the most common situations help to clarify the standard use of many of these unfamiliar codes.

Section 2 represents the next most demanding segment. For example, identifying the Title Proper of a Website is not as self-evident as one might expect. Variations in the title often occur (as in situations where one might chose between "part of" or "the whole" Website; or when the most prominent title begins with a generic phrase such as "Welcome to . . . ;" or when graphics take the place of textual characters in the title). Each of these situations present a challenge which requires a cataloger's sound judgment and expertise. The Statement of Responsibility is another field which requires close attention. Statements such as "maintained by" or "created by" are misleading since they do not constitute a formal statement of responsibility unless they are prominently displayed on the title screen. The fact that they appear at all–although in another section of the Website–adds to the confusion about how best to account for these statements within the cataloging record.

The other sections vary in degree of complexity. Section 6 deserves special consideration, particularly in the lesson on Publication Dates, since a prominently displayed copyright date does not necessarily reflect the actual publication date of the Website. Section 8 (Notes) is important because of the specific notes designed only for Internet resources: 538 (Mode of Access/System Details), 516 (Type of Computer File/Data), 530 (Additional Formats), and 500 (Source of Title Proper/Item Description). It is important that the cataloger understand the function of each note and whether its use is applicable, or even optional, in the local catalog. Section 9 (Electronic Location & Access) explains the usage of subfields $a, $u and $2 in the 856 field. Nancy Olson's CIR includes an appendix with more examples of additional subfields.

The sections which are easiest to assimilate are those dealing with rules already familiar to an experienced cataloger. These include Section 3–Edition Statement; Section 7–Series Statement; Section 10–Main and Added Entries; and Section 11–Subject Headings and Classification.

ADVANTAGES OF THE ONLINE COURSE

Some catalogers may be unconvinced as to the value of taking an online course to learn cataloging procedures. Below are some of the advantages that contribute to the effectiveness of this particular course:

- *Accessibility.* This is by far the greatest advantage of taking an online course. Anyone connected to an Internet browser can link to the OCLC course at any time of the day. Registration is done from the OCLC Institute's e-learning Website (http://www.oclc.org/institute/elearning/oll/CIRuMA/index.htm). Once enrolled, a login code and password are assigned and the course is accessible for a one-year period. This allows the student to review and revisit lessons as often as required.
- *Convenience.* CIRMA provides a quick way to acquire specialized skills while eliminating the need to travel long distances, spend valuable time and expend large sums of money while doing so.

- *Authenticity.* The authenticity of the course content is unequivocal. OCLC, in conjunction with the Library of Congress, the British Library and the National Library of Canada, is an active member of the library consortium which maintains the cataloging standards we follow.
- *Visualization.* Understanding is enhanced by the use of actual Web pages to illustrate the most common, as well as challenging, situations. The use of title screen images helps to clarify situations in which the source of data may not be easily deduced from a theoretical example.
- *No prerequisites.* As stated on OLL's Frequently Asked Questions Website (see URL above), "There are no prerequisites, affiliation requirements with any specific professional organization or association nor any technology requirements such as downloads."

MINOR DISADVANTAGES OF THE ONLINE COURSE

The advantages of taking this online course outweigh the disadvantages, but there are certain areas in which people may find the stand-alone course deficient:

- lack of interaction with instructors and other course participants
- lack of guidance in problematic situations
- no take-home manuals or literature
- no follow-up (to gauge the participant's progress)

There is also no discussion on the topics which are closely related to Internet resources cataloging: URL maintenance, resource selection, Website reliability/instability, content variability, holdings considerations. These topics, however, are adequately covered in the library literature mentioned earlier. While these limitations may be disappointing to some people, most catalogers will find the course very rewarding in spite of them. A few suggestions on how to make up for these limitations would be: (1) have several catalogers from the same institution enroll simultaneously to insure interaction and feedback; (2) print up the more challenging sections of the course (printing directions, for "reference" purposes, are given throughout the course); (3) monitor your progress by keeping your own statistics as you begin to include these resources in your workflow.

CONCLUSION

The launching of a new (Web-based) method of instruction for cataloging standards and procedures could not have arrived at a more critical moment in our profession. Catalogers are well aware of the decline in library school programs requiring coursework in cataloging (Spillane, 1999).[12] Further research on the current status of the faculty teaching cataloging at these library schools would be very useful. It would help dispel or confirm the sobering pronouncements on the future of cataloging if we learned how many qualified cataloging professors are due to retire within the next decade and how many professors are in place to take over for them. (Nancy Olson, for example, is retired.)

Catalogers should also be aware of the in-depth instruction presently being offered at these library schools to students who will one day join our ranks as catalogers. An article by Professor Ingrid Hsieh-Yee[13] describes one such cataloging program offered at the Catholic University of America in which Internet resources play a major part. Students can take up to three courses in the organization of Internet resources beginning with the basics in cataloging principles and progressing to the application of metadata schemes such as Dublin Core, TEI and EAD. While these students appear to be in an enviable position, receiving such an extensive introduction to Internet resources cataloging, they still lack the one thing that will permit them to make use of their new-found knowledge to the fullest extent: years of cataloging experience. The OCLC course offers working catalogers an educational opportunity to marry their expertise to the latest advancements in our profession. Our most fundamental duty–providing the most advanced means of information delivery to our patrons–depends on it.

We would do well to embrace Web-based education for the specific ways it can benefit us as professional catalogers:

- it is an effective way to receive training in general cataloging standards and procedures;
- it is an effective way to learn the latest developments in specialized formats;
- it permits us to keep our skills honed to meet future challenges in the profession;
- the technology is such that changes and upgrades can be communicated to catalogers with minimal delay.

A course like CIRMA will whet catalogers' appetites for more online courses. The demand exists for further instruction in areas other than Internet resources cataloging. When prompted to "design the ideal cataloging course" on the AUTOCAT listserv on May 15, 2001, many catalogers offered their specific wish lists for the following areas: practical MARC instruction on non-book materials; full hands-on instruction of authority control; uniform titles; serials; maps; subject heading analysis and creation; alternate metadata standards; bound-withs (what they are, how to catalog them); Government documents; how to use the various [Classification] Tables, and when.

Now is the optimal time for the development of a standardized program of online cataloging education. Cooperation between OCLC, the Library of Congress, ALA and library schools would help to further this goal. A standardized program of online cataloging education would serve the needs of anyone interested in cataloging regardless of level of expertise or geographic location. For now, however, the educational requirements of working catalogers should be the first priority simply because working catalogers are the ones who will make the best use of such online courses. "Cataloging Internet Resources using MARC21 and *AACR2*" serves this purpose by offering a basic introduction to new cataloging procedures. This introductory experience is essential to catalogers who are increasingly being called upon by their institution and their patrons to provide up-to-date access to these much sought-after resources.

ENDNOTES

1. *Online Learning Library Series*, [http://www.oclc.org/institute/elearning/oll/CIRuMA/index.htm]. Accessed 3/14/02. As of this writing, the course has been revised and expanded to include the cataloging of Internet Serials resources. For details on the revised and expanded Version 2 of the course, see http://www.oclc.org/institute/elearning/oll/CIRuMA/release_notes.htm.

2. Amy K. Weiss and Timothy V. Carstens, "The Year's Work in Cataloging, 1999," *Library Resources & Technical Services* 45, no. 1 (January 2001): 47-58.

3. The Selected Bibliography that follows includes a number of such articles. Those offering an administrative/institutional viewpoint are: Gerhard, 1997; Johns, 1997; Neumeister, 1997; Ward 2001; for a traditional viewpoint, highlighting the OPAC, see: Ward & VanderPol, 2000; Zhang, 2000; Lam, 2000; for a perspective on how to apply standard cataloging practice, see: Jul, 1998; Chase & Dygert, 2000. There are also articles dealing with the development of new cataloging standards for Internet resources: Greenberg, 2000; Grant Campbell, 2001; and recommending how to evaluate and select Websites before including them in the local catalog: Weber, 1999.

4. Kristin H. Gerhard, "Cataloging Internet Resources: Practical Issues and Concerns," *The Serials Librarian* 32, no. 1/2 (1997): 123-137.
5. Diane Ward, "Internet Resource Cataloging: the SUNY Buffalo Librairies' Response," *OCLC Systems & Services* 17, Issue 1 (2001): 19-25.
6. Yvonne W. Zhang, "Cataloging Internet Resources: A Workshop on Cataloging Internet Resources for Your Local Catalog," *Serials Review* 25, no. 1 (1999): 138-140.
7. Enrollment for the workshop in Jacksonville, Florida, was limited to 25 participants at a cost of $80/day for non-members and $40/day for members of the Northeast Florida Library Information Network (NEFLIN).
8. *Serials Cataloging Cooperative Training Program,* [http://www.loc.gov/acq/conser/scctp/home.html]. Accessed 3/14/02.
9. D. Grant Campbell, "Straining the Standards: How Cataloging Websites for Curriculum Support Poses Fresh Problems for the *Anglo-American Cataloging Rules,*" *Journal of Internet Cataloging* 3, no. 1 (2000): 79-92.
10. *Cataloging Internet Resources: A Manual and Practical Guide*, 2nd ed. Ed. Nancy B. Olson. (Dublin, OH: OCLC Online Computer Library Center, 1997) [Online] http://www.purl.org/oclc/cataloging-internet. Accessed 3/14/02.
11. Michael Shepherd and Carolyn Watters, "The Evolution of Cybergenres," In *Proceedings of the Thirty-first Hawaii International Conference on System Sciences, Volume II: Digital Documents Track.* Los Alamitos: IEEE Computer Society (1998) p. 97-109. [Journal online] Accessed from IEEE Xplore on 10/14/01.
12. Jodi Lynn Spillane, "Comparison of Required Introductory Cataloging Courses, 1986 to 1999," *Library Resources & Technical Services* 43: 223-30.
13. Ingrid Hsieh-Yee, "Organizing Internet resources: Teaching Cataloging Standards and Beyond," *OCLC Systems & Services* 16, no. 3 (2000): 130-143.

SELECTED BIBLIOGRAPHY

Chase, Linda, and Claire Dygert. "Organizing Web-Based Resources." *The Serials Librarian* 34, no. 3/4 (2000): 277-286.
Greenberg, Jane. "Metadata Questions in Evolving Internet-Based Educational Terrain." *Journal of Internet Cataloging* 3, no. 1 (2000): 1-11.
Johns, Cecily. "Cataloging Internet Resources: An Administrative View." *Journal of Internet Cataloging* 1, no. 1 (1997): 17-23.
Jul, Erik. "Cataloging Internet Resources: An Assessment and Prospectus." *The Serials Librarian* 34, no. 1/2 (1998): 91-104.
Lam, Vinh-The. "Cataloging Internet Resources: Why, What, How." *Cataloging & Classification Quarterly* 29, no. 3 (2000): 49-61.
Neumeister, Susan M. "Cataloging Internet Resources: A Practitioner's Viewpoint." *Journal of Internet Cataloging* 1, no. 1 (1997): 25-43.
Olson, Nancy B. "Cataloging Remote Electronic Resources." *Cataloging & Classification Quarterly* 31, no. 2 (2001): 101-137.
Ward, David, and Diane VanderPol. "Librarian, Catalog Thy Work! Getting Started Integrating Internet Resources into OPACs." *Journal of Internet Cataloging* 3, no. 4 (2000): 51-61.

Weber, Mary Beth. "Factors to be Considered in the Selection and Cataloging of Internet Resources." *Library Hi Tech* 17, no. 3 (1999): 298-303.

Zhang, Allison. "Cataloging Internet Resources Using the Voyager System." *OCLC Systems & Services* 16, no. 3 (2000): 107-117.

APPENDIX A*

Cataloging Internet Resources Using MARC21 and AACR2

OCLC Online Library Learning series

Part 1: Getting Started

Part 2: Guided Tour through Two MARC Records for Internet Resources

Part 3: Twenty-eight Interactive Lessons

Section 1: **MARC Leader and Control Fields**

> Lesson 1: Type of Record: Leader/06 (Type)
> Lesson 2: Bibliographic Level: Leader/07 (BLvl)
> Lesson 3: Fixed Length Data Elements: Control Field 008 (fixed field)
> Lesson 4: Type of Computer File: 008/26 (File)
> Lesson 5: Fixed-Length Data Elements for Additional Material Characteristics: Control Field 006
> Lesson 6: Physical Description Fixed Field: Control Field 007

Section 2: **Title and Statement of Responsibility**

> Lesson 1: Title Proper for Monographic Internet Resources Lesson
> Lesson 2: General Material Designation
> Lesson 3: Parallel Titles and Other Title Information
> Lesson 4: Statement of Responsibility
> Lesson 5: Varying Form of Title

Section 3: **Edition Statement**

> Lesson 1: Edition Statements for Monographic Resources Lesson View Sample

Section 4: **Computer File Characteristics**

> Lesson 1: AACR2 Options
> Lesson 2: ISBD(ER) Options

Section 5: **Issue Designation for Serials** *(Forthcoming in next release)*

Section 6: **Place, Publisher, and Dates of Publication**

Lesson 1: Place of Publication and Publisher
Lesson 2: Date(s) of Publication for Monographic Resources
Lesson 3: 008 Dates Coding for Monographic Resources

Section 7: **Series Statement**

Lesson 1: Series Statement

Section 8: **Notes**

Lesson 1: Computer File Notes
Lesson 2: Description Identification Notes
Lesson 3: Other Notes

Section 9: **Electronic Location and Access-MARC 856 Field**

Lesson 1: Indicators
Lesson 2: Subfields
Lesson 3: Multiple Access Methods

Section 10: **Main and Added Entries**

Lesson 1: Main Entry
Lesson 2: Added Entries

Section 11: **Subject Headings and Classification**

Lesson 1: Subject Headings
Lesson 2: Classification

* This outline is a synopsis of the course content as it appears at:
http://www.oclc.org/institute/elearning/oll/CIRuMA/course_contents.htm.

The Program for Cooperative Cataloging and Training for Catalogers

Carol G. Hixson
William A. Garrison

SUMMARY. This paper examines the training programs developed by the Program for Cooperative Cataloging (PCC) and gives a historical overview. Future training activities and needs are also discussed. *[Article copies available for a fee from The Haworth Document Delivery Service: 1-800- HAWORTH. E-mail address: <getinfo@haworthpressinc.com> Website: <http://www. HaworthPress.com> © 2002 by The Haworth Press, Inc. All rights reserved.]*

KEYWORDS. Cataloging, training, continuing education, authority work, cooperative cataloging

HISTORICAL BACKGROUND

Historically, training for catalogers has occurred either in library science programs or on the job at individual institutions. Courses in cata-

Carol G. Hixson, MS in Information Studies, is Head of Cataloging, University of Oregon, Eugene, OR and Chair, PCC Standing Committee on Training (E-mail address: chixson@oregon.uoregon.edu). William A. Garrison, MLIS, MA in Latin, is Head of Cataloging, University of Colorado at Boulder Libraries and a member of the PCC Standing Committee on Training (E-mail address: garrisow@spot.colorado.edu).

[Haworth co-indexing entry note]: "The Program for Cooperative Cataloging and Training for Catalogers." Hixson, Carol G., and William A. Garrison. Co-published simultaneously in *Cataloging & Classification Quarterly* (The Haworth Information Press, an imprint of The Haworth Press, Inc.) Vol. 34, No. 3, 2002, pp. 355-365; and: *Education for Cataloging and the Organization of Information: Pitfalls and the Pendulum* (ed: Janet Swan Hill) The Haworth Information Press, an imprint of The Haworth Press, Inc., 2002, pp. 355-365. Single or multiple copies of this article are available for a fee from The Haworth Document Delivery Service [1-800-HAWORTH, 9:00 a.m. - 5:00 p.m. (EST). E-mail address: getinfo@haworthpressinc.com].

loging offered in schools of library and information science have unfortunately decreased in numbers in recent years, and there has been growing dissatisfaction in libraries with the training that catalogers have received as part of their master's degree programs. Libraries have felt that they are shouldering a larger portion of the burden in training entry-level catalogers than should be necessary. Efforts to improve the situation have met with little success. Lynn Howarth, Dean of the Faculty of Information Studies at the University of Toronto, wrote in a recent article that, "At the 1999 ALA Congress on Professional Education, entry-level cataloging education was identified by employer institutions as particularly problematic, and inadequate to sustain staffing requirements for libraries in the United States."[1]

As one means of addressing the perceived lack of adequate training for cataloging, there have been continuing education programs conducted by schools of library and information science over the years, and various professional associations have offered continuing education workshops. Among the most highly regarded and useful of the workshops given by professional associations were the ALA Resources and Technical Services Division's (RTSD, the former name of the current Association for Library Collections and Technical Services (ALCTS)) *AACR2* Institutes and the Authorities Institutes. The *AACR2* institutes were designed and developed collaboratively by the Library of Congress (LC) and RTSD to address the nationwide need for training for the impending implementation of the second edition of the *Anglo American Cataloguing Rules (AACR2)*. The Authorities Institutes which quickly followed were inspired by the popularity of the *AACR2* series. While these institutes (sometimes called "road shows") met with great success, and were highly praised by catalogers, they were held in only a few locations across the country, and ran for one or two years. They were never updated and never offered again after their initial bookings. Because of the limited number of locations in which they were offered, they were also expensive for attendees.

PCC TRAINING PROGRAMS

The Library of Congress continued a training role for non-LC catalogers through some of its programs in cooperative cataloging, most notably the National Coordinated Cataloging Program (NCCP), which relied exclusively on training and review done by LC. NCCP's predecessor program, the Name Authority Cooperative (NACO), which had been in existence since the late 1970s, also relied entirely on training conducted at the Library of Congress by catalogers in LC's Regional and Cooperative Cataloging Division. In 1994, the Program for Cooperative Cataloging (PCC) became the successor to the Cooperative Cataloging Council.[2] The PCC realized that the program's ultimate success would depend on the availability of a significant training component. Several of the task groups of the Cooperative Cataloging Council had made recommendations about training and standards, and in 1994-95 the PCC and its committees began to look at training for catalogers who were going to participate in the programs of the PCC. The programs identified as most needing training to be developed were the Bibliographic Cooperative (BIBCO), NACO, and the Subject Authority Cooperative (SACO). The Cooperative Online Serials Program (CONSER), was not made part of the PCC until 1997, but it already had significant experience in the development of training materials for CONSER participants.

The PCC formed three standing committees: the Standing Committee on Automation, the Standing Committee on Standards, and the Standing Committee on Training.[3] The Standing Committee on Training (STC), in conjunction with staff at the Library of Congress, began developing training materials for BIBCO, NACO and SACO. It was recognized that the training needed to be decentralized and no longer exclusively conducted by catalogers at the Library of Congress nor held exclusively at LC. In response to this conclusion, the PCC developed "train the trainer" programs for both BIBCO and NACO. In May 1995, the first Training the NACO Trainer workshop was held, and in September 1995, the first Training the BIBCO Trainer workshop was conducted.

In addition to realizing the necessity for decentralized training for PCC participants, the PCC also recognized that training needed to be cost effective and affordable for participating institutions. As a part of an effort to reduce costs, the trainers who participated in the "train the trainer" programs were selected from various parts of the country. The intention was that an individual institution joining the PCC would be able to bring in a trainer from its own region, and in that way reduce its training expenses. With all of the above in mind, the PCC began to develop its training programs for participating institutions.

Cataloging Now! Institutes

In 1997 and 1998, the PCC Standing Committee on Training developed a curriculum to promote the values of the PCC and the rationale behind the core record. In a continuation of the cooperative relationship between LC and ALCTS that started with the *AACR2* Institutes, beginning in 1978, ALCTS managed the presentation of a series of regional institutes entitled "Cataloging Now! An ALCTS Institute on the PCC Core Record." A rotating cast of presenters, four at each institute, introduced the concept of the core record in a plenary session, and in separate breakout sessions, they addressed specific issues for catalog librarians, administrators, and public services librarians.

The strength of the Cataloging Now! series rested with the carefully defined curriculum and the well-prepared trainers who were able to step in for one another, assuring that no one person had to bear the brunt of making all the presentations. The fact that there were multiple trainers using a common curriculum made it possible to reduce travel required for the trainers and thus helped keep costs down. Attendees were pleased with the clear presentation of the basic principles and rationale for the core record, as well as the introduction to the PCC, which was still new to many. Among criticisms received were that too many of the sessions were evangelical in tone and that not enough practical information was presented. Suggestions for future sessions focused almost entirely on specific topics for catalogers, such as authority control, subject analysis, special formats cataloging and LC classification. The final report from ALCTS to the PCC Standing Committee on Training noted that most attendees seemed to feel that training in cataloging values was important, but only as a corollary to hands-on review of cataloging rules and practices.

NACO Training

NACO training materials were primarily developed by staff in the Cataloging Policy Support Office and the Regional and Cooperative Cataloging Division at the Library of Congress. NACO training occupies one full week of intensive workshops and practice carried on on-site. The basic outline of the training is seen below:

1. Day One–General introduction to NACO and the PCC, the MARC21 Authorities Format, various cataloging tools, searching

in bibliographic utilities, normalization rules and authority record creation procedures.

2. Day Two–Personal names, *AACR2* Chapter 22, LC Rule Interpretations for Chapter 22, *AACR2* Chapter 26 and LC Rule Interpretations for Chapter 26 specific to personal names, personal name exercises.

3. Day Three–Corporate names, *AACR2* Chapter 24, LC Rule Interpretations for Chapter 24, *AACR2* Chapter 26 and LC Rule Interpretations for Chapter 26 for corporate names, corporate name exercises.

4. Day Four–Geographic names, *AACR2* Chapter 23, LC Rule Interpretations for Chapter 23, geographic name exercises; Uniform titles, *AACR2* Chapter 25, LC Rule Interpretations for Chapter 25, uniform title exercises; Exercises for changes to existing name authority records and reference evaluation exercises.

5. Day Five–Introduction to SACO (if desired by an institution), discussion of revision process and communication process between an institution and its trainer, introduction to the Library of Congress catalogs and resources, the contents of the PCC Website.

Each day consists of morning lectures on the topics mentioned above with an afternoon session reserved for practice in creating new, and changing existing authority records, and in establishing new headings.

NACO training is not designed to teach catalogers how to catalog but rather to understand and apply those rules in *AACR2* chapters 22-26 and their corresponding Library of Congress Rule Interpretations (LCRIs) that may pose problems in heading construction and evaluation. A *NACO Participants' Manual* augments the cataloging code and rule interpretations.[4]

BIBCO Training

In order for a library to be a full BIBCO member of the PCC, it must have had NACO training and must also have been designated independent in its contributions for NACO. (A library is granted independent status only after a period of close review of its contributions has established that it is capable of contributing records with a high level of accuracy and knowledge.)

Training materials for BIBCO were developed by the PCC Standing Committee on Training in conjunction with staff in LC's Regional and Cooperative Cataloging Division. These materials have evolved over time to respond to the needs determined by trainers and have been modified as needed. BIBCO training usually lasts two to three days and consists of an introduction to the core record standards, along with examples of various material types (e.g., books, videos, electronic resources, scores, and sound recordings) cataloged at both the full and core standards. In addition, because a BIBCO library that uses Library of Congress Subject Headings (LCSH) and Library of Congress Classification (LCC) must also contribute LC subject authority and LC classification proposals as needed, the training materials also have a component covering creation of new LC subject headings and new Library of Congress Classification numbers.

It became clear fairly early in the existence of the BIBCO Program that many practicing catalogers participating in the training lacked an understanding of the core record concepts, especially in the area of subject analysis. The core record standard calls for subject headings to be added at the appropriate level of specificity. This concept differs considerably from the older "minimal level" cataloging where broader or more general subject analysis could be performed. Perhaps because of their earlier familiarity with minimal level cataloging, it was not clear to many of those participating in the training that performing subject cataloging at the appropriate level of specificity meant that new subject headings and new classification numbers might need to be proposed and used in bibliographic records to be submitted through BIBCO. Thus it is that the subject heading and classification proposal process is now offered as part of BIBCO training.

As with NACO training, BIBCO training does not teach catalogers how to catalog. Instead, it emphasizes the need for catalogers to use judgment in their cataloging activities and in the creation of bibliographic records.

A *BIBCO Participants' Manual,* to be the BIBCO equivalent of the *NACO Participant's Manual* is currently being prepared by the PCC Standing Committee on Training. It should be completed in 2002. In 2001, David Banush of Cornell University was charged by the Policy Committee of the PCC to conduct a survey on cataloger attitudes relating to the core record. In addition to collecting data and making recommendations about the core record, Banush also used the opportunity to make broader recommendations about the BIBCO Program and the developing BIBCO documentation.[5] He recommended, among other things, that BIBCO training and documentation be redesigned to emphasize the mechanics of record creation, paying particular attention to the differences between full and core records. He also recommended that the core record be de-emphasized in training, marketing, and practice. His recommendations supported the direction already undertaken by the SCT, and many of his specific recommendations have already been implemented.

SACO Training

At this time there is no separate on-site training program for the creation of LC subject heading and classification proposals. The Library of Congress has recently been offering workshops in the creation of LC subject headings in conjunction with ALA conferences. These workshops concentrate on specific subject areas for the creation of proposals. As mentioned above, there is a portion of the BIBCO training that concentrates on when new subject heading proposals and classification number proposals are necessary and which introduces catalogers to the various tools and memoranda they must consult in order to create proposals.

In 2001, Adam Schiff, from the University of Washington, wrote the first *SACO Participants' Manual*, which is now available on the Web.[6] This is the first time that a codification of procedure and process has been created specifically for both PCC participants and more generally for anyone interested in creating LC subject proposals. Basically, a cataloger in any institution may contribute LC subject proposals without the institution having to be a PCC member. This is in contrast to NACO and BIBCO where the institution must be a PCC member and must have completed the appropriate training.

Series Training

To date, training in the creation of series authority records is solely conducted by staff at the Library of Congress. The content of the training is determined by the Library of Congress. A three day series training workshop is conducted at the Library of Congress at least once a year. Alternatively, an institution may have a trainer from the Library of Congress conduct training on site. A training manual for series authority record creation and maintenance exists, but this manual is not generally available.

CONSER Training

The longest-lived of the PCC components, although the last to join the fold officially, is CONSER. The CONSER program has played a significant role in training catalogers from its early days. Founded in the 1970s as a project to convert 200,000 serial records into machine-readable form, its initial participants were the Library of Congress, the National Library of Canada, the National Library of Medicine, the National Agricultural Library, Cornell University, the State University of New York, the New York State Library, the University of California, the University of Minnesota and Yale University. In 1975, participants received Library of Congress training. They began their work online in 1976. The Library of Congress and the National Library of Canada agreed to become Centers of Responsibility whose role it was to verify certain data elements in each record.

When membership expanded beyond the founders, new CONSER members always went to the Library of Congress, usually for two weeks, to receive detailed individual training and review by serial catalogers within LC. No other CONSER members did any training. There was no curriculum or standard practice. There was no CONSER cataloging manual, and much of the information about expectations for CONSER records was passed on during the one-on-one training. Training was handled in this fashion because at first there were few members. As thought was given to further expanding the number of institutions involved in CONSER, however, the program called on its members to develop a standard curriculum.[7] The decision to call on the membership to assist with the training effort is one that is now a hallmark of both the CONSER program and the PCC. Today, responsibility for training new member institutions is not borne exclusively by the Library of Congress but is rather shared among CONSER members. New member institutions are still expected to attend training sessions at the Library of Congress or elsewhere or to cover travel and per diem for a trainer to come to them.

Documentation has long been considered a key component of training and continuing education within the CONSER program. Although the CONSER Coordinator played a key role in writing much of the documentation, participants also played an active role, covering particular aspects or topics that became modules within the *CONSER Editing Guide* and *CONSER Cataloging Manual*. CONSER documentation is so complete and authoritative that it is used not only by CONSER members but also used by thousands of serial catalogers who are not CONSER participants but who are seeking guidance in all aspects of serial cataloging.

In mid-1999, in a move that the then PCC Chair, Brian Schottlaender, described as "groundbreaking,"[8] CONSER again raised the bar for training with the inauguration of the Serials Cataloging Cooperative Training Program (SCCTP). The basic premise of the SCCTP is that providing training to catalogers and other librarians should be a cooperative endeavor that makes the best use of the skills and abilities of a variety of partners. As Hirons and Hixson detail in their October 2001 *White Paper on PCC Role in Continuing Education for Catalogers*, the "SCCTP model consists of the following components: (1) course development by experts in the field, under contract, funded by LC's Cataloging Distribution Service and monitored by the CONSER Coordinator; (2) training of experienced librarians to give the workshops; (3) working with training providers to sponsor courses and listing those workshops on the SCCTP Web site; (4) ongoing evaluation and review based on course evaluations and comments from trainers. In addition, there is an SCCTP Advisory group which provides ongoing oversight."[9] The SCCTP is groundbreaking because, while initially envisioned and directed by a PCC program, its focus has gone well beyond current PCC members. A fundamental reason for the success of the program is the overwhelming support of the cataloging community. Significant numbers of CONSER and non-CONSER catalogers have volunteered to develop materials, become trainers, and serve as reviewers and advisors. Another successful aspect of SCCTP is that the planning and conducting of individual workshops is left to networks and library associations that have identified a regional or local need for the training. SCCTP has worked collaboratively with many different organizations in providing workshops, including ALCTS, the North American Serials Interest Group (NASIG), OCLC, and its regional networks. While course development takes significant time and effort, once it is done and the trainers are trained, there is little for the coordinating staff within the PCC to do. As of 2002, SCCTP had offered workshops in Basic Serials Cataloging, Serial Holdings and Electronic Serials Workshops. A course on Advanced Serials Cataloging is under development.

Lynne Howarth notes "the SCCTP is . . . an exemplary model for continuing professional development in that it has emphasized cooperation, and built on existing collaborative educational infrastructure. . . . Constrained by a relatively modest budget, the SCCTP has, nonetheless, 'thought big,' but 'acted small,' building incrementally on a base program, and iteratively enhancing existing modules as serials, serials cataloging, and serials standards continue to evolve."[10]

Task Group on Educational Needs of the Cataloging Community

In April 2000, the PCC Chair of Standing Committee on Training formed the Task Group on Educational Needs of the Cataloging Community.[11] Chaired by Peter Fletcher of Tulane University, the Task Group was charged, among other things, to investigate the educational needs of the cataloging community and to recommend specific training topics and the mechanisms for carrying out the training. In August of 2000, the Task Group sent out a survey to various cataloging-related listservs, both within and outside the PCC, to solicit from practicing catalogers their opinion as to their training needs. Based on the approximately 80 responses received, the group's final report, issued March 6, 2001, identified the primary areas where survey respondents felt a need for training. These areas were series authorities, name authorities, subject cataloging, electronic resources, classification, and non-books formats descriptive cataloging. The group recommended that the SCCTP model of training be followed as these needs were addressed.

New Joint PCC/ALCTS Effort

Using the results of the Task Group survey as a call to action, and using the success of the SCCTP as a model, the PCC's Standing Committee on Cataloging began to investigate a new collaboration with ALCTS to develop one or more of the continuing education courses identified by practicing catalogers. The timing was fortuitous, because ALCTS had just placed a major emphasis on continuing education, as outlined in a position paper in June 2000.[12] The ALCTS Education Committee had been charged with identifying suitable topics for continuing education, as well as suggesting people who could pull together workshops, pre-conferences, and programs. Some of the topics identified by ALCTS members relating to cataloging were precisely those identified in the Task Group survey. As a result of these two investigative efforts, in June of 2001, members of ALCTS Cataloging & Classification Section, Subject Analysis Committee (SAC) and the SCT began to discuss possible collaboration in the development of a continuing education course on subject analysis. Both the ALCTS Board and the PCC Policy Committee approved of the collaborative effort and a joint working group has been formed. The target date for unveiling the completed course is June 2003.

PCC Success

Approximately ten libraries were involved in the NCCP program prior to the inception of the PCC in 1994. The PCC has expanded considerably since then. The program has become international in scope, with over two hundred institutions participating in BIBCO, NACO, and CONSER. Training activities have been conducted around the world at libraries in Hong Kong, New Zealand, South Africa, the United Kingdom and Latin America. The PCC continues to expand and will continue to develop training programs for catalogers, both those participating directly in the cooperative programs, and, following the pattern of CONSER and SCCTP, also to other catalogers.

ENDNOTES

1. Howarth, Lynne C., "(Re)making the Serials Cataloger: The SCCTP Within an Educational Framework" *Cataloging & Classification Quarterly*, v. 30(4) 2000: 31-32.

2. The history of the Cooperative Cataloging Council and its task groups can be found in: *Towards a new beginning in cooperative cataloging: The history, progress, and future of the Cooperative Cataloging Council*. Washington, DC: Library of Congress Cataloging Distribution Service for the Regional & Cooperative Cataloging Division, 1994.

3. Information about the PCC and its standing committees can be found on the PCC web site at: *http://lcweb.loc.gov/catdir/pcc/*.

4. *Library of Congress NACO Participants' Manual*. 2nd ed. Washington, DC: Library of Congress, Cataloging Distribution Service, 1996. The Manual is also available in pdf format on the PCC website at: *http://www.loc.gov/catdir/pcc/naco/npm2ed.pdf*. It should be noted that this edition of the manual may contain outdated information.

5. Banush, David, BIBCO Core Record Study: Final Report Prepared for the PCC Policy Committee, June 11, 2001, available at: *http://www.loc.gov/catdir/pcc/bibco/coretudefinal.html*.

6. Schiff, Adam L. *SACO Participants' Manual*. Washington, DC: Library of Congress, Cataloging Distribution Service, 2001. Available in pdf format at: *http://www.loc.gov/catdir/pcc/saco/sacomanual.pdf*.

7. E-mail from Jean Hirons, March 5, 2002.

8. "CONSER at 25: Program celebrates anniversary with training initiative," *Library of Congress Information Bulletin*, v.57, no.8 (Aug. '98), p. 213.

9. Hirons, Jean and Carol Hixson, White Paper on PCC Role in Continuing Education for Catalogers, prepared October 5, 2001 for PCC Policy Committee Discussion, available at: *http://www.loc.gov/catdir/pcc/whitepapertrng.html*.

10. Howarth, Lynne C., "(Re) making the Serials Cataloger," p. 34-35.

11. Charge and reports of the Task Group on Educational Needs of the Cataloging Community are available at: *http://www.loc.gov/catdir/pcc/training.html*.

12. ALCTS and Continuing Education, June 2000. Available at: *http://www.ala.org/alcts/now/ce.pdf*.

Catalog Training for People Who Are Not Catalogers: The Colorado Digitization Project Experience

Sue Kriegsman

SUMMARY. The Colorado Digitization Project is a cooperative endeavor designed to enable creation of a virtual library of unique resources and historical collections in Colorado through assisting all types of Cultural Heritage Institutions in the State to scan and make available on the Internet images of materials and artifacts within their collections. An important component of the project is educational, and includes teaching staff in all types of institutions about access, cataloging and metadata. *[Article copies available for a fee from The Haworth Document Delivery Service: 1-800-HAWORTH. E-mail address: <getinfo@haworthpressinc.com> Website: <http://www.HaworthPress.com> © 2002 by The Haworth Press, Inc. All rights reserved.]*

KEYWORDS. Metadata training, continuing education, cataloging training, Colorado Digitization Project

---

Sue Kriegsman was formerly the Operations Coordinator for the Colorado Digitization Project and is currently the Digital Library Projects Manager, Harvard University Library.

[Haworth co-indexing entry note]: "Catalog Training for People Who Are Not Catalogers: The Colorado Digitization Project Experience." Kriegsman, Sue. Co-published simultaneously in *Cataloging & Classification Quarterly* (The Haworth Information Press, an imprint of The Haworth Press, Inc.) Vol. 34, No. 3, 2002, pp. 367-374; and: *Education for Cataloging and the Organization of Information: Pitfalls and the Pendulum* (ed: Janet Swan Hill) The Haworth Information Press, an imprint of The Haworth Press, Inc., 2002, pp. 367-374. Single or multiple copies of this article are available for a fee from The Haworth Document Delivery Service [1-800-HAWORTH, 9:00 a.m. - 5:00 p.m. (EST). E-mail address: getinfo@haworthpressinc.com].

INTRODUCTION

Cataloging training outside of library school is expanding as the need to control structured data not created or retained by libraries increases. The standards for cataloging are expanding to include the needs of non-library based organizations. Collaboration on projects between libraries and other organization types has added the need for a new teaching environment and set of cataloging guidelines. This has become especially evident with collaborative digitization projects.

The Colorado Digitization Project (CDP) has spent the last two years teaching the Dublin Core metadata standard to staff and volunteers in libraries, archives, museums and historical societies. The CDP is a collaborative project among Colorado's libraries, museums, archives and historical societies to develop a virtual collection of Colorado's unique resources and special collections. The goal is to teach different cultural heritage organizations how to work together and increase access to their historical collections through digitization. The CDP has created, and facilitates, a centralized database of catalog records from all of the participating projects (*http://coloradodigital.coalliance.org*). Among other things, the CDP gives incentive grants for digitization and provides education to the organizations on how to proceed with their projects. But there are some basic requirements each grant recipient must fulfill. First of all, the project must be a partnership between different institution types. For example, a library can partner with a museum, or a museum can partner with a historical society, or an archive can partner with a library: any combination of what CDP refers to as CHIs (pronounced chEEse) Cultural Heritage Institutions: libraries, museums, archives, and historical societies.

The other stipulation is that the projects follow a set of guidelines or standards for all aspects of their digitization (*http://coloradodigital. coalliance.org/standard.html*). Most of the organizations involved with digitization projects are engaged in the project to create access to their unique collections by scanning materials. Scanning requirements are therefore usually at the top of the list of things to consider. These standards include image resolution, pixel dimensions, file formats, and storage. But scanning standards are only part of the battle in a digitization project. There is also cataloging. Without cataloging, the digitized items are not easily accessible in a database. In order to provide comprehensive access to the digital collections, CDP-affiliated organizations are required to follow a set of cataloging standards, and are strongly encouraged to attend a full-day workshop that includes hands-on training for the application of the standards. Grantees do not always give a lot of thought to the question of retrieval before committing to the project, and as a result, the workshop audiences for digitization projects are frequently surprised to find themselves immersed in cataloging standards as well as scanning.

TEACHING CATALOGING TO A DIVERSE AUDIENCE

Over two years, the CDP has worked with a wide variety of people along with the usual assortment of CHIs, including paleontologists, bricks and mortar museum people (those who move and reconstruct buildings), school teachers, botanists, and archeologists. This breadth of reach led the CDP to devise ways to engage a diverse audience in cataloging, including:

- Demonstrate the need for standards.
- Use language and terminology familiar to everyone.
- Learn the culture of the different organizations.
- Make the time for training worthwhile.
- Use a variety of teaching techniques.

Rule #1: Demonstrate the Need for Standards

At the beginning of a new project it can be difficult to anticipate all of the possible project components. This is especially true if the project is part of a brand-new and developing field like digitization. On the surface of a digitization project is scanning; beneath that lie legal issues, workflow, staffing, image delivery, data storage, preservation of the original material and cataloging. It becomes critical to identify the need for cataloging standards right at the beginning of the project. The CDP offers an Introduction to Digitization workshop where during the course of a day most aspects of a digitization project are reviewed. Cataloging is given importance equal to scanning during the workshop. Without cataloging, the digitized items will not be found in a database. And cataloging without standards will also result in a faulty database because search results will not be an accurate reflection of the collection. Cataloging according to a documented standard is the hidden glue that holds a digitization project together and makes it available to users.

Another technique to encourage projects to follow cataloging standards is to link mandatory education components to the funding of the project. This might sound cruel and heartless, but if an organization is not aware of the significance of creating cataloging records for digital objects, then it may dismiss the need for the training. In the environment of a digitization project the images themselves are considered the most important component and it is necessary to express the importance of the other project pieces as well. Many small volunteer-run organizations do not have any kind of electronic inventory control or cataloging system and do not initially see the need to provide equal, if not more, attention to item descriptions as to the scanning. But in order to receive project funding the organization must attend training and adhere to a standard; the requirement is a good way to emphasize the importance of cataloging standards.

The goal is to entice the audience and explain the issues of why metadata is important. The format of the CDP workshop begins by introducing many different types of metadata standards such as the Text Encoding Initiative, SGML, and AACR2. We review the importance and purpose of each one. There is also discussion of databases, Internet searches, and library catalogs, all of which have underlying metadata. This provides a solid background on related activities in different contexts and demonstrates that many forms of cataloging standards are already in use by a variety of industries.

Rule #2: Use Language and Terminology Familiar to Everyone

When working with many CHI types the term "cataloging" is not appropriate. Cataloging is associated with technical services departments in traditional libraries and seems to repel each organization that is not a traditional library. Museums, archives, and historical societies do not necessarily associate cataloging with their organizational primary functions. And in the case of the CDP, it might be a reference librarian who is in charge of a digitization project; reference librarians may feel it is not their responsibility to enter into the territory of catalogers. So even within a traditional library, the term cataloging can be intimidating.

If it can't be called cataloging, then what is it? In the realm of electronic records and digital objects a new term has sprung up. Metadata. Structured data about data. It's not a great definition but at least everyone from all CHIs can learn about it together. Discussing metadata creates the common ground to reach all audiences equally. "Come to a workshop on the introduction of metadata" and reference librarians, curators, historians, catalogers, and archivists will all turn up with equal curiosity.

So what makes good metadata? Again, in a diverse environment there is no one clear answer. Should there be a 245 field in every record? An object name? A heading? If you ask a librarian, museum curator, or an archivist they will each give a different answer. So once again, the terminology is going to dictate what organization and culture is selected and unintentionally privileged. But what is the significance of 245s, object names, and headings? They are titles. This is where a new metadata standard comes into play, one that illustrates the concepts of descriptive standards in simple terms not affiliated with any one type of organization. A new, unaffiliated standard is a way to get down to the basics and learn where the different organizational cultures cross paths in describing collections. The CDP selected Dublin Core to teach to a diverse audience of project participants about the significance of metadata standards. Dublin Core is a set of fifteen elements that make up the basics of a good metadata record. Dublin Core uses common, every day terminology, perceived as owned by any one industry. Title is the term Dublin Core uses to describe the element where an object or item should be named. Title. It's simple and universally understood.

Rule #3: Learn the Culture of the Different Organizations

Simply because a common language has been established doesn't mean all the problems of educating a diverse audience are solved. Now that the museums, historical societies, archives and libraries understand the term Title in the same way, the museums raise a concern. Museums do not create titles for previously unnamed objects. It makes perfect sense once a curator explains it. What if Picasso didn't title any of his paintings? It wouldn't really be up to the owning museum to make up a title. Instead, when a painting is hung up for exhibition the small identifier card next to the painting would read "Untitled, oil on canvas."

Museums, or any other CHIs, should not be expected to change their institutional culture to fit the needs of a metadata record. Instead, it is up to the instructor to bring a common language to the discussion so options can be discussed openly and clearly. Everyone can use the common language to express institutional culture. Discussions of the differences between organizational cultures will lead to fewer miscommunications down the road as CHIs continue to work together.

The CDP begins each workshop by asking each person to introduce themselves and discuss briefly what their organization is doing for a digitization project. This simple technique allows everyone in the room to know what CHI types are represented. Not only is it good for the workshop participants to meet each other but it also lets the instructor know how to cater to the participants. Librarians have different reference points for cataloging than a museum curator will have. The instructor will know what perspectives to address based on who is in attendance. For instance, if there is only one archivist in a room of librarians and the discussion turns too much to MARC "tag talk" then the instructor will interpret the discussion for the archivist and make sure that the archivist perspective is also discussed with the group.

Rule #4: Make the Time for Training Worthwhile

Training people for professionally related activities means the training is usually done on work time. This type of education outside of a traditional classroom setting must be relevant to work-based activities, not alienating to the audience, quick, precise, and memorable. There usually isn't time for homework or too much outside reading. For the CDP, teaching metadata using the Dublin Core standard met the criteria for training a diverse audience under these circumstances. Dublin Core is not only the basis for the CDP database, and neutral with regard to organization type; it is also concise enough to be taught in one day. The CDP workshop is structured to include hands-on activities that can be done during the workshop and back at the home institution (memorable). Dublin Core is not as complex as MARC but many of the concepts are the same–Title = 245, Subject = 650, Creator = 100. For a museum volunteer who has never done any descriptive work before, there is a lot to learn about standards and how to execute them. The Dublin Core provides a format in which to discuss and show examples about metadata standards in a one-day workshop.

Rule #5: Use a Variety of Teaching Techniques

In a diverse audience representing different CHIs there are people with different strengths and weaknesses. One person could be very visually inclined but another might learn best by reading and asking questions. Some people might prefer to learn by hearing information and stories. Yet another person might be a combination of the visual and listening learners. In a traditional classroom setting there are take-home reading assignments, research, projects, and presentations. A work-related workshop does not always offer any outside activities and therefore does not let each student learn in their own best way. The instructor must find a way to reach each student and get the points across quickly and accurately.

During the day of a CDP workshop there are class discussions, small group discussions, and hands-on exercises. The material is presented as a lecture with illustrative stories and is accompanied by looking at Web sites and images. There is background reading assigned before attending the workshop but the material during the workshop is taught with the assumption that not all of the reading was done by the attendees. If the background reading was completed prior to the workshop then the day is an opportunity to review the material and ask specific questions. The hope is that there is something available for everyone's learning needs.

Discussion is a big part of the CDP workshop. The day provides a forum to bring up specific questions and concerns. There are discussions about scanning vendors, archival suppliers, database packages, online controlled vocabulary lists, the best way to format names in a database, and encoded archival description. Not everything that comes up for discussion is on the agenda, but discussion is the opportunity to tailor the content of the workshop exactly the needs of the people in attendance. All of the issues on the agenda are still covered but the topics covered in depth vary from group to group.

A benefit of the discussions is networking. People who are participating in digitization projects are almost always surprised to find themselves learning about metadata. But they attend the workshops and follow the standards and try to learn as much as possible in a short amount of time. There is nothing more encouraging than knowing you are not the only one in the world who finds the whole concept of metadata intimidating. Even more commonly, people begin to ask questions in a class and find many other people have the same question. Or better yet, someone else has an answer. Because people attend courses that are related to work it is helpful to find a peer group to turn to when the instructor is gone at the end of the day. Since many students are in working environments focusing on a specific need for metadata, the students will frequently have a lot to add to a day of teaching.

Everyone, including the instructor, should take advantage of the experiences of the group.

CONCLUSION

The diversity of people who need to learn about cataloging is growing as their institutions take on projects that formerly would have been handled by libraries. Photographs, maps, manuscripts, exhibits, ephemera, and anything else that can be digitized are going up on Web sites. The more material added to the Web site the greater the need to organize the data. A paleontologist shouldn't have to take a semester of cataloging in order to make the department's fossil collection available digitally to researchers world-wide. New programs are being devised to fit the needs of this new cataloging user. It is up to the teachers of these new programs to know their audience and provide a forum that is welcoming to all attendees.

The Community of Catalogers:
Its Role in the Education of Catalogers

Judith Hopkins

SUMMARY. The community of catalogers (defined as "those who work with you") plays a relatively small role in the formal education process. It plays a greater role in training as new hires talk to their new colleagues, subscribe to electronic discussion lists (especially focused lists such as the Passport for Windows list, LCWeb, AUTOCAT, etc.) and become involved in professional associations, cooperative projects, etc. Its greatest role, however, is in the area of informal continuing education. That is especially true for electronic discussion lists such as AUTOCAT. Such lists fill a gap in the education/training continuum: how to find quick, specific answers to questions when your library lacks either the personnel or print or electronic resources to provide them. They extend the community of catalogers from those who work with you to the entire world. *[Article copies available for a fee from The Haworth Document Delivery Service: 1-800-HAWORTH. E-mail address: <getinfo@haworthpressinc.com> Website: <http://www.HaworthPress.com> © 2002 by The Haworth Press, Inc. All rights reserved.]*

KEYWORDS. Cataloging education, continuing education, colleagues, electronic discussion lists

---

Judith Hopkins is Technical Services Research and Analysis Officer, State University of New York at Buffalo. She is also the list owner of AUTOCAT.

[Haworth co-indexing entry note]: "The Community of Catalogers: Its Role in the Education of Catalogers." Hopkins, Judith. Co-published simultaneously in *Cataloging & Classification Quarterly* (The Haworth Information Press, an imprint of The Haworth Press, Inc.) Vol. 34, No. 3, 2002, pp. 375-381; and: *Education for Cataloging and the Organization of Information: Pitfalls and the Pendulum* (ed: Janet Swan Hill) The Haworth Information Press, an imprint of The Haworth Press, Inc., 2002, pp. 375-381. Single or multiple copies of this article are available for a fee from The Haworth Document Delivery Service [1-800-HAWORTH, 9:00 a.m. - 5:00 p.m. (EST). E-mail address: getinfo@haworthpressinc.com].

EDUCATION AND TRAINING

We tend to think of education as an instructional delivery mechanism whose components are a teacher, students, and knowledge transfer occurring in a classroom or laboratory setting, either as part of a degree program (such as that leading to the M.L.S. or its equivalents) or through a continuing education program. Even in these days when distance education is growing in popularity, those elements still exist even though the teacher and the students may be distant from each other and the classroom is only virtual. The knowledge transferred can be entirely theoretical or be a combination of theory and practice, including hands-on instruction, but the emphasis is on the general rather than the specific.

Training, on the other hand, is usually thought of as an instructional delivery process which takes place in a work environment, with varying degrees of formality, ranging from a classroom-type setting to the give and take between a senior member of the staff and a junior member. Focus is on the practical and procedural, with emphasis on the practices and procedures of the local institution.

One thing both education and training in their traditional forms have in common is that knowledge is transferred from a person with certain specified and required qualifications such as degrees and/or levels of experience to those who lack those degrees or experience. Another common element is a time frame in which that knowledge transfer is expected to be completed. That can be the traditional four years of an American baccalaureate program, the one to two years of a post-baccalaureate Master's degree program, the one semester length of a single course, the days or weeks of a workshop, and the average though more open-ended length of the period in which training is expected to occur.

For catalogers, education occurs primarily within the confines (whether real or virtual) of a library school whether or not that school has the word 'library' in its name. That education is added onto the whole corpus of knowledge that the individual students have acquired up to that point in formal education, work experience, and varied life experiences. Because the various schools offer programs that differ in the amounts of cataloging instruction they offer or that students are required to take, and because such offerings are usually theoretical, the new M.L.S. holders who take jobs as catalogers usually require on-the-job training in their first jobs. Even experienced catalogers need some training in local procedures, different automated systems, etc., when they move to new jobs. Whether they get such training is questionable. Some large libraries such as the Library of Congress have formal training programs for new staff. Others have senior staff who revise work, and provide some amount of training.

Many new graduates, however, are hired to work in environments where they may be the only cataloger or even the only librarian. While I was not able to find any firm statistics on the number of libraries with only one cataloger who has the M.L.S. or equivalent degree, an informal survey on AUTOCAT during the second week of December 2001 showed that 57 (43%) of the 134 respondents worked in libraries with two or more degreed catalogers (many of which had only two) and 68 (51% or over half) worked in libraries with only one degreed cataloger. The other nine respondents (7%) worked in libraries where there were no degreed catalogers and six of those were the only persons on the staff doing cataloging. Thus, 75 (56%) of all the respondents worked in libraries with 1 or no degreed catalogers.

Fifty (37%) of the respondents worked in university libraries. An additional 29 also worked in academe, 19 in college libraries and ten in community college libraries. Twenty-seven more worked in public libraries, plus two in school library processing centers, and 26 in special libraries of various kinds.

Where do these catalogers get help when they need it? The help needed can be considered to fall into two categories: general current awareness (of trends, new tools, policy changes at LC or the utilities, etc.) and specific (and immediate) current awareness (how do I catalog this particular item? How do I choose among these classes when classifying a work on this topic? What is the meaning of this class number which I found on a CIP record but which isn't in the edition of the classification schedule which my library has? What is the difference in meaning between subject headings A and B, both of which I have found on records in OCLC? Where do I find the resources to do this project which my director has just assigned to me?)

In a 1985 article[1] James W. Williams of the University of Illinois at Urbana-Champaign described a variety of resources that the cataloger could use for informal continuing education. In sum, this advice could be reduced to reading library science journals (along with memberships in professional organizations which usually came with subscriptions to journals). This remains an important source of general current awareness but does nothing to resolve the need for specific current awareness.

THE COMMUNITY OF CATALOGERS

What is meant by the "community of catalogers"? The short answer is "the people you work with." That has always been true, as catalogers have learned from other staff members in their libraries, whether or not those staff members were degreed. The group of people you worked with could be extended to include staff members from other libraries in your community who did similar work and whom you could telephone or chat with at local professional meetings. Today, through technology, it can be extended to include any librarian anywhere around the world.

Some catalogers have always been fortunate enough to have mentors, whether from library school, libraries where they have previously worked, or socially. These people could be trusted to help when one experienced new situations or ran into problems.

Those librarians who attend meetings of professional associations, whether at the local, state, regional, national or international level can make contacts with people of similar interests who can be appealed to when questions arise.

Many catalogers participate in cooperative projects like the Program for Cooperative Cataloging (PCC).

The drawbacks to these resources are that they may be limited in number, may have backgrounds and experiences similar to yours (and thus share the same gaps in knowledge), may take time to get in touch with and get answers from, not to mention your dislike of bothering the same people over and over again whenever you need help.

The community of catalogers plays a relatively small role in the formal education process. It plays a greater role in training as new hires talk to their new colleagues, subscribe to electronic discussion lists (especially focussed lists such as the Passport for Windows list, LCWeb, AUTOCAT, etc.) and become involved in professional associations, cooperative projects, etc. Its greatest role, however, is in continuing education. That is especially true for electronic discussion lists such as AUTOCAT.

THE COMMUNITY OF CATALOGERS AND TECHNOLOGY

In the last decade technology has opened up several new sources of help, such as electronic Web sites. A number of institutions and/or individuals maintain Web sites where documentation of professional interest is maintained. (Examples include the Cataloger's Reference Shelf, maintained by The Library Corporation: *http://www.TLCdelivers.com/tlc/crs/crs0000.htm* where MARC formats and code lists, plus a variety of specialized cataloging manuals can be found, and Technical Processing Online Tools (TPOT) maintained by the University of California at San Diego: *http://oclcgate.ucsd.edu/.*) Of course the Library of Congress (LC) maintains its own Web sites such as those of the Cataloging Policy and Support Office (*http://www.loc.gov/catdir/cpso/*) and the Network Development and MARC Standards Office (*http://www.loc.gov/marc/*) plus that of the Program for Cooperative Cataloging (*http://www.loc.gov/catdir/pcc/*) as do utilities such as OCLC (for its Web documentation go to *http://www.oclc.org/oclc/cataloging/documentation.htm*). Also of great help are the Web sites for individuals and corporate bodies who wrote, edited, translated, or published the items we are cataloging.

In addition there are numerous non-library oriented Web sites which serve as resources for such data as calendars, geographic information, online dictionaries, political and biographical information, etc. Examples include The Internet Library for Librarians which provides access to a variety of tools: almanacs, dictionaries, books of quotations, etc. (*http://www.itcompany.com/inforetriever/* and the GEOnet Names Server (*http://164.214.2.59/gns/html/*).

One new tool is the Weblog or, for short, blog,[2] a Web-based tool for sharing links to interesting resources with like-minded colleagues. There is at least one devoted to cataloging resources: *http://catalogablog.blogspot.com/.* Peter Scott maintains a list of over 60 library Weblogs (plus citations to articles on library Weblogs) at *http://libdex.com/weblogs.html.*

The impact of technology is felt even on well-established methodologies such as involvement in professional associations. Web-pages bring association activities closer to both association members and non-members. One example is the Web-page of the Association of Library Collections & Technical Services (ALCTS): *http://www.ala.org/alcts/.* Some groups are even considering providing for virtual committee membership to increase the involvement of those members who don't go to conferences but who wish to be involved in association activities.

One of the most useful sources of immediate aid is the electronic discussion list.[3] While such lists may be organized around affiliation (library school, work site, organizational memberships) or hobbies and interests (cat lovers, gardeners, readers of mysteries), the lists based on professional interest are the primary ones of relevance to this paper. Within the library field there are lists aimed at people with various specialties. For catalogers there are a number of lists to which they can subscribe (e.g., OLAC-LIST for online audiovisual catalogers; the PCC list for PCC participants) but the most general list is AUTOCAT[4] (for library cataloging and authority control topics) with about 3,900 subscribers in some 46 countries.

On lists such as AUTOCAT catalogers (and this term is used here to include all those who do cataloging work in libraries or elsewhere, regardless of degree or lack thereof, regardless of work site or amount of experience, plus, of course, students of library science and a few non-catalogers who are interested in the topic) can describe their problems and expect to get help within hours (and often within minutes). Geographic restrictions are non-existent. In one recent example, a librarian in Chile asked for advice on AUTOCAT and quickly got a response from a librarian in Australia.

In 1993 I conducted an informal survey on AUTOCAT on the basic uses of the Internet (by which I chiefly meant electronic discussion lists) for catalogers. Several basic uses were identified:[5]

- Keeps you up-to-date with current trends and issues
- Source of quick answers to specific questions
- Lessens isolation

Among the specific uses mentioned were that an electronic discussion list:

- Compensated for a lack of cataloging tools and other resources in one's library,
- Reinforced what one learned in cataloging classes,
- Provided a broad range of views on any question, and
- Is more focused than journals.

Most subscribers to such large lists rarely if ever post questions or provide answers, but they read those that others have posted and learn from them. Others post frequently, either with questions or with answers. Others post rarely but are delighted when they can answer a question that has been posed. Here are some selected recent comments volunteered by subscribers to AUTOCAT during a discussion of cataloging education:

- "Many times AUTOCAT has done me more good than any cataloging class I ever had. I enjoy reading the messages and seeing if I can track down the answer myself. When my co-workers ask me 'how did you know that?' more often than not my answer is 'I learned it on AUTOCAT.' "(Amy Stults, Oct. 26, 2001)

- "I feel as though I am 'reading cataloging' in the sense that people once 'read law' by apprenticing themselves to a practicing lawyer." (Message from unidentified para-professional, forwarded by Ian Fairclough, Nov. 2, 2001)
- "Without AUTOCAT, I feel 'isolated.' With it, I feel like I'm working in an office with other catalogers." (Mary Saunders, personal communication, Oct. 30, 2001)
- "[In choosing a new hire] I'd also look for a person who had demonstrated an interest in ongoing education–had they attended workshops sponsored by their state library association or local consortium, etc. For that matter, are they subscribed to AUTOCAT?" (Jane Myers, Oct. 31, 2001)

Electronic discussion lists such as AUTOCAT thus fill a gap in the education/training continuum: how to find quick, specific answers to questions when your library lacks either the personnel or print or electronic resources to provide them. They extend the community of catalogers from those who work with you to the entire world.

ENDNOTES

1. James W. Williams, "Current awareness for catalogers: sources for informal continuing education," *Illinois Libraries* 67:444-447 (May 1985).

2. Walt Crawford, " 'You *must* read this': library weblogs," *American Libraries* 32, no. 9:74-76 (October 2001).

3. Walt Crawford, "Library lists: building on e-mail," *American Libraries* 32, no. 10:56-58 (November 2001).

4. The AUTOCAT Web site is at *http://ublib.buffalo.edu/libraries/units/cts/ autocat/*.

5. Judith Hopkins, "Re: Cataloging uses of the Internet," AUTOCAT posting number 14042, dated Feb. 22, 1994. Obtain by sending the message: GETPOST AUTOCAT 14042 to *LISTSERV@LISTSERV.ACSU.BUFFALO.EDU*.

Index

Page numbers followed by f indicate figures; those followed by t indicate tables.

383

STC. *See* Standing Committee on
    Training (STC)
Sterling Memorial Library, 44
Stockwell, Admiral, 13
Storytelling, for catalogers and
    managers, 256
Subject access, librarians' understanding
    of, importance of, 224
Subject Analysis Committee (SAC), 364
Subject Analysis course, University of
    Pittsburgh's School of
    Information Sciences (SIS),
    226-227
Subject Approach to Information, 105
Subject Authority Cooperative
    (SACO), 357
Subject cataloging, teaching of, 223-232
    classwork in, 229-230
    concreteness of, 226-227
    goals for courses in, 225-226
    grading issues in, 230-231
    order of topics introduced in,
        227-229
    theory vs. practice in, 224-225
*Subject Cataloging Manual: Subject
    Headings,* 228
Subject courses, 85-86,86t
SUNY Buffalo, 341
Supervising, in technical services, 259

Task Group on Educational Needs of the
    Cataloging Community, 364
Taylor, A.G., xviii,63,72,104,105,
    223,235,319-320
Teaching, of cataloging and
    classification, reasons for,
    1-13. *See also* Cataloging;
    Classification
Technical Processing Online Tools
    (TPOT), 379
Technical services
    communication in, 261
    evaluation in, 259

job options in, 259-260
management style in, 261
personnel issues for, 259-261
recruiting in, 259
supervising in, 259
TEI, 340
Texas A&M University, 315
Texas Woman's University, 302
Text ENcoding Initiative, 204,211-212
"Textbooks Used in Bibliographic
    Control Education Courses,"
    76
*The Anglo-American Cataloging Rules,
    Second Edition,* 104,105,106
*The No Significant Difference
    Phenomenon,* 304
The Who Live at Leeds, 49
Thesaurus Construction and Use, 106
Thesaurus construction/controlled
    vocabulary courses, 89
Threlkeld, R., 303,305
TopClass, 316
Toreki, R., 316
Toys "R" Us, 300
TPOT. *See* Technical Processing
    Online Tools (TPOT)
Trainer Report, 49
Trojan War, 264
Tulane University, 364
Turvey, M.R., xvii,165
Twain, M., 36

UNCG. *See* University of North
    Carolina at Greensboro
    (UNCG)
UNCG cataloging course, LIS
    graduates' perspectives on,
    145-164. *See also* Cataloging
    education, UNCG LIS
    graduates' perspectives on
UNCG Institute and Review Board,
    148
University at Buffalo Libraries, 296
University of Arizon, 301